MW00818271

"In *The World Transparent*, Nina Butorac selects themes from the works of profound Christian thinkers, from St. Paul to St. Augustine to Thomas Merton, and illuminates these themes by way of classic and top-drawer movies . . . What emerges for the reader is an understanding of the powerful relevance of Christian thought to the universal plight of humanity. For the restless heart, the essential message of hope through Christ's two great commandments, love of God and love of neighbor, resonates on every page of this beautifully crafted work."

—LAWRENCE CARMIGNANI
University of Washington

"A well-written work that utilizes the movies as modern-day parables to illustrate the many principal themes in our Christian faith. Nina Butorac presents a faithful interpretation of church teachings while daring to go to the heart of sacramental theology. Our Christian identity, as sacramental bearers of Christ, is the essential theme that is named, challenged, and celebrated in the pages of this book . . . I highly recommend this work to teachers, students, pastors, parents, and individuals wishing to share and grow in their faith."

—DANIEL SYVERSTAD, OP
Former provincial, Western Dominican Province

"An excellent analysis of the art form of storytelling through movies and the way in which cinema can 'hold up a mirror' to the world and the human condition. Butorac exhibits a deep knowledge of the tradition of the Catholic Church with respect to the arts, sacraments, virtues, and other theological matters and how they are treated in the world of film . . . Movies have an outstanding ability to tell stories that show the ways in which the divine is bursting forth into the world, and *The World Transparent* is an excellent resource for those who are interested in film studies."

—PATRICK SHERRARD
Priest administrator, St. Catherine Parish

The World Transparent

Other Works by Nina Butorac

Sacramental Letters: Themes in Catholic Literature

Alyosha.com

The World Transparent

A Catechesis at the Movies

Nina Butorac

WIPF & STOCK · Eugene, Oregon

Wipf & Stock
An Imprint of Wipf and Stock Publishers
199 W. 8th Ave., Suite 3
Eugene, OR 97401

www.wipfandstock.com

PAPERBACK ISBN: 978-1-7252-9699-2
HARDCOVER ISBN: 978-1-7252-9698-5
EBOOK ISBN: 978-1-7252-9700-5

05/13/21

All biblical extracts are from the New American Bible, 1986, unless otherwise cited.

For my mother, the magisterial matron of the home;
and for my father, the arbiter of prudence.

"For you, a thousand times over!"

Contents

Author's Note

*** *SPOILER ALERT* ***

Please take note: *These are not movie reviews!* The forty films presented here will be examined closely and openly discussed, as they are meant to stand as illustrations—like a parable—in order to highlight the Christian themes featured in each chapter. I must presume that these films are already familiar to the reader. Many are classics, all are excellent, but some may be completely new to the reader. Hence this SPOILER ALERT.

As we move through the process of Christian formation, the plot of each film will be retold as a story, including the twists, the characters, and the unexpected surprises, in order to draw out those themes. If the reader has *not* seen the film, and wishes to enjoy the movie unspoiled, I encourage them to do so before reading the section illustrated by that particular film; or otherwise skip that segment and move on through the rest of the chapter. I don't wish to ruin the fun, but I do mean to examine the content.

Preface

THE WORLD TRANSPARENT EXAMINES the spiritual themes that have populated our Western and Christian tradition for many centuries. From a Catholic, sacramental standpoint, the reader will learn the function of allegory as it relates to our two-tiered experience of reality, and how this duality is depicted in symbolic art and modern film. Using forty well-loved films as illustrations, *The World Transparent* endeavors to guide the reader through a process of formation and towards a mature understanding of the Christian faith; not only as an intellectual exploration, but as a spiritually lived experience.

Its focus is on the *virtues*, as they help to form us to live purposeful lives and attain happiness; on *conscience*, as it directs our judgment and moral actions; on *grace*, as it lifts up our nature and works to perfect it; on the *sacraments,* as they confer the graces that enable us to meet life's confrontations and struggles; and on the *theological virtues* of faith, hope, and love, as they immerse us in the order of grace and direct us to the source of our redemption in Christ. Each of these sacred themes is augmented by beauty and by the sacramental qualities found in great art, in powerful stories, and shot through, eminently, by classic, masterful film.

Acknowledgements

WITH MUCH AFFECTION, I wish to thank Larry Carmignani, who carefully reviewed this manuscript and offered his insightful comments and ideas; and Alco Canfield, who helped to correct and edit the original draft. I am also indebted to Fr. Patrick Sherrard, for his support, comments, and valuable direction. In gratitude for their unwavering friendship and encouragement, I thank Gela Gibbons and Fr. Daniel Syverstad, OP, who continue to push me to do my best.

Finally, my indebtedness to Thomas Merton and his writings is apparent on every page of this book, and in every day of my life. With tremendous gratitude, I write his name with honor.

1

The World Transparent

We are living in a world that is absolutely transparent,
and God is shining through it all the time.[1]

—*THOMAS MERTON*

The Stuff of Art

I ENJOY PAINTING. I especially enjoy painting portraits in oils. Not very long ago I was speaking with a parishioner at my church who took an interest in my art work. She had recently converted from some evangelical Christian sect to Catholicism and was very earnest in her new-found faith. I showed her a few photos of some portraits I had painted, but as she flipped through them she expressed her disappointment. "Don't you ever paint anything *spiritual?*" she wondered. "Of course," I exclaimed, "I paint *people!*" She handed the photos back to me with a tight smile.

So I have been thinking about this exchange. What on earth—and I do mean earth—would a spiritual painting look like, anyway? Would it be some abstract landscape with puffy clouds, sunbeams, and rainbows? Or maybe a spiral of infinite triangles? Perhaps she was looking for angels—those celestial beings who are often portrayed with human bodies and big wings. Of course, there is nothing particularly spiritual about

---

1. Merton, *Essential Writings*, 67.

wings and she had already rejected human beings. In some essential way, I suspect that her conversion to Catholicism is not yet complete. She seems to be missing a very crucial point.

The only way an artist can take very tangible paint and turn it into something spiritual is through symbolism; by alluding to sanctity through some physical sign or image. And while the spiritual might be expressed more easily through poetry or music—as words and composition lend themselves to thought and emotion—it is much tougher to turn the physical stuff of the earth into something godly. The vast amount of bad religious art certainly attests to this! We can only sculpt, paint, carve, build, and photograph with the materials we have, such as they are. Even light burning into a strip of celluloid is a physical substance. But light can do marvelous things when it captures a thing of beauty, and beauty is what the artist is really after.

When the Catholic Church proclaims that human life is sacred, it is making a radical claim; but it is an assertion no more radical than Jesus' own, who claimed us for God. The beauty of our human creation, our human story, even the human face in portraiture, can reveal tremendous spiritual depth. When an artist captures this well, the work itself will elicit a whisper of the Incarnation—of God made man—which is, and who is, the heart of everything.

We come to this tremendous insight by way of three great traditions: the Jewish tradition of sacred revelation, the Greek tradition of metaphysics (the study of reality), and the Christian tradition, which emerges from the earlier two. So let us take a very brief look at the ideas that bolster this claim of human sanctity.

Classical Western thought proposes that all things, by virtue of their existence, come from or participate in the divine. Jewish tradition describes God as the Creator, the Lord God who is One, utterly sacred and set apart in holiness, with a name too hallowed to name. This Creator God acts within the history of his people, speaks through his prophets, and guides the people by way of sacred law.

Greek tradition, beginning with Plato, defines the deity as complete perfection, where perfect forms (ideas) exist in the mind of God. The things that imperfect people perceive in the world are only shadows of the real; imperfect particulars of the perfect forms that emanate from the sacred realm. Aristotle, who was a student of Plato, maintains Plato's God of perfection, defining God as supreme being and the unmoved mover of the universe. Yet Aristotle sets God outside the world of human affairs as one disengaged and too perfect to contemplate anything other than his own perfect self. Aristotle's God is not a Creator God because reality has always existed. This reality, for Aristotle, is a two-tiered affair, composed of "whatness" and "existence," where a thing is some *kind* of thing, and that it also *exists*. A book, for example, is a book because it has a certain quality, it is made up of certain parts and it has a certain purpose; but it must also *exist* in order to *be* a book. "What" plus "is" equals "real." Even the pattern of our thoughts and language are based on this equation.

St. Thomas Aquinas, in the thirteenth century, will take this Aristotelian notion—that reality functions on two levels—and propose a metaphysics that is based on a *sacramental* understanding of reality. He does this by defining God as the "existence" portion of the formula. God is pure *being*; complete, simple, and absolute *esse*. So, for anything to exist at all, its existence must be entirely contingent upon God. God saturates the reality we experience because that reality exists, and because we exist, and because God is existence. God keeps everything existing. God is not only the Creator, not only the perfect and supreme being, God is the constant sustainer of everything that is.

What sets this sacramental theology apart from the Judeo and pagan traditions is the Christian doctrine of the Incarnation. Christian theology asserts (and not without scandal) that God entered creation in the person of Jesus Christ, and that this Incarnation eternally sanctifies all of humanity. The sacred divinity of God is in the world, and never apart from the world, so long as the world exists.[2] Because of this sanctification, the entire natural order can be seen as a *sacramental sign*, where the world as a symbol, or the universe as a mirror, points to and reflects the glory of God.

When Thomas Merton says that we are living in a world that is absolutely transparent, this is what he means; that God is shining through all of creation, in nature and in art—in every created thing—and at all times. Merton is not supposing that we will see God in the things of the world, he is saying that God *is* there whether we can see him or not. The ability to see this divinity in created things is a pure gift, he tells us, and

2. This is the sacramental viewpoint, where creation is recognized as an unfolding reality that is imbued with the hidden presence of God. However, it should not be confused with *pantheism,* the belief that all things *are* God. That pantheistic notion is incompatible with the Catholic faith. For further reading on this topic, see "Collapsing the Sacred and the Profane: Pan-Sacramental & Panentheistic Possibilities in Aquinas and Their Implications for Spirituality," by Hans Gustafson, in *The Heythrop Journal* (2011) 1–14.

we are either blessed with this gift or we are not. If not, we must rely upon the witness of others who are so blessed, most especially the mystic or the saint or the artist.

This is the sacramental theology of St. Thomas, in a very tight nutshell, and it will be the foundation of our sacramental study. What we look for in the world—in unity, in truth, and in beauty—is an order saturated with the living God. God is the spark at the center of all being, and this spark is what the artist works to reveal. We do not create truth, we discover it. We do not create beauty, we uncover it; great artists revere it, but they do not make it. That reality is already there. The role of the artist, then, is to penetrate the surface of reality to what is most real, most true, and most beautiful, and then make it apparent.

It would seem to be a rather tricky task to combine something as ordinary as a night at the movies with sacred theology. And indeed, we may be concocting a terrible mixture of the sacred with the profane. But when we consider film as an *art form*—which it certainly is, one that is focused on our created world, our human story, and our human character—then we should see how essential this doubling-up is to a sacramental world view. The sacramental imagination does not separate the sacred from the profane. The sacramental imagination maintains that there *is* no separation, because the world is not profane, it is sanctified. Like a great cathedral, great film not only imitates the beauty of the natural order, it augments it. It magnifies our human condition with structure, light, color, music, and imagery; and it enhances our ability to glimpse a sacred order that we might not otherwise see. When the characters are engaging and the script smart, the lighting perfectly sculpted and the music soaring, a film can elicit great spiritual power. It can take us into a realm we did not know existed and then fill us with awe. This is the spark of beauty and the sacred realm of God; but it is also a human realm. It is double because reality is double, and we are a part of that duality.

The Parables of Jesus

The human story is at the heart of every faith tradition. Our encounters with God throughout history are retold as stories: in the words set down in Holy Scriptures, in prayer and music and chant, and in the plays enacted on stage by ancient peoples. Even Jesus illustrated his teachings with very graphic, symbolic stories. We call them "parables," but the parables that Jesus told were simply stories about people and events structured to reveal, *allegorically*, the kingdom of God.

A parable is a tale that is rich in symbolism. And while sometimes Jesus explained the symbols he was using, there are times when he purposely did not. We can see this in the Parable of the Sower, recounted in three of the gospels.[3] In this parable, Jesus tells of a sower who went out to spread good seed. He sows it rather recklessly, abundantly, on rocky soil, along a well used path, among brambles, and in the good earth. The seeds wither on the rocky ground, they are trampled and eaten by birds on the path, and they are strangled by the brambles. But in the good earth the seeds bear abundant good fruit.

Jesus will later explain the parable to his disciples: how the sower represents the kingdom of God, the seed is the word of God, and the ground is likened to the hearts and minds of those who hear the word, as well as the circumstances that surround them. While this teaching is, of course, important, it is curious that Jesus does not explain the symbolic meaning to his listeners, but only later to his disciples. Those who first heard the parable were left to discover for themselves the richness of the story's imagery. Jesus tells his disciples that *they* must become the teachers of sacramental stories, and he instructs them in the method and interpretive meaning. If Jesus had told his listeners outright what the seed and earth signified, it would have destroyed the subtlety of the message and deflated its power. Then his listeners would not need to make the effort to understand its symbolic message and they would lose the absolutely crucial experience of insight; that "ah ha!" moment when meaning congeals. This moment of discovery is a gift of the Holy Spirit, and it is a necessary grace for spiritual growth.

But the apostles themselves don't always get it. They complain about these confusing stories. When will Jesus just *speak plainly?*[4] Jesus chides his followers for their thick-headedness. If they cannot discern the symbols in a simple parable, how will they ever understand his other teachings? He will later condemn the Sadducees and Pharisees, who ask him to perform a miraculous sign from heaven in order to prove himself to them. But he refuses. No sign will be given to those "blind guides."

3. Matt 13:1–23, Mark 4:1–20, Luke 8:4–15.

4. John 16:29.

They may be able to interpret the appearance of the sky and predict the weather, but they are incapable of interpreting "the signs of the times."[5] Jesus is stating plainly here that the signs do exist, and not only in stories. These signs clearly exist in the world, and they signify the momentous and hidden meaning of the age. So we really *ought* to be paying attention.

Throughout our religious tradition, creation is understood as something completely saturated with meaning that often gives itself away. It is underpinned with significance and purpose and waits with "eager expectation"[6] to be revealed. This revelation is what the sacramental perspective is conditioned to see. It is what Jesus tried to teach to his disciples who were blessed to see what others could not. But if we regard our aesthetic study of signs and symbols as tedious schoolwork meant only for academics, then we would be missing a huge part of what it means to be a Catholic and a Christian.

In human life, signs and symbols occupy an important place. As a being at once body and spirit, man expresses and perceives spiritual realities through physical signs and symbols . . . The same holds true for his relationship with God. God speaks to man through the visible creation.[7]

—CATECHISM OF THE CATHOLIC CHURCH

Awakening to See

It is not surprising that human beings avoid discomfort. Like suffering, it can be debilitating, dangerous, and even traumatic. It can also kill us. So it is our natural inclination to shun pain, even at all costs. We have built up a society that is committed to reducing suffering, and rightly so, but as we are lulled by these rocking arms of contentment—with enough to eat, enough to drink, enough to wear, and enough to love—we can drift into a slumber that leaves us vulnerable to dissipation and attack. The well-fed rabbit that is caged and coddled may end up as tomorrow's dinner! And by the time the trick is played it will be too late. How can we warn the rabbit that all is not as it seems? How can we shock it into attentiveness?

5. Matt 16:3.

6. Rom 8:19.

7. *Catechism of the Catholic Church*, #1146–47.

We can teach and preach and lecture to the contented bunny, but unless it sees the danger and allows itself to be startled by it, it will not venture from its cozy cage. It is the same way with us.

Our first film will introduce us to the dangers of contentment, and hopefully warn us against those comforts and busy distractions that can lull us into a blind stupor. The main characters are professional artists of the theatre and excellent mentors for a launch into our study of film; but these are guides who seem to have lost their way. Like Dante, they have somehow strayed into the Dark Wood of Error and are now clamoring for a way out. They meet at a very elegant French restaurant where they engage in a long conversation about the theatre, the world, and the sacramental quality that the artist is summoned to reveal.

My Dinner With André[8]

My Dinner With André introduces us to two well-known personalities of the New York stage: Wallace Shawn (Wally) and André Gregory, founder of the *Manhattan Project* theatre group and a renowned director. The characters depicted in the film are exaggerated versions of these two very real people, and their dialogue is based on the conversations that they had shared together over the years. It is, perhaps, not the easiest film to begin with, as it is nuanced and subtle and a little dated, but if we can grasp what André Gregory is attempting to express in this work, we will be better positioned to appreciate the teachings and the films that follow.

Our story begins with Wally—a modest, underemployed playwright—walking along the busy streets of New York City. He boards a graffiti infested subway car to meet his friend, André, for dinner. The graffiti in the car is overwhelming, nonsensical; an array of chaotic, painted-over signs and scripts that are impossible to decipher. Wally is dreading this dinner engagement. He has been avoiding André for years, because it is well known in the theatre circles that the man has suffered some kind of mental collapse. One friend overheard André at a party, explaining how he once talked with trees, or some crazy thing like that. Another friend told Wally that he had found André weeping uncontrollably in the street one evening, and he urged Wally to go see him at once.

---

8. *My Dinner With André*, directed by Louis Malle. A George W. George Production, 1981. Rated "PG," I presume for the use of one particular anatomical word; "Not Rated" by other rating entities.

But how can Wally enjoy dining with a man who is suffering such obvious emotional pain? He's not a doctor. What can he possibly say to him?

In the narrative voice-over, Wally admits his incompetence. He can barely manage his own life. What can he do for André? He bemoans his life as a playwright and an unemployed actor. But if we listen carefully (and few seem to) we should note the absurdity of Wally's complaints. "The life of a playwright is tough," he says. He had to get up at 10:00 a.m. that morning in order to make some important phone calls. Then he had to go to the "Xerox shop" to make copies of his new play, and then to the post office to mail them off. There were "dozens of things to do." Meanwhile, Wally's girlfriend, Deby, has to work part-time as a waitress just to pay their bills! He would much rather spend the evening at home and eat a delicious meal that Deby would prepare for him. We ought to laugh at Wally's cozy little miseries, but we don't. That's important. We tend to take Wally at his word: he has it pretty tough, alright.

When Wally enters the fancy French restaurant we can see that he is clearly out of his league. Dressed in rumpled corduroy, he is met by a finely groomed maître de and directed to the bar. He shoves his hands into the square pockets of his jacket and ambles to the bar. Two beautiful women giggle as he passes and he turns, presuming they are laughing at him. He looks about, fidgeting.

Then André sweeps in, full of life and laughter. He whisks up Wally in his arms, gives him a manly bear-hug, and grins as proudly as a prodigal dad. The first thing Wally says to his exuberant friend is: "Well, you look terrific!" Ever the honest one, André replies: "Well, I *feel* terrible!" and they both laugh awkwardly. It is awkward because it is false. Wally said what he was expected to say when two long-parted friends meet again. But it isn't real, or true, or perceptive, or even *caring*. André doesn't point this out, though. He is too kind to correct his friend. But he doesn't let the polite pretense stand, either, hence the laughter and the awkward grins.

The friends are then ushered to a remote table and the conversation begins. Wally decides that the best way to get through the evening is to ask questions. That way he won't have to do much of the talking. André is a talkative whirlwind, so he obliges Wally with a two-hour monologue, interrupted only by the sober waiter who serves them, and Wally's occasional quips of "Gee, then what?"

During the course of this conversation André tells of the workshops he created and attended while in his emotionally fragile state. It is not always easy to sort these stories out. It is a strange discussion as André relates his failings, as well as those moments when he felt most alive. Since he had undergone an emotional breakdown, the stories of this experience are filled with hallucinations, theatrical stunts, compulsive travel, communal adventures, and bizarre, mystical experiences. He tells of his time in Poland, where his improv group formed a "beehive" and sang a prayer of St. Francis to express their gratitude to God, or tossed a teddy bear about a gathered circle and cheered, or danced wildly in the forest like Indians. His time in Poland ends when his friends administer a "christening" for him, and he receives a new name. André then relates how he traveled to the Sahara desert and was so miserable that he ate the sand. He describes the magical antics of a Japanese monk who was once an ascetic, but got fat living in New York and sported Gucci shoes under his robes. He describes his experience at a Christmas Mass where some strange, blue-skinned, flower-bedecked creature appeared to comfort him. What stands out for André, who considered himself completely dead inside, was the sacramental theatre of the christening. He says it is the only time he felt most alive.

He later tells of his compulsion to fashion a symbolic flag, one that would "pick up the vibrations" of his life. But the flag that the designer made for him turned out to be so powerful and overwhelming that André's wife would not allow it in the house. So he gave it to a friend who became so distressed that she burned it. There was nothing particularly horrible about the flag, yet it seemed to have picked up some very dark vibrations.

While all of this sounds a little loony, echoing our post-hippy era of the 1970s, there is something deeper going on here, something compelling. Sure, the psychedelic overload can be easily scoffed at, but those are only the images (the signs) of an inferred, hidden reality. It is the process of recognizing these signs (the blue creature, the flag, the christening, the coincidences that entangle the episode on *The Little Prince*) that is important, and we should be attentive to them. How do the signs drive the story? How do they impact the two characters? Where are the signs directing us to look? Deciphering the symbolic play of these images and symbols is a practice for the literary and spiritually astute. Yet André's adventures are so jumbled and so frantically narrated that we, the listeners, begin to experience his turmoil along with him. The parables of Jesus are simple in comparison! This, too, is intentional.

André is basically saying that our world is inverted, chaotic, and so deceptive that we are mistaking a dream-world for reality itself; and that it sometimes takes a madman to see it. His own exploits, which were certainly psychotic and strange, helped him to see through this dream-world to a holy, sanctified reality; the God-saturated world. He calls it a "William Blake world" (William Blake, who had visions of God). André's perspective is completely sacramental. He even gives us a bit of Martin Buber's sacramental theology from Hasidic mysticism, claiming that there are spirits chained in everything, in you and in me and even in this table, and that *prayer* liberates these spirits. André concludes that every action of ours, therefore, should be "a prayer, a sacrament in the world." Not so hippy, this!

Well, if this sacramental quality in the world really is the case, then André confesses that his entire life has been an absolute disaster; and he himself a complete failure. He is visibly shaking as he admits this now, he is so distressed. He declares that he should be seized and arrested like Albert Speer—Hitler's architect—and tried before the world court, because he has cooperated with, and helped build-up, such evil.

He then relates how he became involved in a mock-burial, allowing himself to be abducted by actors, stripped naked, forced to run blindfolded through the fields in Montauk, and then literally buried alive in an eight foot grave—covered over with boards, then canvas, then dirt—only to be resurrected after thirty minutes in the tomb. Afterwards, he was driven back through the fields to a great celebration, where the participants danced around a campfire until dawn. The point of this experience was to be shocked back to life again. Only then was he able to look at his life with any real honesty.

At this point in André's narrative Wally feels the need to speak up. He says that he considers himself to be a pretty friendly, nice guy. He doesn't want to dwell on suffering or on starving Africans—and he is able to blot them out of his perception—but he is still basically a good guy. He asserts that there must surely be some good, some meaning left in the world. It can't all be hopeless. As an artist and playwright, Wally thinks that theatre can still bring people into contact with the real, but André disagrees. That is what the theatre *should* do, but it doesn't anymore. We are all bored. Our need for comfort has lulled us into the dream-world. "The process that creates this boredom in the world now may very well be a self-perpetuating unconscious form of brainwashing, created by a world totalitarian government based on money," André growls, and this is much more dangerous than one thinks. Someone who is bored is asleep, he reasons, and someone who is asleep will not say "no!"

That's a lot to take in. Wally is waffling. If that's the case, he counters, then what can the artist do in this "Orwellian nightmare?" Because, not everyone can be taken to Mount Everest for some mystical experience. And isn't a cigar store in New York just as real as Mount Everest? Wally says, "I think if you could become fully aware of what existed in the cigar store next door to this restaurant, it would blow your brains out. I mean, isn't there just as much reality to be perceived in a cigar store as there is on Mount Everest?" André absolutely agrees, but the problem is that no one can *see* the cigar store anymore.

Then André relates how he once considered using a real severed head from the city morgue as a prop for the play he was staging at Yale (*The Bacchae*), and how he proposed tossing it into the audience just to shock them into experiencing the horror that was taking place on stage.

Pointedly, Wally rebels. This is all too much. He doesn't understand what André is even talking about. It is all absurd. Those prophetic messages and signs that André has been alluding to are just "coincidences!" Wally loves his comfortable life, why can't André? Wally enjoys his life with Deby: he writes his little stage plays, he is reading the autobiography of Charlton Hesston, and he looks forward to waking up to that cold cup of coffee he left on the kitchen counter the night before. And if a cockroach has died in it over night then, well, then he is just *disappointed.*[9] Yet André seems to be suggesting that no one can have a meaningful life these days.

André listens and smiles and nods, ever patient with his friend's confusion. The problem, André repeats, is that people can't see things clearly anymore. Then he tells how, after his mother died—when he was completely undone by grief—how seven or eight of his friends commented on "how wonderful" he looked! (This should remind us of Wally's first greeting: "Well, you look terrific!") André insists that this inability to see another person's pain, even that of a close friend who is suffering tremendous grief, is "psychically killing" us.

Wally sympathizes, and yet he is exactly the kind of friend (the earnest, smart, and loving friend, but still one so blind) that André is lamenting! Wally, of all people, *should* be able to see clearly! But he has fallen into a blind trance because he has been lulled to sleep by contentment.

9. Did you laugh? Consider the borders of Wally's life: What is "tough" is waking up at 10:00 a.m. to make some phone calls and mail some letters. What makes him happy is waking up to a cold cup of coffee that a cockroach didn't die in. There is not a lot of room for meaningful expansion here!

Comically, Wally will explain how he really does appreciate his comforts. In fact, he's looking for *more* comfort in his life, not less, because "life is very abrasive." The very thought of losing his electric blanket, for example, alarms him. He needs his electric blanket because New York nights are cold! Even though, he admits, that it does change him; it changes the way he sleeps, and it changes the way he dreams.

"But that kind of comfort separates you from reality in a very direct way," André warns him. When you are cold, you can develop some compassion for other people in the world who are cold. "What does it mean to live in an environment where something as massive as the seasons don't in any way affect us? . . . Don't you see that comfort can be dangerous?"

Wally stares.

André continues, paternally, and suggests that a person who is only living his life by habit—comfortably, mechanically—is not really living at all. And if that's the case, then he really does need to make a change, become a hobo and take to the road. If our life, or our marriage, or our work, is just mechanical drudgery, then we have lost "the sacramental element" and are not really living; we are just acting out a role.

This is what André discovered as a result of his breakdown, in his workshops, and through his intentional, bizarre experiences. He had to cut out all of the distractions in his life, eliminate all the noise, and listen to what was inside him. He had to shock himself into a new awakening. It took a christening, a trek through the desert, a mock-burial and a necessary resurrection before he could even begin to discover his true self. Only now is he honestly able to recognize the people in his life—his wife, his children, his friends—and truly love them. Without the interconnection of an *attentive* human relationship, how can anyone really know what the word "love" means?

The dinner ends on this inconclusive note. André pays for their meal and Wally takes a taxi cab home. Along the way he notices the buildings, the streets, and the shops of his childhood, as if for the first time; those things he could not see in the underground subway ride when he was still blind. "There wasn't a street or building that wasn't connected to some memory in my mind. There I was buying a suit with my father. There I was buying an ice cream soda after school." When he gets back to his apartment Deby is home from work, and he tells her all about his dinner with André.

Wally is beginning to see more clearly, now. He doesn't notice the change that has taken place in him, but we do.

When life becomes mechanical and mundane, André suggests that one has to change it, become a hobo, take to the road. Why the road? Why the travels? Why all of the peculiar, intentional stunts? *My Dinner With André* does not actually answer these questions, it just points to them as the means to a new awakening.

Wally does change, if only slightly, but it is an essential beginning for him. He is starting to see reality as something *connected* to the memories of his mind. He is more attentive now, more caring, and he is developing a new sense of wonder; the wonder he knew as a child when the world was still a marvelous place. This wonder, this new way of seeing, is at the heart of the sacramental imagination. It is a perspective that allows us to recognize, at least in glimpses, the sacred realm of God.

Acquiring this perspective, should we wish to avoid some of André's fanatical romps, always begins with an honest look at ourselves.

2

Ourselves

The Beginning Voyage

WHEN ANDRÉ SUGGESTS THAT one must take to the road should life become too mundane, he is proposing a spiritual voyage as much as he is world travel, and a spiritual voyage always begins with an honest examination of one's self. After all, we would not begin a sea voyage without first checking the rigging of the ship, its structural soundness, the integrity of the compass, or the reliability of the helm. The spiritual pilgrim begins, too, with a review of his or her own condition: what is true, what is beautiful, what is good—these things the pilgrim keeps close. But what is broken, or frayed, or misdirected, or false—these things must be dealt with. While we cannot cure our own brokenness, we can change our direction, mend what is tattered, and chuck what is deceptive over the side.

Because we are flawed people—inheritors of a fallen humanity—and because we are wounded by a world that is uncaring and blind, we tend to hide what is ailing. We prefer to wrap layers of illusion around our damaged selves like bandages around a soiled wound. It is a common practice and we all do it. We are attracted to the good and the beautiful, so we want to be good and beautiful, too. But the image we then project to the world is a false image of someone who does not even exist. What is worse, we may come to believe in our own deceptions and rely upon our own illusions to hold us aright. In so doing, we allow our wounds to fester beneath their hardened cast, and then healing is impossible.

Our first task, then, is to challenge these illusions and begin the essential work of unwinding their deceptive casings. As we journey towards a true, authentic, and well-formed wholeness—our true self—we must begin with self-reflection, learning to recognize the artificial features of our false self.

The False Self

To say I was born in sin is to say I came
into the world with a false self.[1]
—*THOMAS MERTON*

We live in shells of falsity. We project masks of goodness, success, happiness, and prosperity for others to see and admire. We project these traits because we desire them, and we desire them because they are good. But the false self projects only an illusion of goodness, because it has not managed to achieve the things it desires. It wants desperately to see itself as good and honorable, and it wants others to see it, too. Yet we know that goodness and honor are earned qualities that require work and sacrifice. And since it is easier to project an image of success than it is to achieve it, we often take that easier path. But the image that the false self is projecting is an empty mask, because there is no true person behind it. The false self is just a complex hodgepodge of willfulness, desire, appetite, and sickly satisfaction.

To make matters worse, the false self lives in a world that is filtered through its own distorted perception, barely able to discern truth from false fashions. It is as mesmerized as a child in a candy store, wanting every good thing it sees. And the proprietors of this candy store have made it their business to keep the false self dazzled by distractions that do not feed its starving soul. Through the marketing of their products, their entertainments, their remedies, and their propaganda, these proprietors pitch their wares in order to bolster an ailing self-esteem. André Gregory warned us that this is a form of brain-washing. Thomas Merton warns us that these salesmen "have rushed forward hopefully to announce their message of comfort. Seldom concerned with the afterlife, whether good or evil, as befits men of our time, they want to set things right for us here

1. Merton, *New Seeds of Contemplation*, 33.

and now. They want us, at all costs, to be inspired, uplifted."[2] But theirs is an empty promise, an empty comfort, because it is the false self that is presumably lifted up and worshipped, when there is nothing to the false self at all, only its trappings. "And the worship of nothing is hell."[3]

To move from the self of illusion to the self of true being—the person God created us to be—is a lifelong process of formation. It is not easily achieved, if it is achieved at all. It requires prayer, reflection, repentance, penance, sacrifice, and the integrity of conscience. One must, after all, seek the truth; and seeking after the truth will require admitting error and changing directions, until what is true and what is good and what is beautiful drops like ripened fruit into our hands.

When St. Thomas writes that "the good is what we desire," he is stating a simple fact of human reality. We all desire what is good. Our desires may be tainted or perverted by sin and human weakness, but the good itself remains good.

So when we are told, over and over again, that financial success, social respect, spousal love, filial devotion, and the admiration of our children are all wholly good things, we accept this teaching as true and obvious. It is, after all, part of the American dream; the dream of all peoples. However, should our spousal relations turn cold, or our children rebellious, or our finances collapse into debt and failure, then the false self will double-down and attempt to project a grand illusion of success, even to the point of absurdity. The false self will boast clownish images of happiness and fulfillment, lest our neighbor, or our friend, or our boss, or our family, see through to our naked, shameful selves, and find nothing there worth loving. These counterfeit projections are a recipe for disaster, because they cannot survive a world created by God in truth. We haven't the ability or the strength to maintain the illusions, especially when our souls are not being nourished by what is real.

2. Merton, *The Inner Experience*, 1.

3. Merton, *New Seeds of Contemplation*, 26.

Death of a Salesman [4]

This theme of the false self, undone by the deceptive comforts and promises of society (and the devil), is impressively portrayed in Arthur Miller's *Death of a Salesman*. The play is so powerful, so astute, so painfully tragic in every sense of the word, that it will drain you. It plunges its audience into the reality of the damaged human psyche, of broken family dynamics, and the suffering brought on by sin and the malformed structures of a society dazzled by success, giving it an authenticity few dramas ever achieve.

Here we have a family broken by degradation and failure, by faithlessness and deceit, and by tremendous self-illusion. Chief among the deluded is the father, Willy Loman, who can no longer sell his company's brand and must struggle to get by after his firm has cut off his salary, forcing him to survive on commissions alone. Willy is sinking into madness.

We have his doting wife, Linda, a powerless, kind-hearted, yet dim-seeming woman who reinforces all of her husband's illusions of success, out of love. She flatters the egos of her grown sons equally well, proclaiming them good boys when they truly are not. Linda prefers willful blindness over truth, because she has learned that the truth is too painful to bear. Her husband, Willy, is demeaning and abusive towards her and their sons, so she has learned the soft tactics of an enabling, battered wife.

The oldest son, Biff, is his father's pride and joy. Biff was an athlete in school, intelligent, funny, popular; a boy full of promise and hope. But Biff has been wounded, deeply wounded, and so he has abandoned the family to find goodness and truth in a drifting life out west.

The younger son, Happy, is a clown of a man; an immature, hedonistic fool who lives his life on the surface of pleasure and frivolous disregard.

These four must come together and decide how they can once again live as a family in order to help their ailing father and desperate mother survive, while their own crippling defects get in the way. Only Biff is able to see that they are flawed people, and he tries to get the others to see it, too; about themselves and the suffocating environment of New York City that perpetuates their poverty. Biff knows that he is a weak, sorry, wreck of a man, but none of the others will admit their own failings. No, the false self is a comfortable place to be, and they believe they can keep up their illusions for a lifetime.

---

4. *Death of a Salesman*, directed by Volker Schlondorff, H. M. Television Company. A Roxbury and Punch Production of Arthur Miller's play (an adaptation). NY, 1985. Rated "PG" for adult themes.

As their wounds fester, things grow worse, especially for Willy, who is too proud to take a job that Charley, his envied neighbor, offers him. What's more, Willy cannot admit that his own sons are emotional cripples; that they can barely hold a job much less achieve the stature and success he prizes most. Willy projects himself as a big man, beloved by all his clients, a back-slapping giant of a man whose sons will soon follow the path he has laid out for them. But Willy has wrecked his car so many times on the long road trips to Boston that even he begins to wonder what is wrong with him. He can't keep his eyes on the road. Is he losing his mind? As he bounds from introspection to fury to doting kindness and boastful pride—drifting into flash-backs that he mistakes for reality, calling out to his brother, Ben,[5] who has recently died—Willy is demonstrating clear signs of psychosis. He is aware of his deterioration, and he looks to suicide as his only way out of the mental turmoil and financial ruin. When Willy realizes that he is worth more money dead than alive, he drops subtle references to an insurance policy that might secure his family's future. The evidence for his plan of self-destruction is hidden behind the electrical panel in the basement: a rubber hose and brass nozzle that can be fitted to the gas line on the water heater.

Linda reveals this shocking discovery to Biff when she is alone with him after a family battle. Jarred by the revelation that his father is planning to kill himself, Biff must come to grips with the agony that is behind his father's failure and shame. In turn, Linda must face the truth about her broken family and her worthless sons. Something must be done to help Willy, and they are the only ones who can do it. With a fury pent up by a lifetime of anger, she confronts her two grown boys:

> "I don't say he's a great man. Willy Loman never made a lot of money. His name was never in the paper. He's not the finest character that ever lived. But he's a human being, and a terrible thing is happening to him. So attention must be paid. He's not to be allowed to fall into his grave like an old dog. Attention, attention must finally be paid to such a person . . . You called him

5. Willy's older brother, Ben, was an opportune capitalist. His great boast, repeated often in the play, gives us some idea of his character and values: "When I was seventeen I walked into the jungle, and when I was twenty-one I walked out. And by God I was rich!" He flaunts the riches he acquired in Alaskan timber and African diamonds (note the exploitive enterprises) and suggests that riches can be gained easily with the right know-how. Ben's ghost in the story is only a phantom playing in Willy's sick mind, yet he serves as a diabolical presence throughout the drama, luring Willy into calamity as he dazzles him with easily gotten wealth.

crazy . . . a lot of people think he's lost his balance. But you don't have to be very smart to know what his trouble is. The man is exhausted. A small man can be just as exhausted as a great man. He works for a company thirty-six years this March, opens up unheard-of territories to their trademark, and now in his old age they take his salary away. Are they any worse than his sons? . . . How long can that go on? How long? You see what I'm sitting here and waiting for? And you tell me he has no character? The man who never worked a day but for your benefit."

Biff and Happy are chastised by this scolding, and they agree to try harder, but they must work within the narrow confines of their own incompetence. Happy suggests they start a line in athletic equipment, the "Loman Line," while Biff agrees to interview for a job in sales, an interview that Biff justifiably fears. Afterwards, the boys will take their father out to dinner, just the three of them, to celebrate Biff's triumph. How can anything go wrong?

But of course it does go wrong, terribly wrong. Happy invites two fancy women to their table, hoping to ditch the old man as soon as they can, and then Biff tells his father that he botched the job interview. Willy comes unglued. He rages at Biff for being such a miserable failure and shoves him to the floor. Unable to bear his father's insults and fury, Biff leaves, telling Happy that he must take care of their father now, because he cannot. But Happy slips out of the restaurant with the two women at his first chance, leaving Willy alone and raving on the men's room floor.

The epiphany, the insight, now comes as we learn the source of Biff's wounding and enter into his father's shame. This young man—who adored his father, who cherished his mother, who had such talent and such promise—was destroyed by an incident that is now revealed to us in foggy flashbacks.

Willy hears knocking on the men's room door. The waiters at the restaurant are asking if he is alright. But the scene changes, and we are transported back to a hotel room in Boston where there is knocking at the door and a woman's giggling laughter. Inside Willy's dark memory we observe a lovely, scantily dressed woman, pawing with Willy on the hotel bed. He kisses her, fondles her, and then the knocking returns. Willy hurries his lady friend into the bathroom and closes her in, shushing her sweetly. Then he goes to open the front door and is shocked to find Biff standing there, all the way up from New York. Biff tells his Dad that he had to see him, that he has failed his math class and now he can't graduate from high school. He needs his father to come home immediately and talk to the math teacher about fixing his grades. But when the twittering woman peeks out from behind the bathroom door, Biff falls to stunned silence. Willy waves her off. She is from the room next door, he lies. She is just a buyer from the room next door. But Biff is no fool, he knows that she is there for all the usual reasons, and he sinks to the floor. Willy's story changes, "they're just painting her room," and then it changes again. Biff cannot bear his father's excuses, and he begins to cry, not only at the betrayal of his mother (Willy gives the young woman a box of nylon stockings that were meant for Linda and sends her away down the hall) but at the betrayal of his own admiration and love for his father. Willy's shaky words offer no comfort: "Now look, Biff, when you grow up you'll understand about these things." "You mustn't overemphasize a thing like this." "She's nothing to me, Biff. I was lonely." These words are like a thousand cuts into the very flesh of his son, who sobs uncontrollably. "I order you to stop crying!" Willy now commands him, but that does not work either. He goes to console his boy but Biff rises and struggles free of his father's attempted embrace. "Don't touch me you—liar! . . . You fake! You phony little fake! You fake!"

Rarely does fiction deliver the human fall from grace more aptly than in these revelatory scenes. Even forgiveness seems powerless to mend what is so badly broken. Both father and son are destroyed. Biff will not graduate high school, and he will not go on to college on a promised scholarship. He severs his relationship with his father and ruins his own future. He will leave the family and go out west where things are real. But his wounded eyes, forced open by this deception, can barely begin to direct him.

When we return from the flashback to present day, the boys come home to an enraged mother. Learning that Willy had been discarded on the men's room floor, Linda lashes out at her despicable sons and demands that they leave the house at once. Happy offers her flowers (left over from his night out) which she hurls to the floor. Willy tries to drift away to an unreal garden, but Biff draws them all together and then slams a hose onto the kitchen table—the instrument that Willy planned to use to end his life—and confronts his family with the awful reality. "There has never been ten minutes of truth spoken in this house!" he cries truthfully, and so he will set things straight. He tells them who they are, he tells them their truth; but most earnestly he confesses his own truth. That he has stolen his way out of every job he ever had, and that he and his father are nothing special, they are only dime-a-dozen people. Willy cannot endure this outing and wails: "I am not a dime-a-dozen!" clinging ferociously to his misplaced pride, and only that.

When Thomas Merton writes about the false self, he does so in order to invite his readers to a higher reality: the reality of the true self. This true self, which seeks union with God, must renounce or remove or work through all of those illusions that keep him or her rooted in a false persona, because what is false is not of God, and so there can be no union there. But this de-masking, this turning from the false self to the true, presumes that the spiritual pilgrim *desires* God over fantasy and truth over fiction. It isn't always the case. When truth is too painful to bear—as it often is—many sad souls take comfort in their make-believe worlds, as we see here in *Death of a Salesman*. Willy Loman's sins are not rooted in his weaknesses so much as they are rooted in his *falsehoods*. Willy lives by the lie; it is the lie that sells his products and it is the lie that destroys him.

Biff's epiphany comes when he sees that his father is a phony; but the greater, more destructive revelation is that his father is a *liar*, one who has betrayed his family and who continually down-plays his deceptions rather than admit a fault. "You mustn't overemphasize these things!" he pleads, almost lovingly. But deceit, infidelity, betrayal, adultery; can these things be *overemphasized*? What destroys this family is the lying boast that Willy Loman is a great man; that he is a big shot (when he is a failure), an admired employee (when they laugh at him and then take his job away), a devoted husband (when he is an abusive cheat), a proud father (when he is demeaning and cruel), and an achiever of the American dream (when he is destroyed by that counterfeit commodity). Willy's greatest loss is the loss of his beloved boy's admiration and love. Biff struggles to forgive him, to find a way to let the old man go (and be allowed to go), but how can he forgive a sin that his father will not even acknowledge? And how can Willy acknowledge what he absolutely refuses to see? And how can he ever see what he has so artfully disguised?

To his great credit, Biff does embrace his father, even as he vows to leave him; and he kisses him in a gesture that reveals tremendous love. The old man is touched. "He likes me," Willy admits tenderly. The family, placated now, can retire upstairs to their beds; but not Willy. Revitalized by Biff's kindness—though still steeped in delusion—Willy speeds off after his illustrious, phantom brother, who entices him with twenty thousand dollars worth of diamonds; or the twenty thousand dollars from his life insurance policy. Willy then dies in a wheel-screeching car wreck off stage.

The final scene over Willy's gravesite depicts the mourners who have now slipped back into their false personas, accomplices in a well worn charade. This family's pretentions, which they have carefully crafted and freely embraced, will last the rest of their lifetimes. Biff may find the truth eventually. He has at least the wisdom to question what is false, but we do not know what will become of him. He may never grow beyond his renunciation of a fallen world. Happy will stay in New York, vowing to "beat this racket!" and become the "number-one-man." As for Linda—who was content with just a little and only wanted Willy to be contented, too—for Linda there will only be grief and the empty shell of a home.

"I made the last payment on the house today," she tells Willy's headstone. "Today, dear. And there'll be nobody home."

All About Eve [6]

In *All About Eve* we encounter another story dealing with false realities as they work to destroy a soul who is not unlike Willy Loman. Set within the glitzy backdrop of the New York stage, it is the story of an aging actress, Margo Channing, who must come to terms with her loss of youth and beauty in an industry which overemphasizes both. Margo's director and beau, Bill Sampson (a man eight years her junior), is supportive and kind, loving and faithful, but Margo suspects he is dishonest. And while she relies heavily upon her friends and fans to bolster her fragile ego, she presumes all along that there is something amiss.

When an admiring young woman enters Margo's world and gushes her great esteem for the stage star, Margo is charmed. She takes this budding actress, Eve Harrison, under her wing—dismissing the warnings of her prudent maid, her loyal friends, and her honest lover—so she can wallow in the accolades of this, her greatest fan. Those who know and love Margo are shoved rudely to the wings. Only the darling Eve, who flatters Margo's delicate self-worth, is fully trusted.

But indeed, something *is* amiss. It turns out that Eve is hardly a sweetheart. Eve is cunning, Eve is shrewd, and Eve is on the make. She uses her beauty and her connection to Margo to attract the attention of the theatre producers, and then attains the coveted role of Margo's understudy in Margo's new play. She later arranges for Margo, who has never

6. *All About Eve*, directed by Joseph Mankiewicz. A Daryl Zanuck Production, 1950. Not rated, though younger children probably won't like it.

missed a theatre performance in her long career, to be delayed by a suspiciously sabotaged car at a resort too far away. Then Eve takes the stage in Margo's place and with great success.

Yet Eve does not achieve this success on her own. She has an attentive accomplice. Addison DeWitt—a slick, erudite, columnist and theatre critic—sees clearly the sinister side of Eve as if he were Satan himself (indeed, there is a remarkable resemblance), and Satan has no illusions![7] He is his own true self. He has no pity for Eve's fallen nature, neither is he charmed by her feminine wiles or softened by her tears. He is attracted only to her power—and she will wield considerable power in the theatre circles—and to her stellar skills as an actress. DeWitt praises Eve's talents in his column, dismissing Margo as an over-appreciated has-been, one who was really too old for the part, and celebrates Eve Harrison as the theatre's great rising star.

DeWitt intends to fully own Eve, and he has no qualms in telling her so. But this dark honesty does not damage their relationship, it only sets things straight. When Eve steps out of line, DeWitt commands her to obedience. When she laughs in his face, he strikes her (the devil will not be mocked). When she feigns indignant fury, he calls out her lies and her foolishness at daring to lie to him. "You're an improbable person, Eve, and so am I. We have that in common. Also our contempt for humanity and inability to love and be loved, insatiable ambition . . . and talent. We deserve each other." And it is true. As we have seen, the lovely young Eve will cheat, lie, obstruct, connive, flirt, flatter, blackmail, and claw her way to the top of the New York stage scene. She might even kill to become a superstar. Yes, even that. DeWitt rightly calls her "a killer." She is well groomed for her partnership with Satan, to whom she has sold her soul, and he sees to it that she is rewarded with success.

On the occasion of Eve's crowning awards celebration, after Eve has snubbed her own party and gone her lonely way home, a beautiful admirer is found waiting to greet her. The young woman was able to sneak into Eve's home and wait for her, so she might gush forth her grand admiration. This final scene mirrors that first encounter between Eve and Margo, when Eve flattered her idol with audacious praise. The scene ends with a brilliant image of this new Eve bowing before a three-way mirror that reflects an infinity of new Eves, just like her; Eves who are, after all,

---

7. A sign worth noting is the theatrical marquee that advertises a performance of "The Devil's Disciple," just before Margo enters the theatre where DeWitt awaits her, and where Eve has just brilliantly read a part as Margo's understudy.

legion. So we are shown, by way of reflection and repetition, that the false self—along with conceit and deception and Satan and sin—will endlessly perpetuate itself in a world that sets pride on a pedestal and exalts fame.

But these successful scoundrels are not the champions in this story. The champion in this story is Margo—aging, fading Margo—even in her fallen, disgraced, and has-been state. She is the true heroine because, though once hoodwinked by flattery, she has uncovered her own vulnerability and has learned the necessary virtue of humility. As it turns out, Margo's truth-speaking friends are true in their love for her as well, and so she chooses love and vulnerability and truth over pride, embittered nerve, and celebrity. "No more make-believe," Margo toasts her friends and Bill, her worthy fiancé, "off stage or on."

In the story examples given so far, we discover that the false self can be blinded by comfort (Wally, in *My Dinner with André*), crippled by self-deception (Willy, in *Death of a Salesman*), and deluded by flattery (Margo, in *All About Eve*). Of the leading characters in these films, it is Wally and Margo who give us the greatest reason for hope. This is because Wally has begun to see things more clearly, and Margo has put aside her "make-believe" self and is learning to value truth; and she appreciates the friends who are bold enough to speak it. She recognizes and accepts the love of her true companions who will support her in her self discovery, just as Wally appreciates André. Both are turning to a new, more honest life, and we expect that they will each find authentic happiness.

We may recall, in the Parable of the Sower, how some of the seed fell on rocky ground (which we might interpret as falling on the parched soil of the false self) and how some fell among the brambles where the grain sprang up, but was choked to death by thorny weeds. Here, it is not so much the *self* that is faulty, but the environment or the circumstances wherein the self lives. Our society, our culture, and our homes can be suffocating to the struggling soul yearning for happiness. Original sin does not just stain our souls, it mars the whole of our world.

In the next film, we are introduced to another form of delusion, the one we are conditioned to accept through the circumstances of our lives; either by powerful social expectations or by the faulty, unchallenged traditions of our culture. In other words, those masks we have acquired through no real fault of our own.

The King of Masks [8]

I was born in a mask. I came into existence under a sign of contradiction, being someone that I was never intended to be and therefore a denial of what I am supposed to be.[9]

—*THOMAS MERTON*

In *The King of Masks*, we meet humble Wang, a lonely old man who has lost his wife and his cherished son, and who makes his meager living as a street performer. Wang is a skilled master in the ancient art of *Sichuan*: the telling of stories using facial masks made of silk. Like a magician, the *Sichuan* artist can change his masks—from worried to happy to sad to fierce—in a split second, thus illustrating the fairytale stories he tells that frighten and delight his audiences.

Master Wang is very traditional and very loving, but he is troubled because he does not have an heir. His art is a family heirloom, passed on from father to son for generations. The ancient tradition holds that the master can never reveal his secrets to an outsider, and never to a daughter.

One day, in the midst of his sidewalk masquerade, a renowned female-impersonator of the Chinese opera stops to watch Wang's performance. The celebrity, Master Liang, is extremely impressed with the old man's skills and tosses him a valuable silver coin. Then he invites him to tea, perhaps hoping to learn his secrets. There, Wang unburdens his heart to Liang, telling him of his sorrow at losing his hereditary line, and how his craft will now be lost because he has no son to carry on the tradition. He humbly declines to teach his skills to an outsider, though he is embarrassed to confess this to the generous opera star who has been so good to him. But the effeminate performer insists that it was never his intention to learn the great master's skills. He proclaims his own unworthiness, stating that he is, after all, "half woman." But he encourages Wang to go

8. *The King of Masks*, directed by Wu Tianming. Samuel Goldwyn Film, a Shaw Brothers (H.K.) Production, 1996. Not rated, but suitable for children old enough to read the subtitles. (Mandarin).

9. Merton, *New Seeds of Contemplation*, 33–34.

and adopt a son, using the gifted money to purchase an heir at the Market for Unwanted Children. Grateful and delighted, Wang goes to this ominous marketplace to find a boy that he can adopt. On the way he stops to purchase a statue of a mother goddess who, the vender assures him, will bless the old man with a son.

When Wang arrives at the market, he is immediately swarmed by desperate little girls who cling to him, begging that he adopt them and take them to his home. They will be good, respectful daughters and work very hard for him. But no, no, he does not want a girl—in fact, no one does—he needs to adopt a boy. It is essential to keep up the sacred tradition. Mothers beg him to take their girls, they do not ask for any money, just that he please feed them. It is heart breaking. But there are no boys, and Wang heads for the exit, downcast and discouraged. Then he hears the cry of a child from behind him: "Grandpa!" Wang turns slowly. There, perched high on a step in order to be seen, is a boy of about eight years old. The child cries out "Grandpa!" once again, and Wang hurries over, looks him over, and then buys him immediately with the silver coin.

How happy they are! They are both overjoyed. Wang takes the little one home to his river barge where he lives along the shore. He washes him and buys him new clothes, but he is alarmed to discover deep bruises on the boy's arms. He is furious that anyone would ever abuse a little child. As the days go by the two grow close, and Wang begins to teach the boy, Doggie, the art of painting and crafting silk masks. Doggie is very smart and obedient and he learns quickly.

One day in the city streets, when old Wang is accidently wounded by a knife, he asks the child to pee on the bleeding cut to stop the bleeding and sterilize the wound. Doggie refuses to do this. The old man is taken aback. Is this child so disobedient that he would refuse, after all he has done for him? He commands the boy to do as he is told, but Doggie sobs and confesses that he cannot obey. It is impossible, because he is not really a boy at all but a girl in disguise. With her hair cut short and dressed in boys' clothing she had disguised herself as a boy because no one at the marketplace ever wanted to keep a girl. She was bought and sold seven times, abused, and then thrown away in her eight short years of life.

Old Wang, however, is not sympathetic. Indeed, he is outraged at having been deceived and cheated out of his money, and at having lost his only chance for an heir. Callously, the old man casts Doggie off and rows away in his barge-home, leaving her alone on the shore. But Doggie is a bold little character. She cries out to him from the wharf, begging that he let her stay. Then she throws herself into the river to swim after his slow moving boat. She will be his servant if not his grandson, she cries from the waters, she will cook his meals and clean his home, if only he will take her back. Alarmed at her daring stunt and fearing she will drown, the old man rescues her and gruffly agrees, but he insists that she must call him "boss" from now on, and never "Grandpa." The relationship is weakly mended, but it is not the same. Wang now teaches Doggie acrobatics so she will be able to earn her keep as a street performer, but he refuses to teach her the craft of *Sichuan*.

One evening the two attend the Chinese opera to watch their friend, Master Liang, the famous female impersonator, perform as a Bodhisattva princess who descends into hell clinging to a long cord, so to rescue her dead father. By this sacrificial act the princess achieves Nirvana, resurrecting from Hades and death. Both Wang and Doggie are transfixed by the great performance. Back at home on the river scow, Doggie asks again why she cannot learn the craft of mask making. The old man tells her it is because she is not a boy. "What does a boy have that I don't have?" she demands to know. "You do not have a teapot spout," he explains, smiling secretly. She goes to retrieve his little statue of the mother goddess and bravely scolds him. "Then how is it that you can *worship* a woman with bosoms who has no teapot spout?!"

The story continues on through many adventures and troubles, culminating in a great sacrifice that Doggie makes to save old Wang, who has been arrested on suspicion of kidnapping (a prominent little boy who had been snatched by traffickers). Like Bodhisattva, Doggie risks her life by descending on a long rope to confront Master Liang in his mansion home, begging him to use his influence to liberate old Wang from his false accusers. She threatens to cut the tether if he refuses. But the amused onlookers suppose it is just a stunt, until Doggie does cut the rope and is only saved from death by Master Liang's great leaping catch.

Moved by her remarkable courage, Liang and his military friends intercede for old Wang and he is released. The kidnapped boy is returned to his family, and Master Wang goes back to his street performances; only now we note with great delight that Doggie has joined him, not as an acrobat, but as a *Sichuan* artist behind her own remarkable mask.

The *King of Masks* challenges us to question our essential identity. It is certainly a powerful social commentary on the oppression of women and traditional gender roles, but really it is more. Who are we, and who are we created to be? Are we immaterial souls that are masked in flesh, gender, teapot spouts, bosoms, makeup, costumes, traditions, family names, professions, colors, and race? Are we merely actors on a stage, playing out our roles in masked obedience to some ancient, unexamined script? Are the roles and masks that are beyond our crafting even important? What of love and self-sacrifice? The Bodhisattva princess descended into hell to rescue her father, thereby achieving Nirvana and sanctity in heaven. Doesn't Doggie do the very same for Master Wang? Where is the grace and nobility that underpins our fleshy, bodily being, and isn't that perhaps the greater reality? The allegorical play on masks and identity that occurs throughout this film should challenge the viewer to consider what is really essential about our human nature, and not the trappings that disguise and hide us, however they are imposed.

The True Self

But there is no substance under the things with which I (the false self) am clothed. I am hollow, and my structure of pleasures and ambitions has no foundation. I am objectified in them. But they are all destined by their very contingency to be destroyed. And when they are gone there will be nothing left of me but my own nakedness and emptiness and hollowness, to tell me that I am my own mistake.[10]

—*THOMAS MERTON*

The false self is often shocked into oblivion by suffering and loss. Then we are left with the awful, naked reality that we are not what we pretended to be. When this happens, we may choose to double-down and intensify our projected false image (often with rage, as we see in Willy Loman), or succumb to misery and grief and deflated acceptance (the Loman family). A wiser option is to recognize our vulnerability and *dare* to be real. When we do (as we see in Margo Channing), we may begin to learn the lessons of humility. It is this virtue that softly turns our vision inward, allowing

10. Merton, *New Seeds of Contemplation*, 35.

us to examine our conscience, our values, and our worth. Suffering and loss are often the flames that forge this new creation; this person that God intended all along. We can catch a glimpse of this rebirth in the bold actions of Doggie, a child who suffered tremendously, yet was no longer afraid of rejection or even death. In the face of extreme oppression, she asserts her human dignity, and then finally *demands* it! (I suspect that there is something in you that cheered her on!) Since we are all created with great dignity and the grace of free will, we share in the work of our own creation; as individual persons and as a human community. It is challenging work to build an authentic character, but it is a work always guided by love, because God is love.

Anastasia [11]

The theme of the lost self searching for truth is a universal theme. Literature and film are replete with wandering pilgrims, coming-of-age children, trauma-driven heroes, and a great multitude of souls on the edge of madness. It is a theme we may have learned from the existentialist thinkers of the twentieth century, and it is illustrated in the countless films that ushered in our post-modern era. Yet, one can go back as far as Dante and find him lost in the Dark Wood of Error. For that matter, one can go back to Job, or to Adam and Eve, wracked with loss and tossed out of their natural homes. Lostness is a universal experience because it is our human condition, and because our creation is not yet complete.

Perhaps one of the finest films to take up this theme of alienation is *Anastasia*, the 1956 classic that depicts our human disaffections in a world gone mad with war.

The story (though much romanticized) is taken from the real life rumor that Anastasia, youngest daughter of Czar Nicholas II, had survived the assassination of her family by the Bolsheviks in 1918, and was wandering through post-war Europe, a victim of amnesia and mental trauma.[12] The image of the "Lost Madonna" is a beloved cultural icon of Russian literature, and this could explain the popular fervor that roiled

11. *Anastasia*, directed by Anatole Litvak. A 20th Century Fox Production, 1956. Not rated, but suitable for any age.

12. Anna Anderson, the woman who claimed to be Anastasia, was later found to be unrelated to the Romanov family through advanced DNA testing done in the 1990s. The remains of the real Anastasia were likely exhumed from a wooded gravesite in Russia, in 1995, where the DNA evidence proved their royal lineage.

behind these rumors. There is something in us that wants Anastasia to live. There was also a lot of money to be made by heartless imposters maneuvering to claim her name.

The film version of this story is beautifully staged and perfectly acted, but what makes it a classic work of art is the screenplay, which is brilliant, even literary.

Our movie opens with a young woman on the edge of despair, leaning forward over the dark waters of the Seine, about to throw herself into the river to drown. She is rescued by a Russian exile who has been charged with finding an heir to what is left of the Romanov fortune. If he and his two accomplices cannot find a surviving heir, they are to concoct a believable one, an imposter they can use to dupe the Dowager Empress Maria Feodorovna. Only the empress can legally identify and designate a successor to the Romanov line, and that successor would then be able to claim some ten million pounds that is being held in the Bank of England.

The three conspiring Russians are strictly scallywags: Chernov, a sniveling ex-banker and coward; Petrovin, a failed doctor of divinity; and General Bounine, an over-bearing military officer of the defeated White Army.[13] All are penniless and desperate characters, having fled Russia after the revolution.

Since the rescued young woman "fits the uniform" and can remember very little of her own past (and she also seems a touch mad), they decide to make her over as the Grand Duchess Anastasia Nicolaevna. With nowhere else to turn the woman, who calls herself Anna, goes along with the charade. Though reluctant to swindle anyone, she reasons that it will be good to have a roof over her head, enough food to eat, and a modest sense of belonging.

It is General Bounine who takes charge of her training, schooling her in the family's history and its imperial refinements. He is a strict and unforgiving taskmaster, demanding perfection from poor Anna, who struggles to learn all the required poise, manners, and memories of a past not hers.

Or is it? This is where the story pivots, as Anna begins to recollect episodes out of Anastasia's past that she could not have learned from Bounine. Are these real memories of her own childhood, or memories from stories she had heard somewhere else? Now Anna's struggle must turn inward. Who is she, really? What is her real name, her true family,

13. One might note that they each represent one of the three pillars of Imperial Russia: vanquished wealth, vanquished religion, and a vanquished military.

her authentic self? She honestly does not know. She only remembers an explosion and many hospitals, and flashes of images that baffle her.

General Bounine invites a cast of expatriated Russian dignitaries to sign a declaration confirming Anna's identity as Anastasia Nicolaevna. It is telling that most of them truly *want* this woman to be the young heiress. They are eager to believe her story and attest to it under oath. But they want it because they desire all of the wealth and finery connected to the old world, and because they may profit by it, too, somehow. Even the Russian Prince Paul, nephew to Empress Maria Feodorovna, is smitten by the illusion of glamour and affluence that Anastasia represents. Her influence could certainly bolster the allowance that his Auntie already allows him. When Prince Paul and Anna are first introduced, he is dazzled by her beauty and grace; but the prince is a flatterer and something of a rogue, and he surely courts this mysterious young woman to get at the inheritance which he expects to gain through her affections. As Anna wisely observes to him while they waltz together: "The poor know, at least, when they are being loved for themselves."

The great challenge in all of this will be convincing Maria Feodorovna, Anastasia's grandmother, of Anna's royal blood. Unfortunately, the empress will not condescend to see her. It is understandable enough, false heirs have been pounding at her door for years. "The firing squads were such poor shots it's amazing the revolution succeeded!" she quips bitterly.

Through some wrangling and charming of the empress' lady-in-waiting (a fabulous character!) General Bounine arranges to have Anna attend the same opera as the empress. He seats her in a tier strategically positioned across the stage from the empress, where the old woman might steal a better look. It is a smart move and the empress, out of curiosity or perhaps deep longing, peers through her opera glasses at Anna and is struck by the young woman's resemblance to her grandchild. We can see her hard features soften, if only for a moment.

Though the empress is as tough as nails, she has also suffered great sorrow and is tragically isolated in her old age. Weakening, she consents to General Bounine's logic and his persistent requests, and so she allows Anna an audience. Their meeting is one of the finest scenes in all of cinema. Here is the traumatized young woman, seeking the truth about her life; and here is the traumatized old woman, knowing the truth full well, and despising it. Though the honest desperation in each woman's search is authentic—the two do admit their shared suffering and their great need for love—still, neither is willing to compromise the truth for a comfortable and convenient illusion. As a result, the meeting does not go well. "I am as weary of these spectral grandchildren as I am false hope," the empress laments, and it is true. When Anna speaks lovingly of her sisters, the empress bristles and accuses her of fraud. She calls her "imposter!" because she cannot bear to hear her family's names repeated with such warmth by this "cheap little actress."

"You call me that!" Anna moans, wilting under the rejection. The empress stiffly offers to arrange another meeting, at a time when they are both stronger; but no, Anna reasons, the empress would only harden in her resolve, and Anna could not endure another rebuff. Unwittingly, she begins to cough back her tears.

The old woman asks, tenderly now, if she is alright. Is she ill? But Anna shakes her head. She was ill but not any longer, though it is kind of the empress to ask. She tells the old woman that she is just a little frightened, and that she always coughs when she is frightened.

The empress is taken aback. "Say that again."

"That I cough when I am frightened?"

"When you were a little girl, you coughed when you were frightened. Malenkaia! Malenkaia![14] You have come from so very far away, and I have waited so long." The two embrace and they weep together. "No, no, no. Don't cry. There's no need to be frightened. No, don't speak. You are safe, Anastasia. You are with me. You're home! The phantoms can go. The closed rooms can be opened."

At the end of this scene, in the midst of their embrace, the empress is heard to murmur to the walls: "Oh, but please, if it should not be you, don't ever tell me."

Sometimes love and need can triumph over truth and, as the empress foresaw, "the truth serves only a world that lives by it."

Still, our story does not end with this discovery. It would be too fanciful, too sentimental, and altogether too deceptive if it did! This story has great integrity, and so we are more deeply challenged.

A great gala is now planned to celebrate and present the Grand Duchess Anastasia Nicolaevna to the world. Prince Paul wants to use the occasion to announce their engagement. All the socialites are dizzy with old-world excitement. "It is madness without the moon!" But the astute empress is not moved by the fanfare. "Yes, I can smell the mothballs," she grumbles. Though there is great merriment, the empress wryly suspects that some deception is brewing.

14. The childhood nickname for Anastasia.

As she prepares Anna for her coronation she comments on Anna's somber mood, challenging her granddaughter to speak her truth. What does she really want? Is it a life with *Paul?* But Anna demurs, she wants to please her grandmother, that is all. But it is not enough. "You must find the things from which other women make their happiness," the empress instructs her. "The world moves on, Malenkaia . . . and we must move with it, or be left to molder with the past. I *am* the past. I like it. It's sweet and familiar. The present is cold and foreign. And the future . . . fortunately, I don't need to concern myself with that. But you do. It's yours." She gives her the jeweled necklace of Catherine the Great and then sends her into the green room where she had already instructed General Bounine to wait.

It is time. The empress approaches the great stairway with Prince Paul, presumably to proclaim Anastasia as her granddaughter and heir, and to announce Anastasia's engagement to her nephew prince. But at the moment of their grand entry it is discovered that Anastasia is gone, she has fled the green room and has run off with General Bounine!

Prince Paul is thoroughly and stupidly stunned. "I don't understand," he mutters, fading.

"You never did!"

"So, she wasn't Anastasia after all?"

Empress Maria Feodorovna stiffens with a knowing smile. "Wasn't she?" she smirks, tilting her head and leaving the crucial question hanging in the air.

We are, in our romantic way, pleased that Anastasia has run off with General Bounine, choosing love over a false sense of duty. We understand that she got what she wanted and needed most, love and the truth. The old empress got what she wanted, too, which was love and the truth. Only those false bunglers, those hangers-on who wanted sparkling illusion and wealth and a grander station in life got nothing. And that is just what they deserved, as "*they are all destined by their very contingency to be destroyed.*"[15] So to them—the gaping, expectant, gala guests—the empress has something to say.

"Whatever will you say?" Paul wonders as he escorts the empress down the majestic staircase to the rush of an orchestral anthem.

"Say? Oh, I will say: 'The play is over. Go home.'"

---

15. Merton, *New Seeds of Contemplation*, 35.

Anna is first driven by madness to the edge of destruction. Her past, unknown traumas led her to the very brink of suicide. Like Willy Loman, she is wounded and bandaged in layers of ill-fitted cloth that project a deceptive image of herself to the world. But unlike Loman, she does not choose these trappings to bolster a vain self-image. Like Margo and Eve, she willingly steps upon the pedestal of fame, but unlike them Anna aspires only to learn the truth about her identity—and if it happens to be that of a princess then so be it. This is what we are left with: the belief that she is Anastasia, but the real truth that it no longer matters. She has found love, and love will nurture her to become what she is meant to be, her true self.

Granted, this is a fanciful ending, but the wisdom and dignity and deep satisfaction of the dowager empress portrays this happily-ever-after moment as something akin to noble.

My Life as a Dog [16]

"It's not so bad if you think about it.
It could have been worse."

—*INGEMAR*

Anastasia discovers her truth with the help of honest humility and the empress' sharp wisdom. Though she is used by greedy, dishonest men, she never allows herself to sink to their level or betray her true self. Her reward (one can only hope) is a lifetime of love.

In our next film, *My Life as a Dog,* we meet Ingemar, a young boy who must suffer the loss of everyone he has ever loved: a father who has abandoned him, a mother who is dying of tuberculosis (and emotionally erratic), an older brother who is hardened and cruel, and his little dog, Siskan, who is sent to the pound. Like an unwanted dog, Ingemar is shuffled from home to home while his mother slowly dies in the hospital. He is an odd little kid and he and his brother are not wanted by the social worker who must take them in out of pity or obligation. So he is moved again. Ingemar finally ends up at his uncle's place in a little mountain village far from home.

16. *My Life as a Dog,* directed by Lasse Hallström. A Waldemar Bergendahl Production, 1985. Rated "PG 13" with some nudity and sexual references.

The film is interspersed with Ingemar's voice-over reflections as he tries to keep his life in manageable perspective. He is grieving and in great pain over his losses, but he soothes his aching heart with reassurances that are close to prayers of gratitude. "It could have been worse," he reasons. Consider that man who casually walked across an athletic field one afternoon and got a javelin through his chest. "I'll bet he was surprised!" Or the Russian space dog, Laika, who was sent into orbit in a Sputnik satellite with great patriotic fervor, and then left to starve or freeze to death in space. "They never intended to bring her back," he notes. These chilling reflections give us an idea of the inner workings of Ingemar's heart. He hurts terribly, but things could always be a lot worse.

Ingemar's uncle is also an odd sort, living with his wife and in-laws in a rather peculiar town filled with rather peculiar people. There is Ingemar's new friend, Manne, a boy with green (copper bleached) hair; a girl who dresses like a boy; an old man who is fixated on ladies underwear ads; and another decrepit old neighbor, Fransson, who is fixated on fixing his roof. Layer upon layer of human charm! Ingemar does not stand out among these odd people, and he takes comfort in their company.

After school he helps out at the town's one industry, a glass factory, which is a warm place to be on a cold winter day in Sweden. He develops a school-boy crush on the buxom blonde glass polisher, who seems to be the light in every other workman's eye! He learns to box with the neighbor kids in Manne's barn, and he helps his uncle build a little shack outside their crowded rented home. There, his uncle can get away from his wife and in-laws, and together they play "I've Got a Lovely Bunch of Coconuts" on the record player, *ad infinitum*, driving his poor wife nuts. These little peccadilloes light up the film.

Ingemar's life would be happy in this place if only Siskan, his little terrier, could live with him, too. He pleads with his uncle to go and retrieve his dog from the kennel where she had been left, but the uncle is evasive, carefully steering around the issue with feigned deafness and sudden distractions.

As children are often cruel, and because Ingemar is so vulnerable, he learns the truth about Siskan at a birthday party, after he and his tom-boy girl friend get into a quarrel. Furious at his bizarre behavior (of barking like a dog and chasing the girls on his hands and knees), she tells him that his own dog is dead, that it was killed at the kennel and everybody knows it. Poor Ingemar flies into a rage. He flees the party and locks himself in his uncle's shack where he will stay and shiver throughout the frozen night. Though the uncle begs him to come inside the house, Ingemar only barks at him like an enraged terrier from behind the locked door. His uncle doesn't know what to do, and so he leaves a thermos and blanket for Ingemar at the doorway and goes to bed. In the morning, when Ingemar still refuses to come out of the shack, the uncle breaks down the door and discovers the boy weeping softly. Ingemar begs his uncle to tell him that he was not the cause of his mother's death, and the uncle lamely assures him that "No, it was not you." Then Ingemar cries deeply into the pillow, and utters the question that has been burning in his wounded heart all along: "Why didn't you want me, Mama?" he sobs, "Why didn't you want me?" Here the finite and the infinite seem to congeal. All of Ingemar's sorrows and hopes and loves converge in this frozen moment, in this frozen shack, and he is undone by anguish, abandonment, and dread. Ingemar's awkward uncle tries to console the boy, but he can barely do more than sit there, murmuring without sense. These contrasting tensions are what give *My Life as a Dog* its depth and its sparkle; we suffer, and we do not understand.

Then a shout goes up from the neighborhood kids. "Ingemar! Come see! Come see! Old Fransson has gone for a swim in the river!" All of the townsfolk come running out of their houses, plowing through the snow to the frozen river. Ingemar creeps along, too. There they find Fransson, the old roofer, submerged to his neck in the icy waters. They try to coax the crazy man from his frigid bath, forming a human chain to reach him. Ingemar watches as they lure the reluctant Fransson to shore, towel him off, wrap him in blankets, set him by a flaming furnace at the glass factory, and pour some potent potion into his mouth, uncorked from a silver flask. And then Ingemar smiles. It is a slow smile, a shy and simple smile, but it is a good smile, too. He knows now that he is home, and that these endearing people, these characters who have rescued this goofy old man, will be there to rescue him, too. This is the significant sign, this is the infinite gesture of love. Ingemar, who was shuttled from place to place like an unwanted dog—a dog that is easily destroyed in a kennel or left to starve to death in space—has come home to the warmth of *human communion*, even and especially in its peculiarity.

The Burmese Harp [17]

*"The soil of Burma is red,
and so are its rocks."*

To seek the true self, we must honestly assess our human condition as well as our human values. We must unmask those false images that we have concocted, by choice or by circumstance, and set aside the trappings that are not essential to our true nature—as we saw in the *King of Masks*.

But that is only the beginning of our search for authenticity.

Our Judeo-Christian tradition asserts that human beings were created in the image and likeness of God. The Catholic faith teaches that we have an inherited sanctity uniquely imbued in our actual flesh, because the Incarnation of Christ—God taking on human form in the person of Jesus Christ—has sanctified the human body. The church places particular emphasis on the human body as the instrument through which our salvation is accomplished. It is the temple of the Holy Spirit, and should be treated as such. This applies not only to how we comport ourselves, but how we treat others. If this is true, and I believe it is, then it must also be true for all people, everywhere, regardless of their own beliefs.

So let us turn now to the beautiful Japanese film, *The Burmese Harp*, which places particular emphasis on, and reverence for, the human body; even in the aftermath of grisly death.

Filmed in 1956, *The Burmese Harp* deals with the end of WWII as it is seen through the eyes of a defeated Japanese platoon. The film boldly presents two conflicting choices for the conquered armies that are stranded in Burma after the war's end: Should they continue fighting to the death, for love of country and to honor those who have already died—in which case many more lives will be lost; or should they surrender in shame and return home to Japan, to rebuild their homeland after its near annihilation? In between these two just choices there is a third, sacred option, one which our hero, Mizushima, will take upon himself.

The film is based on the novel, *The Harp of Burma*, which is a beloved, sweet fable that was written for a young Japanese audience after the war. But it is also a fable in the more negative sense of the word, as it

17. *The Burmese Harp*, directed by Kon Ichikawa. Produced by Masayuki Takagi, Nikkatsu Corporation, 1956. (Japanese). Not rated, suitable for any age able to read the subtitles.

presents this horrible episode in Asian history as an innocent tale of noble comrades in arms. We should know that the Burmese suffered great atrocities at the hands of the Japanese soldiers, and that these atrocities are never even suggested in this story. But as a film, *The Burmese Harp* is powerful enough in its message to overcome this flaw. We may need to suspend our objections long enough to realize that, while there is terrible cruelty in war, there are also those good soldiers—saints even—who deserve to have their sacrifices acknowledged and honored and praised; even in spite of the atrocities committed by lesser men. You will find such a saint in *The Burmese Harp* and discover, I hope, a new perspective on what it means to revere the image of God in man.

Our story opens with a platoon of soldiers, a band of some twenty Japanese troops, on their final push to Thailand through the deep mountain jungles of Burma. They are good soldiers and fond of singing together to raise their spirits. Their leader, Captain Inouye, studied music and was a choral director before the war, and he has taught his company well. Their forward scout, Private Mizushima, is skilled at playing a Burmese harp, which lends an eerie purity to their mournful songs of home and family. He is also gently teased by his comrades for looking more like a Burmese peasant than a Japanese soldier, when he advances ahead of them disguised in traditional Burmese garb.

As the unit settles down to rest in a peasant village they are startled by the approach of enemy troops moving through the dense jungle. The captain quickly commands them all to sing and clap their hands so the enemy will not know that they are aware of them. This gives the Japanese time to prepare for battle. As they take up their arms and load their weapons, they begin singing "There is No Place Like Home,"[18] a tune well known to the approaching British regiment. The enemy responds by singing the same song back to them, only with English words. Amazed by the unity of their music, the Japanese and British come slowly together, singing soulfully, and no shots are fired.

Now the Japanese learn from their enemy that Imperial Japan has surrendered, and that the war has finally ended. They surrender to the British regiment and are marched south toward a detention camp in Mudon where they will await their fate as prisoners of war.

On the way to the camp they are told by their captors that there are still many Japanese units that refuse to surrender and who are still

---

18. A song well known to many cultures, apparently!

fighting from unshakable high caves in the mountain region. Mizushima, the advance scout, volunteers to go to these Japanese units and explain to them that the war is over and that they should surrender and return to Japan to rebuild their country. But when he reaches the caves he finds that his countrymen refuse to accept defeat. They accuse Mizushima of being a British spy and of collaborating with the enemy. Imperial Japan would never surrender! And for them to do so now would bring great dishonor to the soldiers who have already died. Mizushima tries to persuade them by stating it is better to rebuild Japan than to die for no reason at all. But they lunge to attack him at the same time the British resume their barrage on the fortified caves. Unlucky Mizushima is now trapped between his raging countrymen and his warring captors. When a mortar round explodes inside the cave all of the unyielding Japanese soldiers are destroyed, and Mizushima is thrown to the rocks below where he is knocked unconscious.

After the assault, our captured Japanese platoon fear that Mizushima has also been killed in the fighting, and they must leave his body behind and continue south with their captors. But Mizushima was only stunned. He is found by a wandering Burmese Buddhist, a monk who brings him to his cell and nurses him back to health. Mizushima then steals the holy man's vestments and disguises himself as a monk, casting off his Japanese uniform. Now he can walk in plain sight through Burma, without fear of being attacked, so he can reunite with his comrades in Mudon.

The journey is weeks long and Mizushima is starving. In his travels he discovers the bodies of many dead Japanese soldiers. Dutifully, he incinerates their corpses and buries those he can, but the task is monumental and he needs to keep moving south.

When Mizushima reaches a great river outside of Mudon, he is horrified to find hundreds of corpses piled like driftwood along the muddy banks where they had floated down from the hills. He cannot tend to them all, he must find his platoon.

Back at the prison camp his comrades have accepted the likelihood that their beloved Mizushima is dead. But when a solemn monk is spotted passing their work crew on a bridge, they are convinced it is Mizushima. The resemblance is uncanny. Then he is spotted again, in a monastic funeral procession carrying the cremated remains of an unknown soldier in a square, white sarcophagus. He carries it in the manner of the Japanese and not as the Burmese Buddhists carry their revered dead. The witnesses are convinced that this monk is their own Mizushima. Some who hear the story believe the witnesses, but others do not.

Then Captain Inouye devises a plan to send a message to Mizushima by way of a local trader, an old woman who barters in small items with the captives. The captain purchases a parrot from the old woman and teaches the bird to speak his message to Mizushima in Japanese: "Mizushima, let us return to Japan together." The plan succeeds, for the next time the strange monk is observed, he is seen walking with two parrots riding on his shoulder.

Mizushima's conversion to a monastic life is told in a series of flashbacks, and through them we learn that he had every intention of returning home with his comrades when he first arrived in Mudon. But then he chanced upon a Christian funeral outside of an English hospital, where a Japanese soldier—an enemy soldier to these British—is buried with great honor and hymns of prayer. Mizushima returns to the monastery and collapses in distress. Images of the Japanese corpses—swollen, half-rotted, eaten by buzzards, covered in flies—all return to him now and pull at his heart. He returns to the great river and begins to bury the hundreds of corpses that were washed ashore there, one body at a time. The gentle Burmese fishermen and ferrymen stand aside, reverently, to watch. Then, succumbing to their own devout urgings, they begin to dig and help the holy monk entomb these unfortunate remains. When Mizushima unearths a Burmese ruby in the muddy sand, a fisherman notes that it is very strange to find such a stone so near the river; it must be the grateful spirit of all these dead. Mizushima clutches the ruby to his heart.

Back at the detention camp, word has gone out that the captives will soon be repatriated back to Japan, and they must prepare to leave. It is a joyous time, but the men are still distressed at the fate of Mizushima. Then the monk appears with his harp, standing outside their wire fence, and plays a sad farewell song. They know it is Mizushima and cry out to him, but he does not respond to them, he just sadly turns away.

The old woman trader visits for the last time, carrying with her a new parrot, the brother of the first. It squawks its message from Mizushima: "No, I can't go back!" She also hands the captain a letter from Mitzushima.

Why has our hero disguised himself as a monk? Is he a deserter, a coward who is afraid to return home? Or has he learned, through his travels in the Buddhist countryside, that he has a higher calling?

After the freed captives board the ship and are well on their way home, the good captain takes out the letter and reads it to his men. In it,

Mizushima explains why he cannot return to Japan with them, though he longs to go home with his comrades. He explains how, in his travels through the Burmese mountains and in the lowlands ravaged by war, he came across hundreds of rotting corpses. He could not abandon these Japanese soldiers to such a dishonor. He writes:

> "I cannot leave the bodies of my comrades lying scattered along the hills and rivers of Burma . . . Why must the world suffer such misery? Why must there be such inexplicable pain? As the days passed, I came to understand . . . That our work is simply to ease the great suffering of the world. To have the courage to face suffering, senselessness and irrationality without fear, to find strength to create peace by one's own example."

Mizushima tells them that he has been accepted into the Buddhist monastery and that he will study to become a priest. Note that he is responding, not just to a desire, but to a calling; an irrepressible summons to ministry as a Buddhist priest. He will form himself in prayer and in penance, dedicating his labors to burying the dead, so that every Japanese soldier in Burma will receive an honorable rest. There are thousands of Japanese war-dead, and Mizushima knows that his mission will last his lifetime; but as he awakens to his true self—a vocation he cannot refuse—he will create some peace by his own example, as he cares for his dead brothers on their sacred voyage home.

In the six films that we have examined in this chapter, we should note that there is a discernable progression towards the good. We began at the lowest rung, with that champion of illusion, Willy Loman. Because his values are so conflicting, so self-serving, and so shallow, he fails to achieve the good he always wanted for himself and for his family. Willy has very little self-awareness. He is consumed with misplaced pride and disconnected rage, allowing himself to be enticed by the devil, even to his own destruction.

Margo Channing, however, manages to side-step the wiles of the devil who has been tempting her with promised fame, and accepts her own truth by way of a learned humility and a genuine desire to love and be loved. Humility undoes her self-pride, thwarting the devil and his empty promises.

Old Wang is humble and even good, but he must learn the lessons of justice. When the child that he has rejected—because of unfair and unchallenged traditions—boldly saves his life, he recognizes her tremendous courage and human dignity, a dignity she rightly asserts. Wang is humble, but he was blind to conventional injustice. He had to learn the value of justice by the example Doggie set for him. The search for the true self begins with humility and a desire for what is good. Yet, one can be humble and still comfortably blind to what is real.

Anna, in *Anastasia*, is deeply humble—even wretchedly so—but she wants only the truth about herself, and love if it should come to her. Both do, and it is just.

Ingemar, like all children, begins his life with great humility. He never hardens through suffering, as his brother does, but accepts it humbly—as the way things are—knowing, by way of a prudential outlook, that things could be a lot worse. Prudence is a powerful virtue, and we trust that Ingemar will grow into a man of great sensitivity and integrity, aided by the love of his new family and his supporting community.

Finally, we have Mizushima, a cheerful young soldier who discovers the horrors of war and the great desecration that war inflicts on human life. Mizushima is humble, caring, and reverent. He is also loyal to his country and to his comrades in arms. But Mizushima is called to a higher good, and so he sets his sights and his response to that call over all other human affections. His true self is a grace given to him through his assent to a holy vocation.

Sometimes the masks and the disguises we wear can smother our true selves, and sometimes we blend into them: fit the uniform, bark the language, or steal the vestments. It is not about the disguise, it is about the truth that is hidden underneath; who we are and how we respond to the God who is constantly calling.

Our desire for the good is at the core of our human nature because we are created in the image of God who *is* absolute Good. This desire drives our lives. Though we are flawed creatures who cannot always discern the good in every situation, we are still moved by it. This really is at the heart of our integrity. The first principle of the natural law is: "Do good, avoid evil." A very simple formula for very complicated times. But we cannot do good without first knowing the truth about the way things are, and we can't know that truth unless we are willing and able to see it. As St. Thomas tells us, the good presupposes the true, which is to say, the true (self) precedes the good (self).

Now that we have discarded our self-illusions and recognize our desire for what is good—an honest self that lives its true purpose in a world it can truly see—we should be delighted to learn that we have guides, given to each generation, who have recognized and named and mapped out the good path ahead of us. The ancient Greeks and Romans extolled the virtues as the worthy means to human happiness; the Jewish people gave us the law, the prophets, and the wisdom literature of the Bible; the early Christian thinkers joined these traditions to form a theology of grace and discipleship—a theology which teaches how we are created in the image of God, fallen through sin, gifted by grace, confronted by evil, and redeemed by Christ—that we might find our true place and purpose as co-heirs with Christ in unity with God.

3

Our Guides

On Virtue, Vice, and Sin

THE DESIRE TO LIVE a moral life, to be a person of integrity and good character, is a desire shared and valued throughout history and within our many faith traditions. In Greek thought, Plato identifies four *cardinal virtues* in his *Republic*, describing these virtues—or good habits—as prudence, justice, temperance, and fortitude.[1] Through the teachings of Socrates, Plato promotes these virtues as acquired skills that lead to moral excellence and true happiness in this life.

Aristotle will follow Plato with his *Nichomachean Ethics*, presenting the virtues in greater detail as he catalogs them in a structure that also considers their corresponding vices. Aristotle's formula for happiness is in living a purposeful life, achieving one's potential, and in developing a *balance* that allows one to become "the best version" of one's self.

In his *Nicomachean Table*, Aristotle lists twelve spheres of action or feeling, and introduces twelve vices (bad habits) of excess and twelve contrasting vices of deficiency. In between these vices he places the virtues; twelve good habits that act as the "golden mean," the centering fulcrum, which temper our excessive and deficient behaviors. The following table depicts this for us graphically. Note how the spheres of action align with each virtue, and how these virtues balance out their two opposing extremes.

1. Hamilton, *The Collected Dialogues of Plato*, 426–35.

	Sphere of Action or Feeling	Vice of Excess	Virtue Balance (Mean)	Vice of Deficiency
1	Fear and Confidence	Rashness	Courage	Cowardice
2	Pleasure and Pain	Self-Indulgence	Temperance	Insensibility
3	Getting and Spending (minor)	Prodigality	Liberality	Illiberality
4	Getting and Spending (major)	Vulgarity	Magnificence	Pettiness
5	Honor and Dishonor (minor)	Vanity	Magnanimity	Pusillanimity
6	Honor and Dishonor (major)	Ambition	Proper Ambition	Lack of Ambition
7	Anger	Irascibility	Good Temper	Lack of Spirit
8	Self-expression	Boastfulness	Truthfulness	Mock Modesty
9	Conversation	Buffoonery	Wittiness	Boorishness
10	Social Conduct	Obsequiousness	Friendliness	Cantankerousness
11	Shame	Shyness	Modesty	Shamelessness
12	Indignation	Envy	Righteous Indignation	Malicious Spitefulness

The Judaic wisdom tradition, which was influenced by Greek thought, echoes Plato's cardinal virtues in the Wisdom of Solomon, stating: "she (wisdom) teaches moderation and prudence, justice and fortitude, and nothing in life is more useful for men than these;"[2] and again in the fourth book of Maccabees: "Now the kinds of wisdom are right

2. Wis 8:7.

judgment, justice, courage and self control. Right judgment is supreme over all of these since, by means of it, reason rules over the emotions."[3]

St. Paul, in his first letter to the Corinthians, describes and establishes the most important of Christian virtues: faith, hope, and love (charity), what we refer to now as the *theological virtues.*[4] The early Christian fathers later expounded upon these three holy virtues, and reintroduced some of the earlier pagan virtues found in Plato and Aristotle, which they adapted into a Christian ethic. In the same way, these Christian thinkers drew from the inventory of pagan vices and composed their own catalog of cardinal ills.

Around 400 AD, the Roman Christian poet, Aurelius Prudentius Clemens, assembled the virtues and vices and personified them in his allegorical poem, *Psychomachia.* In it, Prudentius presents the virtues as angelic characters (all feminine, as was conditioned by the Latin feminine noun) who battle against their corresponding vices. This poetic structure suggests that the virtues, as practiced good habits, can act as remedies against the vices, which might otherwise lead the soul to hell. (Of course, the idea that an angelic being like "Patience" would engage in bloody combat against "Wrath" seems too far out of character for such a serene virtue. Prudentius avoids this mischaracterization by having Patience linger patiently on the field of battle while Wrath rages and shrieks and batters poor Patience upon her helmeted head, all to no avail. Exhausted and undone, and with all of her furious weaponry in ruins, Wrath hurls herself upon her own broken sword and dies.)

In medieval times, the collected virtues were used as penitential aids to confessor priests, serving as a guide for assigning an effective and helpful penance to the faithful. If, for example, a penitent confessed the sin of theft—a sin rooted in the vice of greed or envy—a penance rooted in the corresponding virtues of charity or gratitude might be imposed to help the penitent overcome the temptation to steal.

Over the centuries, many models have been constructed to show the contrasting relationship between vice and virtue. Some are similar to the one personified in Prudentius' poem. Others allow for a deeper scrutiny into the relationship between vice and its corresponding virtue. St. Thomas plunges this depth (as only St. Thomas can) by expanding upon

3. 4 Macc 1:18–19.

4. 1 Cor 13:1–13.

the Christian notion of sin and developing the cardinal and theological virtues found in Holy Scriptures and in St. Paul.

Below is a model of this evolving understanding of the virtues. The first column shows the four cardinal virtues which were listed by Plato and echoed in the wisdom books of the Bible. The seven "saving" virtues are extensions of these first four. By aligning the seven capital vices (or seven deadly sins, as St. Gregory the Great defined them) with their corresponding virtues, the chart shows how these vices can be remedied by the virtues. In this model, virtue is not a middle ground between two excesses, as we saw in Aristotle's table, but therapy for the wounded; practiced good habits that can strengthen our ability to stave off temptations. In the right hand column, adjacent to the lists of seven, are the three theological virtues coined by St. Paul.

Four Cardinal Virtues (Plato, Judaic Wisdom Literature)	Seven Saving Virtues		Seven Capital Vices (Deadly Sins)	Three Theological Virtues (St. Paul)
Prudence	Humility	*heals*	Pride	FAITH
Justice	Gratitude	*heals*	Envy	HOPE
Temperance	Patience	*heals*	Wrath	LOVE
Fortitude	Diligence	*heals*	Sloth	
	Charity	*heals*	Greed	
	Temperance	*heals*	Gluttony	
	Chastity	*heals*	Lust	

While the concepts of vice and virtue are pagan in origin, the belief that the virtues can act as healing exercises against sin is a valuable Christian notion. This relationship can help to form us as Christian disciples. Of course, we should not adopt the Pelagian[5] notion that we are

---

5. Pelagius, 354–420 AD. A British monk who taught that human beings could achieve human perfection without divine grace. St. Jerome and St. Augustine famously contested his views and Palagianism was condemned at the Council of Carthage in 418 AD.

earning our salvation through good behavior, wholly on our own; that is not the point. The seven saving virtues are *good habits* that strengthen us against sin. Salvation requires grace. This is why St. Thomas draws out and defines the three theological virtues of faith, hope, and love as actions of God, interconnected to his loving grace. They are theological because they are dependent and sourced in God, through the redemptive action of Christ, and the gifts of the Holy Spirit. (We will expand on these theological virtues in the last chapter of this book.)

The ancient pagans regarded human failings as weaknesses, as tragic flaws, and as vices that hinder the heroic character from achieving excellence and true happiness. Sin, however, is a far greater evil than mere human weakness.

In Hebrew tradition, a sin is an offense against God and the prescribed law. "The law of Moses expresses many truths naturally accessible to reason . . . The precepts of the Decalogue lay the foundations for the vocation of man fashioned in the image of God; they prohibit what is contrary to the love of God and neighbor and prescribe what is essential to it."[6] This carries through to our Christian tradition, as the old law prepared the people for the new gospel law of love. Jesus instructed the people to "keep the commandments." Yet, when Jesus was accused of breaking the law of Moses (the law of the Sabbath when he healed the sick) Jesus retorted that "the Sabbath was made for man, not man for the Sabbath."[7] Christ was the fulfillment of the old law, not its adversary. In his teachings he emphasized two commandments of the heart as the greatest among all the commandments: love of God and love of neighbor. When he preached the Sermon on the Mount he gave us clear instructions (in the Beatitudes) of what we should do to live according to the *heart*, not as subjects to the precepts of the religious code but to the precepts of *love*.

The author of the letter to the Hebrews tells us that our union with Christ has liberated us from the prescribed law. Citing Jeremiah, it introduces us to the new law of the new covenant: the law of grace, the law of love, the law of the Holy Spirit. ". . . I will conclude a new covenant with the house of Israel . . . I will put my laws in their minds and I will write

6. *Catechism of the Catholic Church*, #1961–62.

7. Mark 2:27.

them upon their hearts."[8] St. Paul tells us plainly: "For sin is not to have any power over you, since you are not under the law but under grace."[9] The entire law of the gospel is summed up in Christ's new commandment: "Love one another. As I have loved you, so you should love one another."[10]

Sin, therefore, in this Christian context, is not found in our human weaknesses or in our breaking of the Mosaic law prescribing our behavior, so much as it is found in the choices we make *against the law of love*. It is a transgression of the heart. This means it is an intentional act, freely chosen, that counters the love of God. Since we are made in the image of God and given the God-like freedom to choose our own actions, our true moral character is dependent upon that liberty. St. Paul places great emphasis on human freedom and on the law of love that Christ taught. For the Christian, sin is not just a failing that stymies our human growth, because the flesh dies away. Sin poses a far greater danger to our souls, because our souls do not die away. Sin is, therefore, *the greatest evil we can do*, as it is always a choice we make from our gifted freedom and against the law of love.

In the next few films, we will progress from the darker evil of sin toward the learned virtues of solidarity, humility, and fortitude. We will continue on to the brighter saving virtues of patience and justice—guided by the reins of prudence and the compass of conscience—and then to the saving powers of grace.

We begin with *House of Sand and Fog* and the consequences of sin. Sin, by its destructive nature, will hurl the main players into a great calamity. The following film, *Flight of the Phoenix*, will show how cooperation and solidarity—in league with a few virtues—can overcome our debilitating vices and bring a cantankerous community to new life. As we progress into the light, we will discover in *Captains Courageous* how the saving virtues, taught and exercised patiently and with love, can aid us in our struggle against sin. As the virtues are guided by prudence, we will look at human justice and human mercy in two paired films, *Twelve Angry Men* and its Russian remake, '*12*.' Finally, we will consider

8. Heb 8:8, 10. (Jer 33:33)
9. Rom 6:14.
10. John 13:34.

the formation of our conscience and how the law that is written on our hearts prepares us to act as moral people; this in *A Man for All Seasons*.

House of Sand and Fog[11]

House of Sand and Fog reveals how sin works against our souls to destroy us. It captures especially the insidious nature of sin—even our most venial offenses—and shows how these evils can fester like an infection when left unchecked, and how they will continue to bloat until at last they erupt into catastrophe.

Just as we find in most tragedies, each of the four main characters is marked with a fatal flaw, a sinful stain, that grows out of humanity's original disobedience to the law of love. These characters can be neatly framed as personifying one or more of the seven deadly sins.[12]

We begin with Colonel Behrani, an Iranian immigrant and former military prince, who was forced to flee Iran with his family when the Shah was deposed. Now living in San Francisco, he must work two menial jobs in order to keep his wife in luxury and maintain his own upright status. As the film begins, we learn that Behrani has just married his daughter off to a good family, and how he is striving now to save enough money to buy a house as investment property for his family's future. He will use this investment to purchase more real estate and provide for his son's education. Behrani is a proud man who, through determination and fortitude, will work to regain all that was taken from him by the revolution.

Behrani's mellow wife, Nadi, is a kind woman who tries to endure this imposed exile in America. She is also very proud, insisting that she will not live "like an Arab!" And she is a little too attached to the comforts she has always known. To dull her emotional pain, she finds comfort in luxury and in sedatives.

Their very sweet son, Esmail, who is about fifteen years old, acts as a moderating balance to his parents' extremes. He can be seen as a "Golden Mean" of temperance and calm.

The other main player in this tragedy is Kathy Nicolo, an attractive young woman who has sunk into misery after her husband deserts

---

11. *House of Sand and Fog*, directed by Vadim Perelman. Bisgrove Entertainment, Cobalt Media Group Production, 2003. Rated "R" for language, a sexual scene, and a murder/suicide.

12. Pride, envy, wrath, sloth, greed, gluttony, lust.

her. Because of her long, depressive state, she has let her life fall apart; putting off her mother's nagging calls and letting the mail pile up in her doorway for weeks, unopened. When some county deputies show up at her home to evict her, she is shocked and outraged. Apparently, the house—which belonged to her late father—is being seized by the county for some unpaid business taxes. These taxes were mistakenly imposed on the property by the county, so Kathy's home is being confiscated through no fault of her own. Though blameless, she cannot afford or even manage to legally contest the county's claim against her. We learn that Colonel Behrani has purchased the house at auction for a quarter of its value.

Lester Burdon is the county deputy who has been sent to evict Kathy from the dwelling. Seeing that she has nowhere to go, that she is being treated unjustly, and that she is quite pretty, he gallantly steps in to assist her. Lester helps move her things into a storage unit while she rents a motel room on her maxed-out credit card. Though Lester is married with two children, he is very much drawn to the helpless woman. Lester is the lusty knight in shining armor.

When the Behranis move into the home, these four lives become entangled and knotted together, and then the circumstances grow more dire. Kathy is booted from the motel room for non-payment and is forced to live in her car. Behrani is incensed at the county's suggestion that he sell back the home. Each character now hardens within the shell of their own sinful natures. Proud Behrani is intractable and full of rage. He will not be thwarted by a weak American woman who cannot meet her responsibilities. Her issue is with the county, not with him. Nadi is traumatized by Kathy's hapless attempts to force her way back into the home. Nadi's kindness allows her to tend to Kathy when the young woman is injured, and when she later sinks into despair, but Nadi's fidelity to her husband's authority, her fear of being deported, and her own pleasure in owning a home with a beautiful ocean view, do taint her moral judgment. Though she can feel pity for Kathy, she dare not challenge her husband's unyielding position. Instead, she escapes through her medications.

As we watch these characters congeal in their sins, or splinter as a result of them, we should note that there are also many moments of offered grace. Each of the main four characters is given a chance to redirect themselves and turn against the vices that are pulling them into calamity.

Lester leaves his wife for Kathy, and together they move into a friend's cabin in the woods where they set up house. Infatuation has turned into adultery. Lester's good wife confronts him at the sheriff's station. With their two young children in the car, she pleads with her husband to please come home. He brushes her off sharply, unable to bear her righteous tears or the cries of his innocent kids. She then attacks him, slapping him repeatedly for being such a fool, and in agony she sinks to the pavement, sobbing. This is where his lust has led him. This is the direct consequence of his sin. He could turn back, change direction, repent, but he does not choose that better path.

Kathy, who has been working on her recovery from alcoholism, succumbs to a glass of wine that Lester buys for her at a restaurant. At first she turns it down, alluding to her sobriety, but Lester goads her to have just one glass: "You're a big girl," he reasons, craftily. They finish the bottle and Kathy falls back into her addiction.

But it is Colonel Behrani who is given, time and time again, the opportunity to turn things around and do the right thing. He could give Kathy her just due. He could sell the house back to her. He could make a small profit rather than a great one. But pride will not bow down to justice. Pride can only be defeated by humility, which Behrani will not abide. He was humiliated by the revolution, he will not be humbled in his new life, not ever again.

It is his beautiful young son, Esmail, who tries to direct his father's actions back to kindness and mercy. He protects his mother from his father's wrath when Behrani knocks her to the floor. He tells his father that he *feels sorry* for Kathy, hoping that charity might soften his father's heart. But Behrani counters his son's graces with cold and clear logic. The woman lost the house because she was irresponsible; that is her due. The county sold the house by mistake because they are incompetent; that is their problem. Why should he and his family suffer because of the mistakes of others? "We must be lions in our hearts," he tells his son. Here we should note how Behrani, in his pride, can rationalize justice and turn it into a weapon, and that he has no room in his lion's heart for mercy. He cares only for the good of his family (a noble good), and most especially for the good of his son, whom he adores. This is pride taken to its extreme, and it is deadly because it presumes a human eminence that is god-like, and is therefore blasphemous.

As their willful, misdirected steps begin to career out of control, events spiral into disaster. A distraught and drunken Kathy parks her car in Behrani's driveway and tries to shoot herself with Lester's pistol. She only fails because the gun is not loaded. Horrified, Behrani carries her into his home. She is filthy, sick, drunk, and raving. Nadi leads her into the bath to bathe her, but when Kathy is left alone she swallows a whole bottle of Nadi's pills and slides into unconsciousness. Now Lester comes by the house. He spots Kathy's car and then sees Esmail staring at his pistol on the kitchen table. Horrified, Lester breaks into the home and grabs his gun, loading it quickly. Anything could happen now. This can't end well. When he sees the Behranis carrying Kathy from the bathroom, he accuses Behrani of foul play and aims his weapon at the terrified couple. It is Esmail who hurriedly explains that Kathy took a whole bottle of his mother's pills. Nadi says that Kathy vomited up the pills, but she is intoxicated and sick. Lester then locks the family in the bathroom where they must stay and await the dawn. In the morning, he will take Behrani to the county courthouse and force him to sign the house over to Kathy. Behrani will do it, too, because he, Lester, will demand it; and because he will have his gun pointed at the colonel's back.

We are relieved that no one is hurt and that this drama will end in some kind of compromise, even if the compromise has to be forced. We may even think that Lester, the white knight, has saved the day; he certainly thinks so! But we would be terribly wrong. Lester believes he is a good man and a servant of justice, but really he is only serving his own corrupted appetites; and this he cannot see.

The next morning Lester tells Behrani to drive him and Esmail to the county courthouse where he will turn the house back over to Kathy. But Behrani suggests a different plan. He says he will sell the house back to the county for the amount he paid for it. He will then sign over the county's check to Lester and Kathy. In return, Kathy will sign the deed of the house back to Behrani. This way the Behranis can keep the house and Lester and Kathy can start a new life together. Lester considers it. It seems workable, though a little confusing. And though it will require him to trust the Iranian colonel, it could give him the one thing he desires most. So he agrees.

But our knight is so nervous and suspicious that he loses his cool when the three of them reach the top of the courthouse steps. Lester tucks his pistol into his belt behind his back and spins Behrani around against a pillar, warning him not to try anything stupid when they get inside. But before he can finish his lecture, Esmail grabs the gun out of Lester's belt and points it at the deputy. Lester turns, giving Behrani a chance to grab Lester in a choke hold.

Behrani then spies two officers climbing up the stairs and cries out to them for help. But the deputies misjudge the scene. They only see a kid pointing a pistol at one of their own, so they draw their weapons and order Esmail to drop his gun. Confused, Esmail turns with the gun still pointed in his hands, and the officers shoot him through the chest. Esmail falls headlong onto the stairs, a vast pool of blood widening underneath him. His father shrieks.

We are so shocked by this event that the rest of the movie hardly seems to matter at all. This was completely unexpected. The sinful four were the just targets, any one of them, but that humble, wise, innocent boy? No, never. He is a lamb. A slaughtered lamb. Of course, that is also the whole point.

In his agony, Behrani—who worked two jobs to support his wife in luxury, to marry off his daughter to a good family, to provide a college education for his growing son, and to live in dignity when his dignity was ripped from him—now clutches his face and wails: "I want only my son! I want only my son!" Here is a man who had no room in his heart for mercy and whose own measure of justice was calculating and cold. Now he realizes that all he has ever wanted was his son, whom he loves more than his own life.

In the hospital, where Esmail is dying, Behrani bows to the ground at last in prayer—rocking with his forehead to the floor—pleading that his son's life be spared. He will renew his submission to Allah; he will return to a life of prayer; he will make a vow, a nazr, to God:

> "My nazr, hear me, please to hear me. I will give everything to one who is less fortunate. Yes! I will make it for the broken bird. Please, God, I'm making nazr to this woman. To Kathy Nicolo. And I, to you I promise, if you heal my son, I will return her father's house. I will also give to her all the money I have. My God, Khoda. I make nazr only for my son. Please, I want only for my son. I beg you. I will do whatever is your will. I will purchase ten kilos of the finest seed and I will find an American mosque and I will feed them to all the birds outside. I will let the birds cover me and peck out my eyes! Please God, my nazr is in your hands!"

But the answer is "no" and the boy dies.

Inexplicably, at least to my mind, this loss is not enough. Behrani must be annihilated. True, he cannot return to Nadi with the news that Esmail is dead. That is impossible. Instead, he chooses to escape this unbearable pain, for himself and for Nadi, as his only other option. So he prepares a poison that he puts in Nadi's tea, and continues to comfort her with the illusion that the house is now theirs and that all will be well.

In this tranquil moment, he makes a kind of confession, admitting that he has lead his family so far astray, but now they will return home. Nadi drifts into a coma and dies peacefully, and then Behrani strangles himself to death.

Why are we treated to this bleak murder/suicide at the end of the film? Were their sins of pride and luxury so abhorrent? Is there no hope of redemption for these two tragic people? Behrani suffers his loss, repents with tremendous remorse, and is still condemned. Each of our four main characters fall to the brink of hell in this story, and no one is redeemed. Lester loses his family and goes to prison. Kathy seems to just spin off into oblivion. She does survive, however, and she admits to the authorities that the house is not hers. Yet she seems too stricken to move beyond that small acknowledgement—and we are given few clues as to where this admission takes her.

Flannery O'Connor wrote: "There is something in us, as storytellers and as listeners to stories, that demands the redemptive act, that demands that what falls at least be offered the chance to be restored."[13] But that does not happen here.

For our purposes, it is enough that *House of Sand and Fog* shows us the grave consequences of sin. The sinners do suffer the wages of their transgressions, that's true, but the innocent suffer, too. Our culture tends to overlook those wages, relegating the price of sin to some extraneous religious dogma that is not for them. But this film does not allow us the luxury of that perspective. This story is too shocking, and we are meant to be shocked by it. We are meant to see that our sins are real, that they are insidious powers which will grow in their destructiveness, and that this destruction will impose a ferocious cost on the guilty and the innocent alike.

While it is certainly astute to deliver such a message, I still find it unsettling that redemption has no voice in this story. Esmail could have been that redeemer, he seemed groomed for it, but he manages only to be the poor, slaughtered lamb.

Yet there is a motif, a recurrence of symbolic imagery in this film that we have not yet touched upon. I present it last because I did not wish to overwhelm the reader with yet another layer of complexity, but it is important! Throughout this film we see many images and allusions to birds. The opening scenes give us a joyful look at childhood, with the two little Behrani children cavorting on the beach with their mother. There

13. O'Connor, *Mystery and Manners,* 48.

are gulls there, playing in the Caspian breeze. But at a distance, there is Colonel Behrani, carving out his own paradise with chainsaws and cutting down the trees to improve his grand view. Later, in their new home, a dove lights upon the birdbath and charms Nadi. The dove is a peaceful little reminder of better days. Yet again, there is Behrani, carving out his own paradise and building a stairway that blocks the birdbath to improve his grand view. When Kathy tries to kill herself in the driveway, Behrani is horrified. He carries her into the house and tells Esmail that they must care for Kathy now. She is a "broken bird." He repeats the proverb his grandfather told him, that when a bird flies into your home it is a blessing, because it is an angel in disguise. Behrani's heart is softening, but it is too late, as we soon learn. Then, after the shooting, when Behrani prays for the life of his son, his vow to Allah is for Kathy Nicolo, the "broken bird." Behrani pledges to give her everything he owns. He vows to feed the birds of an American mosque with the finest seed, and let the birds cover him and peck out his eyes! What a powerful prayer! What a powerful image! These birds must not be ignored! When Kathy is shown disheveled, spinning alone on the pier, the camera pans to the water where a twisted, dead seagull floats in blood. Finally, when Behrani returns to Nadi from the hospital and awakens her from her drugged sleep, she tells him that she dreamt of a bird "trapped in our empty house. It was trying to find a way out. It fluttered around hitting the walls. I could feel the air from the wings on my face. I opened the window and it flew away." This bird of paradise is *Esmail,* not Kathy. Behrani misunderstood. The angel was in his home all along, trying to escape the walls of his imprisonment. What Behrani had tried to carve out by force was already given to him by grace. Esmail's death makes real this revelation of grace: that all his father ever really wanted was "only my son."

Flight of the Phoenix [14]

In our next film, *Flight of the Phoenix,* we are presented with a similar character study that dabbles in the personification of the vices and in the failings of human relationships. It also shows how the virtues can rescue the characters from their crushing faults and from the muddled mess they make of things.

14. *Flight of the Phoenix,* directed by Robert Aldrich. An Associates and Aldrich Production, 1965. Rated "PG 13" for mild cussing and mild violence.

Flight of the Phoenix takes off from the very start with a transport plane in peril. The plane is caught in a sandstorm over the Arabian desert and is forced off course, only to make a hard-landing in the middle of nowhere. Two passengers die in the crash, another suffers a shattered leg and dies slowly from the infection that results. The remaining characters are an assortment of rough men, about a dozen, who must somehow escape their predicament in the desert dunes. We can view each survivor—with just a little forcing—as representing one of the pagan vices or the Christian deadly sins.

Human sins are not all equal in their ability to corrupt. As we saw with Colonel Behrani, the greatest sin of all is pride. Pride is the root of corruption as it extends its tentacles into every human weakness in its need to grow greater. Appropriately, its corresponding virtue, humility, is often described as the greatest of the virtues. St. Thomas quotes from the homily of St. Gregory, that ". . . he who gathers the other virtues without humility is as one who carries straw against the wind."[15]

Among our tattered castaways is the plane's pilot, Captain Frank Towns, who is not only reeking of pride, he is eaten up with guilt for having crashed his aircraft with loss of life and on account of his own bad judgment. He scrawls the reason for the mishap in his flight log as "pilot error," and then underlines it twice. Guilt and pride are a cantankerous combination, and Captain Towns is certainly a cantankerous man. Humility might restore his balance, but he would rather dig his own grave and hit himself over the head with the shovel than submit to a humbling correction. His adversary, Heinrich Dorfmann (another prideful man but one who is tempered by diligence and patience), points out Towns' failings with keen accuracy, telling the captain to his face: "You act as if stupidity were a virtue."

The first officer and navigator, Lew Moran, is a struggling alcoholic, and Captain Towns is quick to blame Lew's drinking for directing them into the sandstorm in the first place. Towns blames Lew out of anger and frustration, and because of his own overriding guilt, but it does great damage to their friendship. Intemperance is chastised by wrath, but one vice cannot correct another. It is only the desert setting itself that imposes a forced temperance on Lew, which he accepts humbly, and he becomes a rather likeable chap as a result of it.

---

15. Pegis, *Basic Writings of St. Thomas Aquinas*, 469.

Diligence and sloth march side by side in the characters of Captain Harris, an Australian military officer, and his attendant, Sergeant Watson. But contrary to the usual formula, Sergeant Watson manages to survive the ordeal, even though he is cowardly, deceptive, lazy, and disloyal. His heroic commander strides off into the wilderness to find help, only to return on the verge of death. He is later murdered when he goes to investigate a raiding party of Arabs who camp near the crash site. One must wonder why the slothful sergeant survives the ordeal and brave Captain Harris does not. Perhaps it is because Harris relies upon his own arrogance, and will not take advice from an authority (Captain Towns) who clearly knows the situation better than he does. Or maybe it is just because cowards often do survive, and brave men often perish.

The other characters are smaller versions of vice and virtue. There is the silly Ratbags, a buffoon to the point of absurdity; the courageous Dr. Renaud, who cares too much and is murdered for the sake of his ministry; a big Trucker Cobb, who is mentally and emotionally unstable, and who dies as a result of his impetuous rush to join Captain Harris on his desert trek; a mild Mr. Standish, who has little to offer but prayer; a few minor players who die off quickly; a sweet monkey and Bellamy, his gentle keeper; and then Heinrich Dorfmann, the young German engineer.

The real conflict and drama of the story lies in the hostile relationship that develops between Captain Towns and Heinrich Dorfmann. This conflict may be exacerbated by the post-war times, as Towns likely has little affection for Germans in general and this one in particular. Or it may be due to the usual bad blood that can occur between an aging elder who has lost his way and a young hot-shot who knows it all. But when we pit the two powerful prides against one another (when neither will succumb, either to reason, guilt, compassion, justice, or mercy—much less humility) then the whole universe is in peril. Here we have that particular great conflict presented on screen.

What we learn from *Flight of the Phoenix* is that each individual man, steeped in his own particular sins and unwilling to be moved beyond his own obstinate will, dies uselessly when he acts alone. There is nothing these men can do on their own to escape their predicament. It is only after they submit to another man's authority, put their trust in the virtues of another human being, that they are able to construct a workable plan. This plan is a massive endeavor that demands the combined virtues of each castaway, especially humility and diligence. They must also put their confidence in a man whom they clearly despise (Dorfmann) and submit to his direction. That is not easily done, but with diligence, patience, temperance, and fortitude, they learn the hard lesson of *solidarity* as together they rebuild the airplane.

The twist comes when the men learn that Dorfmann is not the aeronautical engineer (a rightful authority) that they thought he was. They discover that the German designs *model* airplanes, the kind hobbyists build from balsa kits! Still, as Dorfmann explains in an offhanded quip, "the principles are the same." Our marooned bunch have no choice but to accept Dorfmann and follow him, and he has no choice but to put the whole dirty lot of them to purposeful work. Some of these castaways are injured, some are weak, some are defiant, and some are all but useless; but those who are stronger, more patient, and more knowledgeable are able to lift up the weaker sorts—who are at least able to keep the batteries charged and the lights working—and so they make a success of the project. This is solidarity.

What we should learn from the film is that the virtues, working in harmony with one another, can create a force for good that no weakness or evil can destroy. Together, the virtuous can achieve great things. With grace, they can lift up nature—even soar—or at least transport a rabble of faulty, quarrelsome men from death to safety. Remember, even the vice-laden Sergeant Watson made it out alive, but then, so did the monkey!

Captains Courageous [16]

A virtue is an habitual and firm disposition to do the good. [17]

—CATECHISM OF THE CATHOLIC CHURCH

If *House of Sand and Fog* and *Flight of the Phoenix* depict characters that manifest some aspect of the seven deadly sins with a smattering of nascent virtues, then *Captains Courageous* works well as a companion film. For here we have characters who manifest the qualities of the seven saving virtues with a smattering of juvenile vice.

The movie was made in 1937, and it can be a little saccharine. The first thirty minutes or so are chafingly childish, but I ask for your patience

16. *Captains Courageous*, directed by Victor Fleming. A Metro-Goldwyn-Mayer Production, 1937. Not rated, but invite the kids!

17. *Catechism of the Catholic Church*, #1733.

(a virtue!) to see it through. Our main character, Harvey Cheyne, needs to be fleshed out as a thoroughly loathsome, spoiled brat, and that takes a little doing. But once he falls off an ocean liner into the North Atlantic the film improves considerably.

This is a Rudyard Kipling tale (although it is much more serene on the screen than it is in the original story) so we might expect a little moralizing. What we discover in *Captains Courageous* is the education of young Harvey Cheyne, a boy who has grown up in lavish over-indulgence and who has received little moral guidance from his busy, wealthy father. Harvey has no personal integrity beyond the shallow esteem that money buys for him.

After Harvey is expelled from school for his belligerent and unruly behavior, his father decides to take him to Europe for the summer break. Onboard the ocean liner, Harvey boasts to a couple of kids that he can quaff down five or six ice cream sodas if he wanted to. (Kipling's story has Harvey smoking cigars, but you get the idea.) On a dare, he does just that, and of course the sodas make him sick. Harvey escapes to the stern of the ship holding his stomach when he stumbles and falls overboard.

He is fished out of the sea by a Portuguese fisherman who is jigging for cod in a small, fog-bound dory. The fisherman, Manuel Fidello, then rows the boy over to a big schooner and cheerfully brags to his American captain and crew, "I get fish with hair on him!"

Harvey recuperates aboard the fishing schooner where he must spend the next three months of the summer's fishing season. There he encounters a boatload of moral masters.

There is Captain Troop, a fair minded New Englander who lays down the rules gently but also firmly. He does not believe a word of Harvey's boastful account: that his dad practically owns the ocean liner that he fell off of, and how his father will pay the captain handsomely if he would just take him back to New York. Captain Troop waves that off as a fancy fish story and explains that "it wouldn't be just" to deprive a whole crew of its wages based on the yarn told by an upset boy. He invites Harvey to join the crew, and promises to pay him nine whole dollars for his three months work. But seeing as how he isn't believed, Harvey scoffs at the offer and refuses to lift a finger. "Well, do as you've a mind to about that," Troop grumbles.

There is the captain's son, Dan, a few years older than Harvey, who sets a fine example for how a hard working young man ought to act. He gives Harvey a set of his own work clothes, but Harvey whines that "this stuff itches." "Wait'll you wear them awhile, they'll shrink to your tonnage," Dan quips; a not-so-subtle hint that Harvey will soon adapt to the uncomfortable ways of integrity.

But it is Manuel, the joyful fisherman who rescued Harvey, who takes the boy under his wing and teaches him the value of honesty and self-worth. He does so by way of the virtues. Since Harvey refuses to work the crew shun him as a "Jonah" (a passenger on a fishing vessel) and Jonahs always bring bad luck. To dispel this impression, Manuel gets the boy to do a little labor by forcibly taking the kid's hands, scooping up a severed fish head from the deck, and dropping it over the side rail. "Now you can go down and eat," he says, kicking him below and telling Captain Troop that he did some work. "You made me do something!" the child protests, but Manuel doesn't seem bothered by the distinction. "That was work." So the boy is allowed to eat with the crew. He soon joins the black cook and helps out in the galley. He would like to chop bait with the crewmen, as it looks like it would be fun to sing with them as they cut up the herring, but Harvey's awkward attempt to join in is an embarrassment. He mishandles the knife and sings out of turn. Still, he is learning to respect this team of diligent men. He can see for himself the value of their labor, and he is beginning to desire what is true and good.

What Harvey wants most, however, is to go fishing with Manuel as his dory mate. He boasts that he can row a boat because he learned how to row in school. Manuel only scoffs, saying a kid doesn't know anything about boats. Harvey grows irate at this put-down and then rattles off the names of all the rigging on the schooner, which he had learned from a book in Captain Troop's quarters. He then stomps off in a rubber-booted rage. Manuel is impressed, "That one smart kid!"

Encouraged by Harvey's effort to learn, and noting his willingness to toil as a humble galley grunt, Manuel figures that Harvey has worked his way out of being a Jonah. So he takes the boy out in his dory to fish. Ever anxious and overly eager, Harvey must learn patience as he handles the oars. After a few failed attempts he manages it. It is the same while fishing. Harvey anxiously yanks the hand-line too soon, pulling the bait from the fish's mouth and losing it. Manuel teaches him to wait, let the fish take the bait, then strike with the line. In time, they begin hauling in a fine catch.

Besides these little lessons in patience and practical fishing, Harvey also learns something of Manuel's faith, and this is important. "Do you think they fish in heaven?" he wonders, after hearing about the death of Manuel's father, who was drowned at sea. "Sure they fish in heaven," Manuel retorts. "What else they do? . . . And when they run out of fish, the Savior, he makes more!" Harvey had never considered the possibility that heaven was as nice as life here.

But what might have been a solid bonding experience for the two fishermen turns ugly when a fellow crewman, Long Jack, gets tangled in his trawl and is pulled over the side of his own fishing dory. Harvey laughs, explaining how he purposefully tangled the trawl so that Long Jack would lose on a bet they had made the night before. Long Jack is pierced several times by the hooks, and these will have to be cut out of his flesh with a knife. He might have been killed by the tangled tackle when it pulled him overboard. Disgusted by Harvey's prank, Manuel returns the fish that Harvey caught to the sea, and then rows the kid back to the schooner. "Give him hand maybe," he tells Troop, "he got no way to cheat himself over side."

The juxtaposing of Harvey's vices—which are many—with the virtues he needs to learn, is at constant play in this film. But Manuel teaches the boy more than the good virtues. He introduces Harvey to Christian values, and chief among them is repentance. Harvey is filled with remorse over Long Jack's injuries. He never meant for him to get hurt, he just wanted to win the bet and have a little fun. It is a child's prank and Harvey apologizes to Long Jack, admitting the whole thing "like regular grown fella!" Manuel proclaims. Long Jack is not as impressed.

In time, Harvey learns the ropes, developing strong muscles for rowing and hauling in cod, and strong virtues that propel him forward to happiness. Now Harvey, who has fallen (off the ocean liner and about an arm's reach from grace) is offered this most loving chance to be lifted up and set aright. And if this was merely a morality play, Harvey's new beginnings would probably end the story. But *Captains Courageous* does take us further, and it is a better story because of it. Harvey not only needs to learn the virtues, he needs to be saved. There is a powerful Christian message in this tale, one that takes us beyond mere rescue; what we saw in *Flight of the Phoenix*.

Let us consider Captain Troop. Here is a very likeable man, full of wisdom, tradition, charm, and compassion. But our captain has a fatal flaw. He is a proud man. To a certain extent his pride is well placed. He is proud of his son, Dan, of young Harvey (when he merits it), of his good crew, and of his intrepid schooner, the *We're Here*. But Troop is just a little too proud of himself, too, and he jeopardizes the lives of his crew by cutting across a shallow shoal in order to beat the *Jenny Cushman* (a rival schooner) home to Gloucester. Once in open water, the two ships barrel home in a gale.[18] Unwilling to be bested by his opponent, Captain Troop orders his crew to cut across the *Jenny Cushman's* bow when the *Cushman* has the nautical right-of-way. It is a bold, dangerous, and completely *illegal* tactic. But Captain Troop is deeply pleased when they pass the *Cushman* under full sail, and when his rival blows out a foresail in the process. Now they will be the first ship home for sure. Like Harvey, Captain Troop had to cheat to win. We might snicker a bit, thinking this trick was just daring and bold and our team deserves the victory, but that is as childish as Harvey's stunt, when he tangled Long Jack's trawl.

Troop's illegal maneuver is under-emphasized in the film, and that is unfortunate, because the story's tragedy is a direct result of Troop's arrogance. Heavily loaded with a hold full of cod, in high winds and under full sail, the rigging of the *We're Here* is under tremendous stress. Troop orders Manuel and Long Jack aloft to reef the sails, but as they climb the mast the stays part, the mast splits, and the whole top-rigging comes crashing into the sea, taking Manuel with it. Long Jack jumps clear, but Manuel is fouled in the backstay, which cuts deep into his flesh, sawing his body in half. Captain Troop must free the rigging by chopping through the backstay with an axe. But this will not release Manuel, it will only allow the tangled sails and rigging to sink free of the vessel. There is no way they can rescue Manuel, who shouts out to the cook in Portuguese that "the whole bottom half of him is gone" but he doesn't want the kid to know. It is a horror. Harvey is beside himself. He cannot understand why they are not trying to save Manuel. Caring only for his friend, he boldly clamors onto the broken mast and tries to reach him, but Manuel waves the boy back and tells him not to worry. "I alright. I go now to fish with my father. We have many good times, so you smile now." The cables are then cut through and the ship is released, while the waters swirl around the sunken rigging that has taken Manuel to his death.

Our hero is gone, and the crippled schooner must now limp its way home to Gloucester.

The next scene shows Harvey receiving his pay from Captain Troop back in port. Harvey is grateful for his meager wages and he uses the money to buy a candle holder for Manuel and his father, which he

---

18. The seafaring scenes in this film are not only stupendous, they are an heirloom of classic film. They are also a fitting memorial to the fine sailing craft that once plied the Grand Banks for cod.

arranges for them in the church. The priest encourages the boy to say a prayer, but he is not sure how. "Can I say whatever I want?" "Anything," the priest tells him. So Harvey learns to pray, gazing up at an unseen cross: "Look, if 'tis that way, the way Manuel said, could you fix it so that one day there will be an extra seat in Manuel's father's dory, with him and Manuel? Because, because I just got to be with Manuel. I got to! I guess that's all I wanted to ask. Well, please."

Harvey has learned many of the virtues that build good character, but he is now discovering much more. Remember, we do not earn our way to heaven, and the virtues cannot save us. We are saved by grace and by the sacrificial love of Jesus on the cross. Christ is our redemption. Harvey is just now finding this out through Manuel's own example, his teachings, his joys, and his sacrifice. Harvey is also learning something of the theological virtues that will guide him as a disciple of Christ. He has learned to love, and to hope, and to put his faith in God. Joined now by his father, together they pray for Manuel and for all those "who go down to the sea in ships" at a community memorial. Then Harvey returns to his father's love and tells him his story. Presumably, the father has learned something valuable, too.

On Prudence and Justice

A learned good habit can help us to avoid sin and lift us out of ignorance, but we must first recognize the sin in ourselves, as well as the inherent danger of sin's consequences. In *House of Sand and Fog*, we saw the shocking destruction that resulted from some seemingly minor faults and attitudes that then escalated, moment by moment, into disaster; where even the innocent were slain. In *Flight of the Phoenix* and *Captains Courageous*, we begin to see the value of solidarity and cooperative effort, along with the power of the virtues working to accomplish hard tasks and forming a noble character. Yet it is true that these last two films are rather simple in their moral teaching. Simplicity is a good starting point, but life is always more intricate and complex. Our own experiences are probably closer to those found in *Death of a Salesman* and *House of Sand and Fog* than they are to the rescue dramas aboard the *Phoenix* or the *We're Here*.

Responding to these complexities, philosophers throughout history have woven the virtues into their own complicated fabric; from Plato's writings on the cardinal virtues, to the wisdom literature of the Judaic tradition which reintroduces these ideas to a law-saturated culture. In the writings of St. Paul we hear these virtues echoed: "Finally, brothers, whatever is true, whatever is honorable, whatever is just, whatever is pure, whatever is lovely, whatever is gracious, if there is any excellence and if there is anything worthy of praise, think about these things."[19] The early fathers of the church exhorted Christian disciples to put these virtues into practice and strive to be morally fit against the mortal dangers of sin.

A millennium later, St. Thomas expands the tapestry of pagan virtues, insisting that the pagan philosophers did not have the grace of Christian revelation, and so were limited in their views, relying on human reason alone. He restructures the virtues into a hierarchy where humility is first among them, because humility is needed before one can acquire any of the others. Harvey Cheyne, for example, could not have learned virtue without first accepting, in humility, the wisdom of his teachers: Manuel and the crew of the *We're Here.* The same is true of Captain Towns of the *Phoenix,* though it was a much more difficult lesson for him. Towns, a fading older man with great pride and considerable knowledge, had to humbly submit to the authority of the younger man in order to save the lives of those he had stranded.

When Plato ordered the cardinal virtues (of prudence, justice, courage, and temperance), he also structured them in a hierarchy of importance. Of the four, he places prudence as the principal guiding virtue. This may strike us as rather odd. To our modern minds, the word "prudence" has a negative connotation. It is a disparaging term, often confused with behaving like a prude: a bitter old bird who has long since lost her passion for life. This is entirely not the case! Prudence is the preeminent "charioteer" of the cardinal virtues. She guides the thundering team with stability, reason, wisdom, discernment, and right-judgment. Like Aristotle's Golden Mean, prudence balances the excesses, but she also directs the will and the passions. Prudence ascertains the *truth* of things, not only from a standpoint of seeing what is true, but of grasping the importance of things, and prioritizing what is most essential. Truth, remember, precedes the good.

In Christian tradition, prudence guides the judgment of our *conscience,* so that we are able to discern the wise, just, and moral action. Prudence *is* that discernment. It is the operation of our reasoning faculties, actively working with the revealed law of God and according to the

19. Phil 4:8

law written on our hearts. Prudence is not a passive virtue, prudence is "right reason in *action*."[20] This action is vital! For it is one thing to know the truth of a situation, and quite another to *act* upon that knowledge. This is the crucial difference between study and achievement; between orthodoxy and orthopraxy; or between a model airplane design and a flying aircraft! We may be wise in our thinking, but how do our thoughts and beliefs manifest themselves in our conduct towards God and our neighbor? It is fine to profess "justice for all," for example, but quite another thing to *do* justice.

Case in point: Have you ever been called to jury duty? Did you actually want to go? Was your experience in the jury room a good one? Were the other jurors prudent, thoughtful, and fair? What was the outcome of your deliberation? Did you achieve a conviction for the guilty, acquittal for the innocent, or satisfaction in knowing you did your best? Was justice served?

This leads us to the second cardinal virtue, justice. What is justice? Simply put, justice is that virtue most concerned with rendering "to each his due." The just person seeks to order things properly, rightly, and in a fair manner. If prudence seeks to know the way things are, justice seeks to know the way things are *meant to be*. (Of course, how things are meant to be is a very slippery judgment in itself!) Philosophers, legal scholars, legislators, and faith traditions have worked tirelessly to ascertain what is just, and to codify their findings into laws that are fair; rendering to each his or her due (within a context of due process) in order to resolve human conflicts and re-establish right relations. And since justice is a virtue that is exercised by both individuals *and* societies, these laws are based upon the principles we value as a people; among which are peace, freedom, security, and human dignity.

The next two movies we will consider, side-by-side, take the viewer into the jury room and put the virtue of justice into action as it is guided by the flawed, prudential judgment of twelve all-too-human jurors.

---

20. *Catechism of the Catholic Church*, #1806.

Twelve Angry Men [21] and '*12*'[22]

These two tremendous films, *Twelve Angry Men* and '*12*' (a Russian remake of the American classic), examine the workings of prudential judgment in the minds of twelve muddled jurors. Here are two cultures telling the same story in two very different ways and in very different times. Both are powerful dramas that attempt to uncover the unseen motive and events surrounding an unseen murder. The case is similar in each film: a young man, marginally foreign, is accused of killing his elder. It seems to be an open and shut case, and the jurors are expected to reach an easy verdict.

We begin with the 1957 American classic, *Twelve Angry Men*; a film that is driven almost entirely by its script and its very fine acting. It is shot in black and white, stripped bare of potent images, yet thoroughly steeped in *story*. It unfolds like a suspense novel, written in black and white and gripping with suspense. The screenplay does not provide us with any historical context or even much of a plot. Instead we find ourselves sequestered in a sparse room that is filled to the brim with character and psychology and the earnest magnificence of the human face.

Twelve Angry Men begins with a judge's instructions to an all-male jury. Though we never see the trial, we can assemble the details of the case from the arguments these jurors will make. We learn that a young street tough—a Puerto Rican youth—has been accused of murdering his father with a switchblade knife. By reconstructing the murder scene, the jurors replay the murder as it was described in court by the key witnesses. Just as important as the case, however, are the personal stories told by each juror as they argue their positions, distort the facts, and lay bare their own biases, faults, and sins.

When this gang of twelve first assemble there is little doubt among them that the accused is guilty, so they are eager to take a quick vote and get along home. They have spent six days listening to the lawyers and the witnesses, and the facts are clear and indisputable. However, when they do take their vote, they discover that there is one lone hold-out who has voted "not guilty," and that stops their hurry-home cold.

---

21. *Twelve Angry Men*, directed by Sidney Lumet. An Orion-Nova Production,1957. Not rated, but probably not suitable for young children, though they probably wouldn't like it anyway.

22. '*12*', directed by Nikita Mikhalkov. Three T Productions, 2007. (Russian) Rated "PG" for strong language and violent images.

The hold-out is a thoughtful gentleman, mild in manner, but earnest in his position. He states that the fate of the young defendant deserves some discussion on their part. The boy's life is at stake. Can they not weigh his life against one hour of their own inconvenience? The other men grumble but they comply, and the details of the case are reassessed. By introducing the element of doubt, and by challenging the jurors to consider other possibilities, the hold-out juror (he is not named until the end of the film and is only referred to as Juror #8) is able to reveal a few cracks in the prosecution's case and sow seeds of uncertainty in the minds of the other men. In so doing, he manages to sway one elderly juror over to his side. Now there are two men voting "not guilty."

The remaining ten are outraged. It is a hot day, the hottest day of the year. The room is stifling. They want to get home. This trial has gone on long enough and they have businesses to tend to and a ball game to watch. Tempers flare, but reason does triumph, and this is the key point. In this film, it is prudence ("right reason in action") and the love of justice that prevail over the selfish wants and hurried judgments of the lesser men. More jurors are won over as our hero continues to conduct a scientific examination of the case. This rational, keenly American approach to justice is based upon empirical evidence and conducted through a very orderly method of elimination. Juror #8 presents each condemning fact of the case and then challenges it thoroughly. He uses doubt as his pruning tool to snip away every questionable twig of presumption; and then grafts new possibilities onto the changing vine. When every belief is challenged and the whole vine is shaken, what remains is the truth. If very little remains, then reasonable doubt must hold sway.

Like Behrani's cool justice in *House of Sand and Fog*, this logical approach does not consider mercy. No one suggests that they forgive the accused young man. But unlike Behrani, this approach to justice is executed by a man who is thoroughly detached, objective, decent, and humble in his conduct.

As the testimony of each witness at the trial is challenged, then re-enacted and found wanting, their testimonies must be dismissed. Eventually, most of the jurors find little left with which to convict the boy. Now, as if cornered, the passions of the remaining men explode with vile, personal attacks. Those who changed their vote to "not guilty" are accused of disloyalty, stupidity, arrogance, and betrayal. But when the last remaining juror to vote "guilty" finds himself alone, he literally self-destructs in a raving tantrum, revealing a heart that is deeply wounded, at odds with its own best loves, and wholly corrupted by hatred, racial bigotry, and self-loathing. Like Wrath in Prudentius' poem, this last juror destroys himself in a fit of rage, throwing himself on his own broken sword, exhausted and sobbing.

In the end the young accused is acquitted and allowed to go free.

> *You are not under the law*
> *but under grace.*[23]
>
> —ST. PAUL

Let us now transport ourselves fifty years into the future. We are in twenty-first century Russia. The Soviet Union has collapsed and Russia is staggering in disarray, confusion, and disrepair. Twelve jurors are assembled to deliberate on a case not unlike the one presented in *Twelve Angry Men*.

A young man is accused of murdering his benefactor, a family friend who took him in when he was orphaned by war. The accused is a Chechen youth, a people despised by these Russians. The jury room is set up in a school gymnasium that is adjacent to the courthouse. It is a temporary arrangement, the bailiff explains, as he leads the jurors down the hallway of the school that is bustling with kids. "The courthouse is undergoing renovations." (The setting seems to suggest that justice under the old Soviet regime is in ruins, though it is now being restored, and that maybe these men have something to learn.) The jurors spill into the wide, empty gym.

In an offset moment we watch a middle-aged man take something from his wallet and place it on a shelf where the athletic trophies are displayed. Then he moves quietly away.

The other jurors frolic in the gym like school kids, shooting baskets, toying with a broken television set, and playing on a piano that is hung behind a protective cage. "Even the piano is behind bars," one juror observes, laughing. Maybe the bars are there to protect the instrument from the rough play of the kids. Another juror suggests that the bars are there to keep the piano from hurting the children. Image and allegory are rich in this film, so it is worth our while to speculate on these peculiar remarks.

---

23. Rom 6:14.

Although the circumstances of the trial are similar to those found in *Twelve Angry Men*, this Russian version is fully fleshed out, vibrant, historically relevant, rowdy, and robust. Like a Dostoyevsky novel, '*12*' bursts with passion and misdirected tangents. While our American film rests on the cool, masculine marble of the Enlightenment, '*12*' is an iconographic display of sacramental imagery, like a rambunctious child straining in the grasp of an exhausted Mother Russia.

Another way that '*12*' distances itself from its American cousin is in how it depicts the life events of the young accused. The Russian film portrays the boy's experiences in war-torn Chechnya. Though his suffering is only shown from a distance, in flashback moments that pop in and out of the jailed boy's memory, we do get to see the one crucial history that is missing from *Twelve Angry Men*: the story of the accused.

Through these flashbacks we learn that this boy, at about the age of ten, saw his parents murdered, his home and farm burned, his dog killed, his cities bombed, and everything that was ever true and beautiful in his life destroyed. He lived through it. He starved through it. He hid in corpse strewn basements through it all until a family friend, a Russian officer he calls "Uncle Volodya," rescues him. The graphic violence that we witness through his eyes is not only shocking and powerful, it is iconic—literally like an icon—a sacramental image that is underpinned with grace, with sanctity, and with God-made-man sacredness. In the Orthodox faith, an icon is not just a work of art, an icon is a bearer of grace.

Back in the jury room gym, the camera pans to the hidden something on the metal shelf and then pans away.

But down to business. Our Russian jurors are very eager to go home. That vicious Chechen kid is obviously guilty, why fool around? Still, for propriety's sake, they will take a vote. To the surprise of eleven eager men, one juror votes "not guilty." It is the same man (Juror #1, this time) with the kind face who placed an unseen item on the shelf when he first entered the gym. He says they are moving too fast, that the accused young man deserves at least one conversation before his fate is decided. Now the story overlaps our American version. And while these jurors are more colorful than their American counterparts, they still quarrel and bicker and insult one another in like fashion as they review the votes.

Unsure of his next move, our Juror #1 pauses. It is a crucial pause. He waits (what is he waiting for?), he ponders (prudently sizing up the situation that he is close to losing), he glances over to the shelves and glances back again (why?), then he decides to speak his truth to these strangers. With marked humility he will confess his life to them.

He begins by saying he was once a successful man. He was happily married, working as a technical engineer and earning a modest wage as a civil servant. He might have made a lot more money working for some foreign tech firm, but he was proud to be serving his government and his country. Unfortunately, he was mistreated by his employer and his ideas were stolen, and then he fell into heavy drinking. He became an alcoholic, losing his job and his wife to his addiction. In his bouts of drunkenness, which he does not fail to detail, he was beaten and jailed and sickened and raving. He wanted to die. "It was scary." Then one day on a train, when he was close to death, a kind woman rescued him. She believed in him, lifted him up, and essentially said to him: "Live!" Through her grace and by her love and effort he was able to break the bonds of his addiction. He could never have done it without her or on his own. They married and today they have two small children. He is now a reformed, successful, and happy man. But he is also a changed man. He now knows the depth of human suffering. So this boy, he argues, this accused foreigner who can barely speak Russian, deserves that same care and mercy, because he has *dignity*, "because he is a human being."

The other jurors are stunned. What kind of an argument is this?

A little sparrow that is trapped inside the gym swoops down over their heads and they all duck, startled, and then they have a good laugh. The camera pans back to the shelves. Another juror changes his vote to "not guilty."

The story moves from the jury room to the jailed boy. He paces the floor of his unheated cell. He counts the distance between the walls with his steps. He dances a proud dance. He is freezing cold. His active mind flashes with images: the face of his mild mother, ferocious rifle fire, the dead bodies of his parents, that one scene—repeated seven times—of the rain after a street battle, the dead soldiers, the burning bus, *that dog and the bone he carries!* So many images to reckon with! So full of meaty, carnal flesh!

These are, in many ways, Christian images and sacramental signs. That is no ordinary bird, and a scene that is repeated seven times in a film is worth noting!

As the jurors continue their debate, each one takes a turn at telling his own life story: there is the Jewish son of a Holocaust survivor (who reasons well but is despised for his "Jewish tricks"), a stage actor (who makes people laugh so he can keep himself from crying), a Caucasian surgeon (who is accused of buying his medical diploma), a simple mind-ed plumber and a man-child producer (who are both terribly confused by the other jurors' arguments), a love-sick middle-aged man who writes poetry and knows he's a fool in love, an artist, and a caustic cab driver. Each man reveals a small part of himself, giving us a deeper insight into his motives and his judgments.

As they did in *Twelve Angry Men*, these jurors stage a re-enactment of the murder scene, and the court witnesses are similarly challenged and dismissed. So more jurors move, one by one, from "guilty" to "not guilty." The others grow enraged, betraying deep racial hatred as the driving force behind their rush to judgment. This play-acting infuriates the cab driver most of all. It is all such fantasy! He decides to stage his own drama, as-suming the role of the knife-wielding "savage" in order to demonstrate the angle of the kid's attack. He physically drags the ridiculed surgeon to stand in place of the murdered uncle. Then, with authentic fury and slapping his own face to heighten his ire, the cabby comes at the doctor with the knife raised in his hand. Shrieking with rage he imitates the boy's assault and lunges at his victim. The lights bang and go out, there is a flash—distorted faces scream and flicker on the screen—and we all jump. When the lights return things are calmer (we are calmer!) and the violent man resumes his place at the long table, wiping away a glob of bird feces that has struck him in the head.

From the midst of this imposed calm the old evidence is re-examined and a new theory is considered. The men construct a complicated hypoth-esis that seems to fit with the inconsistent testimonies of the witnesses. As their theory develops and the pieces fall into place, the jurors begin to suspect that the Chechen boy was framed; set up by corrupt players who wanted the uncle dead, the boy in prison, and the building they were living in vacated—all to profit from some real estate swindle. Most of the hold-out jurors are won over by this new conjecture and they decide to acquit.

Now there is only one man remaining. It is the low, hateful cabby. Exhausted by outrage and undone by what seems a plausible explanation, he leaves the other men, goes to a darkened corner, and unburdens his heart. He confesses to the abuse he inflicted on his own son—beating him senseless—while the child only smiled and blinked his eyes. The boy never protested, he never answered back. He only smiled and blinked, no matter how hard his father beat him. Until one day, driven by some strange impulse, the cabbie hurries home to find his son hiding in the closet with a noose in his hand, ready to hang himself. The child survives, but the raging, racist juror now sobs in agony at what nearly took place, and at what he has become.

The American film ends with the acquittal, remember, and with Juror #8 striding out of the courtroom, well satisfied. The camera angle is shot from the height of a flag pole, and we watch as our hero descends the courthouse steps and blends into the city scene on foot. It is an effective and powerful image meant to honor the American legal system. All is good here. Our system of empirical evidence and rational argument works. Justice is served and the innocent are set free. Or at least, that is its message.

In marked contrast, '12' does not treat us to such patriotic pride. Russia is in ruins. The Soviet experiment was a disaster. The enemy is at the gate and plotting from within. The civil courts barely function, corruption is rampant, and our jurors are all exhausted, broken men. Yet, when the final vote is taken, they raise their hands and vote "not guilty."

End of story? No, indeed, there is still one *new* hold-out. The chairman of the jury, the one who called for the vote, now raises his hand to vote "guilty" against the boy; not because he thinks the youth is responsible for his uncle's death, but because he fears for the young man's life. He explains it this way: If the young Chechen is freed, considering the circumstances of the murder and the frame-up, he will likely be killed by those same criminals who murdered his uncle. It would be better if the young man went to prison where his enemies could never lay hands on him; because freedom would only lead to his murder. The eleven jurors suggest that maybe they can watch over the boy together, and somehow protect him from harm. But this idea is dismissed. The thugs who want him dead would still come after him, and these busy, traveling, professional, and weak men could never protect the youth. Then the chairman decides that he alone will guard the boy and help him find his uncle's killers. He is, after all, an honored officer of the Russian army, and no one would dare to threaten him.

So it is done. Exonerated by justice, set free by mercy, and protected by sacrificial love, the boy will surely thrive. But let us pause here a moment and consider how human love would not have triumphed without the grace of that one woman who rescued the alcoholic she encountered on a train, and without the courage of that same man, the juror who stood against all the others and spoke his truth to them. It would not have triumphed without the chairman's appeal to mercy over justice, and without the intervention of the mother of the infant Christ—because *she* has been the focus of the wandering camera's eye all along.

The verdict is in: "not guilty." The mobsters who were watching the trial closely are stunned, the prosecutor is stunned, and the accused boy wipes his eyes in disbelief. Now the jurors we have come to know so well go their own way and scatter in the snowy streets. Only the chairman sits with the freed youth on the wintery steps of the courthouse. "Would you recognize them?" he asks, meaning the thugs who killed his uncle.

"Of course. I will never forget them," he replies.

"We will find them. We will, I promise."

As for our hero, Juror #1, in the final scene we see him reenter the darkened gym. He walks over to the steel shelving to retrieve the small icon of the Mother of God that he had placed there earlier, to watch over their chaotic assembly. The little sparrow that had been pestering them all evening hops up beside her. The juror recognizes the bird, then goes over to the windows and opens two high panels. Snow billows in through the open portals. He returns for the icon, kisses it, and slips it back into his wallet. Then he addresses the fledgling: "If you want to fly away, fly away. If you want to stay, stay. You have to make up your own mind."

We are delighted to see the tiny bird flutter to the open window frame, ponder its options for a moment, and then flit out into the darkened streets; the Holy Ghost released into our violent world! God's love poured forth.

Our hero leaves the gym quietly. There is no need, in true humility, for pride or satisfaction. It was not his power of reasoning, or critical science, or even the quality of Russian justice that gave life back to that boy. It was a pure gift, an act of God at work in the human heart, a sacramental grace.

We flashback, one more time, to the rain, the burned out bus, the dead soldiers, and the dog with the bone that is a human arm. These words are etched across the screen:

> "The law is all powerful and constant. But what can be done
> when mercy has greater force than the law?"

> —B. TOSIA[24]

"God, I'm blind!"

---

24. "B. Tosia" There seems to be no such person, and it is assumed that this is a cryptic pseudonym for the writer and director (and the actor who plays the Chairman), Nikita Mikhalkov.

While it is true that virtuous habits exercise our good character, we should also recognize—by way of our own experiences in a complex world—that human goodness is always wounded by sin, and we cannot sufficiently maintain our moral balance in all ways and at all times. Human goodness must also look to, and pray for, the *grace* of God; grace here meaning the pure gift of God's own goodness and help. This is where our Judeo/Christian theology parts ways with pagan and secular sensibilities. Justice, without the grace of mercy, is still an important virtue and an essential human good, but the measure of human justice is always incomplete, and we can somehow intuit this.

Let us reconsider Colonel Behrani and his just dealings with Kathy Nicolo. Behrani was lawful and reasonable but he was not merciful, and his son, Esmail, knew it. "We will remain lions in our hearts," Behrani tells him, instructing his son in the ways of courage and human justice. And though Esmail is merciful in his own heart, he chooses to act like a lion, grabbing the deputy's gun in order to enforce his father's strong justice, and so dies as a consequence of its inherent human flaws.

Because we suffer in a complex world and are wounded by our own sinful nature, we need grace. We need the gift—not only our deserved due portion, but the absolute *gift*—of mercy. Without it, even justice can turn cold and cruel and catastrophic. With it, we unite our freedom to God's purpose. With it, we are saved. With it, we set the Spirit of God loose upon the world.

> *The Voice of God is heard in Paradise: . . . What was cruel*
> *has become merciful. What is now merciful was never cruel.*
> *I have always overshadowed Jonas with My mercy,*
> *and cruelty I know not at all. Have you had sight of me,*
> *Jonas My child? Mercy within mercy within mercy.*[25]
>
> —THOMAS MERTON

25. Merton, *The Sign of Jonas*, 351–52.

Considering Conscience

The Catechism of the Catholic Church states that prudence "guides the judgment of conscience."[26] Now that we have a better understanding of prudence as a virtue, we can see how it is closely tied to justice and to our duty as moral people. In a similar way, prudence guides us as we grow in knowledge and understanding. By the wise, discerning compass of prudence, we can adjust our course and begin to form ourselves into the true, *good* people God intended us to be, even before we were made.[27] This process of becoming—of growing into our true selves—allows us to literally participate in our own creation. With the aid of practiced good habits we gain in wisdom. By the grace of God we are gifted with choice and freedom. It is this prudential activity, of wisdom acting in freedom, that guides the judgment of our conscience.

So then, what exactly is conscience? As children we might have seen those old cartoons that showed a good little angel sitting on one shoulder of our hero, and a bad little devil sitting on the other, both whispering advice and temptations into our good hero's ears. It is a goofy image, but it does depict conscience as a voice cajoling our moral actions, and that gets the point across pretty well to a young mind! Conscience *is* an inner voice, yet it is more, as we shall see.

But before we go there, let us first consider what conscience is not. We might define conscience as an uneasy feeling, an emotional response to some good or evil action, or a moral judgment made against another person. We might also equate it with feelings of guilt and remorse (these feelings do *result* from a bad decision on our part, but they are not the first workings of conscience). Defining conscience as a *feeling* is misleading and wrong. Conscience is not a feeling. Conscience is a *judgment of reason*. It is a faculty of the mind. It is the active process of our moral decision making; that action we take when we discern what we should or should not do. It is our best judgment based upon our apprehension of the divine law. How do we know what that divine law is? Well, we certainly cannot know the mind of God, but we can discern this law through prayer and reflection, through our understanding of the natural law (to do good and avoid evil), by our lived experiences,

---

26. *Catechism of the Catholic Church*, #1806.

27. "Before I formed you in the womb I knew you." Jer 1:5.

and according to the law that is written on our hearts.[28] Our discernment includes the study of Holy Scriptures and the authoritative teachings of the church, as well as the pursuit of secular, human learning: through philosophy, science, medicine, history, law, and the arts. We cannot make good, intelligent judgments in ignorance, and conscience *is* a judgment of reason.

Conscience is also a *principle of freedom,* because it is our inherent dignity to act freely as we have been gifted by God. And since conscience is the process of discerning moral judgments (to act or not to act in a given situation), that judgment must be made in freedom. A choice that is not freely made is not a choice; it is either an accident or an act forced upon us, and conscience must never be forced or coerced. Our conscience can only work when we are free to decide what to do.

The "Pastoral Constitution on the Church in the Modern World" proclaims that "Conscience is the most secret core and sanctuary of the human person."[29] *Conscience is where we hear the voice of God.* It is, therefore, our absolute moral duty to form our conscience accordingly, and this is a lifelong task. A well-formed conscience is not something we can learn from a book, or memorize from a list of rules, or acquire without effort. And it is certainly not an appetite that moves us to do whatever we *want* to do. No, conscience must be honest and wise in its judgments, just as we must be discerning in our engagements with the world, our neighbor, and with God. Since it is our duty to form a mature, moral conscience, let us briefly walk through the steps that guide this formation.

We begin at the very core of our being, where we *listen to the voice of God in prayer* and through interior reflection. St. Ignatius encouraged his followers to conduct a daily "examination of conscience," which is the practice of reviewing the day's events and our actions therein. How have we hurt another person or offended God? What were the consequences of that action? Are we sorry for the offense, and how will we make amends? This examination of conscience is also the beginning prayer at every Catholic Mass.

We should make a concerted effort to *study the Holy Scriptures,* especially the gospels, and form our conscience according to the teachings

---

28. "(The Gentiles) show that the demands of the law are written in their hearts, while their conscience also bears witness and their conflicting thoughts accuse or even defend them." Rom 2:15.

29. *Catechism of the Catholic Church,* #1776, quoting the "Pastoral Constitution on the Church in the Modern World" *(Gaudium et Spes).*

of Christ: To do to another as we would have them do to us; to keep
the commandments; to love God with all of our heart, soul, mind, and
strength, and to love our neighbor as ourselves. A mature conscience is
drawn to these teachings.

We are to study and *receive the teachings of the church* with an open
mind, with trust, and with deep respect. The church is the Body of Christ
and the memory of sacred revelation. She has over two thousand years of
experience with human frailty and the consequences of sin. And she has
been charged with keeping and teaching the wisdom of her great thinkers
and saints. Furthermore, the tradition of the church honors the teachings of Hebrew law, its history, the commandments, and the voice of the
prophets. Because conscience is a judgment of *reason,* it follows that we
should study and respect this tremendous tradition of thought, experience, and revelation. By the same token, we should not apply a rigid,
blind adherence to church teachings, as this kind of legalism is counter
to a mature faith. Certainly a well formed conscience should fall in line
with church teachings, but conscience is called to be *formed* by those
teachings, not overruled by them. "Pay careful attention" to the church's
teachings, regard them with "deep respect," this is what is asked of us
from the church teachers themselves.[30] While our conscience must be
formed according to reason, and not subjugated by blind obedience, we
must remember that the church has a right to her conscience, and teaches
according to her own deep wisdom.

Because conscience is the sanctuary of God, we must form our
conscience in goodness and in truth; and because conscience is where
we hear the voice of God, that voice will always draw us toward what
is perfectly true and perfectly good, God himself. Therefore, above all,
we must *love the truth and seek it earnestly*, shunning every falsehood,
because what is true is of God. We must also intend the good with our
whole hearts, doing those things which move us in the direction of the
divine law, because the divine law is the goodness of God.

It is proper and necessary to *consult the human disciplines* of philosophy, science, history, art, medicine, the law, etc., in order to grow
in wisdom, as these disciplines are the repository of human knowledge.

---

30. The Theological Commission that worked on the "Pastoral Constitution on
the Church in the Modern World" *(Gaudium et Spes)* during Vatican II changed the
language of the draft from: "the faithful ought to form their consciences according to
the Church's sacred teaching" (which was considered too restrictive) to: "In forming
their consciences, the faithful must pay careful attention to Church teachings."

We must form our conscience according to what our reason judges to be true; not only the truth we learn through our own experiences and study, but the truth we learn from the knowledge gained by other people throughout history.

We should *receive the civil laws with an open mind and with respect.* Conversely, a just society must enact civil laws that respect the conscience of its citizenry. A law that goes against the moral law is no law at all; and a law that compels a citizen to act against his or her conscience is vacuous, empty, and unbinding.

A well formed conscience carefully *examines the circumstances* surrounding any moral action. We must also *consider the consequences of our action,* how our actions will be received by others, and be prepared to *take full responsibility* for our deeds.

Our *conscience is not infallible*; it can make mistakes. We might be fooled by false prophets or false teachers; and we can certainly fool ourselves while suppressing the voice of our conscience. An erroneous conscience is the consequence of a badly formed conscience; and we are duty-bound to form our conscience so that we are able to make good decisions. Still, *even an erroneous conscience must be followed and obeyed.* The moral failing is not in obeying one's erroneous conscience, the moral failing is in not forming one's conscience properly to begin with—either through laziness, or defiance, or willful ignorance.[31] Too often I hear that one must obey a "well formed" or "right" conscience. This is misleading. It suggests that we should not follow our weak or erroneous conscience. On the contrary, we must follow our conscience whether it was well-formed or not! And then we must get back to work reforming it. If conscience is a principle of freedom, as the church proclaims, then freedom must allow for error and mistakes.

How do we know when we have acted in accordance with a good conscience? We know because we will experience *peace of mind.* If we were to transgress our conscience we would experience regret, remorse, and guilt. These are messages from that sanctuary of our being, that place where God speaks, and they must be seriously regarded so that our *transgressions can be reconciled.*

---

31. "Certainly one must follow an erroneous conscience. But the departure from truth which took place beforehand and now takes its revenge is the actual guilt which first lulls man into false security and then abandons him in the trackless waste." Cardinal Joseph Ratzinger (Pope Emeritus Benedict XVI). "Conscience and Truth."

What should we do if we offend against our conscience? The sacrament of penance is the sacrament that absolves us from sin, when we are contrite and resolve not to repeat the offense. Remember, an examination of conscience precedes our spoken confession. This is the sacramental moment, along with absolution—the grace filled gift—which we receive as a consequence of our remorse and repentance. Only God knows how honestly we have made that act of contrition.

These are the teachings of the Catholic Church. Yet I suspect if one were to ask the average Catholic which moral entity they should obey above all, the magisterium or their own conscience, they would likely say "the magisterium," which is the teaching authority of the church. They probably think that the magisterium is a scholarly band of wise bishops listening to the voice of the Holy Spirit and repeating that voice back to the faithful. And in many ways, of course, it is! But by "magisterium" we mean the *whole* teaching authority of the church, which includes the theologians and laity. It is more of a conversation than a ruling body, and its role is to *instruct* the faithful. Why "instruct" and not "rule over?" Because the moral entity one must obey over everything else (in primacy) is one's conscience. Conscience is the final moral arbiter. Yes, we have the moral obligation to form our conscience, but it is our conscience that we must finally obey over any moral teaching or law, even that of the magisterium. That is the magisterial teaching of the Catholic Church. But even these teachings can be abused; by those who assume that they can go against church teaching because they disagree with them, without ever having read the church's documents or positions, much less studied, prayed, or reflected on them; and by those who believe that absolute obedience is the only response required of them and others. Both extremes are dangerous, and both lay bare a culpable and poorly formed conscience.

Building a Just Society

It is one thing to form and honor our inner conscience, but what about the conscience of society itself? How can we build a just society—which is the duty of the laity—according to the moral law and the demands of justice?

As we recall, conscience is a *judgment of reason* and a *principle of freedom*. These are foundational human values which must be upheld by a just society. Because the primacy of conscience is grounded in our human dignity, human societies must therefore be founded on that dignity. Governments should give every citizen a voice in their own governing while defending the human rights of its citizenry. That is the principal role of government: to defend our human rights (which are derived from our human dignity) and to promote the common good (what God has given to humanity in freedom, and a bounty that is justly distributed). All people are equal in human dignity (being equally human) and therefore, in justice, they must stand equal before the law. Civil authorities must not only recognize this, they must codify it into their constitutions and legal structures (i.e., the Bill of Rights; the Universal Declaration of Human Rights), so that no one stands above the law. This is what we mean when we say we govern by the rule of law. Human dignity, freedom, justice, equality, opportunity; these are the hallmarks of a just society, with conscience as its foundation. Civil authorities, therefore, have no right to compel a citizen to act against his or her conscience—except in those cases where the law must protect the rights and safety of others.

Theologies and ideologies often part ways at this point, leading to considerable confusion. For example, the church supports an individual's right to object and refrain from conscripted military service, or from partaking in immoral legal, medical, or business practices, according to the dictates of their individual conscience. Yet it is often the case that the law must weigh the freedom of one citizen's actions against the rights and freedoms of another. These cases ought to challenge us to consider the complexities underlying our social framework, yet they do not diminish the significance of the role that conscience plays in a free and democratic order.[32]

---

32. For example, one might argue that a baker is free to refuse service to a gay couple who are wishing to purchase a cake for their wedding, owing to the baker's religious faith that opposes gay marriage. Yet, would that same baker be justified in denying service to an inter-racial couple, if inter-racial marriage violated his or her religious beliefs? While we must uphold religious freedom as a human right, that right must be justly applied to all faiths. In addition, not every right is primary or absolute. There are also the rights of the marrying couples to consider. What if some religious practices called for the sexual mutilation of children, or the use of dangerous, psychedelic drugs, or human sacrifice for that matter? The point here is not to diminish the demands of conscience in a just society, or to weaken the law's duty to protect the freedom of our conscience; the point is to show that moral discernments are not simple tasks. The world is complex, and our prudential judgments must be formed well enough to account for these complexities. Even when we employ a well-meaning heart and the powers of reason to moral law, we may still fall short of what is just (and certainly what is merciful).

In truth, you can stir up a lot of controversy by upholding these teachings on conscience. They are not always popular, especially with kings and governments corrupted by their own coercing powers. In days past, one might even be executed for claiming that individual conscience is above the civil law. That is a very old story, and one which now serves as our introductory leap into *A Man For All Seasons*, the story of Sir Thomas More, Chancellor of England, saint, and martyr for the freedom of conscience.

A Man For All Seasons[33]

Sir Thomas More lived in the times of King Henry VIII. He was a brilliant lawyer, a gifted statesman, a loving family man, and a devout Catholic, which was the faith of England in those days. This was before Henry's schism and his proclamation that the king is supreme over the church, and not the other way around.[34] When the church is made subservient to the crown there is the great danger that the primacy of conscience, left undefended, will be deposed by dysfunctional parliaments and autocratic kings.

The historical setting and basic storyline of the film is probably familiar to most readers. King Henry VIII wants to divorce his first wife, Catherine of Aragon—who has not produced a male heir—so he can marry Anne Boleyn, a younger woman who has attracted the king's wandering attention. Henry decides to have his first marriage annulled, which is the proper legal procedure. But Rome will not grant the annulment

---

The church teaches that we should not coerce the conscience of any human being, we can only instruct them (including the rebuke of sin), pray for them, and support them with love. By the same token, we all have the right to live in a secure society. Therefore a criminal may be arrested and secured in prison (after a fair trial) to protect others from the harm he might otherwise do. This is not the same thing as coercing the conscience of the convicted. On the other hand, torture is the absolute coercion of another's conscience, the sole purpose of which is to destroy the will of the victim. That is why torture can never be justified.

The church insists that every human being has God-given human rights, but that not all rights are equal in their authority. There is a hierarchy of human rights. Human life is paramount, for example, and therefore any willful destruction of human life, such as abortion by choice, must always be opposed. Discerning how all of our human and civil rights interact in the social landscape is a continuing process that requires the well-formed conscience of society itself, bridled by the guiding reins of dear prudence.

33. *A Man for All Seasons*, directed by Fred Zinnermann. A Fred Zinnermann Production, 1966. Rated "G" for all ages, but the kids might not enjoy it.

34. See Thomas Becket in *Becket*.

as there are no compelling grounds for it, and the king's chancellor at the time, Cardinal Wolsey, will not go against Rome. As it happens, the cardinal's time on earth is reaching its end, and when he dies King Henry decides to make Sir Thomas More his Lord Chancellor of the Realm.

With grand regalia, Henry VIII pays a visit to More's estate in Chelsea in order to discuss the matter of his marriage. It is a situation most urgent to the king, as he and England need a male heir. Of course, he does not suggest that his own desires and passion for Anne Boleyn are influencing his motives. Rather, he emphasizes the necessity of an heir, for the good of the realm, and he justifies a divorce from Queen Catherine based upon her inability to produce one. More listens to Henry's case, but he is hesitant.

When the king's argument fails to sway Sir Thomas, Henry suggests that his marriage to Catherine was illicit from the start. He had married his brother's widow, and for this he needed a dispensation from Rome, which he received. Sir Thomas has already noted the folly of the king's request in seeking a dispensation from the dispensation, but Henry now insists that the first dispensation went against the law in Leviticus, and he ineptly tries to defend his position on biblical grounds. More feigns sympathy, but he must humbly admit that he is no theologian and that these matters are best left to the canon lawyers in Rome.

What we might recognize in this exchange is Henry's fumbling presentation of an argument he has formed from his own studies. The king is attempting to override church law with a personal interpretation he has devised from the biblical law. Yet it is clear to Thomas that the king is only going after what he desires, Anne Boleyn, and that Henry is trying to justify his position by arguing backwards from his desired conclusion. In so doing, Henry lays bare his own awkward reasoning and the confusion of his conscience. Sir Thomas sees through the king's missteps and rightly suggests that he take the issue up with authorities who have greater knowledge of such matters. Of course the king refuses to do this, as he knows full well what the authorities will conclude, as they have already concluded it: that his first marriage was proper and licit.

Unable to persuade Sir Thomas with argument, Henry leans on More for his loyalty. Sir Thomas is a man of integrity and he is highly respected. His support would surely clinch the deal. But if Henry can't have More's support, he will settle for his silence. "I will have *no opposition*," he states emphatically, and that concludes their discourse. In an exchange of glances, Sir Thomas assents to silence. He will not speak his position, not even to his family, and he will find safety in secrecy.

More's family struggles to understand his silence. Their bewilderment helps us to untangle the complexity of More's thought on conscience and the rule of law, and on the perilous position he must take as the king's silent chancellor. These are dangerous times. A zealous William Roper—the young man who will marry More's daughter, Margaret—points to the presence of spies in the household and among Thomas' friends. In particular he singles out Richard Rich, a lackey who is looking to advance his position at any cost. Roper challenges Sir Thomas to arrest Richard Rich, because he is a bad man.

> *Sir Thomas More:* "There is no law against that. (He is free to go,) and go he should if he were the devil himself until he broke the law."
>
> *William Roper:* "Now you give the devil benefit of the law?"
>
> *Sir Thomas More:* "Yes. What would you do? Would you cut a great road through the law to get after the devil?"
>
> *William Roper:* "Yes! I'd cut down every law in England to do that!"
>
> *Sir Thomas More:* "Oh? And when the last law was down and the devil turned round on you, where would you hide, the laws all being flat? This country is planted thick with laws from coast to coast, man's laws, not God's. But if you cut them down . . . do you really think you could stand upright in the winds that would blow then? Yes, I would give the devil benefit of the law for my own safety's sake!"

So King Henry, by an act of his newly created Parliament, is made Supreme Head of the Church of England, fomenting the English schism against the Catholic Church. Sir Thomas responds by resigning his office as chancellor, without stating why he resigns.

Henry is now free to marry Anne Boleyn after granting for himself the annulment that he desired. Even so, the king still needs to establish the legitimate status of his new marriage before the court and his subjects and the world. He insists, therefore, that all of his statesmen sign an oath, an Act of Succession, recognizing his second marriage as lawful and proclaiming his future children as legal heirs to the throne. Sir Thomas, however, refuses to sign the document; nor will he make any contrary statement regarding

Henry's marital status. Clearly Thomas cannot sign an oath swearing to believe what he does not believe, as that would be a lie before God; and he cannot publicly condemn the marriage, as that would be treason against the king and could get him killed. Instead, he remains silent as his only prudent course, and he insists that his family do likewise.

But Sir Thomas has enemies and his silence no longer protects him. The laws have shifted, the devil has turned, and on a trumped-up charge of bribery—arranged by the king's chief minister, Sir Thomas Cromwell and his toady, Richard Rich—More is summoned and examined. As the false charges cannot be supported by evidence, or hold up against More's clever arguments, he is released. But he is just as quickly re-arrested and imprisoned in the tower of London on a new and vague charge of "ingratitude to the king." Cromwell even threatens More with torture if he does not sign the oath, but More steadily refuses.

At this point, the Duke of Norfolk, Thomas' old friend and the king's newest chancellor, attempts to sway Thomas into signing for the sake of their good fellowship. In a telling exchange, he pleads with Thomas to go along with the rest of them and avoid further punishment:

> *The Duke of Norfolk:* "Oh, confound all this. I'm not a scholar. I don't know whether the marriage was lawful or not but dammit, Thomas, look at these names! Why can't you do as I did, and come with us, for fellowship?"

> *Sir Thomas More:* "And when we die, and you are sent to heaven for doing your conscience, and I am sent to hell for not doing mine, will you come with me, for fellowship?"

A Man For All Seasons does a commendable job in drawing out Sir Thomas More's views on the primacy of conscience and the rule of law. It is a remarkably intelligent script that is so crisp and intriguing that the viewer is never bogged down by the legal intricacies.

Sir Thomas cannot go against his conscience and swear an oath that legitimizes Henry's second marriage. Yet in fairness and in principle he does not condemn those who do sign it, presuming they signed according to their conscience. Thomas allows that the Duke of Norfolk will attain heaven, even though the Duke publically opposes the church's position. Consider this closely. Here are two moral choices, one contrary to church teaching and one adhering to it. Both actions oppose one another, yet neither decision can condemn the two men, because they are each acting according to their conscience. *That* is the essential power of conscience!

It is not relativism. Conscience does not determine the objective moral good of the act itself, conscience determines the subjective moral goodness of the person acting. Conscience is the final moral arbiter, the last authority, speaking for the well-meaning, good intent of the soul standing alone before God.

In the end, of course, Sir Thomas More is found guilty of treason (the victim of Cromwell's malicious undermining and Sir Richard's purchased perjury) and is put to death; the first real martyr for conscience.[35] Bear in mind that Sir Thomas was not executed because he opposed the king. In fact, he *refused* to oppose the king! But he also refused to publically swear an oath that supported the marriage, which would have been a lie, an intrinsic evil, and wholly against his conscience.

A Man For All Seasons is an excellent lesson for our times, where the rule of law is cut down by unprincipled men and where conscience is distorted and coerced by wicked powers. It is also quite adept at showing how opposing views can be morally held when they are earnestly considered, studied, and honestly proclaimed, to the detriment of no one's immortal soul.

Henry VIII's final legacy, the fruit of his appetites and his power, was to divide the church in schism, outlawing Catholicism in England and placing the Church of England under the imperial authority. But when a king is the final arbiter of the moral order, his whims and his errors become as powerful as the law, and then the *rule of law*—and the primacy of conscience which upholds it—turns irrelevant ("the laws all being flat") and is relegated to the dusty shelves of history and an underfunded academia.

Conscience is the aboriginal Vicar of Christ.[36]

—*SAINT JOHN HENRY CARDINAL NEWMAN*

---

35. Sir Thomas More was canonized Saint Thomas More in 1935.

36. *Catechism of the Catholic Church*, #1778, quoting Newman's "Letter to the Duke of Norfolk."

4

Grace

"And I say to thee: thou art Peter;
and upon this rock I will build my church,
and the gates of hell shall not prevail against it."[1]

—*JESUS CHRIST*

IT IS AMAZING HOW often I have heard this pronouncement explained by earnest Christians who thoughtlessly distort the words of Jesus. For some reason people tend to twist it around to mean its complete opposite! They say that *hell* is battering the gates of the church, that the church is under attack, and so we must boldly and ruthlessly guard the portals against hell's assault. Even priests (the less gifted ones) have preached this message from the pulpit. But that is not what Jesus is saying here, not at all. Read the words carefully. There are no walls around the church. The church is the Body of Christ, the People of God, and Christ has not walled himself off from anyone. Walls keep people out (or forcibly in). Gates select and admit and release, but there are no gates into the church or out of it. Those doors are open and people are invited to enter or free to leave according to their own lights. Freedom is essential to our human dignity. God beckons, but he does not destroy our liberty to refuse him.

---

1. Matt 16:18. (Douay-Rheims)

Hell is the walled-in place. *Hell* is the gated community. Hell allows us no freedom and no escape. It only admits the damned through its sinister gates and then keeps them there. What Jesus is saying to Peter is that he, Peter, is the foundation of the church, because he, Peter, proclaimed that Jesus was the Christ, the son of the living God. The gates of *hell and death* are the portals that will not hold up, not withstand, not prevail against the saving grace of God and his church. The gates of hell and death will fail by the merciful action of Christ crucified on the cross out of love. As there are no walls or gates around Christ and his church, we do violence to the church and to Christ when we endeavor to keep people away, or divide ourselves into menacing tribes or culture warriors.

As for the gates of heaven, well for heaven's sake, the gates of heaven are everywhere! This is the message of grace found in the sacraments of the church and in the sacramental signs that flower all around us. Thomas Merton tells us, in his oft-quoted journal entry, that people are all going around shining like the sun.

> At the center of our being is a point of nothingness which is untouched by sin and by illusion, a point of pure truth, a point or spark which belongs entirely to God . . . This little point of nothingness and of absolute poverty is the pure glory of God in us . . . It is like a pure diamond, blazing with the invisible light of heaven. It is in everybody, and if we could see it we would see these billions of points of light coming together in the face and blaze of a sun that would make all the darkness and cruelty of life vanish completely . . . I have no program for this seeing. It is only given. But the gate of heaven is everywhere.[2]

Put simply, grace is everywhere because "Grace is a *participation in the life of God*,"[3] and God is everywhere.

The Quality of Grace

When we exercise the cardinal virtues we may well achieve human excellence, but that prominence is always open to corruption. The ancient Greeks knew that there was an Achilles' heel, a fatal flaw, a heroic weakness, even at the core of our excellence. This is the human condition. The virtues, without grace, form a fine edifice that can withstand many

---

2. Merton, *Conjectures of a Guilty Bystander*, 146.

3. *Catechism of the Catholic Church*, #1997. (Emphasis in text).

assaults, but the mortar that holds the bricks together can also become the weakest link that collapses the entire structure. A virtue that gives a person strength has, built into its very nature, the flaw that may destroy him. The virtuous man, for example, may come to take pride in his own excellence, a pride that blasts away the foundation (humility) of his own formation! And then poor humility has to go back to work and rebuild the thing, brick by brick.

This is the stuff of tragic literature. When the ancient Greeks told of this tragic element in their dramas, it was often through the warning voice of the "Greek chorus," who sang out to caution an over-confident hero, advising him to tread lightly and walk humbly, lest he stumble. Rarely does the hero listen, and mighty is his fall.

Another kind of hero, the one found more readily in the Christian tradition, is the humble, broken, and destitute sinner. Here is the well-meaning person, stained with original sin, who has reached the lowest point of existence; like our Juror #1 in the Russian film, '12.' This man was so close to mortal destruction that he could only be rescued by the power of God. That rescue and that power is *grace*.

The grace of God in this context is often portrayed through a feminine character; and this is fitting when we consider grace as a favor that is caring, nurturing, and kind. By the same token, grace can come galloping in like a furious matron wielding a broom, chasing away the devil as if he were selling mischief door-to-door.[4] More exquisite, I think, is the icon of grace who is steady, enduring, foundational, and salvific. This is the loving power we find in *Roma*, a film that portrays a small, humble nanny as the only centering force in a family that is flying to pieces.

Roma[5]

Roma can be a puzzling film. It is beautiful, brooding, and strange—even compelling—yet it is painfully lacking in story. Quite honestly, there is no story or even much of a plot, at least in the conventional sense. Instead we have a chapter in the life of an upper-class family living in Mexico City, and of their indigenous servant, Cleo. It is a fascinating chapter, however,

4. This ferocious grace is wonderfully portrayed by Ma Joad, in *The Grapes of Wrath*.

5. *Roma*, directed by Alfonso Cuarón. Produced by Alfonso Cuarón, Gabriela Rodriguez, and Nicolás Celis; Netflix, 2018. (Spanish). Rated "R" for graphic nudity, language, and some disturbing imagery.

giving us a rare look inside the heart and culture of Mexico. And while it is a period piece (1971), it doesn't have to be. It can still happen today, and it does, every day.

In *Roma* we have a prosperous family that is spiraling into chaos. The father has left the home and is supposedly on a business trip, but he has actually abandoned his wife and four kids for a wilder life, and he sends no money home. The mother tries to cope with the situation, but she is distraught and lashes out at the servants while struggling with her own personal crisis.

Around this fractured family swirls a huge city that is itself fraying and in distress: there is student unrest, mass protests, violence, and hit-squad murders. There are brass bands playing in the streets and parading for the sake of some holiday, yet no one seems to notice them or care. Mexican military men practice the martial arts as if they were preparing for combat, but they are awkward and clumsy and fall over. Only Cleo, who watches her young man from the sidelines, is able to hold her balance in the difficult yoga pose. The children in the family quarrel, as kids do, but the youngest boy says odd things about his former life as a sailor who was drowned at sea. Nothing really fits. It is as if Mexico herself is trying to adapt to the many cultures and desires and corruptive vices that have invaded her. This is graphically and comically portrayed by the father's oversized, American-built car as it struggles and jockeys into place in the tiny Mexican garage. What are we to make of all this peculiar disarray?

There is only one place to look. For in the middle of the mayhem there is Cleo, ever centered, ever balanced. She is the mild, enduring rock of stability amid all of the brokenness. The children cling to her as their family unravels. The young man she dates on her days off uses her for sex, but he has no love for her. He exhibits his machismo in a bizarre, full-frontal naked dance, but she can only giggle at his flapping cockiness. Then he abandons her when she becomes pregnant, as if his indifference is normal behavior. Cleo's employer, the cuckolded wife and mother, embraces Cleo and comforts her, saying: "We women have to stay together," and insisting that she can keep her job through the pregnancy. Though Cleo will lose the baby, she knows that she is safe for now and needed in the household. So she won't have to return to her village in shame.

The saving action of grace in this film occurs when the mother takes Cleo and the children to the ocean for a holiday. The kids swim out too far into the heavy waves, and Cleo—who cannot swim—risks her life to rescue them. It is a powerful scene, and frightening, yet we never lose faith in Cleo's saving grace.

Our heroine is, like Mexico herself, exploited, used, loved, abandoned, long-suffering, and cherished. She is the heart of mild, calm balance; ever just, ever saving, ever meek. She is like the *Virgen de Guadalupe*, a truly feminine daughter of power and grace. She is like Jesus, ever present and worthy of our trust. That is the story. It is beautiful, but don't expect it to sweep you off your feet and dance for you. It does not. It simply endures.

First Reformed [6]

There is in all visible things an invisible fecundity, a dimmed light, a meek namelessness, a hidden wholeness. This mysterious Unity and Integrity is Wisdom, the Mother of all, Natura naturans. *There is in all things an inexhaustible sweetness and purity, a silence that is a fount of action and joy. It rises up in wordless gentleness and flows out to me from the unseen roots of all created being, welcoming me tenderly, saluting me with indescribable humility. This is at once my own being, my own nature, and the Gift of my Creator's Thought and Art within me, speaking as Hagia Sophia, speaking as my sister, Wisdom.* [7]

—THOMAS MERTON

As a work of art, *First Reformed* is wrapped in many layers of meaning. On the surface its story is simple enough, with an intelligent script and some unexpected plot twists. And though it is stark in its depiction of religious faith, this austerity moves the film along at a thoughtful, contemplative pace.

What is particularly unique about *First Reformed* is how well it captures the spiritual experience itself, in all of its spectral hues. Once we viewers move from the surface glimmer of the storyline and sink into

6. *First Reformed*, directed by Paul Schrader. A Killer Films Production, 2017. Rated "R" for disturbing imagery and mature themes, including a suicide.

7. Merton, *Hagia Sophia*. I would encourage readers to study Thomas Merton's prose poem, *Hagia Sophia*, to gain a deeper insight into *First Reformed* and my interpretation of this film. Merton is mentioned, directly or indirectly, three times in this movie, and that is no accident!

the film's depths—to the level of its underlying themes—we should note an unsettling disturbance in our own emotional center. Suddenly the anchors of culture, faith, politics, and human wisdom give way, and we are set adrift. At this level we grow uncomfortable and perplexed. We don't seem to have a metaphorical compass to cope with the unmooring that is taking place, and we do experience this dissidence. What is happening to us? What is going on? What does all this *mean*? It is dark here, psychotic, and a little creepy.

What the characters and the audience are experiencing is a plunge into the spiritual depths of anguish, even evil. There is a pervading sense of lostness and anxiety that emerges, one that seems essential to the movie's theme of suffering. It is mysterious because suffering is mysterious. The mood is captured by the stark settings, the slow scenes, the gripping dialogues, and a humming build-up to some impending doom.

First Reformed takes us through the dark night of lost faith by way of a very honest, tragic, and broken good man. Here we meet Reverend Toller, a minister who is grappling with his own grief, guilt, and failing health. He is very much like Juror #1, in the Russian film '*12*', before he encountered grace. He seems on the verge of death. It is scary.

Toller has just been assigned to pastor the tiny congregation of a small New England church, First Reformed. The church is sparsely attended, but it has great historic significance and a noble past. It was once a part of the Underground Railroad that helped Southern negroes escape slavery, and people still come to tour the historic landmark. But as a church First Reformed is dying. The mega-church in town oversees this tiny ecclesial heirloom, but it attracts the greater crowds to its mega stage.

After services one day, Reverend Toller is approached by a young pregnant woman. She asks Toller if he might please come speak with her husband, Michael. Her husband is a despondent young man, caring, but overwhelmed by the evil he sees all around him. He does not want to bring a child into the world. He has studied the environmental sciences and knows that the earth is dying from deforestation, carbon emissions, and global warming. He sees how human greed is responsible for this destruction, and he has been jailed for his acts of protest against the destroyers. Michael wants his wife, Mary, to terminate her pregnancy. It would be unfair to raise a child in this environment, he reasons. Their child would only have to suffer the loss of every created good thing because of pollution, famine, war, and disease. But Mary is not willing to do such a thing.

So Reverend Toller visits with Mary's husband to counsel him. He listens, questions, and encourages the young man, but he can see that Michael is in the throes of tremendous despair. Toller knows the signs of that anguish. Gently, he spars with Michael, grappling with his arguments as if he were Jacob wrestling with an angel. Then he asks Michael to consider this paradox: "Wisdom," he tells him, "is holding two contradictory truths in our mind simultaneously: hope and despair. A life without despair is a life without hope. Holding these two ideas in our head is life itself."

Hope and despair are the film's sacramental themes. There is despair over what is broken—God's beautiful creation and human frailty—and hope for what may be redeemed. There is the reality of our human suffering and our grief over a fallen world, but then there is that other reality, our lived lives that participate in God's own existence and are supplanted with sanctifying grace. Somewhere in the center—not at a point of compromise but at a point of precarious, juxtaposing realities—despair and hope converge. It is a duality of earth and heaven, of fallen human wretchedness and perfecting divine grace. It is our history of original sin and the absolute love of the Incarnation, when God enters creation to redeem us. "Grace covers us all," Toller tells Michael. Later that evening Toller writes in his journal that the exchange was "exhilarating."

Sadly, the young man is unable to fathom the paradox. He has given up on life, resigns himself to despair, and violently kills himself as his only way out of hopelessness. Toller must now comfort Michael's widow, but he is clearly struggling with the trauma of this death.

Like Michael, Reverend Toller is broken-hearted and fragile. He has lost his son to war (after encouraging him to enlist) and his wife in a bitter divorce. He must contend with his church leaders who see him as a failure, as well as his own demons of alcoholism and a deep sadness that overshadows his every action. He *pollutes* his body with alcohol, a body that is dying of stomach cancer, and becomes—like the earth—a temple of great devastation.

Then he is covered by grace.

Her name is *Mary* and she literally covers him with a "wordless gentleness" meant to heal him. In a strange, bold gesture she lays her body over his, their hands flatly joined, and together they levitate as one; the unborn child is protected between them as they are raised up in unity. This is not a sexual union but a *mystical* union. This is Adam coming into being at the voice of Holy Wisdom, with all of creation roiling underneath.[8] Mary calls this experience "a magical mystery tour," but in Toller's vision the beauty of the earth turns dark and festers with chemical poisons.

The strange relationship that forms between Toller and Mary is, on the surface, most inappropriate. But we are not meant to view this film on its surface level, we are meant to view it at the allegorical level. Otherwise, the levitation scene is almost corny. But when we consider this experience as an allegory, then the "mystery tour" becomes an *action of grace* that truly rescues Toller. This action is the feminine grace of God working to redeem him. It is the sacramental sign, the sacred insight, and a glimpse at the *promise* of the Incarnation. The Incarnation, and Christ's redemptive love, is the hope that Toller longs for, and it is what gives this film its theological depth.

Now Toller must confront his demons. There is the dreaded diagnosis of an impending death by cancer, and the doting music director who wants to save him from his torments (how harshly he rebukes her! She is like St. Peter to our Lord, a stumbling block to him; one who does not consider God's ways). Toller must also take on the powers that are destroying the earth, as well as his church leaders who are profiting from those powers. He is haunted by Michael's death, and by the suicide vest and explosives that he found among Michael's things; weapons the young man planned to use, apparently, in some violent act against the polluters.

Toller's first instinct—a primitive instinct by all indications—is to take up Michael's cause and destroy the destroyer. He decides to use the vest and blow himself up at First Reform's re-consecration event, along with the evil men who will be attending the service. His life hardly matters, he is dying anyway. This will be an act of his own malformed justice. But notice how he snarls *like one possessed* when his murderous plans are foiled by Mary—Mary, full of grace—who arrives at the church like an innocent child, when he had commanded her to stay away. Toller shrieks in chilling frustration at the sight of her, but he cannot and will not harm her.

So he changes tactics. He will not kill anyone. He will only do violence to himself. That will be enough. Like a penitent Hazel Motes[9] he wraps himself in barbed wire and prepares to destroy himself with a glass full of poison. But this is self-loathing not penance!

---

8. See "Hagia Sophia" in *Emblems in a Season of Fury*, 61–69.

9. Flannery O'Connor's hero in her first novel, *Wise Blood*.

Then grace reappears at his door, like a soft touch, calling him *by name*—and for the first time—into true being. You, o man, are destined to live. You, o man, were purchased at a great price. You, o man, are heir to an unimaginable destiny. Toller's full glass falls from his hand and shatters on the floor. Only now can he express his overwhelming love for this feminine grace, this Holy Wisdom, this saving power of God.

It is by Mary's willing assent that Christ came into the world; it is by her holy response that the devil is thwarted and crushed, shrieking. There is hope for the children of Eve, because Mary is the new Eve, the "unseen pivot of all Nature." She will bring God into the world, the Incarnation, and set "upon the Second Person, the Logos, a crown which is His Human Nature . . . in His mission of inexpressible mercy, to die for us on the Cross."[10]

The cross is the Christian paradox. The cross is the duality of hope and despair. The cross is the union at the center of our human existence. *The cross is life.* So when Toller and Mary embrace in a tender, passionate exchange of a newly discovered love, we should see it—allegorically—as the bond of human frailty with an immaculate gentleness that is more powerful than Satan or death; a grace that is the very life of God within us. This is our human nature: to be human and wounded but destined for God. We are temples of God, temples of the Holy Spirit. We must not destroy this temple or the creation that nurtures it, because all are God's.

Without this allegorical reading, Toller's passionate love for Mary makes very little sense in the film, except as a rather weird, romantic, out-of-place-ending to a pretty dark flick.

It is better to find God on the threshold of despair than to risk
our lives in a complacency that has never felt the need of forgiveness.[11]

—THOMAS MERTON

Sacramental Signs

If ever there was a patron saint for the sacramental, it should be John the Baptist. Jesus claimed that there was no man born of woman who was

10. Merton, "Hagia Sophia" in *Emblems in a Season of Fury*, 61–69.

11. Merton, *No Man is an Island*, 41.

greater than John the Baptist. John's role, as he himself proclaimed, was to be a voice crying in the wilderness. His gesture was to point to the Lamb of God. His grounding was in the wild earth eating locusts. His glory was to be acclaimed by God as the greatest among men.

A sacramental is just this: a proclamation, grounded in the stuff of the earth, that points to God. It is a material sign and a human gesture that signifies a sacred reality. It is not a sacrament *per se*, but it has a similar function. A work of art can be a sacramental sign in the same way that incense can be a sacramental sign. Incense makes visible a trail of smoke, indicative of our prayers lifting up to heaven. It is sweetly scented, as are our pleas that we raise earnestly to God. A story or a painting or a film can do something very similar, through image and symbolic rendering. More profoundly, our own lives can do the same. The point of being Christian is to point to God. We are called to be a sacramental sign in the world and for the world; to be like John the Baptist; to be so filled with grace that it overflows, pouring out to everyone we meet, so that in *us* they will see Christ, too.

We can see this sacramental quality in the life of St. Francis of Assisi, for example. Wounded in his flesh by the stigmata—the very wounds of Christ—St. Francis became a living icon of Christ to the world in his own flesh. Is there a more beloved saint in our canon? And did he not see Christ in the poor, in the sick, in the lowliest of humankind? Did he not see God in the moon and the sun and in all of the creatures of the earth, even in the *rocks*? The life of St. Francis is a thoroughly sacramental imaging of Jesus; Christ, who is the Sacrament of God.

Our imagination is where we encounter God. We don't make God who he is, surely, but we conform our minds and hearts (our imaginations) to God as we understand him, and as he has revealed himself to us. When we form a perspective that is able to see the mystery of God in beauty, wisdom, and truth, we learn how to see that same underlying mystery and grace in the world and in our own lives. If we can recognize the presence of God in all things, we may learn to see Christ in others. And if we can do that well, we will become so beautiful, so grace-filled, that others will be able to see Christ in us. Then *we* become the sacramental sign and the image of Christ to the world. Then we become bearers of grace.

The character Mary in *First Reformed* assumes this sacramental role in a very unique and subtle way. She not only turns Toller's eyes to behold a mystical vision of creation, she directs the grace of that vision like a force to overwhelm him. This is why he shrieks like one possessed at the sight of her entering a church he means to destroy. It is the devil coming out of him. His self-destructive despair is crushed by her indescribable humility. He must honor his own life now and reclaim the sanctity of his human existence. Grace does this. Grace changes a person. It is not just a helpful gift, it turns our lives around, and sometimes inside out. Reverend Toller can now live the paradox he preached: to abide in hope when the world is poisoned by despair. This is life, and it is Mary who gives him this hope. She is the promise. She is the sign. She is, like the Blessed Virgin Mary, so filled with grace that she has become the full and seeded flower of Christ to the world.

The Sacraments

The sacraments of the church are not the only means to grace, they are the *assured* means. It would be misguided to think that there are no other occasions for grace outside of the seven sacraments. "The world is charged with the grandeur of God!"[12] Grace abounds, and the gate of heaven is everywhere. But the sacraments do *confer* grace. They are not just signs of God's loving gift (they are not *simply* an allegory or a symbol, what we might find in a story or film), they *make* God's grace present to the recipient; and in this way they are unique and holy.

The church defines a sacrament as an outward sign, instituted by Christ, that *gives grace.* There are seven sacraments in the Catholic Church: baptism, reconciliation (penance), holy Eucharist (communion), confirmation, matrimony, holy orders, and the anointing of the sick (last rites). These are, essentially, seven outward signs that signify Christ's redemptive action in the world. And while the sign is a visible, outward gesture, the invisible, infinite grace behind each sacrament is the greater reality. When we consider the sacrament of baptism, for example, we can see that water is used to signify the cleansing of the baptized, who are washed clean of original sin. Water also images the pouring out of God's grace upon the newly initiated, sealing them for Christ. The water is clearly and visibly present, but the grace is more real. In this same way, every sacrament is physically enacted, and each is a real encounter with the risen Lord.

Our Christian task is to shine a light on these encounters and point to the Lamb of God, as did John the Baptist. As beneficiaries of the grace

12. Hopkins, *Poems*, 26.

gifted to us in the sacraments—and in the Eucharist especially—we have been dismissed into the world to carry Christ in our flesh to every nation. We are meant to be a physically present, *sacramental* gift to those who do not know Christ, or who struggle with disbelief, or with sin, suffering, and death; so to embody the good news that God awaits us all.

Baptism

The first of the Christian sacraments is baptism. It is first because it was the earliest saving action that Jesus undertook in his mission on earth. It is primary because it initiates the baptized into the church and into the community of believers. And it is foremost because this initiation conditions the soul to receive the other sacraments. We are baptized in order to be cleansed from the stain of original sin and to receive the gifts of the Holy Spirit. As a sacrament, baptism is universally practiced by all Christians, as Jesus instructed us to do.

In the times of John the Baptist, baptism was a full immersion into the waters of the Jordan river. The initiate is tipped backwards into the current, as if falling dead into the grave and covered up. That it is an imitation of death is no accident. The newly baptized is then lifted up out of the waters, raised into the breathable air, and given a new life in Christ; signifying the full bodily resurrection of the faithful at the end of time. As St. Paul tells us, we are baptized into the death of Christ, but also into his resurrection.

Ocean Heaven [13]

Our baptism drowns us in the death of Christ.[14]
—*THOMAS MERTON*

Our next film, *Ocean Heaven*, provides us with some very Christian images of baptism. While it is not a Christian film, and these images might

---

13. *Ocean Heaven*, directed by Xiao Lu Xue. A William Kong Production, 2010. (Mandarin) Not rated, suitable for children old enough to read the subtitles.

14. Merton, *No Man is an Island*, 94–95.

not have been intended, there are still some interesting Christian parallels at work in this drama out of Hong Kong.

The movie opens with a plunge into what seems to be a very watery grave. Two men, a father and his grown son, sit on the bow of a boat with their legs dangling over the side. The older man ties a concrete block to his ankle and the ankle of his smiling, happy son. The boy seems quite contented. The father waits, looks about the blue horizon, sighs, and then throws the block into the sea. It yanks both of them overboard, plunging them deep below the calm waters.

Ocean Heaven is the story of a widowed father and his autistic son. The father, Sam Wang, is a maintenance worker at the local aquarium. His kind boss allows Sam's son, Dafu, to spend the work day swimming about in the giant fish tanks. Dafu loves to swim, he is more at home in the water than on land. He loves the fish and the sea turtles and the joy of floating and spinning freely in the huge, modern tanks. The father suggests to his boss that Dafu "was born in the wrong body," but he says this with great sadness.

As an autistic young man, Dafu can barely express himself. He requires routine, precision, and orderliness at home. He can function, moderately, but he needs his father to dress and feed him, and to take him everywhere he goes. Dafu's autism hinders his ability to communicate his needs or to express any love for his father. He lives within the shell of his own world, and relationships are excruciating to him.

When Sam learns that he is dying of cancer, with only a few months left to live, his first reaction is to drown himself and Dafu in the sea. He wants to take Dafu with him, even into death, because he knows that Dafu cannot manage alone and there is no one else to care for him. His son is too old for an orphanage, too young for a care facility for the elderly, and too capable for an institution that houses the mentally ill. Sam just hasn't the heart to leave his beloved boy in a place that looks more like a prison than a home. But his attempt to kill both himself and Dafu fails, as Dafu quickly unties the ropes that had them bound.

Ashamed of his actions, Sam redoubles his effort to find a decent home for Dafu. He goes from school to school, but is still unsuccessful. Dafu is not easy to manage. He can do a few small things for himself but he cannot live alone and he is capable of flying into dangerous rages when angered.

A neighbor girl, who is very fond of Sam, offers to care for Dafu, but Sam knows that his son would be an unfair burden to her. Sam's kind boss kindly refuses to look after the boy, as he would not be able to give him the proper attention either. Finally, Dafu's old primary school teachers agree to take him in. The school is run by Principal Lui, a woman who is recovering from a stroke and who understands the many challenges that come to those living with a disability. Principal Lui has tremendous respect and sympathy for the dying father. So she arranges for Dafu to board at the school, in a small dorm room, where he can stay for the rest of his life. This is a tremendous comfort to Sam, who moves into the dorm room with Dafu, so that their parting will be gradual.

Because Sam does not want his son to be a heavy burden on the school's faculty, he decides to teach Dafu how to do a few little things for himself: how to count change, ride the bus, boil an egg, and mop the floor at the aquarium so he can have a valuable job and will still be able to swim there. As Sam takes Dafu on errands about the neighborhood, teaching him new skills, a community of compassionate neighbors begins to form around them. These people are signs of welcome, of love and caring, but they are not the only signs.

With the end drawing near, Sam must find a way to comfort Dafu, to give him some kind of faith and belief that his father will always be with him, so Dafu does not grieve too terribly when he dies. Then he has a very keen insight.

In bringing up his son, Sam had always tried to teach Dafu how to think and feel the way *normal* people think and feel. But because his teaching methods keep failing, Sam realizes that he must change the way he instructs his son. He decides to teach Dafu according to *Dafu's* perceptions of reality, not his. Sam considers the peculiar way that Dafu learns, which is not through language or memorization or even repetition, but through *images* and *symbols*.

Let us look at the many images that occupy Dafu's world. He is attracted to beauty, but Dafu has no word for "beauty," nor is he able to understand the abstract concept. He just knows that he is drawn to it. "Flower" is beauty. When we consider this more closely we realize that "flower" is not just beauty, "flower" is also a living thing; a beautiful, living thing. Dafu recognizes the connection, and so he keeps the flowers watered. Water is life.

Another image to consider is the ocean. Dafu loved his mother, but she went away. That is all he knows. He does not know that she drowned herself in the sea. If we look about Dafu's room we will see that his mother is always paired with images of the ocean; his room is filled with sea shells and with photos of his mother at the beach. He loves the aquarium and the creatures there. He swims with the dolphins and the turtles, and he is delighted by them. Water is life *and* mother.

Again, Dafu is attracted to the circus clown, a sweet girl who befriends him. The image of a clown means friendship to Dafu. We grasp this when the girl must leave town to continue her circus travels, and in the way Dafu grieves for her. Because he is unable to express his grief, he spends the afternoon leaning sadly against a life-sized figure of Ronald McDonald at a McDonalds hamburger stand. This image moves us, but it should also prompt our insight into Dafu's association of image with his own deep feelings. Earlier, when the clown-girl pointed up to the sky and told Dafu that her grandmother lived in heaven, he looked up and made the connection. The image of "cloud" now triggers thoughts of heaven for Dafu.

The film is filled with these symbolic pairings of images with emotion because that is how Dafu exists in the world. That is also how art exists and expresses itself in the world, through image and symbolic representations. To take it further, that is how the sacraments operate in the life of the church, as outward signs of invisible grace. It is all interconnected.

Sam has finally come to understand this about his son. So, knowing that his death is imminent, he tells Dafu that turtles "live forever," and that he—the father—is turning into a turtle. He makes a turtle costume for himself and swims with Dafu in the aquarium to reinforce this symbolic pairing. "Turtle" is father. "Turtle" will always be with Dafu. Dafu will never be alone. Father will not leave him orphaned.

After Sam dies his mourning friends and neighbors gather around his gravesite. However, Dafu just wanders away. He doesn't seem to understand the reality of his father's death. When he sees a flower growing alone in the grass nearby he names it: "flower." Then he touches the little yellow daisy and looks skyward. Beauty. Life. Heaven.

This is an intriguing movie, with intimations of tremendous grace that can be found in the sacramental icons at play in Dafu's peculiar mind. Throughout the film there are signs touching on the divine; in the neighbors and friends who care for Dafu, and in the crystal clear waters that envelope him when he swims. Like the newly baptized, Dafu is welcomed into a community and restored to a new life. Though he is a boy at odds with relationships and the normal expression of human feelings, he is not alone. And though we have been schooled in the linear, rational ways of learning and language, we should still be inspired by Dafu's world of imagination and wonder. It is innate in every human being created in the image of God. And it is to these little ones that the Kingdom of God has been entrusted.

In the end our hearts burn, our eyes fill, and our sad mouths stretch into smiles as Dafu embraces the giant sea turtle and waves at us through the glass of the giant fish tank. Can you see?

Dafu was taught by *normals* how to boil an egg; but we have been given, by Dafu, new eyes for sacramental wonder. With this new vision, this new creation, we should see just how fitting was his father's gift of eternal love.

Or are you unaware that we who were baptized into Christ Jesus were baptized into his death? We are indeed buried with him through baptism into death, so that, just as Christ was raised from the dead by the glory of the Father, we too might live in newness of life.[15]

—*ST. PAUL*

It is awkward to use a film that makes no mention of Christ to illustrate the most Christian sacrament of baptism. But we should realize, too, that the church does not baptize Christians, it baptizes the *non-Christian*. If we can see how a film like *Ocean Heaven* hints at the underlying grace of love that the father has for his son, we may begin to recognize a parallel, an allegory, a sign that points us to a deeper reality: that we were created to be more than we are, that we were loved into existence, and that we are sustained in our lives by the grace of God, through the sacraments of the church, and in the community of faith around us. We are baptized into the death of Christ, yes, but we are also baptized into his resurrection. A turtle lives forever, as do our immortal souls. Baptism launches us into this new life in Christ, a new birth and a new creation. In so doing, we are made co-heirs with Christ as the children of God.

The Spirit itself bears witness with our spirit that we are children of God, and if children, then heirs, heirs of God and joint heirs with Christ, if only we suffer with him so that we may also be glorified with him.[16]

—*ST. PAUL*

15. Rom 6:3–4.
16. Rom 8:16–17.

Penance

While it is true that grace permeates creation—because God imbues his work—it is also true that the world we live in is a fallen place. The reality we encounter is, sadly, often harsh and the society we create is frequently brutal. We are sinful creatures and we perpetuate a sinful humanity. The sacrament of baptism cleanses us of the stain of original sin, but the effects of sin remain. Baptism does not remove our tendency to commit sins, as we will, again and again. Because our human dignity is grounded in freedom, this gift of freedom must allow for sin, even though we do not have to choose it. When we do commit a sin, however, our conscience moves us to seek forgiveness, atone for the offense, seek reparation, and enjoy the consolation that our Lord is merciful. Since our transgressions are committed against our neighbor as well as God, we seek forgiveness from both. That is the root of the sacrament of penance. We recognize that we have sinned, we regret the action, we speak the sin to another seeking forgiveness, and resolve not to commit the offense again. We are absolved from the sin by the mercy of God, and we are directed to perform a penance that attempts to restore—as best we can—the damage that was done by our sin; damage to our neighbor as well as to our own soul. This sacrament of penance is beautifully, graphically, and theologically well presented in our next film, *The Mission.*

The Mission[17] (Part I)

The Mission is based on the actual, historical experiences of the early Jesuit missionaries who came to the South American colonies (what is now Paraguay) during the settlement period of the mid-eighteenth century.

The main character, Rodrigo Mendoza, is a slave trader and mercenary. He makes his comfortable living by capturing the native *Guarani* people and selling them into bondage to the Portuguese. Because the *Guarani* have been hunted incessantly, the few that remain have fled deeper and higher into the jungle, above the waterfalls. The Jesuit missionaries have followed them there, and they begin to establish a mission for the native people in this remote region. These missions protect the *Guarani* from capture and from slavery.

17. *The Mission*, directed by Roland Joffé. A Goldcrest Films Production, 1986. Rated "PG" for images of violence in war and some nudity.

When Rodrigo discovers the Jesuits intruding into his hunting grounds, he is angered. From his hideout in the jungle he spies Fr. Gabriel,[18] who also recognizes Rodrigo. "We are going to make Christians of these people," Fr. Gabriel shouts to the huntsman. But Rodrigo replies curtly: "If you have the time."

Rodrigo is a military man, proud, clever, and cunning. The Jesuit missions hamper his trade and he wants them gone. Though Spain has outlawed the slave trade in its territories, Portugal has not. And because the territorial borders in the jungle are nebulous at best, they are easily disregarded. There is good money to be made in the slave-trade and corruption is rampant.

The buying and selling of human beings is morally prohibitive, but that problem is easily resolved when the empowered dehumanize their captives. The colonists of the day claimed that these native people were not human the way Europeans were human. They asserted that the native people were animals, just a few steps above the monkey, and that made their slave trade ethical. Rodrigo Mendoza is a civilized man, upstanding, even gracious, but he does not regard the natives as anything more than beasts to be snared in nets and herded into markets to be sold. They should be whipped when they are disorderly and shot when it is necessary. He is harsh in his treatment of the *Guarani* because he accepts the lie that they are less than human; a lie that makes his enterprise deceptively decent and acceptably profitable.

Rodrigo has a younger brother, Filipe, whom he loves and mentors. He also has his heart set on a beautiful woman, whom he intends to marry. But while Rodrigo is in the jungle hunting human prey, his brother is falling for the same lovely señorita. Filipe's betrayal humiliates Rodrigo and ignites his fury. In a rage, and goaded into action by an impromptu duel, Rodrigo stabs and kills his brother in the street.

Horrified by his bloody deed, Rodrigo is crushed by remorse and grief. He sinks into a deep despair, hoping to die. Because this killing was a duel, the law cannot touch him. So, instead of prison, Rodrigo exiles himself in some dank cloister, refusing to speak to anyone, refusing all consolation, and waiting in a monk's cell for his life to end. He waits six months.

Then he is visited by Fr. Gabriel, the Jesuit who was building the mission above the falls and who had intruded on his spoils. Fr. Gabriel

18. Father Gabriel's character is loosely based on the life of the Paraguayan saint, Roque González de Santa Cruz, SJ.

is not a welcome sight. "Leave, priest," Rodrigo snarls when the Jesuit approaches. "You know what I am."

Fr. Gabriel is not rebuffed. "Yes, I know. You're a mercenary, you're a slave trader, and you killed your brother. I know." Then he adds: "And you loved him. Although you chose a strange way to show it."

Rodrigo flares up in anger and grabs Fr. Gabriel by his tunic. "Are you laughing at me?" he demands to know, throttling the priest. "Are you laughing at me?"

Fr. Gabriel does not back down to this threat and nods his head, "I am laughing, because all I see is laughable." Fr. Gabriel's bravery is commendable and Rodrigo, a life-long soldier, recognizes courage for what it is, and lets him go.

Then Fr. Gabriel challenges Rodrigo to make peace with his conscience and with God. Only then can he be free of his burden of guilt. There is a way to be good again. There is life. But Rodrigo has no faith in life or in himself. The priest exhorts him: "God gave us the burden of freedom. You chose your crime. Do you have the courage to choose your penance? Do you dare do that?"

"For me there is no redemption, no penance hard enough."

"There is. But do you dare to try it?"

"Do *I* dare? Do you dare to see it fail?"

Fr. Gabriel does dare to see it through, and without failure. As he promised, he allows Rodrigo to choose his own penance.

Because his sin is so great, Rodrigo takes on a monumental task to atone for his crimes. He lashes all of his armor and weaponry together in a roped net—the same net he used to snare the *Guarani*—and he attempts to haul this bundle all the way up the falls, scaling the slick wet precipice, to the high jungle. It is a harrowing venture, but Rodrigo is strong, determined, proud, unflinching. He means to drag this absurd baggage behind him like his own dead corpse, his own false self. The struggle is severe because his sins are severe; not only the crime of murder, but the sins he had committed in his life as a slave trader. He will go to the people he assaulted, the families he destroyed, the tribes he decimated. With a band of Jesuits to accompany him, he will scale the waterfall, lugging a warrior load behind him.

At one point, exasperated by Rodrigo's struggle, a Jesuit brother grabs a knife and severs the rope that binds Rodrigo to his penitential burden. The armor tumbles a hundred feet down the crevasse. But Rodrigo is not so easily released. Wordlessly, but with great annoyance, he scuttles down the muddy trail to retrieve the mess, reties the line, and begins his upward trek again. No priest can release him from his reparations. This is a penance he has imposed upon himself and he will see it through.

At the summit of his climb, filthy and covered in mud, he encounters the *Guarani* at their new mission. The men of the tribe recognize Rodrigo as their hated adversary, and the chief sends a young warrior to take hold of the enemy. The warrior grabs a knife and makes ready to cut Rodrigo's throat, who waits steadily for his life to end. That would suit his crime, he thinks. But instead of killing him, the young man demands an accounting, shaking him by the hair and rebuking him in his own language. We do not know what he is saying, but his anger and his indignation is clear enough. When he encounters no resistance from Rodrigo, the chief commands him to cut the ropes that bind the penitent to the instruments of his warring past. The netted cargo crashes down the embankment and plunges into the river. Now Rodrigo is truly freed. His yoke is lifted, his ties are severed. This release does not come from anyone's mild blessing or from any encouraging words. This release comes as an act of pure forgiveness and mercy by the ones who were terribly wronged.

Overcome, Rodrigo breaks down and sobs, crying like a baby; which is to say, like one born again. These tears of contrition are not uncommon after the sacrament of penance, it is a grace of the sacrament and a gift of the Holy Spirit. But the *Guarani* do not know this, and they laugh at the sight of this big, hairy, mud-soaked man—their once hated enemy—sobbing like a little child. They cannot comprehend it. Seeing their laughter, Rodrigo begins to laugh with them. He laughs at himself, as well as at all the evils his pride had built up in him. He laughs and then cries and then accepts Fr. Gabriel's rocking embrace. His exhausting penance, and the stunning act of mercy the *Guarani* have bestowed upon him, have given him back his life.

Holy Orders

The Mission (Part II)

Rodrigo Mendoza stays with the small band of Jesuits above the falls and helps to build the mission there. He shares in their communal life and studies the Scriptures to learn more of Christ's teachings. It is telling that his reading and his reflections center on love, as it is so beautifully expressed in St. Paul's first letter to the Corinthians: "Love is patient, love is kind.

It is not jealous, love is not pompous, it is not inflated, it is not rude, it does not seek its own interests, it is not quick-tempered, it does not brood over injury, it does not rejoice over wrongdoing but rejoices with the truth. It bears all things, believes all things, hopes all things, endures all things. Love never fails."[19] Here we can see how Rodrigo is moving away from his vices—which are accurately catalogued for him in St. Paul's letter—to the virtues that are sustained by love: patience, kindness, humility, temperance, and fortitude. But Rodrigo is also discovering St. Paul's treatise on the theological virtues, which moves his heart greatly: "So faith, hope, love remain, these three; but the greatest of these is love."[20]

In time, Rodrigo asks to be received into the Society of Jesus as a novice, and he is welcomed into the order.

New tensions among the aristocracy, and between Portugal and Spain back in Europe, bring trouble for the missions in the New World. A papal emissary arrives to tell the Jesuits that there has been a transfer of lands from the Spanish held territories to the Portuguese. The Jesuits are told that they must abandon their missions, leave their work among the indigenous people, and allow the natives to be captured and enslaved again, as it is now permitted by Portuguese law. A complicated European conflict forces this situation on the Jesuits, and they are told that they must not resist, as their resistance here would have grave repercussions on the Jesuit order throughout Europe. The Jesuits take vows of obedience and are subordinate to the pope, but their vow of obedience now means that they must abandon their beloved people and allow *Guarani* to be slaughtered and enslaved. What are they going to do? What can anyone do when their two greatest loves conflict?

Most of the Jesuits above the falls decide to fight against the soldiers who will come to destroy their mission. But Fr. Gabriel, who is their superior, commands them not to take up arms. A priest can never attack another human being, and he must never kill. Fr. Gabriel promises the people that he will stay with them, but he will not fight. Rodrigo, however, has not fully reformed his military thinking. He wants to defend the mission with weapons if the soldiers attack. He retrieves his armor from the river where it had fallen, when the *Guarani* cut it loose, and then prepares for battle. Fr. Gabriel forbids him to take up arms, but Rodrigo

19. 1 Cor 13:4–8.
20. 1 Cor 13:13.

is determined. "They want to live, Father. They say that God has left them, he's deserted them. Has he?"

Fr. Gabriel cannot persuade Rodrigo against this tactic. "You should never have become a priest," he murmurs.

"But I am a priest, and they need me."

"Then help them *as* a priest! If you die with blood on your hands, Rodrigo, you betray everything we've done. You promised your life to God. And God is love! . . . If might is right, then love has no place in the world. It may be so, it may be so. But I don't have the strength to live in a world like that, Rodrigo." And so the two friends part; one, to his war making and his shattered vows, and the other to his people.

How should a priest respond? What is his role in the life of the people? What would Jesus do? That really is the overriding question. Every fiber of our fallen being wants to follow Rodrigo into battle against the great evil of slavery. The other Jesuits in the community do, too, and we understand their actions. We cheer for them, even. But when their bows and arrows fail against muskets and cannon, they all die, one by one, along with most of the clever but defeated young men of the *Guarani*.

Fr. Gabriel stays with the rest of the people at their mission, with the women, the sick, the old, and the very young. His role *as a priest* is to administer the sacraments and to perpetuate the sacrifice of Christ in the world. As the visible vicar of Christ he must remain with the people. The shepherd does not run, but neither does he kill. So together, Christ and his people process to their slaughter. The women cradle little statues and little babies in their arms. An old man holds a crucifix aloft and before the torched and burning mission church. Fr. Gabriel lifts high the Blessed Sacrament in its monstrance before the eyes of the Catholic soldiers who have come to kill them. Even the soldiers are shocked at what they are ordered to do.

Rodrigo, whose military defenses have all collapsed, has retreated before the advancing army to the mission grounds. When he stoops to lift a fallen child he is shot two or three times, but it will take him a little while to die. He waits in the dust, then lifts his head, his neck straining and his eyes watching as Fr. Gabriel defies the menacing army with the Body of Christ. Kill these people and you kill Christ. Kill me and you kill Christ. Smoke blurs Rodrigo's vision, maybe it is blood, but when Fr. Gabriel is shot through the heart and spins violently to the earth, Rodrigo sighs and closes his exhausted eyes, dying, one hopes, to the abiding mercy of God.

An old man lifts the Body of Christ out of the dust and proceeds on into the hailstorm of murder.

This is a fictional story of very real events. In 1777 the Jesuit order was suppressed in Europe on the claim that the Jesuits interfered with the commerce and the political shenanigans of the age. But such stories of martyrdom and sanctity continue on a global scale to this day, and these martyrs are cherished in the memory of God's people, and in the canon of the communion of saints.

The Eucharist

When Fr. Gabriel's elevates the Eucharist as the pinnacle of his priestly purpose, he is also offering his own life and body as a sacrifice for the people. Though the other Jesuits also died for the people, they were not acting as priests but as soldiers, because they were willing to kill for the people, too. And soldiering is not the way of Christ. *The Mission* truly is one of the finest films made on the grace of the ordained priesthood; with the Eucharist at the center of this priestly charism. Fr. Gabriel cannot save the lives of the people, but he can take on the sacrifice of Christ. He can perpetuate the sacrifice of Jesus on the cross, in all of its bloody, cruel, and physical reality, but with great faith for the salvation of souls. This is the essence of his holy priesthood, and the center of that essence is the Body of Christ in the Eucharist.

Babette's Feast [21]

Babette's Feast is, perhaps, the one film most often referenced when alluding to the Eucharistic meal. It is a symbolic film that is uncluttered by plot, visually splendid, and very lovely in its presentation of the Eucharist as God's gift and bounty to his people. I understand that it is the favorite film of Pope Francis.

Babette's Feast is the story of two Danish sisters who take in a French refugee, Babette, out of charity and kindness, and because of their need for a cook and housekeeper. Babette loves the two sisters and she serves them for many years, grateful for a home safe from the revolutionary upheavals taking place in France. Though she is puzzled by the sisters'

21. *Babette's Feast,* directed by Gabriel Axer. A Nordisk Film Production, 1987. (French). Rated "G."

reserve and their strict asceticism—a quality that the whole, devout, townsfolk[22] share—she is obedient to their preferred menu of fish porridge (made from reconstituted dried fish and reconstituted dried bread crusts) over tasty French delicacies and exotic spices. Babette was once an honored chef in the finest French restaurants in her day, but now she must bridle her gifts and talents out of respect for the patroness pair.

In an unexpected stroke of good fortune, Babette learns that she has won a French lottery. But rather than use the money to return home to Paris, she sets out to create a sumptuous feast; not only for the kind sisters but for their aging friends and small faith community. Their austere congregation has become a dwindling handful of devotees who are fracturing on account of disagreements and rancor. Babette aims to heal them. Like Moses, she feeds these lost wanderers with the elaborate gift of manna in the desert. Like Christ, she multiplies the portions, treating a total of twelve dinner guests to a great supper. But this is not a meal of dried fish and bread crusts, this is the Eucharistic feast, the bounty, the abundance of God's love. And though her ascetic guests promise one another that they will not display any pleasure in the corporeal treats that Babette prepares—professing their detachment from temporal things while they focus on spiritual rewards—their eyes do sparkle at the strange new flavors they are tasting. When the champagne is uncorked the spirits begin to flow more lustily, there are new delights, new delicacies, new laughter, even joy, and their long held grudges begin to fade and sink into a gentle pool of wine.

The elderly spinsters are awed to learn that dear Babette has spent every dime of her prize money on this one sumptuous banquet of gratitude and thanksgiving, and that it was all for them. Babette explains that, as a chef and as an artist, she relished the opportunity to do her very best. It is in her art that she has expressed the purpose God has called her to fulfill. And so, in a sweet embrace, her patroness tells her that she will "delight the angels."

After the Eucharistic meal, Babette's aging, ascetic revelers go out under the stars, clasp hands in a circle, and sing their praises to God.[23]

---

22. This is the same Inner Mission sect of Danish Lutheranism that is represented by Peter Petersen's small congregation in *Ordet*, as we shall see.

23. How curious and sad that the writer, Isak Dinesen, a nonbeliever, died of malnutrition brought on by insurmountable depression.

Driving Miss Daisy[24]

*"I no longer call you slaves, because a slave does not know what
his master is doing. I have called you friends, because I have told you
everything I have learned from my Father."*[25]

—JESUS CHRIST

Jesus called us his friends. He said "friends" because, as he explained, he had revealed to us what he was about. Friends are not always on equal footing, but they share a common experience, a common ministry, and a common end. If we are true to ourselves and live a good, virtuous life, we may discover our true purpose through the help of our friends; a purpose that has been laid out for us from the beginning of time. A worthy friend does not tear us down, a worthy friend helps us to reach that beatific end. The value and worth of such a friendship is holy.

This theme of holy friendship is what underlies the film, *Driving Miss Daisy.* Here we have a most unlikely and irreverent pairing of two people—divided by race, by gender, by social status, by faith, and by circumstance—who are forced into a relationship that one desperately needs and the other wholly detests. And yet, somehow it works. It works because both Hoke and Miss Daisy are good people. And though they begin their association in strife, they end not only with friendship and love, but with a saving and sacramental gift of life, one to the other.

Miss Daisy is an aging, wealthy, Jewish woman whose busy yet doting son realizes that she should no longer be driving her car after she backed it into the neighbor's hedge. Having her driving privileges revoked is an affront not only to her pride—which she has a lot of—but to her freedom and dignity as well, as it drastically limits her ability to get around and keep control over her own affairs.

Enter Hoke, an elderly, black gentleman in need of a job as a chauffeur. Boolie, the son, hires Hoke to drive his mother to her appointments and to temple. But Daisy is outraged by the arrangement. "I am not prejudiced!" the Georgian matron exclaims, it is just that she was raised modestly, without opulence, and does not wish to be chauffeured around

24. *Driving Miss Daisy*, directed by Bruce Beresford. A Zanuck Company Production, 1989. Rated "PG" for some racist language.

25. John 15:15.

like "the queen of Romania." (Though she does confide to her son that "they all take things," when a can of salmon goes missing and Hoke is suspected.) Miss Daisy has a black serving maid, Idella, but she insists that Idella is different. "We know how to stay out of each other's way."[26]

The story spans almost three decades, from the time when Hoke is first hired in the late 1940s (you can follow the years by the great old cars featured!) to the early 1970s when Hoke and Miss Daisy are each in their fading nineties. And while the film does remark upon the times, it never loses its focus on the unlikely pair who must grapple with the decidedly unfriendly world around them.

Tensions swell over racial hatred in the South—from a bombing at the Jewish temple, to an encounter with two Alabama traffic cops, to the murder of Reverend Martin Luther King—tensions that impact the perimeter of their lives but cannot be ignored. Both Hoke and Daisy are vulnerable to racial hatred, and this may well be the thread that binds them. After Daisy's temple is bombed, and as they return home in the rain, Hoke recollects the time he saw his friend's daddy hanging from a tree where he had been lynched. He tells the tale in grisly detail until Daisy weeps. "This has nothing to do with that," she insists, meaning the temple bombing. "Yes'm," he dutifully replies, knowing full well that it does.

As the relationship moves from master/slave to employer/servant to teacher/student (Miss Daisy teaches Hoke to read) we can begin to see how their dependence upon one another changes, and how they grow into a kind of friendship. This growing dependency and affection keeps moving them forward, shifting into new realities, as if driving them to a higher purpose.

When an ice storm freezes the region in hard ice and knocks out power to the home, Hoke still makes it over to the house with hot coffee and builds them a fire. Daisy tells her son on the phone that he need not worry about her, that Hoke is there and he is "very handy." Boolie is amazed to hear her say "loving things about Hoke." "I didn't say I *loved* him I said he was *handy!*" she snaps, slamming down the phone. But it is true, she does love him, and one can see that they are now bickering and teasing one another like old chums. Friendship, the kind Jesus claimed with his disciples, is key to understanding this story. When Idella dies and Miss Daisy and Hoke attend the funeral, the song that is sung at this black Southern Baptist service is *What a Friend We Have in Jesus*.

26. This suggests an unspoken habit of segregation that Miss Daisy does not recognize, even in her own home.

It is only as the years pile on, as the cars grow sleeker and their eyes grow dimmer, that the two are able to see things more clearly. Daisy's mind fails her, conventions fade, and Hoke's sight weakens so that he can barely drive a car. Yet it is during this most vulnerable time, when their life span seems to be closing in on them, that Daisy takes his gnarled hand and tells him with real love, "Hoke, you are my best friend. You are. You are."

"Yes'm."

In the final scene we learn that the strong-willed Daisy is nearing a hundred years old. Boolie has sold the family home and has moved his mother into a nursing facility. Hoke rarely has the chance to visit her now, since he can no longer drive and the busses don't go out that way. It is Thanksgiving Day, and Boolie has driven Hoke to the nursing home to visit with Daisy. Boolie is his usual blustery self but his mother dismisses him curtly. "Hoke came to see me, not you," she scolds. "Boolie, go charm the nurses!"

Left alone, the two best friends share a restful moment together. There doesn't seem to be much to say. Every convention and code that had divided them has turned to dust, and they are just getting along as best they can. Then Hoke notices that Daisy has not eaten any of her Thanksgiving pie. She shakily fumbles with the spoon but cannot grasp it, so he takes it from her and she allows this final concession, handing over her will to him at last. Like a servant, Hoke cuts the pie, like a friend he lifts it up, like a priest he offers it to her, and like a lover she assents and receives it as a pure gift of grace. She savors it in *thanksgiving*,[27] you can see it in her eyes. She savors joyfully this Eucharistic morsel, as well as the dear, sweet man who offers it to her. And so he feeds her another bite, and then another, and then we all fade to black.

Driving Miss Daisy can be a problematic film. Hoke is so docile that it is difficult to accept him as anything more than a subservient slave. But we must remember that he was born in the nineteenth century, likely a child of slaves, and he has had to accept this forced place in our cruel society—because there were no other choices for him, not if he wanted to survive. He saw his friend's daddy lynched, remember. That is not something one easily forgets. Also, on more than a few occasions, Hoke insists that he be treated with dignity by Miss Daisy, and his mild corrections do change her.

27. "Eucharist" means "thanksgiving."

If it is uncomfortable for us to see Hoke as a docile servant, is it any more difficult to see him as the image of Christ? He does not die for Miss Daisy, but he does endure, lifting her own quarrelsome nature up to the possibilities of grace and a new creation. Hoke quite literally carries Miss Daisy like a cross. "Why don't you let me *carry* you?" he chided, when she refused to let him drive her to the store. And in this final scene we really ought to see intimations of a Eucharistic meal. The Christian themes at work in this film whisper the uncomfortable message that we are to be servants to one another, and that the poor will save the rich as a Eucharistic gift to them, because the poor are the very person of Christ,[28] and because the rich cannot save themselves.

> *The rich exist for the sake of the poor.*
> *The poor exist for the salvation of the rich.*[29]
> —ST. JOHN CHRYSOSTOM

Confirmation

Like baptism and the Eucharist, confirmation is a sacrament of initiation and discipleship. Its outward sign is the anointing of oils on the forehead of the recipient, followed sometimes by a little slap on the cheek, usually delivered by the bishop. The anointing signifies a seal of belonging to Christ, marking the recipient with a sign of consecration. The reason for the slap is to remind them that they are going to suffer in this world and, if they are fortunate, they will suffer for Christ.

The liturgy of confirmation contains a renewal of the promises made at baptism, as confirmation is bound to that first sacrament in a unique way. Indeed, it is necessary for the completion of baptismal grace, wherein the recipients are sealed with the gifts of the Holy Spirit to strengthen them as mature disciples of Christ.[30] This outpouring of the Holy Spirit at confirmation is the inner grace that perpetuates the gifts the apostles

---

28. "Amen, I say to you, whatever you did for one of these least brothers of mine, you did for me." Matt 25:40.

29. Chrysostom, *Sentences*, 38.

30. The seven gifts of the Holy Spirit imparted at confirmation are: wisdom, understanding, counsel, fortitude, knowledge, piety, and the fear of (reverence for) God.

received at Pentecost; those gifts which helped them proclaim the mighty works of God.

Fortified by these graces, the confirmed are called to bear witness to Christ and to defend the faith. As confirmation deepens the graces we received at our baptism, the destiny of the baptized and confirmed Christian is *to become a saint*; that is to say, to attain union with God.

Becket [31]

It is difficult to find a truly excellent film based on the life of a saint. They are out there, but they are rare. The story of St. Thomas Becket in *Becket* is a worthy example that might help to illustrate the graces underlying the sacrament of confirmation (as well as holy orders). It is a well-crafted, intelligent, timely, and even fun movie, with some very poignant and grace-filled scenes. It is beautifully filmed, which one can readily see; it is intelligent, because the complex themes are artfully enfleshed in the manner and the dialogue of its characters; it is fun, because Peter O'Toole and Richard Burton make it so (it might have been rather dreary without these two); and it is timely, as the issue of power and authority between church and state are put to the test, then (Thomas Becket was martyred in 1170 AD) as now.

The church presumes that its authority over the state is a divine right. It still asserts this, though states rarely concur or oblige her. Yet we can see, historically, that without the correcting voice of the church (the sacred realm) defending our human rights and the rights of conscience, the state (the temporal realm) can easily drift into relativism (where there is no absolute morality or reality) and totalitarianism (where the strongest powers project their own reality and inflict their own moral chaos). The best our world can manage is a brokered compromise: a separation of church and state which allows some proportional freedoms and successes for each realm of society.

The complete separation of church and state, however, is a modern invention. It did not exist in the times of King Henry II of England. In the twelfth century the authority of the church over the reigning monarch was well recognized and well established. Of course, this ecclesial authority was often a royal nuisance to any willful monarch. We might recall a

31. *Becket,* directed by Peter Glenville. A Hal Wallis Production, 1964. Rated "PG 13" for some sexual content and violence, but pretty mild by today's standards.

similar conflict (with very similar names and persons!) in *A Man For All Seasons*, and the struggle we witnessed there between King Henry VIII and Sir Thomas More.

In the historical film, *Becket*, we find that King Henry II is also burdened with a most difficult archbishop. Earlier in his reign, Henry had decided to make his best friend, Thomas Becket, his chancellor, so that he might be counseled by a devoted loyalist. This drew bitter resentment from the Norman noblemen who loathed the Saxon Becket. So when the old archbishop dies, Henry has a stroke of genius. He decides to make Becket the new Archbishop of Canterbury. He decides this against Becket's own earnest wishes and to the horror of the Norman churchmen. Becket is not only a despised Saxon, he is a drunkard, a womanizer, and a rogue. How can he be made archbishop when he is not even a priest? But Henry is not slowed down by such ecclesial technicalities. He arranges to have Becket ordained a priest and installed as his new archbishop all on the same day. The church and the kingdom are stunned.

Thomas Becket is also stunned, but he cannot argue his way out of this lunacy, even though he pleads with the king to reconsider. Out of obedience and devotion to his king, he does succumb to Henry's directives, allowing himself to be ordained into the priesthood and made the Archbishop of Canterbury. He thereby receives, worthy or not, the sacrament of holy orders along with its graces.

Once installed, we should notice how Becket changes as he begins to take seriously his new role and office. Though he figures that he can manage the contrary functions of both archbishop and chancellor, there is a difference in his manner now. He had always been a man devoid of ardor, unable to love anyone. He was devoted to the king, but he was unable to show his love, and Henry knew it and grieved. He was attentive to the woman in his life, but unable to show his love, and she also knew it and grieved. Now, even to his own surprise, Thomas Becket has fallen in love with God. This is the work of grace, absolutely; grace in the sacraments and in the gifts that are given to him—especially the gifts of the Holy Spirit—through the sacraments.[32] Although Thomas is still loyal to King Henry, he has put the honor of God first in his life and in his ministry, and that honor has uprooted his subservience to the temporal realm.

---

32. From the messianic prophecy of Isaiah 11:1–3 we read of them: ". . . the Spirit of the Lord shall rest upon him, the spirit of wisdom and understanding, the spirit of counsel and might, the spirit of knowledge and the fear of the Lord."

What Henry had hoped to achieve, which was a submissive church brought to bear by the loyalty of deep friendship, he will lose in triple portions: he never does achieve dominance over the church, and he loses not only his loyal chancellor but his closest and dearest friend. As Archbishop Becket draws closer to God and his call to shepherd the faithful, he grows further from the king and his demand for complete loyalty.[33]

Then their relationship is challenged, not by war or theology, but by their contested authority over a priest who has "debauched a young girl." The civil authorities arrest the priest, preparing to try him in the civil courts. The church, however, forbids these secular powers to usurp her authority over her clergy. The accused priest should be handed over to the bishopric, to be investigated and tried by the ecclesial courts. But before Becket can make his demands known the accused priest is captured by Lord Gilbert's men, who claim that their prisoner had tried to escape. Lord Gilbert then has the priest put to death. For this sacrilegious murder, Lord Gilbert is excommunicated by Archbishop Becket.

Now the battle lines are drawn: King Henry and his noble lords against the church and her archbishop. Henry secretly visits with Thomas, to confer privately with him and hopefully reach a compromise regarding Gilbert's excommunication, but Becket is immoveable. He must defend the church and his clergy. The accused priest would have been fairly tried in the ecclesial courts, but instead he was murdered without trial by vengeful, secular powers. The archbishop cannot look the other way; the honor of God and God's church are at stake. During this exchange Becket comes to realize that he truly cannot serve two masters, and he relinquishes his chancellorship to Henry, returning his ring—the lions of England—to the king in order to tend solely to his flock. The king, who loves Thomas with an "obsessive and unnatural" affection, receives the

---

33. The turmoil in *Becket* illustrates, quite nicely, the doctrine that Pope Gelasius I promulgated in the fourth century. Gelasius developed a social theory that recognized two realms (two swords) of influence: the sacred and the temporal. "Two there are . . . whereby this world is ruled in sovereign fashion. The consecrated authority of the priesthood and the power of the king, and of these two the responsibility of the priests is by so much the weightier . . ." It is crucial to note that by "rule" Gelasius makes clear that the authority of the sacred realm (the church and her priesthood) is an authority of inspiration, which one follows out of conviction (in faith and good conscience); while the power of the temporal realm (the state) is one of coercion, which one follows by way of force or compulsion. Though the authority of the state may well be legitimate, it remains coercive. The greater authority of the church rests upon conscience and the inspiration of faith. (As per McElroy, *The Search for an American Public Theology*, 21–22.)

relinquished ring as a token of their broken trust and his rejected love. "Now I must learn to be alone," he mourns, returning to London.

It has taken time and the force of circumstances to move Becket to accept his true calling and path. He is loyal, but his loyalties had been divided and misdirected. It is the honor of God that he must put first over king, country, and family life, as that honor is what he now freely chooses to serve. The grace of his baptism, completed in the sacrament of confirmation, will help him to serve God's honor, even unto death. The gifts of the Holy Spirit—which are wisdom, understanding, counsel, fortitude, knowledge, piety, and reverence for God—will give him the strength to accomplish his purpose. If we watch Thomas Becket carefully, we can see these graces at work in his struggles with his proper duties and his troubled conscience. Though similar to the seven saving virtues, the gifts of the Holy Spirit should not be confused with those virtues, as these divine graces are directed toward our *sanctification;* helping us to grow *in holiness.* They are heavenly aids, sanctifying gifts, graces that help us to cooperate with God's saving plan.

It is only after Becket accepts his role as something more than a political stunt that he becomes thoroughly overwhelmed with love for God, and all that this love entails. Sanctifying grace gives him the wisdom and understanding to counsel the king, the reverence to administer the duties of his holy office, and the knowledge to speak his truth to the king's lackeys when they attempt to arrest him on some trumped up charge. Grace also gives Becket the fortitude to await a very certain martyrdom.

As for the king, he has sunk into a most miserable despondency. Though he professes his great hatred for Becket, who jilted him, he also confesses his greater, even violent love for him. This turmoil in his heart is damning. And while reveling amongst his noble henchmen one evening, King Henry utters his famous condemnation of Becket, wondering out loud: "Will no one rid me of this meddlesome priest?" Henry is drunk, distraught, and forlorn, but his henchmen take it as a directive to go ahead with their plans to assassinate the archbishop.

They arrive at the cathedral while Becket is at vespers, the evening prayer. They announce their purpose, but the archbishop does not flee. He tells them that it is a sacrilege to bring weapons into God's church. He warns them of the danger to their own immortal souls. But his warnings do not slow their advance, and with determined purpose Thomas Becket is murdered in the cathedral by the many swords of the flawed king: by the frailty of human empowerment, by the fragility of inherited rule, and by the misdirected loyalties of those who would serve but one worldly, weak, and wretched master.

In turn, the church crowns a new martyr to her calendar of saints.

Matrimony

Of the seven sacraments only two, holy orders and matrimony, are grouped together as vocational in their character. While the other sacraments are directed toward the salvation of our own souls, these two sacraments are directed primarily outward, toward the salvation of others. "If (they) contribute as well to personal salvation, it is through the service to others that they do so."[34] The role of the priest is to keep alive the sacramental presence of Christ in the world. This is the role that Fr. Gabriel evinced for us in *The Mission,* for example, and what we can also see in Thomas Becket. In a similar way, the role of the married couple (*as a married couple and not just as two lay people*) is to love each other the way Christ loves the church, and to nurture the children they may bring into the world with this same sacrificial care. As we take a closer look at the sacraments of the church, let us now take a longer look at the sacrament of marriage.

Ryan's Daughter[35]

There are, of course, hundreds of films that deal directly with the theme of marriage (and many of them are comedies, which says something!) but there are few that actually touch on the sacramental quality of marriage as the Catholic Church extols it. Surely Hollywood is the last place one might go looking to find marital virtue. Still, we can discover tremendous grace at work in *Ryan's Daughter,* a film that is as sacramental as it is epic. *Ryan's Daughter* depicts many of the tensions, failings, and passions—as well as the loneliness—of marriage, while preserving that one grace that binds it for life.

The heroine is a young, vibrant, spoiled, and passionate girl, Rosy Ryan, who lives within the confines of a small Irish village and among the confines of its smaller minded villagers. Rosy is the only child of the

34. *Catechism of the Catholic Church,* #1536.

35. *Ryan's Daughter,* directed by David Lean. A Faraway Production, 1970. Rated "R" for sexual situations; some scenes are not suitable for youngsters.

local pub owner, Tom Ryan, who lavishes his "princess" with love, finery, and excess, so that she has become the target of envy and jealous gossip by those less privileged. Rosy's good fortune has not made her haughty, however. She is a lovely girl, intelligent, curious, and kind, but she does carry herself with a difference. She has learned from books and her romance novels that the world is a wonderful, romantic, and beautiful place. But her vision and passions are too far-reaching for this ignorant, cruel, and dying little barnacle of a town.

Boys her age do not interest Rosy in the least. She is looking for something greater, even transcendent. With little to choose from, she falls for her handsome school teacher, a man more than twice her age, but a man of wisdom and a lover of the arts. To Rosy's eyes, Charles Shaughnessy is worldly and exciting. With a scientific mind, a gentle heart for the children he teaches, and a great love for nature and music, Charles awakens in Rosy a longing for beauty and fulfillment. He is a widower, living alone next door to the school, but he is also sensible enough to rebuff the sweet advances of a blossoming young student. When Rosy professes her love for him, Charles tries to calm her fervor with tempered reason, explaining that he is just too mundane and too old for a girl like herself. But Rosy is headstrong and lusty and she adores the man. What can he do? So they marry.

Sadly, he is no bedroom gallant and what Rosy craves—which includes sexual ecstasy, as she explains to Fr. Hugh—is tamed by the drudgery and routine of the home. Though their love is real, it is their life that beats her down. Fr. Hugh, who is a powerful presence in the village, in the story, and in the lives of Rosy and Charles, offers her the best advice an old Irishman can give: "Don't nurse your wishes, Rose. You can't help having them, but don't nurse them." In his own stoic way he is telling her to be satisfied with her lot. Life is work, and poverty, maybe a little joy, then sickness and death. This is the way things are in a fatalistic land. "That's all there is!" he insists. But this is just crippling to Rose. She does the best she can with an impotent husband who spends his day collecting, pressing, and logging dead flowers into his botany books, or teaching little children about the remarkable wide world that they will likely never see, but the stark, dry, burden of life is sapping her vitality, and Rose begins to wilt and languish.

The Great War changes everything when a shell-shocked British officer arrives to recover his nerves at a British camp that has been erected near the village. He is young, handsome, fragile, desperate for comfort, and an arm's reach away from the unhappy Rose.

A sensual and dynamic spark ignites between them and, just as quickly, ugly rumors flare up throughout the town. The people snicker at the dowdy cuckold, Charles Shaughnessy, that professor who thinks he's just so smart; they sneer at Rosy Shaughnessy, whose doting father spoiled her rotten; but they utterly despise the "peg-leg" British officer, as one in lot with all the Brits who have oppressed the Irish people for centuries. This officer, Major Doryan, must deal with the rebellious villagers, with revolutionary arms smugglers, and with his own shattered nerves, all while he is entangled in this adulterous affair with the married Rose.

With so much active turmoil, little attention is paid to the heartbroken Charles. He knows the affair is going on. How can he not know when Rosy leaves his own bed in the middle of the night? He understands that she is fine and young and passionate, and he regrets that she was ever stuck with an old bore like himself. He does not forbid her freedom from the home, and she goes where she wills. He just hopes that the two lovers will burn themselves out and that Rosy will come back to him. Even the viewer rather forgets about this sad nowhere man who waits by his window.

The romance and scandal and intrigue that structures this film is set in the historic times of the Irish rebellion, as the people struggled against their English oppressors along with Tim O'Leary. It is filmed before the expansive backdrop of Western Ireland, with grand vistas and a storm scene that is truly unmatched in cinema. One can view this movie from the historical standpoint of a poor people fighting for their freedom; or from the perspective of liberation theology, where the parish priest is a champion of the struggling oppressed. One can also view it from a moralistic stance, and watch how sin corrupts the hearts of the people and leads to death; or even on a simpler level, as a beautiful love story that ends in heartbreak. But for all of that, our purpose is to focus on the sacrament of marriage, and to use this film to illuminate matrimony's sacramental themes. Perhaps more to the point, we might look at how each aspect of the sacrament is *betrayed* by the flawed, fallen characters we encounter here.

Since marriage is a sacrament, its outward sign is a symbolic representation of an inner grace that is real. The principal sign in marriage is not the wedding or the ring, it is the spoken exchange of vows between the bride and groom. These vows form a covenant, a commitment, that is lifelong. It is a covenant not unlike the covenant God made with Abraham and his people, Israel. It also reflects the new covenant of Christ to his church. It is a promise of love and care and a commitment of lifelong faithfulness. Because this promise mirrors the covenant of Christ to the People of God, it is a commitment unlike any other. The married partners are meant to be Christ to one another, loving with sacrificial love, and enduring patiently the hardships of life—even its drudgery—because of their enduring trust in one another. This covenant helps to transform the couple as one carries the other, like a cross, into unity with God. It is a profound grace, and it is one that Rosy fails to recognize and Charles fails to provide.

In marriage the vows are spoken out loud and in public, as the promise requires witnesses to hear it proclaimed. The sacrament asks the whole community to give ear to this sacred promise and to support the couple in their needs as they reform their lives together. The cohesion of the community behind the new union is like the church responding in love to her covenant with Christ. So let us look at this little Irish village where the people are tawdry and cruel. There are few jobs. The families are impoverished. The young are idle, having no future and no place to go, and so they go looking for trouble. The men drink away their meager earnings and the women gossip and scoff at their neighbors who try to better themselves. This is hardly a supportive community! Indeed, the townsfolk betray Rose and Charles out of sheer envy (a deadly sin), and their betrayal does the greatest damage to the marriage.

Of course, marriage fundamentally entails the sexual union of the wedded pair, and necessarily so. A marriage that cannot or will not be consummated is an unfinished sacrament. It may still be recognized as legal, but it is easily annulled since consummation is needed to complete the sacrament. The purpose of sexual expression in marriage is twofold: to express the bonds of love and to generate new life. Children do not make a marriage, but their presence does affirm a consummated union. Rosy and Charles, from the wedding night forward, seem ill-suited in their sexual intimacy. Though the difficulties are not openly expressed, it is clear that Charles is not a robust lover and Rosy needs and craves physical love. Rosy's infidelity damages the marriage, but Charles' patience gives us some reason to believe that the marriage is not completely destroyed. This is important. Why is Charles' love for Rosy so forgiving? Is it his weakness or is it his strength?

There is another element to marriage that might be overlooked, and that is the role of the church, which claims marriage as a holy sacrament. It is not just a civil contract, though it usually includes that aspect because of its public nature. In the eyes of the church, marriage is a sacrament which gives grace. It is holy. When it is not holy, when it is not sacramentally embraced, it may stumble and break and can throw a well meaning couple (and their children) into some disastrous territory. Even as a sacrament it strains against the notion that we are meant to shoulder our spouses like a cross, with all of their faults and sins, to the gates of heaven![36] That might seem a little extreme but that quality is not missing from the sacramental promise. The married couple do vow to help their partner live up to their God-given purpose, share in their Christian discipleship, and help their spouse attain salvation. What we find in *Ryan's Daughter* is a parish priest who is wholly involved in the lives of his people, and that includes the marriage of Rose and Charles. To our American sensibilities he seems a little *too* involved! He counsels, he directs, he scolds, he slaps, he teaches, he consoles, he pops in and out of their story like a good meddling priest, but he is also a tremendously necessary one! He brings Charles his clothes when Charles wanders down the cold beach in despair, dressed only in his nightshirt. He is surprisingly kind to Rosy, given her unfaithfulness, and works more on her conscience than he does her shame. The ones he confronts with justified fury are the idle townsfolk, who gossip and taunt and let their own jealousies lead them to the precipice of brutality. Hoodwinked by vicious rumors, these locals falsely claim that Rosy has sold out Tim O'Leary to her British lover. They attack and humiliate Rosy, stripping her of her fine clothes and cutting off all of her hair. They not only shame Charles, they bludgeon him to the floor as he tries to save Rosy from their rabid assault.

The failure of the community to sustain this couple, steeped in their own sins as they are, is really greater than the failure of Rosy to live up to her vows; or the failure of Charles to recognize Rosy's needs. And the stupid viciousness of these villagers is a clear consequence of the corrupt social order of the land. The people are poor, ignorant, jobless, bored,

---

36. This is a cross of love, not a cross of oppression. We are not meant to enable an abusive spouse. We saw the fruits of this practice in Linda Loman's own misdirected efforts, in *Death of a Salesman*. Linda flattered the illusions of her raving husband and the egos of her indolent sons. She did not lift them up in truth, she enabled them in their falsehood. We are not meant to coddle the illusions of our loved ones, we are meant to assist their true selves on the difficult road to salvation, as Hoke does for Miss Daisy. We can test the goodness of our efforts by considering: "Is what I do helpful or is it detrimental to my loved one's true purpose?" just as we might challenge our own moral actions. By the same token, we cannot lay all of our own troubles on our spouse and expect those burdens to be carried for us. Each of these tactics is a *failure* of love.

and turned inward like caged animals. Growth is not possible for these people because growth is barely allowed, and that is a grave injustice. When people are not free to grow, they are not free to fulfill their holy purpose. If we contrast the expanse of this gorgeous land with the stony walls of the villagers' hovels, we can see how they are living in a literal dungeon of the mind.

The final factor to consider in marriage is the magnanimous activity that is at work in the sacrament, as in all of the sacraments, and that activity is the transforming grace of God. It brings about a new creation, one that is a braided, three-strand unity, because we are lifted up by our beloved and accompanied by God. It is a unity of I and thou and Thou. And at the very real level of grace, this new creation is indomitable.

What should surprise us at the end of the film—and it does, I think—is the Christ-like love that Charles Shaughnessy has for Rose. He is ever faithful to her in spite of her failings and distractions, and he shares in the suffering that she must endure at the hands of the violent townsfolk. Even Rosy's father, Tom Ryan (a coward and a turncoat), points this out for us when he must say goodbye to his dear daughter. "You know Rose, when you married him, I thought you could have done a lot better. Now I'm not so sure they come much better. Would you tell him that? It's not a thing one fella can easily say to another."

Charles is the Christ of this film, and Rosy is his people. *This* is the covenant. Together, alongside Fr. Hugh—Christ's church on earth—they stride down the street on their final trek out of town. Together they walk the path of the paschal sacrifice, while the townsfolk whistle and jeer from their hovels. Trailing behind them is the village fool, Michael. He is the silent Greek chorus, the frailty, the confusion, and the folly of our human condition.

The old priest helps to carry their belongings as far as the bus stop, and as the Shaughnessys climb aboard the bus Fr. Hugh turns to Charles and speaks his peace: "I think you have it in your mind that you and Rosy ought to part. Yeah, I thought as much. Well, maybe you're right and maybe you aren't, *but I doubt it*. And that's my parting gift to you. That doubt!" He slaps the glass of the closing bus door, behind which stare the startled faces of our heroic duo.

"God bless!" he shouts over the roar of the diesel and a brown cloud of dust. Then he turns to the idiot man who has been entrusted to his care. "I don't know, Michael," he sighs, "I just don't know."

Anointing of the Sick

Shadowlands [37]

Why love if losing hurts so much? I have no answers anymore, only the life I have lived. Twice in that life I've been given the choice: as a boy and as a man. The boy chose safety, the man chooses suffering. The pain now is part of the happiness then. That's the deal.

—*C. S. LEWIS IN SHADOWLANDS*

The world has signed a pact with the devil; it had to . . . The terms are clear: if you want to live, you have to die . . . This is what we know. The rest is gravy. [38]

—*ANNIE DILLARD*

Suffering and death fly in the face of our deepest longing. A good old man I knew well, who had just lost his wife of sixty years, took me by the shoulders after her funeral Mass and wept, "I can't believe it's real!" He was a retired colonel, a career soldier through the course of three wars, but he had never encountered death quite like this. Indeed, until we lose a close loved one, death is just a convenient end to some tidy story, but it hardly seems real. Yet, I think, we don't become fully human until our lives have been properly shaken by it.

Shadowlands takes us through the transforming power of suffering in the life of England's most beloved Christian writer, C. S. Lewis. Lewis was a shy, reclusive, confident, and creative academic who taught literature at Oxford and wrote on Christian themes in his theological works, as well as in his series of children's books (*The Chronicles of Narnia*). He lived an unruffled bachelor's life with his mild mannered brother, Warnie. He taught his classes and delivered his lectures with great mastery and assurance. He wasn't arrogant or boastful or smug, he was simply well-studied and very comfortable in his beliefs.

Enter the Christian-Jewish, ex-communist, married-but-separated, expatriated American, Joy Gresham. Like a whirlwind she upsets Lewis' well arranged apple cart, challenging his ideas in a way that no student,

37. *Shadowlands*, directed by Richard Attenborough, produced by Richard Attenborough. 1993. Rated "PG" for reasons I cannot fathom.

38. Dillard, *Pilgrim at Tinker Creek*, 183.

friend, brother, or colleague would dare try. She is not cantankerous, she is merely bold, smart, and honest. She adores all that is good in Lewis—and there is much that is good—but she sets him straight when he is dishonest with himself, or allows himself to be placated by friends who have been carefully vetted and placed along the outer reaches of his heart. Perplexed but amazed by this "truest" of women, Lewis falls in love, though he scarcely knows how, and they marry; at first only "technically," to allow Joy to remain in England, but later with love and honor.

Joy has a young son, Douglas, who is star-struck at meeting this famous author of his favorite books. At their first encounter Douglas asks if Lewis would please sign his Narnia book. Flattered, Lewis pens what must have been his signature inscription: "The magic never ends." The mild boy is charmed and shows it to his mother. Joy, however, in her bold, smart, and honest fashion, quips: "Well, if it does, sue him."

Douglas' timid character seems to mirror Lewis' own innocence and gentle manner. Yet both will have to reckon with the harsh reality of suffering and death which will put an end to their unruffled faith and magical thinking. When Douglas sneaks into Lewis' attic and pushes through the coats that are hanging in an old wardrobe, he finds that they do not open up to a secret fairyland world, as the wardrobe did in the Narnia stories he loves. There is nothing behind the coats but the hard, wooden backing of a stinking, old cabinet. Douglas knows now that the magic does indeed end, even as his prayers seem to fall on deaf ears. He sighs, "it doesn't work."

To drive the point home there remains that hard, diabolical contract we read in Annie Dillard's quote: "If you want to live, you have to die." When Joy is diagnosed with terminal bone cancer, Lewis must come to terms with her impending death; and not only struggle with his own grief, but with all of the terrible pain and suffering that Joy must endure as well. He cares for her needs, yet in the midst of her agony his own pious musings on the meaning of suffering come roaring back to haunt him. "Pain is God's megaphone to rouse a deaf world," he used to lecture with a triumphant smile. Now, in the face of real agony, Lewis is horrified. He is horrified by Joy's unbearable pain as well as his own weak efforts to explain it; as if he could ever justify the ways of God! As if God should even need his clever defenses! It doesn't work. There is nothing Lewis can do but pray. There is no making sense of any of it. He has no more charming quips to tickle the hearts of his audience, those adoring old ladies and the children who gobbled up his books. Suffering is real and it is a damn mess. It is meant to be shockingly real. Indeed, it is the most real thing we know, when we come to know it at last.

Joy's resolution to the problem of suffering is acceptance, and in recognizing that happiness and grief are part of "the deal." "The happiness now is part of the pain then," she tells Lewis in better days. "That's what makes it real." This is a stoic, almost pagan resolution, but Lewis—at least in the movie—accepts it full force.

Quite honestly, I cannot. I must challenge this presumption. It seems only to skirt the issue of suffering, pushing the problem further down field. Annie Dillard, in the segment quoted earlier, makes a very similar claim, but with one crucial caveat: she calls it a pact with the *devil!* Is this, then, just another proverb of hell? Are we really meant to accept it as a true, Christian teaching?

Let us return to the sacraments and to the gospel. When Jesus took pity on the sick and dying he did not encourage them to accept it as part of some fated contract. He healed them. So much of his ministry was dedicated to teaching that we may forget how active Christ was in *healing* people. The church takes up Christ's healing ministry by caring for the sick, establishing hospitals and religious orders wholly dedicated to their healing, and in easing the suffering of ailing people. The sacrament of the anointing of the sick was instituted for the very purpose of healing those afflicted in body and in spirit; to give them the strength, not only to endure suffering, but to *make it holy.* This anointing has been under-regarded by the church of late, and has often been considered a "last rite" only for the dying. But that was not its original purpose. In the epistle of St. James the author asks: "Is anyone among you sick? He should summon the presbyters of the church, and they should pray over him and anoint him with oil in the name of the Lord, and the prayer of faith will save the sick person, and the Lord will raise him up. If he has committed any sins, he will be forgiven."[39] This is a prayer for healing, restoration, and forgiveness. It is prayer that embraces life, not a prayer of forced stamina or stoic fatalism that so willingly submits itself to the grave.

Is suffering part of our lives? Yes, that is most evident. But why we suffer remains a very real mystery; one that seems to include, at least to me, an unwanted pact with the devil and the mystery of the cross.

---

39. Jas 5:14–15.

Departures[40]

Like *The Burmese Harp*, *Departures* is a Japanese film that honors—to the point of sanctity—the dignity of the human body, even in death. Both films are so filled with reverent imagery and profound respect for human life that it makes me wonder why Christianity never really prospered in Japan. I know that the Catholic faith was repressed by Japanese princes of old who rejected the foreign ideas brought over by the Jesuit missionaries; and I know that its historically Catholic center, Nagasaki, was devastated by the American nuclear bombing in 1945. But even now Catholicism does not really flower in the very fertile soil of Japan. Maybe Christianity is just seen as one lovely fruit among many, but I don't know.

Departures is a beautiful, dignified, and even funny film about a young man, Daigo Kobayashi, who loses his job as a cellist when his city's orchestra folds for lack of funds. Penniless and mortified, he must return to his hometown with his lovely and very supportive wife, Mika, to start a new life. The couple move into his mother's modest home where they can live cheaply. Daigo's mother had died years earlier, and his father ran off when he was just a small boy. He only vaguely remembers his father, and he can't quite recollect his face, but he despises him for having left him and his mother in poverty.

Now, back in his village, Daigo must find a new line of work, as there are no jobs for cellists in this backwater. He answers a newspaper ad for an assistant at a company specializing in "departures." He naïvely thinks it is some kind of travel agency, when in fact the company is a funeral service! But the boss is not an undertaker—at least not as Western people might assume—he is a *Nokanshi*, a master in the ancient, traditional art of dressing and preparing the dead for their final journey. Though Daigo is horrified at the thought of working with dead bodies, our desperate young hero accepts the job.

Now we are taken through the long apprenticeship of Daigo Kobayashi as he learns this most reverential craft. *Nokanshi* is no minimalist expression of Asian mysticism. Daigo's boss is an earthy, food-loving, matter-of-fact practitioner of a voluptuous art-form that he honors well. Though he works with death, he is exuberant about life and all of its

40. *Departures*, directed by Yōjirō Takita. A Tokyo Broadcasting System Production, 2008. (Japanese). Rated "PG 13" for "thematic material," referring to the theme of death, I suppose; death by old age, young age, and the suicidal death of a transvestite youth.

abundant gifts; but he is also a reverential master of a very sacred tradition. He serves as a father figure to Daigo, who can barely manage his own life. Daigo's world is a web of secrets, embarrassments, and unfaced fears. He harbors a buried hatred for his absent father, he sells his cello and must stifle his musical talents, he hides the nature of his job from his wife (who would be repulsed if she knew), and even represses his own feelings of revulsion at having to work with dead bodies. Living a joyful life just isn't in the cards for young Daigo.

But slowly, and through the reverence of this sacramental craft (which is minutely choreographed), Daigo learns the underlying meaning of his practiced gestures: how every fold of the garment, each tying of a bow, each application of oils and perfumes, signifies a hidden reality, and is performed to honor the family's love for their departed parent, sister, or child. That love is at the root of the ancient tradition.

When Daigo discovers the underlying meanings of his gestures and art, he begins to revere them, and soon he assumes the role of a *Nokanshi* master. Now he is no longer ashamed. His wife and friends do not understand him. Mika leaves him (though she does return), and his childhood friend taunts him crudely as one tainted and defiled. But when this same friend loses his own mother, he asks Daigo to please perform the last rites for her and prepare her body for cremation. The beauty of this scene, how Daigo transforms the beloved old working woman into a beautiful, flower-bedecked icon, is itself an image of great splendor.

Daigo's journey is a journey of healing. It is a voyage to authenticity and self-realization as he learns to face the truth about his life. He discovers this truth from his pragmatic boss, their wise secretary, his musical expression (if only to be played on his old child's cello), his loving but naïve wife, and at last from his own father, who has just died, and whom Daigo decides to prepare for burial in the traditional way, as a final gesture of forgiveness and love.

Departures is a story ripe with images that point to the grace of God. These images are not overtly Christian, but their underlying reality of love—at the core of life and as the medium of art—is fully fleshed out and flashing red for anyone so graced to see.

5

Confrontations

ON OUR PATH TO holiness we are often confronted by powers that work to trip us up. These powers seem to be working against our salvation and contrary to God's plan for our lives. They can be divided into three basic themes: suffering, evil, and doubt.

Each of these powers has the capacity to wound us to death or to save us through some hidden action of grace. Suffering, for example, can embitter us and fill our hearts with fear; yet suffering can also purge our pride and instill in us the saving qualities of empathy and compassion. Evil works to deceive and corrupt the human heart, yet it seems to lay the groundwork for tremendous grace, when we have nowhere else to turn but to God. And while doubt can lead us to a paralysis of the spirit, it is also a necessary tool of the intellect, enabling us to discern what is false from what is true, and directing us to choose the truth.

These are all complex notions which we shall try to untangle in this next chapter, as we look at films that are uniquely suited to our theme of confrontations.

Confronted by Suffering

We concluded the last chapter on the sacraments with the anointing of the sick and the question of suffering. It remains a question because suffering really is a mystery. We should not assume that people suffer only as a punishment from God and on account of their sins. While it is true that our sins can cause us to suffer, it is not true that all those who suffer are being punished by God. That would be too simple, too pagan, too fatalistic. Good people suffer too, as we see in the case of Job. The lesson we are meant to take from that Old Testament tale is that we should not presume to know the ways of God. God corrected Job's friends who accused Job of wrong-doing based on his downfall. Suffering is not an indication of evil or sin; it may well be a sign of tremendous grace! Even Jesus, who was all good—who was God—suffered. All we really know is that God's ways are above our ways. It is a mystery.

By the same token, we cannot deny the reality of suffering or underplay its role in our lives. It may work as "God's megaphone to rouse a deaf world," as C. S. Lewis first touted, but that leaves us wondering why we are all deaf in the first place. It may be the "deal," that "pact with the devil" that makes our lived reality more real to us, but the question still remains: why is there this pact at all? Let's be honest, suffering confronts and confounds us. It can destroy our lives, our loves, our faith, and our hope. Yet it is also transformational and the rocky landscape of grace. This is the Christian paradox, as Reverend Toller came to discover; we live on a horizon between hope and despair.

Because suffering is real, our confrontation with it ignites in us a traumatic rejection. We will not have it. We will not endure it. This cannot be. There is something in the ground of our being that knows, intuitively, that suffering should not be a part of our lives. We work desperately to avoid it, but we never succeed. Suffering is real, it is meant to be real; and since we cannot avoid it, we can only take two perilous paths through it: the path that purifies, or the path that destroys. Each path requires a courageous plunge through the surface of suffering and into its underlying reality and depth.

The saint, by her life's example, can lead the way through human anguish; the artist, by his art, can illuminate the path. We need these guides, because we know that our spirit is weak and our vision clouded. As St. Paul tells us, we "see through a glass, darkly."[1] The truth that lies beneath the surface of our experience is hidden. It is the artist's role to polish the glass, spotlight the images, and reveal something of that underlying reality to our awakened eyes. In stories and in film, this is often done by depicting some calamity that jars the characters, forcing them to take notice, to look inward—perhaps for the first time in their lives—and

---

1. 1 Cor 13:12. (KJV)

discover their own frailty and the disorder of their hearts. Only then can they see their tremendous *need* for grace, perhaps even pray for it, and so prepare themselves to receive its saving power.

Nature and the Love of Self

Force Majeure[2]

Force Majeure is a Swedish/French film that hits you over the head (knocks you down, spinning) with a literal and allegorical avalanche. It is, in many ways, an old fashioned morality play that asks a very basic question, a foundational question, a question that is at the root of our moral lives and our civil laws. From a standpoint that is as fundamental as family life, here is the challenge: "In a crisis, who are you going to save, your loved ones or yourself?" That is about as foundational as one can get when forming a moral principle, because everything else flows from the answer given.

If you put yourself first above all others, loved or unknown, then every moral principle you embrace will be based on how its outcome affects *you*. And if everyone were to take this position, then society—even your beloved family—would dissolve into chaos as our communal structures are destroyed. However, if we put others first, society still stands a chance.

To illustrate the point, *Force Majeure* places a family of four into the heart of this moral conundrum—abruptly, magnificently—and then analyzes the actions of each member, in retrospect and repeatedly, until the family structure begins to fracture.

On a sunny afternoon in the French Alps, a vacationing family of four dine on the outside deck of a restaurant that is adjacent to their ski lodge. It is the second day of their vacation and spirits are high. Suddenly, a huge avalanche comes crashing down the mountain slopes. The avalanche is a controlled phenomenon and the father assures everyone that they are safe, that the authorities know what they are doing. At first the diners are enchanted. People grab their phones and cameras to film the event. But the avalanche continues to rise and roar until the whole scene is buried in a massive, exploding white-out. It happens so quickly that the last few seconds show a full-on panic as shadowy patrons leap from their tables and flee. It is visually splendid, even frightening! Everyone screams

2. *Force Majeure*, directed by Ruben Östlund. A Beofilm Production, 2014. (Swedish). Rated "R" for language and brief nudity.

and scatters. The father, Tomas, who had been filming the event, grabs his gloves from the table and bolts. The children cry in the arms of their mother who disappears in the fog. The roaring stops. The mist settles. The sky turns blue again. There is the mother at the table, clinging to her children, and there is Tomas, walking back into the picture.

They laugh nervously. No one is hurt, and wasn't that something? It is only in retrospect, after the trauma settles in, that they begin to question their actions. Tomas is convinced that he did everything right, everything he could possibly do. We, the viewers, are left wondering if his perception of reality isn't just a little bit skewed. His wife, Ebba, is wondering the same thing. She is astonished by her husband's cowardly dash for safety, leaving her and the children behind; and she is further stunned by his complete inability to recount his actions. The two kids seem to know the score, but they are emotionally ill-equipped to deal with a father who puts his own life ahead of theirs. It is only a thread of a plot, but when that thread is pulled things do unravel right along the seam that should have bound the family together in love.

Most of the film revolves around this unraveling and the hidden wounds of the family members, their friends, and the fragile bonds of the couple's marriage; especially a marriage that seems pasted together by sheer will. Ebba is a little too self-assured, and she repeats the story of the avalanche and Tomas' cowardice to their friends at dinner, and then again to his own brother, Mats. Naturally, Tomas is humiliated by her report, but he only digs in deeper, denying his wife's perception of the event. "I do not share your interpretation," he says, stolidly. His brother tries to rationalize and affirm the couple's valid perceptions, but it is no use. Their views are diametrically opposed to one another, and so reason cannot resolve it.

The dispute is finally settled when Ebba suggests that they look at the video replay of the avalanche on Tomas' phone. Tomas protests weakly, but Ebba insists. So they watch, and there in the video everyone can see that Tomas is clearly running away; they can even hear the clatter of his boots as he leaves his wife and children behind in the chaos. Tomas does not watch the video closely, apparently he already knows the truth. He is stunned and deeply ashamed. Later he collapses, admitting to Ebba that he is a terrible person, a deceptive, miserable man who even cheats at video games he plays with the kids. He is a liar, an unfaithful husband, and now he sees that he is a coward as well. So Tomas cries and cries, undone by this needed confession and wailing in remorse. His children crawl into his arms to comfort him and sob with him. But Ebba sits apart in her own chair, with little more to say than "Daddy is just sad."

We have hope for this family now, because Tomas is able to repent. Ebba, however, bears the greater burden. She has found herself in the dangerous position of being correct, of being better, and she separates herself from her family as a gesture of self-assurance. She prefers to ski alone. In time, Ebba will have to grapple with her own self-righteousness.

Tomas' brother, Mats, is ashamed for his brother, but he has no trouble asserting his own good character. He tells his girlfriend that he would never act like Tomas did. So she decides to tease him playfully, suggesting that he might also run away from her in a similar situation. Mats is deeply insulted and defends himself. He tells her that he has *always* put his family first, his ex-wife and his kids back home. Astutely, the girlfriend comments that the ex-wife is taking care of the kids, right? He nods, yeah. "While you're on vacation with a twenty-year-old girl?" Now Mats is left stunned and stammering.

The fact is, we believe we are good people. We are the kind of people who would always pitch in to save others, and certainly we would protect our spouses and children! But *Force Majeure* suggests that we may not be as good as we think we are.

On the departing bus trip down the mountain, the family will face another life-threatening event. The young bus driver is clumsy, inexperienced, and reckless. He cannot manage the steep grade and hairpin turns that twist down the snowy mountainside. He stops the bus, reverses, grinds the gears, and nearly lunges the bus over the edge of a cliff, only to jolt forward into a barrier. The passengers scream. So what does Ebba do? She panics, demanding to be let off the rollicking bus ahead of her own kids and husband. This scene exposes Ebba; she is as much a coward as Tomas ever was. She reacts with panic just as he did during the avalanche. It is a reflex, isn't it? An animal instinct, really. As the passengers all clamor off the bus, they curse the incompetent driver and then trek together down the wet road on foot. They walk in silence. Now Ebba must reflect on her own behavior and wonder if her reaction was just the natural response of any creature caught in a crisis. And it nearly is. Nearly.

Force Majeure ends, like many modern films, with the question left open-ended. It seems to suggest that we really are directed by instinct, that it is only natural to save ourselves first, and that there really is very little we can do about it. Those who would moralize against the notion that we are little more than animals, like Ebba, are only fooling themselves, and they are just as guilty and selfish as the people they condemn when it is their turn to react. We saw it with Tomas, we saw it again with his brother, and we see it now with Ebba. If this is humanity, then it is a selfish, fractured, dismal, mess.

But let us not forget another scene, the one where Tomas rescues his family when they are lost on the mountain during a heavy snowfall. The skiers became separated and Tomas had to go search for Ebba and bring her back to the safety of the fold, when she thought she was able to ski alone. Isn't this who we really are? Because, if no one had ever risked their life to save another, then we truly would be doomed. But thank God there really are such saints, and there always have been.

The second of the two greatest commandments, "love your neighbor as yourself," should clarify our Christian response to the moral question that *Force Majeure* poses; indeed, it *commands* the right response. If our first instinct is to save ourselves, then our prudential judgment should direct us differently, when it is given the time to consider a better course. And it often does take time. We may react according to instincts that help us to survive, but we are also formed by the virtues, directed by our conscience, and gifted by grace to choose a way that is better and best.

Ebba was wrong to judge her husband based on his impulsive, in-the-moment leap to safety. Certainly, she was wrong to humiliate him. When Tomas does reflect and does confess his failings, he reveals that he is a man struggling to grow in goodness. He is the one who leads the family to safety when they were lost on the mountainside. As for Tomas' brother, he is still stunned to think that he is anything but noble, yet his young girlfriend walks ahead of them all in the final scene, and she walks alone. We cannot know what direction these characters will now take in their lives, but the journey down the mountain is silent and ponderous.

Society and the Love of Neighbor

When we view our society as an expansion of the human family, we might see a similar pattern that often roils into global calamities. When life is good, we are good. When danger explodes around us, we trample our own children to escape.

The term "force majeure" literally means a "superior force." This is a legal expression meaning an overpowering force, a force unforeseen—like a flood or an avalanche—or what we English speakers might call "an act of God." "Force majeure" is often used as an escape clause to nullify an insurance policy or a legal contract. Should we imagine that the unforeseen force in this film has the power to void the family's contract of cohesion and love? If that is the case, then can catastrophe also nullify society's moral contract, that we should all care for one another? Does this social contract only work when times are good? So when calamity strikes all bets are off and we can revert back to an "every man for himself" ethic? Is that acceptable? Or are we called to something better? The answers to these questions not only reveal who we are—or who we think we are—they also form the very cornerstone for our social order.

There is one classic film that, in my opinion, stands heads above any other in exploring the moral obligations of society. It dares to challenge the conscience of our moral order, individually and as a community, and asks the same question that *Force Majeure* is asking: "In a crisis, who are you going to save: yourself or the other?"

The Grapes of Wrath pits the great commandment, "love your neighbor," against the frightening intrusion of the stranger, with all of his poverty and all of his needs and all of his desperation. It is a revealing exposé on the ferocious fears that the stranger can ignite in the center of the settled order, just as it exposes the innate goodness of the God-made human heart.

The Grapes of Wrath [3]

The Grapes of Wrath is a drama that is modest in its godliness, subtle in its allegory, and genuinely transcendental in its theology.[4] It is a classic novel by John Steinbeck, perhaps the very finest novel in American letters, but it is an equally classic film.

The story introduces us to the Joad family. These are simple, good, farming people who sharecrop a scrappy piece of land in Oklahoma. The major force of destruction for the family and for their neighbors is a great

3. *The Grapes of Wrath*, directed by John Ford. A Darryl F. Zamuck Production, 1940. Not rated, but suitable for all ages.

4. The director, John Ford, was a Catholic who often allowed his Catholic aesthetics to influence his work. The story's author, John Steinbeck, was a Transcendentalist and very closely involved in the filming of *The Grapes of Wrath*, ensuring that it remained true to his ideals and art. Together, they structured this masterpiece.

drought that has lasted for years. With it came the "dusters," those incessant dry winds that blew the soil away and literally buried the farms in mounds of drifting sand. These billowing dusters descended on the region like an avalanche, looming huge and dark and filling the sky as wide as the state with a fine, deadening dust.[5] Then there is the great depression and the economic collapse of the nation, forcing millions of people out of work. Another force driving against the farmers is the mechanization of agriculture, where one man and a tractor can produce more saleable crops than a dozen families working as croppers. Since the sharecroppers can no longer earn a profit for their corporate landowners, they are told they must leave the land and go somewhere else. But there is nowhere else for the farmers to go. There are no legal avenues of complaint, the corporations are well sheltered, and there is literally no other place in the State of Oklahoma for the families to resettle. So, when the Joads hear that there is work in California picking fruit, they—along with thousands more like them—set out on the road for the land of gold.

The Grapes of Wrath is deeply layered. It is clearly an indictment against the unregulated capitalism that drove the desperate farmers to work for wages that could not even feed them. And it is no accident that the only encampment that has clean, running water with "sanitary units" and Saturday night dances is run by the U.S. government. After weeks on the road, and after being shot at and run out of makeshift camps by angry locals, it is the government camp that provides the Joads with some relief, and where Ma is finally "treated decent." Steinbeck certainly had a socialistic bent, and we might note that the proprietor of the government camp looks suspiciously like Franklin D. Roosevelt. No subtlety, that! But the story also delves into the depths of human suffering. It depicts suffering as rising out of natural (drought) and human (selfishness) causes. It forces us to ask: What is suffering doing to the people; not only to the poor who must endure it, but to the fearful well-off who willingly inflict it? Is suffering merely a terrible burden that the poor must tolerate, or is there some transformational force at work within its mystery?

When we look more closely at the characters in the story, we can see how each one is pitted against some destructive power. Tom Joad, our protagonist, has his own flawed nature to contend with. He is an angry

---

5. The dust clouds were presumed to be natural occurrences. However, scientists now tell us that they were caused by the over-planting of one crop, wheat, which exhausted the soil. The repeated and great demand for wheat came from the global armies that needed to feed their soldiers on the battlefields of Europe during WWI.

young man, intelligent but unschooled, and driven by an all-consuming need for justice. What is happening to his people is unjust, and he meets this injustice with just outrage. But his fury does not work to change anything, and it only sinks him further into trouble and confusion. The older men, Pa and his brother John, are weak in body and broken in spirit. They were good farmers, deeply connected with the land, but hard work has taken its toll on their bodies, and the demolition of their beloved farms has decimated their spirit. Broken in body and in spirit, they can barely function as men. Rose of Sharon is young, in love, and expecting her first child; but she is exhausted by the ordeal and shattered when her useless husband runs off. The youngest son, Al, is a practical, adventurous, detached young man who is "hankering to be off on his own." Then there are the two powerhouse characters: Ma and the ex-preacher, Jim Casey. These two drive the drama and they are the only co-eternal forces that succeed against the powers of evil that they confront. They are also the only ones who can influence, direct, and educate the young Tom Joad.

Ma is the rock. She keeps the family going, holds it together, counsels, scolds, advises, feeds, and waxes philosophic. She keeps a loving whole hold on this fraying little society. Like the church, but perhaps not quite the church, she stakes her claim: "We're the people that live," she pronounces at the end of the film, "They can't wipe us out; they can't lick us. We'll go on forever, Pa, 'cause we're the people!" And while this has its patriotic ring, it may be making an even greater claim: We are the People of God. We are the church! (Though not entirely.)

A church is nothing without Christ. Christ is the groom, the people and church are his bride. So where might we find Christ in this story? An ex-preacher who has *lost* the spirit? It seems unlikely, but there he is, Jim Casey. Ol' J.C. The preacher does have to find his way at first, and he is confounded by the forces that drive the people from the land. He is horrified by the stories of starvation he hears in the transit camps. And he willingly goes to jail in the place of another man, allowing himself to be arrested and sacrificing his own freedom for the sake of a fellow human being. In California, the land of milk and honey, he joins the striking farm workers, claiming that a worker deserves his wages. He preaches that the Holy Spirit is Love, and confesses that "I love everybody so much, I'm fit to bust sometimes!" He considers how every human being is just a small piece of a great big soul (the Oversoul in Transcendentalist thought). In the end he dies for the people, chiding his executioners before they bludgeon him: "Listen, you fellas. You don't know what you're doing. You're helping to starve kids!" Echoes of Christ on the cross.

But the transformational character in this drama is Tom Joad. He is the one we follow, though it takes him some time to learn which direction to take. He is torn between his loyalty to his family and the rage he feels in his guts, the rage that leads him to kill Casey's killer in an unthinking act of revenge. This violent deed is no restitution and Tom knows it. It is Casey's preaching, his wisdom, his self-sacrifice, and his last act of forgiveness that turns Tom enough to "see things clear," as Casey saw them. Tom's own overwhelming need for justice will finally send him off to serve its holy cause. He must leave his family now for the sake of Christ (personified in the person of Jim Casey) and become an everyman. He will be that little bit of the great soul that is everywhere, so then *he* will be everywhere, in solidarity with the poor. "Where ever there's a fight so hungry people can eat, I'll be there. Wherever there's a cop beating up a guy, I'll be there. I'll be in the way guys yell when they're mad. I'll be in the way kids laugh when they're hungry and they know supper's ready. And when the people are eating the stuff they raise and living in the houses they build, I'll be there, too."

To suffer as Christ suffered is to make suffering holy, and those trials will bear great fruit in the lives of other people. Tom's transformation from an angry young man—an ex-con, a dutiful son—into a man with clear vision, is the direct consequence of the lessons he learned from Jim Casey and from Ma. Yet it is their greater example of sacrificial love *in the face of suffering*—suffering that is inflicted by the indifferent forces of nature and human sin—that seals Tom as a disciple of Christ, to carry out his mission of solidarity and justice. This is only the beginning for Tom Joad, but we suspect it is the true purpose that God has called him to fulfill.

Fate and Justice

THOU art indeed just, Lord, if I contend
With thee; but, sir, so what I plead is just.
Why do sinners' ways prosper? and why must
Disappointment all I endeavour end?[6]

—GERARD MANLEY HOPKINS

---

6. "Thou art indeed just, Lord." *Poems of Gerard Manley Hopkins.* XCVII.

Justice and fate walk hand in hand. We are all born at a certain time, in a certain place, and into a certain circumstance. This is our fate. Some are born into riches, others into poverty, but no one merits the wealth of their birth, nor do they deserve their poverty. These conditions are of God's choosing and belong to the mystery of suffering and to God's providential plans. So while some people must struggle with destitution or physical afflictions, it remains the duty of society, *in justice*, to ensure that they do not remain in these dire circumstances. It is a matter of justice that the sick be tended to and healed, if possible. It is a matter of justice that the poor be aided and lifted out of their poverty. It is a matter of justice that the structures of society allow for a fair distribution of the goods of the earth—which are given to us by God—so that all people will have the opportunity to grow in health and goodness and spiritual well-being. The fates must not have the last word.

The Joads suffered because of the poverty they were born into, but the real evil was in the hearts of those who would not share their wealth, or allow them to grow out of their poverty. We saw this earlier in *Ryan's Daughter*, where the townsfolk were constrained and corrupted by ignorance and privation, which were the social consequences of an oppressive ruling order. There is real evil in a governmental system that protects the wealthy and imposes tremendous burdens on those who are pushed aside or out on to the road.

When Jesus was asked why a man begging in the streets was born blind, the people presumed it was because of the blind man's sins, or the sins of his parents. But Jesus answered that this was *not* the case. "Neither he nor his parents sinned; it is so that the works of God might be made visible through him."[7] What are those works? What did Jesus do? Jesus *healed* the blind man, giving him back his sight. We are called to do likewise; to relieve the suffering of others, to heal, to comfort, to share our goods, and to lift others up to the possibility of grace. This is what Hoke does for Miss Daisy, it is what Mary does for Reverend Toller, and it is what Jim Casey and Ma do for Tom Joad.

But what of those who cannot be healed? What about those who are born with a disability, or a deformity, or have been embittered by circumstances beyond their control? How do fate and Providence, sin and justice, fit into our complicated moral lives and our hope for salvation? With our next two films we shall attempt to examine these questions more deeply.

7. John 9:1–41.

Jean de Florette[8]

A malicious heart can wear a congenial veil. It can hide behind a hand-shake, a hug, or a slap on the back. It has no qualms with deception; indeed, it thrives on lies and platitudes. Hamlet called it out: "That one may smile, and smile, and be a villain!" Our next film, *Jean de Florette* calls out the smiling villain as well.

Set in Provence, France, in the 1920s, *Jean de Florette* is the story of two scoundrels of noble birth who conspire to destroy their neighbor in order to acquire his newly inherited lands. César Soubeyran, the patient elder, and his dull, rat-faced nephew, Ugolin, have no regard for human love, friendship, or community. Each has been spurned by human con-tact. César was rejected by his first and only love, Florette, some thirty years earlier; and Ugolin is despised for his stupidity and his inbred ugli-ness. Each is well acquainted with the utility of bitterness and spite, and each covets only money for what it can buy them: a servant instead of a wife; a prostitute instead of a lover; a chronic bachelorhood instead of a family. Their wealth is in their inherited lands—an endowment of God's generous bounty and beauty—and their wealth will be sustained by the cultivation of carnations, which they plan to grow and harvest and sell for a very fine sum.

They have only one hurdle to overcome: carnations need water, lots of it, and their family lands are dry. The two look to a neighboring farm where there is a known spring, and propose to purchase the property cheaply from its aging owner. However, when César offers to buy the land from his gruff neighbor (the brother of Florette) the man balks and in-sults César and his whole damn family, calling them crooks and thieves. Enraged, César pulls the old man down from the olive tree that he had been pruning, spins him by his legs, and bashes his head against a rock. Then he leaves him there to die. Good enough, he will buy the land from its heirs instead.

But the heir is not Florette, César's former sweetheart, as he had ex-pected. Florette has passed away. The heir is her exuberant son, a hunch-back who comes from a rival village with his wife and child to claim the estate. This son, Jean de Florette, arrives filled with joy and a sense of adventure, as if he and his family were entering paradise together.

---

8. *Jean de Florette*, directed by Claude Berri. A Pierre Grunstein, Alain Poiré Production, 1986. (French). Rated "PG" for mature themes, but suitable for anyone old enough to read the subtitles.

For the two scoundrels, it is a considerable setback, and they must make new plans. Together, they decide to sabotage the estate's water supply by cementing over the only irrigating spring there. Then they bide their time like patient buzzards. They will closely watch this bookish clown who thinks he can cultivate a plantation with his science and his magical seeds and with water that just falls from the sky, as if God cared! The two laugh, they drink, they cavort with the vile tavern flies in town who eagerly predict disaster on the deformed, citified fool.

Indeed, while they all do hope for disaster, César and Ugolin know how to conceal their malevolence. Rather than stoke enmity against Jean and his family, as the villagers do, they smile and offer their help and spy and smile on their despised neighbor. César even instructs Ugolin in the ways of treachery. "You must push an enemy downhill," he tells him, "in the direction where he will fall." That way, no one can accuse them of ill will.

Remarkably, Jean de Florette fools them all. He turns out to be a very hard worker, a diligent surveyor, an enthusiastic student of agriculture, and a successful farmer—growing a fine garden and raising rabbits for food and cash. Like Adam in paradise, he seems to walk with God. His beautiful wife adores him. Their pretty daughter, Manon, is a delight to their eyes. All seems so very well and good to their innocent hearts. Jean tells the nosey Ugolin, who envies his success, that he has put his faith in "statistics and Providence."[9]

Nevertheless, when the summer rains fail to come, the crops wilt and the family suffers. Jean prays earnestly to God, begging for rain, because all of his modern methods have turned against him. He was convinced that the right application of agrarian science would yield a good harvest, and he trusted the skies to do their usual work, but now he must turn desperately to prayer. Should we think that God has abandoned Jean de Florette when the rains do not come? Is Providence mocking this good man when the thunderstorm rolls over his parched and dying crops, only to rain on other men's fields? Or is this just the indifferent sky, the silent universe, the godless ether, moving where it moves, unwilled by any divine mover? Jean raises his eyes to heaven and accuses Providence of great injustice: "I'm a hunchback, have you forgotten that? Do you think

---

9. There is a difference between fate, which is blind happenstance, and Providence, which is God's plan as it is revealed in time. Fate does not have a purpose, it is what it is. The Providence of God only acts with purpose toward one great end, which is our salvation. It is also interesting to note that the film's musical theme is taken from Giuseppe Verdi's opera, *La Forza del Destino*, or *The Force of Destiny*.

it's easy?" He shakes his fists, falling to his knees. "There's nobody up there!" he wails in resignation, "There's nobody up there!"

Jean and his family must toil fervently now, from morning to night, trekking up and down the mountain in sweltering heat, packing jugs of water on their donkey and on their own backs, in order to quench their thirsty fields. But it isn't enough. The soil turns to dust, the crops fade, the rabbits die, and their savings bleed dry. Ugolin does not even lend Jean his uncle's mule, which he had promised to do, now that Jean has reached his exhausted end. "I feel sorry for the donkey," one neighbor laughs viciously.

In desperation, Jean begins to dig a well by hand, but he soon hits solid rock and can dig no further. Undefeated, he takes out a mortgage on the farm and with the money he buys enough dynamite to blast the stubborn rock loose. Ever confident, but drinking too much, Jean is excited and giddy with wine. He sets the dynamite in the well and lets his daughter, Manon, light the long fuse while they hide in safety. The blast hurls the shattered rocks skyward, as if to assault the deaf and indifferent heavens. Eagerly, Jean races to the well to see if the explosion has cut through to the water table at last.

But then the rocks descend.

They are not hurled down by an angry God, and they are not drawn to earth by the indifferent force of gravity, either. No, these stones are an assault on Jean by every willful, greedy, avaricious wish that the human heart can conjure when it chooses wealth over charity, treachery over friendship, and power over sacrificial love. Even in his ugly heart, Ugolin knows this is true. When Jean is struck by the falling rocks and dies, Ugolin weeps for him. César is amazed. "Why are you crying?" he laughs, because their tactics have succeeded and they will reap the rewards. But the single spark of goodness that is left in Ugolin answers him: "It is not me who is crying, it is my eyes."

In the end, César takes his nephew to their new estate which he has just purchased from Jean's widow for next to nothing, and Ugolin digs up the blocked-over spring. Like a volcanic flame from hell the waters shoot forth. The two villains laugh and rejoice in the swelling pool, and then the old man cups his hands into the water and pours it over his idiot nephew's head, baptizing his only living kin in a diabolical gesture of triumph, naming him "the King of Carnations."

What they do not know, and only hear, is the anguished shrieking of little Manon, who has witnessed this horrible scene, and has fled the awful visage of such despicable men.

Fate and Mercy

Manon des Sources [10]

The sequel to *Jean de Florette* is *Manon des Sources,* or *Manon of the Spring.* It is equally beautiful, but I suspect it would be a serious stretch to find some salvific moment in this film. Like its predecessor, it is more pagan than Christian, and it is so thoroughly French that it borders on parody. I am not sure if this is a flaw in the film or its particular charm, so I will leave that to my readers. For me, its over-the-top Frenchiness is delightful, and its epic story line—playing out like a Greek tragedy—is deeply moving. This is a very human tale, and this is where it simply shines.

Recalling *Jean de Florette,* we are reintroduced to the same two scoundrels, Ugolin and his uncle, César Soubeyran. These two cohorts purposefully blocked up Jean de Florette's irrigation spring, and waited as his farm withered and died. They were then able to purchase the land cheaply from his widow after Jean's unfortunate death. The two men are both bitter, greedy, self-aggrandizing, lonely, and vile. They drove poor Jean, a deformed hunchback, to his death, and his widow to destitution. Little Manon, Jean's daughter, is left an orphan.

In our sequel, Manon is now grown, living as a simple shepherdess in the same hills, and cared for by a gypsy woman who had befriended her when she was a child. Manon is a beautiful young woman, almost sacred to the local farmers who know, not only her sad story, but their own complicity in her father's ruin and death. They had kept silent when they suspected foul play, and they allowed César and Ugolin to torment her father and hasten his demise. Manon has little to do with the villagers or the neighboring farms. She is a free soul, untouchable, shepherding her little flock of goats and dancing naked in the sun.

But when the miserable Ugolin chances to see this stunning dance, he is smitten with an all-consuming love. Beyond head-over-heels, he is obsessively stricken. Ugolin is an emotionally stunted man, a thick-headed man, terribly homely, and mean on account of it. Should we ever

10. *Manon des Sources,* directed by Claude Berri. A Pierre Grunstein, Alain Poiré Production, 1986. (French). Rated "PG" for mature themes, and one distant nude scene.

wish to pity him, his nastiness reasserts itself and we are once again left with feelings of disgust. But now, unfamiliar with the power of love and overcome by the rush, his passions hurl him into lunacy. He knows that Manon is beautiful and he is a troll, the product of too many marrying cousins, but he is rich and she is poor, so maybe he has a chance. At his uncle's urging, Ugolin buys himself a new hunting outfit, complete with a feathered hat, and he goes courting. But Manon is repulsed by this cretin, not only for his romantic presumptions but because she knows that he had plotted against her father. Ugolin can manage only a few civil words to her before he starts to stammer, unpacking his heart and declaring his sole desire to enslave himself for her love. She flees from him, wisely, as he seems capable of anything! Jilted and dejected, Ugolin heads back to his dark hovel.

He then tries to win Manon with kindness, filling her animal traps with prey that he has killed for her as gifts. But she doesn't know that he is doing this. She gives the gifts to a handsome teacher she meets in the hills, who is also attracted by her beauty, and who is kind like her father was kind. Ugolin weeps to see his offerings handed over to such a rival. While trekking home, he discovers one of Manon's hair ribbons snagged on a shrub, and carries it home as a prize. In wretched secrecy he takes the ribbon and sews it directly into his flesh, over his heart, where it festers as a constant emblem of his devotion.

One day Manon happens to overhear two hunters speak of her father's struggles, and how the entire village knew that the spring had been sabotaged, and yet they did nothing. She is horrified. Out of revenge fueled by grief, she blocks up the hidden source of water for the whole region, an underground river hidden in a limestone cavern, and within an hour the farmers and townsfolk lose their water supply and fly into a panic.

The people immediately blame the government for their misfortune. The mayor of the village—who is only mayor because he owns a telephone—calls in a geological expert who soon arrives for an emergency town meeting. But the forum does not go well. The geologist uses big words that the angry farmers do not understand. He then produces a large map to illustrate his aquatic theories, but the map doesn't even include their spring! The farmers riot and run the rural engineer out of town, then they try to knock the mayor senseless with their canes, demanding that the government provide the water that they all properly paid for. Well, that doesn't work, the authorities flee for their lives, and so the rabble all run to the church. If the government won't help them, as it damn well should, they will just have to pray for a miracle!

At Mass on Sunday, and preaching to a full assembly of desperate people, the priest scolds the villagers from his high pulpit. He tells them that the disaster is a punishment from God for their sins, and exhorts the guilty to repent. César and Ugolin also attend the church service, and Ugolin begins to suffer from the gnawing pangs of conscience, but César does not. It is all foolishness to him. After Mass, some of the villagers accuse César and Ugolin of driving Jean de Florette to his death. It is *their* treachery that has angered God! Manon, who is standing nearby and listening, publically accuses the two of blocking up her father's spring. She saw them dig up the cemented stones after they had bought the property from her mother. César feigns outrage at these charges, but poor Ugolin is beside himself. Seeing Manon once more, and suffering under her accusations, he begs her—for the sake of his life—to marry him and let him love her forever. "What a terrible mixture," he laments, "all my remorse for the harm I caused you and all the happiness I'd like to bring you." But she rejects him, and so he rushes away, only to hang himself from a dying tree.

The people decide that they must pray for a miracle in order to restore their water supply, so they arrange a holy procession from the church to the plaza fountain. They ask Manon to join them, because an orphan's prayers are powerful, they tell her. But Manon is hesitant, struggling with her own conscience, now. How can she pray to undo what she herself has inflicted on the people? Her young admirer, the school teacher, suggests that she act as her father would have acted. Her father was a good man, kind and forgiving. So together Manon and her new love go to the cavern and unblock the underground stream, allowing the waters to flow back down the mountain. They then return to town and join in the prayerful procession. By the time the priest reaches the fountain plaza the water from the hills has filled its cisterns and seeped its way down to the village, gurgling at the fountain's spout; then the waters gush forth. "A miracle!" the devout proclaim. Of course, we know that this is no miracle. It is just the good work of a corrected conscience and an act of mercy from the kind heart of a young woman in love.

It is sad about Ugolin but life goes on and Manon marries her handsome teacher. César, who has buried poor Ugolin in the family plot, now mourns his death. He places fresh carnations on Ugolin's tomb, knowing that he was the last withered branch in the proud Soubeyran line. Now César must die alone and without an heir.

By chance, an elderly blind woman happens upon César at the church yard. She is an old acquaintance of his, Delphine,[11] and like a prophetess she recounts to César the tragic twists that fate has taken in his life. She explains how Florette, César's only love, wrote to him when he was soldiering in Africa, telling him that she was pregnant with his child. But César says he never received such a letter. "In that case, it's a tragedy," the old woman sighs. He presumed she no longer loved him, while she presumed he no longer cared. Florette tried to abort the child with "devil-ish potions," but they did not work. So she hurriedly married another man, the blacksmith in a neighboring village, who would raise the child as his own. The baby was born alive, but it was born a hunchback.

Stricken by the news, César languishes in misery and hopes to die. How cruel and ironic are the fates, the son he had always wanted was the man he had tormented to death! He calls for the priest and confesses his terrible sins, then he dies that same night—but not before leaving all of his wealth and lands to Manon, his grandchild.

In *Jean de Florette* we met Jean, a modern man who was naturally good and loving. Only when the rains failed and his crops died did he raise his eyes in prayer—but Providence had other plans, and the thundering, dry, statistical skies moved on.

Manon des Sources is similar in its theology. The fountain miracle was no magical marvel. It was a miracle of the heart. It was Manon's own repentance and her capacity to forgive even the evil people who hurt her father that brought the water back to the people. As for the church, it is depicted as a trough of buffoonery, not as a conduit of sacramental grace. The devout are laughable, ignorant fools, railing against the government on one hand and clinging to their superstitions on the other. *Manon des Sources* really is a human tale, chock full of meanness and just desserts, fickle fates, pleasing outcomes, and the happily-ever-after ending of beautiful people in love.

Still, I do believe there is something raw and mysterious in the pity we feel for Ugolin, who was wounded by fate and cursed with "a face like a rat." We hope he has found some peaceful rest. As for César—who was also scarred by misfortune and his own thick pride, and who finally does come to some measure of repentance—for César we do expect a small portion of deliverance. He confesses his sins to the priest, admitting that he is "so pathetic I even pity myself." Should we hope that he finds mercy?

11. Perhaps a reference to the prophetic oracle at Delphi.

In the very last scene, after the priest leaves, César dresses himself handsomely and then lays down on his bed to die. He knows that it is time. And he is sure that Jean de Florette, his son there in heaven, will not blame him but will defend him against too harsh a judgment.

The next morning his serving maid discovers his dead body, closes his staring eyes, and makes the sign of the cross in prayer. As we gaze on César in death we can see that he is holding a woman's hair comb in his hand, the only memento he possessed from that one love in his life. Had the fates only been kinder. Ah, but César has already told us, "there is no such thing as fate!" Maybe so. But in these pitiful, loveless lives the fates are all they have; and it seems that they have had the last word. The winds blow, the clouds tumble, and the rains fall on other men's fields.

Oh, but please, I beg you, do look closely at César's dead and open hand before the movie credits roll. There is the comb of his beloved Florette, and there also is a trickle of enlaced beads from a rosary, dim and out of focus, flowing across his palm like droplets from a new sprung spring.

Mine, O thou lord of life, send my roots rain.[12]

—*GERARD MANLEY HOPKINS*

Sanity and Sanctity

The message of the cross is foolishness to those who are perishing,
but to us who are being saved it is the power of God.[13]

—*ST. PAUL*

---

12. Hopkins, *Poems of Gerard Manley Hopkins*, XCVII.

13. 1 Cor 1:18.

Europe '51 [14]

Europe '51 is one of those obscure Italian films that does not get the attention it deserves. Perhaps because it is dark, a little plodding, strange, and—well—*dark*. It is the story of a tragic woman who is sinking into madness. To be more precise, *Europe '51* takes up the mystery of sanctity and the word of the cross.

It begins by presenting the frivolous life of a wealthy couple living in post-war Italy. They are high society people, hosting fancy parties and cavorting on the edge of oblivion. They are oblivious to the poverty all around them, to the struggles of the working class, and to the women widowed by war. But most especially, the couple are oblivious to their moody, adolescent son. His need for attention is waved away as something trivial until, in a fit of despondency, he hurls himself down a staircase in what may be an attempt at suicide. The boy later dies, unexpectedly, from a blood clot to his brain and his mother, Irene, plummets into unbearable grief. Her marriage to her husband, George, has always been an unhappy one, but now it is intolerable. What is worse, she must share her husband's affection with his mother, a cold and arrogant old woman who exhibits little fondness for Irene.

After weeks of mourning, Irene finds some solace in helping a poor family whose child is very ill. The child may die if his family does not buy the medicine he needs, but they are just too poor to afford it. So Irene steps in to purchase the expensive drugs and the child recovers. Moved by the joy and gratitude of the boy's family, Irene begins to take on more missions of mercy. She even spends time with a communist group, going so far as to step in to cover for a factory worker, to help the woman keep her job. At the factory, Irene is horrified by the working conditions there. She begins to minister to more desperate people, tending to a prostitute who is dying of tuberculosis, and helping a washer-woman who has taken a dozen orphaned children into her care. Irene is, as Roberto Rossellini intentionally crafted, a modern day St. Francis.[15]

Of course, Irene's husband and mother-in-law don't know what to make of her bizarre behavior and her long absences from the home. George fears that she is having an affair or, even worse, that she has joined the communist party! They decide that she must be going mad, as no

---

14. *Europe '51*, directed by Roberto Rossellini. A Roberto Rossellini Production, 1952. (Italian). Not rated. Suitable for anyone able to read the subtitles.

15. Roberto Rossellini is the writer as well as the director of *Europe '51*.

sane woman would cavort with such destitute people, or give solace to a dying prostitute, or forgive and comfort a common thief. So they arrange to have Irene committed to an insane asylum. That way they can get her out of their way and restore their social standing among the community of the oblivious.

In the mental ward our heroine suffers greatly. She has been abandoned by her husband, is taunted by the staff, and is ignored by her well-paid lawyers. She must also endure the clinical coldness of her doctors who offer her no treatment other than social isolation, meaning to keep her locked away for the rest of her life. Yet even in lock-down, Irene continues to minister to the least of these, her fellow patients.

Europe '51 is best viewed on three dynamic levels, because that braided cord is its greatest strength. There is the surface story, such as it is, where we follow the plight of Irene Girard through her grief and her struggles, and on to her miserable end. But then there is the spiritual story, one that furtively blurs the borders between foolishness and the cross, while it challenges us to see Irene's ministrations as hallowed actions of grace. Finally there is the film's political level, one depicting modern Italy as a nation that has lost its soul and its sons to fascism and war. Italy has been betrayed by the insensible wealthy classes and, in seeking salvation from the communist ideal, she has stumbled, managing only to imprison her saints.

All three levels work, but Irene's mission of mercy must be held to the light. Though it is not the piety we might expect to see in a religious film of the 1950s, it is holy and real because her actions are good and her intentions are pure. She has a modest attachment to the church and the local priest who befriends her, but he is driven by necessity to leave her in the institution and go away with her family, leaving Irene doubly abandoned. If this woman really is a saint, she is a pathetically poor one. Surely her sanctity strikes a tone that, to our ears, lands a little off-key. She does not want to be entombed in the asylum, and her protests echo our Lord's pleas in the garden of Gethsemane. We might recall that Reverend Toller, from *First Reformed*, also recoiled from the cross. He was accused of being "always in the garden." Maybe that is as far as he could go, as far as grace allowed. Maybe the garden is far enough.

In the end, however, Irene does relinquish her will to the will of God. In the closing scene of the film we watch as she bids farewell from her barred window to the poor people who have come to praise and thank her; those little ones gathered in the street below. These are the same people she had served and saved during her ministry in the world. They are grateful for her aid, these lowly, and they know exactly who they are proclaiming. It is the task of the *laity* to proclaim its saints, and it is the task of the church to affirm them. So, from the height of her high window, Irene touches two fingers to her lips in a sweet farewell—a gesture of benediction and love and devotion—and her sad smile ends this strange and dissident film.

The Christian must not only accept suffering: he must make it holy.[16]
—*THOMAS MERTON*

Suffering always takes us back to the foot of the cross. In reviewing these last five films, we should be able to see a progression from self absorption to self sacrifice to sanctity. We move from the newly examined conscience of Tomas in *Force Majeure* to the education of Tom Joad and the ways of sacrifice in *The Grapes of Wrath*; from the struggle of Jean de Florette with nature and Providence, and against the willful tactics of evil men, to the turning of Manon's conscience, acting with mercy and inheriting César's vast estate. Finally, there is Irene, who willingly accepts the way of the cross as her only response to suffering and to a grief that is otherwise insufferable. It is in her imitation of Christ that Irene has found the path to holiness.

Suffering makes no sense apart from the passion of Christ and the cross. As Thomas Merton tells us, we are called not only to accept suffering but to "make it holy." The only way we can make suffering holy is to offer it as a sacrifice, as our *particular* shared portion of Christ's holy passion; because Christ is intimately bound to our human identity and to the very name we are given in baptism. Indeed, baptism "gives us our personal, incommunicable, vocation to reproduce in our own lives the life and suffering and charity of Christ in a way unknown to anyone else who has ever lived under the sun."[17] We are baptized into the death of Christ, and suffering is—mysteriously—essential to this pinnacle of love.

16. Merton, *No Man is an Island*, 95.

17. Merton, *No Man is an Island*, 95.

Confronted by Evil

Suffering is not evil. Suffering is bearing a burden. The burden may be difficult and painful, even overwhelming, but God gives us the grace to endure it. While it is true that suffering is often the consequence of some moral evil (sin), it is not an evil in itself. Good people suffer, as Jesus suffered, and when we offer our suffering up as an act of love, we are sharing in the passion of Christ.

Evil is quite another matter. Pure evil, as the antithesis of God and God's goodness, does not actually exist. It cannot. Everything that exists shares in God's own Being and existence. Evil is a void. It is the absence of good where the good *ought* to be. According to Catholic theology, even the devil is not *pure* evil, since the devil exists as an angelic being and bears the goodness of his own existence. All that is morally evil in creation is the result of our gifted freedom, including Satan's freedom to rebel against God, and our own free choice to sin. These are the two great evils, human sin and angelic rebellion. We have scrutinized sin rather thoroughly in our earlier chapters, but the devil is quite another matter.

The modern mind is not inclined to conjure or assent to a demonic presence in the world. What earlier peoples claimed as "demonic," moderns attribute to human psychosis—the sick, pathological mind that is capable of unbelievable horror—but horror with human origins. It may well be, though I tend to differ. There are times in life when evil feels very much like a personality; when it seems particularly well-orchestrated with a plan for human destruction, exhibiting malice toward human achievements and corrupting our human will the way disease corrupts a healthy body. The devil is not only in the details, the devil is in the very way we perceive and process and act upon the truth. One does not have to believe in a personal devil to experience this disaffection, but it helps.

That said, belief in some demonic being is not necessary for our study of the next two films on evil. One can still gain from these films a crucial insight into the nature of evil by regarding Satan as a metaphor. It is a rather limiting perspective, I think, but it will suffice so long as one is not lulled into complacency by it. This is especially true when we consider that the very existence of Satan, who he is and how he operates, is the theme at the heart of our next movie: *The Usual Suspects*.

When the Devil Exists

*"The greatest trick the devil ever pulled was convincing
the world he didn't exist."*[18]

—*VERBAL KINT*

The Usual Suspects[19]

The Usual Suspects is a truly diabolical film, yet it is also quite sacramental. It is sacramental because the images and symbolic play structured
throughout the film signify and point to a hidden, deeper reality. It is
diabolical because it is, in a sense, an *inverted* sacramental sign. The film
presents this constant, upside-down flow of images and deceptions, not
to point out God, but to point out Satan himself; a personality so hidden
that we readily doubt his reality.

Our story begins in real time and depicts a horrible event in the San
Pedro harbor. A transport ship has been destroyed, burned to the water
line, with most of its crew members murdered. A small man has been
detained by the Los Angeles police and is being interrogated for what he
might know about the doomed ship. This detainee, Verbal Kint, is a weak
minded, weak bodied, petty crook who is certainly chatty enough, but
not very cooperative. Verbal has been granted "full immunity" by "the
Prince of Darkness himself," so the police cannot hold him for very long.
They can only hope to coax a story out of him and get to the perpetrators.
Kint obliges them with a lengthy retelling of events.

The movie moves back and forth from Verbal Kint's retold story to
the present day interrogation. We have no reason to doubt Kint, and his
stories are fascinating. Throughout the course of his narrative, while he
names his accomplices and details their adventures from New York to
Los Angeles, the detectives in LA are uncovering new evidence about the
destroyed ship. Pay close attention! Because each time new evidence is
discovered and revealed, Kint changes the direction of his own narrative,

---

18. Verbal Kint in *The Usual Suspects,* a reference to Charles Baudelaire's famed
expression.

19. *The Usual Suspects,* directed by Bryan Singer. A Bad Hat Harry Production,
1995. Rated "R" for language, considerable violence, and mature themes.

and his tale takes a new twist and turn. It can get confusing but, as the lieutenant states near the end of the interrogation, you have to sort of step back and take it all in (the mess on his desk, the movie we just watched, the writing on the wall), in order to form an accurate impression of what is really going on.

Flannery O'Connor once said that her fiction is about "the action of grace in territory held largely by the devil."[20] In *The Usual Suspects* we are definitely in the territory of the devil, but the action of grace is surely missing, or heavily underplayed. The dark underworld of the corrupt cops, the criminals that Kint describes, and the thugs who murder with impunity, all depict a thoroughly degraded image of humanity. The extreme violence, the burnt corpses, and the shocking blackmail that even targets children, is breathtaking in its sinister scope. One wonders how human beings can be so vicious. Even the good cops bungle what little grace justice seems to afford them.

Yet, in the shadow of all of this horror lurks Keyser Söze, the mastermind, the mob boss, the demonic chieftain straight out of hell. Verbal trembles when he admits that Söze may have played a role in the murders. He will not identify or put the finger on Söze, as that would be suicide, he just insinuates that there may really be a crime lord behind it all. In one telling scene, he raises his paralyzed arm to the detective and asks: "How do you shoot the devil in the back? What if you miss?"

At first viewing, *The Usual Suspects* can be very difficult to follow. What is real and what is true and what is the twisted retelling of a narrative that changes over time, can confound even the most careful viewer. But it is meant to be confounding. We are meant to be taken in. We are meant to trust the wrong people and believe the drama that is playing out before our eyes. Not only is the devil operating to deceive us, he is directing us to see *only* "the usual suspects," not the hidden, real, and guilty culprit; the one we don't believe in, the one who is as real as we are.

It is only at the very end of the film, when we realize that Verbal Kint is *lying*—and all of his stories were inventions taken from the bulletin board in the lieutenant's office—that we are properly dope-slapped into a different reality. This chilling moment affronts us because it is completely unforeseen. We are shocked to discover that the trick has been played *on us;* that Verbal's deposition (the scenes that make up most of the movie) was a fantastic mix of cons meant only to deflect attention away from

20. O'Connor, *Mystery and Manners,* 118.

him, and point to other dangers that do not even exist. Verbal told his "spook story" to throw the police off his track. Sure, his warnings about Keyser Söze were intriguing, and his outing of Dean Keaton—the corrupt cop—as Keyser Söze is ingenious. Keaton is dead. "I saw him die," Verbal whined. So now the investigators can relax a little. The threat is over, Söze is dead, and Verbal Kint can leave the police station unmolested.

But when the one remaining witness to the events on the destroyed ship, a man burnt and dying, finishes his description of Keyser Söze to the police artist from his hospital bed, the rendered image is sent over the fax machine to the LAPD. We watch as it prints out, and there is Verbal Kint's face, emerging in the printer tray.

All we know now is this: that Keyser Söze is the devil and that Verbal Kint is Keyser Söze. Verbal Kint, the deformed liar, the fraud, the con-man and trickster; he is the mob boss who willingly slaughtered a boatload of men in order to cover up the murder of that one critical witness. He is the devil who killed the only man, the Guatemalan, who could *prove him real*. This is the twist, the trick, the inversion of the sacramental sign that stuns us just long enough for the devil to get away.

The Usual Suspects is an extremely well-crafted movie. It is a flashing beacon that warns us not to be taken in by the tricks of the devil. Satan is a liar before anything else, and Jesus named him the "father of lies." The devil's first lie is his irrational claim that he does not even exist. Of course, he can't make that claim without first existing. And Jesus affirmed the devil's existence when he said: "I saw Satan fall like lightning from the sky."[21]

The reason for the devil's lies is to work against our love of the truth and our salvation. When Jesus proclaimed that he is the Truth—not just a speaker of truth but the Truth itself—then it must follow that every lie told is a distortion of God's own truth. Truth is reality, after all, it is life. If everything that is made is made according to the Word of God, then this Word gives life to everything living. The Word gives meaning, even as words themselves give meaning. Yet a lie has no real meaning. It points to a non-reality, to non-life. A lie is a kind of anti-word, and so an anti-Christ.[22] Deception not only works against truth, it creates its own diabolical reality, one that cannot be real; and we who are truth seekers find this non-reality so confounding that it leaves us shaking.

---

21. Luke 10:18.

22. There is something frivolous, something sinister, and something inverted, in the name "Verbal." It seems to make a mockery of the "Word of God," who is Christ.

We should not forget the lesson we learned from Eve Harrington, in *All About Eve.* We should not forget that these kinds are legion. Because if we cannot recognize the depth of evil, or if we are willing to tolerate deception for the sake of success or some presumed higher good, then we are in grave danger of consorting with the wiles of the devil. And we will likely be thoroughly stunned when the devil turns on us, because he will, leaving us with nothing within nothing within nothing.

And then "like that **poof** he's gone."

Lying is linked to the tragedy of sin and its perverse consequences, which have had, and continue to have, devastating effects on the lives of individuals and nations. We need but think of the events of the past century, when aberrant ideological and political systems willfully twisted the truth and brought about the exploitation and murder of an appalling number of men and women . . . After experiences like these, how can we fail to be seriously concerned about lies in our own times, lies which are the framework for menacing scenarios of death in many parts of the world? Any authentic search for peace must begin with the realization that the problem of truth and untruth is the concern of every man and woman; it is decisive for the peaceful future of our planet.[23]

—*POPE EMERITUS BENEDICT XVI*

To Beat the Devil

How far does one have to go to find the root of sin and human evil? Scripture tells us it is the love of money; though money itself is not evil, as many good things can be done with it when it is shared. But the *love* of money is a love of wealth for its own sake, and wealth becomes useless after a certain point. How much stuff do people really need? Still, there are those who always seem to crave more. So we have to wonder, what is it they are actually craving?

When a person takes no real joy in things, because they already have too much, they may find that their only satisfaction is in power. And this is what money ultimately buys: the power to assert one's will over another. The desire for this kind of power is a corruption of the will, the sanctuary

23. Benedict XVI, Pope Emeritus, "In Truth, Peace."

of God. It seeks to subjugate the weaker person into powerlessness (denying them their human dignity), and its impossible, final goal is to subjugate God. The Tree of Knowledge was all about becoming gods, remember. The root of evil exists within that perversion of the will which desires godhood for itself. It is the original sin. And its effects are felt everywhere.

Fargo [24]

This leads us to consider *Fargo*, an amazing film that takes us on a dangerous journey into the depths of human corruption. Like *The Usual Suspects*, it is replete with imagery that is often inverted and horribly violent. Yet, unlike *The Usual Suspects*, *Fargo* points to the psychotic, sick, human mind, not to Satan. It treks through human degradation the way Dante trekked through the circles of hell, layer after dreaded layer. And while Dante's hell spirals around Satan, Dante's pilgrimage is focused on the human tragedy of the damned, not on the Prince of Darkness himself. In a similar way, *Fargo* emphasizes the human tragedy of the nearly damned. Its focus is on the human character; the very good, the very weak, the very oppressive, and the very sickening bad.

The story begins with a less-than-clever fraud perpetrated by an under-achieving car salesman and two seedy hoodlums. These three arrange to stage a kidnapping of the salesman's own wife for the ransom money that her father will pay them and that they can then divide. But the kidnapping goes terribly wrong and a state trooper is murdered by the kidnappers when he pulls them over for a traffic infraction. Two innocent witnesses, who happened to drive by the icy scene, are also shot dead.

The story then introduces us to a loving couple who are expecting, very soon, their first child. They are an Edenic pair, but the traditional family roles of this Midwest duo are reversed. The very pregnant wife, Marge Gunderson, is the Chief of Police in their small, Minnesota town, and the gentle, sweet husband, Norm, stays at home and paints ducks. (Though the film portrays the criminal workings of human sin, it has its own odd humor, too.) Marge is now called in to investigate the roadside murders.

As for the kidnappers, they are both comic and vile. Carl is talkative, homely, greedy, and stupid; a wannabe small tough-guy who is willing

---

24. *Fargo*, directed by Joel and Ethan Coen. A PolyGram Filmed Entertainment Production, 1996. Rated "R" for language and considerable violence, with two sexual scenes.

to stage an abduction for some easy dough. But he is nothing like his partner in crime, Gaear, who is a pure psychopath.

The car salesman, Jerry Lundegaard, is a middling man, a bit of a dullard, living under the oppressive thumb of his wife's wealthy father. Though he is weak, Lundegaard struggles to assert his manly dignity which his father-in-law has so ruthlessly quashed. This is why he concocts the fake kidnapping of his wife, so he can get enough money to buy his way out from under her old man. But because Lundegaard is a coward and a fool, he acts in ways contrary to courage and honesty, using stealth and deception as his weapons of choice. As a car salesman, he is very skilled at both.

Lundegaard's wife is an oblivious fool who cannot or will not see the damage that is being done to her family by her domineering dad. The real evil in their lives is this man's over-bearing reign. But the Lundegaards dare not offend him because they rely on his influence and his money to maintain their comfortable living. To them, the false image of a happy family is more important than the reality of their failures and their stupidity. They are a good example of the false-self couple.

But let us return now to the crime scene where, in the middle of a blizzard, the state trooper and the two young witnesses have been shot dead. During her investigation our police chief, Marge, discovers clues that direct her south to Minneapolis where she interviews some possible leads: two prostitutes who are as bubbly as high school cheerleaders, our guilty car salesman who charms her and skillfully evades her questions, and a gruff native American mechanic who tells her nothing. She comes up dry.

In an odd and out-of-place scene at a Minneapolis restaurant, Marge takes a break from her investigation. She has agreed to have dinner with an old high school chum, Mike Yanagita, who tells her the sad story of his wife's death. He is a kind, pathetic, and lonely man—a man as out-of-place in Minneapolis as the scene seems to be in the movie—but it is here that Marge has her epiphany. She is very moved by her friend's tragic story and his grief, and she offers him her kind sympathy.

Later, when Marge chats on the phone with another high school friend, she learns that Mike's wife didn't die. They were never even married! He lives with his parents. And she is doing just fine, but she had to move out of town because Mike kept bugging her. Ah-ha! There is the clue. Marge is a good and uncomplicated woman, but she is also a police chief and nobody's fool.

The next day she goes back to the car dealership to speak with Jerry Lundegaard again, only this time she thoroughly challenges the evasive story he told her the day before, asking him for documentation to corroborate his earlier claims. In a panic, he flees the interview and so now she has her man!

What did Marge realize after her dinner with her school friend, Mike? That people lie. That they lie very easily and very convincingly. Indeed, some people are so skilled at lying that even she—a seasoned cop—can be taken in when her guard is down and she isn't expecting it. Did we not experience this same revelation in *The Usual Suspects?* This is Marge's epiphany: that even *good* people lie.

Now the hunt is on. She questions an elderly man who had reported to police that some "funny looking fella" was boasting in a bar, and gave away his hideout in a cabin by the lake. Marge closes in.

Sensing trouble, the kidnappers grow alarmed. More people are killed. Carl gets shot in the face by the old father-in-law who is then killed after delivering the ransom money. The bleeding, face-shot Carl shoots a parking lot attendant out of sheer rage, and then buries half the money to hide it from his partner. He then quarrels with his psychopathic cohort (who has killed the kidnapped wife because she kept screaming), and storms out the door of their cabin hideout, intending to take the car. The psychopath, furious over the quarrel, grabs an ax and kills Carl.

Enough blood and murder? Not yet.

As Marge moves in on the fiends, she waddles through the snow only to find the psychopath shoving the severed leg of his partner into a roaring wood chipper, shooting pink slurry onto a bloody mound.

Ok. That's enough. Our heroine draws her gun, the madman runs, she shoots, and he falls wounded. She somehow gets him into the squad car and they drive away.

Meanwhile, in another part of town, the police are knocking on a motel room door. A familiar voice cheerfully calls out: "Just a minute!" The police storm through the door and Jerry Lundegaard is grabbed as he tries to escape out a window in his underwear. The cops manhandle him into submission on the bed, cuffing his hands behind his back while he shrieks with all the agony of his destroyed life.

We might think that this spiral into hell would have ended with the capture of Gaear, the psychopath, but the wails of Jerry Lundegaard should remind us that the danger never really ends. *Fargo* illustrates how evil can rise out of every void where the good ought to be. We see this in the film's chronicle of faulty characters: in the psychotic, sick mind, where a healthy mind ought to be; in the vile, self-loathing ego where a wholesome ego ought to be; in the deceptive false-self where a true self ought to be; in the ignorant, blind fool, where wisdom ought to be; and in the contemptuous oppressor, where a loving and liberating heart ought to be.

Sin is the greatest evil and the greatest void, because sin entails a tremendous failing in faith. Without faith, we try to take by force what has already been gifted to us by grace. Then our lives and our graced bodies, created in the image of God, can end up pulverized in a wood chipper. This is what Marge cannot understand. So many people dead, "and for what?" she laments to her captive, "For a little bit of money. There's more to life than a little money you know. Don't you *know* that? And here you are, and it's a beautiful day."

Fortunately, we get one last charming view of our human potential in the closing scene of the film. Marge is now back home, cuddled in bed with her pudgy husband, Norm. She has had quite a traumatic week in the city away from home, but Norm tells her that one of his duck paintings has made it onto a postage stamp. "It's just the three-cent," he wags his head humbly, but she bolsters him: "It's terrific!" Norm sighs, "People don't much use the three-cent." "Oh, for Pete's sake, of course they do! Whenever they raise the postage people need the little stamps, when they're stuck with a bunch of the old ones . . . I'm so proud of you, Norm." He smiles and pats her round tummy. "Two more months," he says, and then he tells her that he loves her.

There is evil in the world, there is sin and psychosis, but there are evil powers, too. The powers exist. The devil exists. Yet the devil's undoing will be accomplished by every human action that mirrors the humility and the goodness and the innocence of Christ. Against innocence, the devil is powerless, and humility thwarts the devil in his pride. Marge and Norm, in their sweet humility, settle this violent adventure, and give us each a little bit of hope for our human destiny. As St. Thomas tells us, to exercise any of the virtues without humility is like trying to carry straw through a windstorm—or a blizzard.

When the Law is Evil

In *The Grapes of Wrath*, Tom Joad laments that it isn't the law that is working against them—these poor travelers—but the law's vigilante defenders. "They're working away our spirits, trying to make us cringe and crawl, taking away our *decency*." When people act out of fear to chase away the destitute, we can understand their fears and their need to protect the things they love. Their actions are certainly sinful, but society is not necessarily to blame. It is only when people begin to organize as a power in order to subvert the purpose of society—which is to protect the vulnerable—that a different kind of evil raises its menacing head. Social evils are an intentional form of power that are crafted to subvert justice, and conspire to do great harm to the weaker man, woman, or child. Governments are meant to administer justice to the people: to provide for the common good, to enhance opportunity, and to protect our human rights. But when this function is corrupted by malevolent powers the outcome is injustice, which can only lead to greater evils.

In the *King of Masks* we saw this happen in a society that devalued women and girls, so they became chattel to be sold at market prices. In *The Grapes of Wrath* we saw this again with the displaced farmers who were honest and good and hardworking, but were forced to starve when the economic structures failed or were subverted. In *Driving Miss Daisy* we saw how systematic racism kept poor people of color working essentially as slaves, and how even wealthy racial minorities were terrorized. When the law devalues any portion of human dignity it degrades us all. Then the whole social structure fractures, turning from what it *ought* to be in justice, to something menacing and evil; a void where justice should prevail.

In our next two films we will take a closer look at the corruption of the social order, and how the law itself can be deformed, inflicting tremendous evil against our human dignity. It should leave us wondering: when the *law* is evil, what can be done?

Au Revoir les Enfants [25]

Au Revoir les Enfants is Louis Malle's autobiographical account of his experience in a Catholic boys' school during the Nazi occupation of France. He tells his story from a very raucous, adolescent point of view, and through the character of Julien Quentin.

Julien attends a boarding school for wealthy boys run by the Discalced Carmelite fathers, and directed by the Carmelite friar, Père Jean.

---

25. *Au Revoir Les Enfants*, directed by Louis Malle. A Louis Malle Production, 1987. (French). Rated "PG" for rough language and adolescent hijinks.

Unbeknownst to Julien, Père Jean has been hiding Jewish students in the school to protect them from the Nazis. As a favor, he asks Julien to befriend a new student, Jean Bonnet, who is a very gifted young man but vulnerable to the other boys' taunts. Though the two do not hit it off at first, being French toughs and highly competitive, they eventually form a bond of friendship that is constantly tested, shaken, and reaffirmed.

While the story centers on these two boys, there is much more going on in the background. The French kids are rowdy, raunchy, and undisciplined. Their school masters hardly seem to notice. The gimpy kitchen helper, Joseph—a slow and lower class youth—is tormented by the pampered rich boys, but he is also a valuable go-between in their black market trade of jam and vitamin crackers for cigarettes and girly photos. There is nothing new under the sun! Though this might seem like typical adolescent fun, it does have its own dark underside with its own terrible consequences. When Joseph is fired from his kitchen job—because he was also selling the school's food supplies on the black market—he becomes a Nazi collaborator, which instantly makes him an important man and pays him well.

Meanwhile, our attention is on the friendship that is forming between Julian and Jean. (Why should we care about that creepy Joseph?) The two boys play piano together, lust over their female music teacher together, brawl in schoolyard battles on wooden stilts, and play a wild treasure hunting game that gets them both lost in the woods. Ironically, it is the "good Catholic" Bavarian Nazis who find them and bring them back to the school safely.

On the surface, *Au Revoir les Enfants* is a story that seems to distract us from the horrors of war. How can we not enjoy the horse play of rowdy boys and their friendships? Even in the bomb shelter, while the region is being pummeled and explosions shake the underground, the school boys sing and pray and sock each other. In the grip of the Nazi occupation the resistance grows as naturally among the French people as rebellion flowers in pre-teen toughs. These French *are* undisciplined. They are not like the Germans. But it is their unruly nature that keeps them one step out of step with the occupying forces and nurtures their rebellious spirit.

When the law is immoral it is not necessary to follow the law. Indeed, it is only moral to resist it, refute it, and disobey it. "An unjust law is no law at all."[26] This teaching of St. Augustine's, repeated by St. Thomas,

---

26. Augustine, "On Free Choice of the Will," Book 1, § 5.

leaves its mark in France.[27] The Germans seemed to have lost sight of its moral message, or else they opposed it entirely. Yet the theme of rebellion against *unjust* laws is key to understanding our film. When the Nazi commander addresses the boys in the school's court yard, after pulling them all out of their classes, he reasserts the erroneous view that duty must always come before justice.

The Gestapo have just raided the school and they are rounding up the hidden Jewish boys, the hidden French resisters, and those courageous priests who provided them sanctuary against the laws of the occupation. When a German soldier takes three young girls out of the church and into his custody, the commander orders him to let the girls go, as they were only looking to go to confession. But then he turns to the boys and explains: "That soldier did his duty . . . The strength of the German soldier is his discipline. That's what you French lack, discipline." It is true. For two hours we have experienced nothing but their undisciplined tomfoolery; yet it is the rowdy disorder of the French boys that kept the Jewish boys safe, as it gave the clergy and the resistance fighters a chaotic cover for their saving actions.

Jean Bonnet (Jean Kipplestein), Julien's good friend, is one of three Jewish boys who are arrested by the Nazis that day. The fired cook, Joseph, has turned them all in. He was well paid.

In the final scene, the Nazis lead the boys out through the courtyard gate along with Père Jean, the headmaster.[28] The assembly of boys cry out together: *"Au revoir, mon Père!"* Julian lifts his hand to wave goodbye, his eyes glassing over in grief and disbelief. Then Louis Malle concludes his story in a voice-over, as the gate closes and Julien's eyes swell with tears: "Bonnet, Negus, and Dupre died at Auschwitz; Father Jean at Mauthausen . . . More than forty years have passed, but I will remember every second of that January morning until I die."

When Society Errs

In the twentieth century, fascism and the Nazis were defeated through resistance, revolution, and war. There was a tremendous price to pay,

---

27. It is also quoted by Martin Luther King, Jr. in his "Letter from a Birmingham Jail."

28. Historically, this is Père Jacques de Jésus, OCD. For his sacrificial heroism, Père Jacques was named "Righteous Among the Nations" by the State of Israel in 1985; in 1990 the process for his canonization was begun.

but the laws that were evil—against the Jewish people and those who struggled to resist oppression—were overturned. New democratic governments followed and order did triumph, but at a devastating cost.

What might we do in a different reality, in an unlikely time and landscape? What can we do, for example, when society and culture has embraced some errant, moral principle as a solution to suffering, sickness, and death? How does one confront an *institutional* evil when the rest of society accepts it as good? Is our social morality bound only by some agreed upon social contract? If this were so, then we would have to accept whatever contract the majority imposed, even genocide. Or are there, perhaps, some deeper principles that guide, not only our lives, but our social governance as well?

Since history and current events might provide us with topics too hot to consider without prejudice, let us look at a slightly different reality; one that is true to the principles we may hold dear, but which exposes the intrinsic flaws that still lurk within those principles. This is the backdrop for our next film, *Never Let Me Go*.

Never Let Me Go [29]

Never Let Me Go is an ominous, science fiction film out of Britain that would make an excellent jumping off point for a robust discussion about human life, its dignity, destiny, and needed legal protections. If one wanted to promote a genuine debate on Catholic ethical teachings and its condemnation of abortion, euthanasia, and fetal research, this film would be a fascinating vehicle to use.[30]

Although *Never Let Me Go* is a dystopian drama, it is not futuristic or fantastic. The times actually parallel our own, but the story takes place in a reality that is somehow different from ours. England is still England, yet it has apparently taken its utilitarian principles of morality to their logical ends, *ad absurdum*; on into the absurd.

Utilitarianism is an ethical theory that basically states: "whatever works is good." If an action produces the greatest amount of good for the greatest number of people then that action is considered a moral good. It is very commonsensical, and it permeates English and American society

29. *Never Let Me Go*, directed by Mark Romanek. A DNA Films Production, 2010. Rated "R" for some sexual situations and references.

30. Though I doubt it would work out well, given my experience with these things.

to the teeth, but it is not Catholic. American Catholics struggle with this dissonance, whether they realize it or not, because they have been raised in a utilitarian culture. They can support torture, for example, because a tortured man might give up information that saves many lives. Even though the church condemns torture as a grave and intrinsic evil, it can still make sense to American Catholics because the *utility* of that horrible practice results in more good for more people. "If we want this good result, then we can do this evil thing to attain it." The end, to the utilitarian, justifies the means.

Catholic teaching claims just the opposite: the end never justifies the means. This is why the church condemns all violations against human life and dignity, from abortion to torture to the death penalty to euthanasia. (It becomes more complex when self-defense is introduced, but for now this is enough to ponder.)

Our film, *Never Let Me Go*, tells the story of three children raised to adulthood in a peculiar little boarding school in the country. It is a poor school but it is the children's whole world. They do not know their parents, or even if they have parents, as they never leave the school grounds. They only know the school, with its emphasis on good health and artistic achievement, as their home. They find love among their fellow students and by winning the approval of their stern but kind instructors. If it is disturbing, it doesn't seem to be *too* sinister. Yet we do suspect that something is terribly wrong.

When a young new teacher begins to instruct her class of earnest students, she realizes that these eager kids do not know who they are. "Study isn't important," she tells them, and their artwork isn't important, either. This amazes the children. All of their lives they had been taught that artistic expression was absolutely crucial for their future success, and they believed it. Why wouldn't they? But the young teacher decides to break with the institution's rules and tell the children the truth. "None of you will do anything but live the life that has already been set out for you. You will become adults, but only briefly. Before you are old, before you are even middle-aged, you will start to donate your vital organs. That's what you were created to do." The organs of these children will keep the rest of society alive. That is their life's only purpose.

Of course the new teacher is fired immediately, but the children are left to struggle with the unsettling news.

It is interesting to see how easily the kids accept their role in this society. If that's the way things are then that's the way things are. For the greater good, they will make the sacrifice; it is their duty, even ennobling. Like young soldiers going off to war, they are scared, excited, told they are called to a great service, commemorated, honored, and corralled into camps.

The story surrounds three main characters, and it entails a love triangle that is meant to keep the drama moving, but it is only surface stuff and silly. The three, who are now grown and all close friends, are moved into cottages to await their call.

Kathy, the narrating character, volunteers to be a "carer" for the others. This allows her more freedom in the outside world, to tend to and bolster her donating patients. Kathy's role will also allow her a few more years of life.

Tommy, her beloved friend, begins his donations. Perhaps a kidney, perhaps a lung. We are never told, it is kept very shadowy. But he recovers and continues his life as an artist, well nurtured by the society that feeds on him.

It is Ruth, the third friend in our story's threesome—Kathy's best friend and rival—who succumbs to the hardship of her first donation. She is in the hospital struggling to recover and dealing with the agonies of failing health, a failed career, and simmering rebellion. Kathy visits to soothe and encourage her, but Ruth is defiant. She says there are rumors among the donor class that their idyllic childhood school has been shut down, and that it was the last of its kind. New donors are now being hooked up to life support, like batteries in a warehouse, perhaps never even allowed to gain consciousness.

If Kathy ever struggles with the immorality of this social order, it is not shown. She seems to passively accept who she is and her purpose in society. Indeed, she serves as a crucial tool in that society, a nurse who is trained to comfort and console those who might otherwise rebel. That must never happen. Rebellion is not an option.

After Ruth's death and organ harvestation, Kathy and Tommy discover that they are truly in love and—because they heard a rumor that true love can defer their donations—they seek out the ancient head mistress of their school to plead for a deferment. Tommy brings all of his art work with him, to show her and prove to her his worthiness of heart.

These final scenes are remarkable. Though we suspected that malice was somehow lurking in the heart of the wrinkled old directress, it becomes clear that she had been the children's best champion all along. These children are *clones*, you see, and not naturally conceived people. Society, in all of its kindness, allowed them a childhood of sorts in the experimental schools. But Ruth was right, those schools are all gone now and the cloned bodies of these creatures will be reared in laboratories, kept alive to grow to maturity, and then harvested, without ever gaining awareness. Awareness might lead to rebellion. The head mistress doesn't say all of this, but by now the audience has figured it out.

Tommy eagerly displays his art across the old woman's tea table, hoping to convince the mistress that he is capable of love, and therefore he is worthy of life. But Kathy taps his shoulder. "There are no deferments," she tells him. He is puzzled. The head mistress confirms it. "There are no deferments," she echoes. "If you asked people in society to go backwards, to accept death and disease again, they would simply say 'no.' The schools and the art galleries were our attempt to answer a question that no one is asking anymore. We weren't trying to show if there was love in your souls; but that you even *had* souls at all."

Tommy is stunned. Kathy nods, accepting. Then they both gather up his drawings and leave.

On a lonely road, as darkness falls, an anxious Tommy asks Kathy to stop the car. He gets out, goes forward into the beam of the headlights, staggers, turns, and then shrieks his anguish and terror to the skies. This is a tremendously powerful scene. It is gut wrenching. It somehow culminates and exposes all of the dread that the film had so neatly concealed, and then expresses it as sheer human horror.

Stoic Kathy takes him in her arms.

But time and soldiers and clinics and smug societies march on. Tommy gives his third and last donation. Kathy watches him die on the operating table. She will soon begin her own donations, and die like her friends. In a narrative voice-over, in the last scene, Kathy ponders death as something that comes to everyone. Like Hamlet, she accepts an early death, believing that the readiness is all. It takes a moral outlook grounded in utility to accept the grave as easily as one accepts a warm bed, especially when that death is ordered by societal powers that feed, literally feed, off of one's slaughtered flesh. It is true that we must always be ready for death, but the greater moral terror is how ready we are to dehumanize those we wish to kill.

The sanctity of human life is a message so subtle in this film that many will likely miss it. If they don't miss it, they may not like hearing it. Human beings are not commodities to be exploited, used, or killed; not as fetuses, or slaves, or marketable children, or cheap labor, or cannon fodder, or body parts.[31] Neither should they be pushed into their graves to preserve some public or private gain.[32]

We are made in the image of God, sanctified by the Incarnation of Christ, and wholly sacred. The role of government in any just society is to protect the rights of every human being on account of this sanctity. For without justice, as St. Augustine tells us, the government would be just a bunch of crooks.[33]

Confronted by Doubt

The children in *Never Let Me Go* were not bothered by doubt. They dutifully accepted their role as organ donors for the good of society. This is, perhaps, the most horrific aspect of the film. They fully believed that they were less than human. They believed what the authorities (their teachers, their government, their society) wanted them to believe, because it worked for the good of most people. That their deaths were the end product of a faulty moral code never enters their young, uneducated minds. It would be catastrophic for them to question the moral order when it serves so many people with good health and a long life. Only Ruth *doubted* the legitimacy of such a system, but Ruth did not live long enough to resist or rebel against the injustice she rightly perceived.

When the utility of death (or injury, or oppression) is deemed necessary for the good of the many (those who have the power to manipulate the social order), then the vulnerable will always be the first to die, and social evil will triumph. But this evil would not have the last word if dissenting doubt is allowed to transform our minds and hearts, changing us from beguiled children to mature, prudent, and courageous adults.

---

31. In some parts of the world, the organs of executed prisoners have been harvested for transplant into the more obedient citizenry.

32. We ought to reconsider Willy Loman, in *Death of a Salesman*. He may have been emotionally frail and steeped in sin, but he maintained his human dignity to the end. "You can't eat the orange and throw the peel away!" he shouts to his bottom-line boss, "A man is not a piece of fruit!" And again to his son: "I am not a dime-a-dozen, I am Willy Loman!" There is arrogance here, sure, but there is also his most vital assertion of an inherent human dignity; a dignity that cannot be taken away, and a dignity that uniquely names us.

33. "Without justice, what are kingdoms but great bands of robbers?" Augustine, *City of God*, Book IV, 4.

The Doubt That is True

Our faith is tested by doubt, but it would be foolish to assume that doubt is somehow a weakness or a sin. Doubt is necessary in order to test the validity of any belief or trust, especially when we trust others to tell us the truth. Others may be lying. Or they may be flattering us while they drain away our savings or our lives! If we do not use doubt to discern the truth in what we have been told, we might easily fall prey to lies and propaganda. Doubt is an essential tool for sorting out what is true from what is false. We do owe respect to all proper authorities that offer guidance and wise teachings: to Holy Scripture, the traditions of the church, the law, our instructors, as well as our family and friends. Yet we also need to test every teaching against the parameters of truth, and weigh them carefully. This is how prudential judgment operates.

In our next two films we will be looking at the role that doubt plays in our lives; as a tool that works to inform our intellect, and as a fixed resolution that can destroy our souls.

Fireworks Wednesday [34]

The Catechism of the Catholic Church states that, as a consequence of original sin: "the harmony in which (Adam and Eve) had found themselves . . . is now destroyed: the control of the soul's spiritual faculties over the body is shattered; the union of man and woman becomes subject to tensions, their relations henceforth marked by lust and domination." [35] Ya think?

Fireworks Wednesday, which comes to us from modern day Iran, is an intriguing look at a shattered marriage that brooks little hope for redemption. This brokenness is witnessed through the curious eyes of a delightful young woman, Rouhi, who is soon to be married to a fine young man. Rouhi is a sweet, mischievous, and intelligent girl who works as a temporary maid cleaning the houses of Tehran's suburban well-to-do. She is excited about her upcoming marriage, and though we can see that her joy is real, it has a childlike quality that is also a little naïve.

When Rouhi is sent by her agency to an apartment dwelling across town, she discovers that the couple who live there are in great distress. The front room is in shambles. Furniture has been knocked over, windows

34. *Fireworks Wednesday,* directed by Asghar Farhadi. Produced by Jamal Saadatian, 2006. (Farsi). Not rated. Suitable for anyone able to read the subtitles.

35. *Catechism of the Catholic Church,* #400.

smashed, and the frantic husband is on the phone making a flurry of phone calls and shouting angry retorts. As a lowly maid, Rouhi knows to mind her own business and keep to her work, but she can't help but listen in and wonder over the events that have led to such an uproar.

We learn in broken pieces that the wife, Mozhdeh, is accusing her husband of having an affair. His denials and rages must have caused the broken windows and destruction that Roohi is now clearing away.

Because Rouhi is sympathetic to the wife's pain, she agrees to do the distraught woman a favor and spy on a female neighbor who lives alone in the same building, so she might learn the identity of the adulteress. This neighbor is an attractive beautician who takes clients into her home salon. Mozhdeh cooks up a scheme to send Rouhi to the woman's apartment to have her eyebrows shaped—as a wedding gift, she suggests—but also to learn whatever she can about the floozy. Delighted to be part of this secret fun, Rouhi eagerly accepts her new assignment.

But Rouhi's meddling backfires, and the couple are only thrown deeper into suspicion, denial, and destructive behavior that has a damaging impact on their child.

Both Mozhdeh and her husband, Morteza, are convincing in their claims of guilt and innocence. Like Rouhi, we viewers tend to side with Mozhdeh—the likely victim—until it becomes clear that her paranoia and suspicions have gotten the best of her. She counts the number of hang-up phone messages that are recorded on their phone; she listens for evidence of her rival's conduct through the exhaust vent in the bathroom; she concocts the spying mission for her hired maid to undertake; until we begin to suspect that it is Mozhdeh who has lost her sense of proportion and perhaps her grip on reality. Is she going mad?

In a similar way, we presume early on that the husband is the adulterer and a violent man, given the condition of the shattered apartment. But we soon discover that he is actually a very patient and rational and gentle man—seemingly decent—but at his wits end because of his jealous and volatile wife. Then, when new evidence emerges to the contrary, our sympathies flip back again to Mozhdeh, who may be overly stressed but she is likely the one who has been wronged. Rouhi undergoes this same back and forth struggle between suspicion, guilt, doubt, and truth.

When the spying mission turns up nothing, Mozhdeh takes to her sick bed and asks Rouhi to go pick up her son at school. With Rouhi away, Mozhdeh disguises herself in Rouhi's chador (cloak) and goes to check on her husband, to see if he really is at his office where he said he would be. But Morteza recognizes his wife in the chador and he runs outside and strikes her repeatedly in the street, to the horror of his co-workers and to his own immense shame.

Unhurt but humiliated, Mozhdeh runs home. She is now convinced that her husband is innocent (he was indeed at work and not with a mistress), so she retreats to her sick bed.

In Iran, Fireworks Wednesday is a national holiday, a New Year celebration, and the couple's child wants to go see the big fireworks show. With his wife in bed, Morteza asks if Rouhi will help him take his son to the evening event, promising to pay her for the extra hours. Then he will drive her home. She agrees, but she is wary.

At the celebration Rouhi is left alone with the boy for a very long time, not knowing where Morteza has disappeared to. He returns at last, takes his son home, and then drives Rouhi across town to where her fiancé is waiting.

But here is the clincher: When Morteza left Rouhi at the fair, he went off to visit his mistress, the beautician that Mozhdeh had suspected all along. They talk in the car, and the beautician breaks off the affair and leaves him. Dejected, Morteza slinks back to the fireworks show—but Rouhi sees and recognizes the beautician's unique cigarette lighter, which she left in Morteza's car.

When Rouhi returns to her betrothed, she returns as much in love with him as ever, though she has changed just enough to appreciate that things are not always as they seem. She is not embittered by her experience, she is just wiser, having gained new insights that will surely nurture her own relationship and marriage.

Sadly, though reconciled with her husband, Mozhdeh has sunk further into despair. If her husband's infidelity was all in her head, then how psychotic is she? And didn't Rouhi give her the strangest look when they returned from the fireworks show? Yet now we viewers know that Mozhdeh was not imaging things; that she was correct in her suspicion, and her doubt was warranted.

In the final scene we see her crawl into bed with her sleeping child, never to return to her husband, who calls to his wife from their own cold room.

Marriage is, above anything else, a covenant of trust. When trust is betrayed, though the relationship can be mended, it can never be the same. For Rouhi, her goodness sees her through the ordeal and she gains in prudential wisdom. For Mozhdeh, her suspicions bear a bitter fruit, but she was good and sought the truth, and so she still has her cherished child. As for Morteza—the adulterer, the liar, and the betrayer—he will lose not only his mistress and his wife, but his little son as well. What sin hath wrought, even from the very beginning.

The Doubt That is False

Mozhdeh was driven to emotional anguish because she doubted her false husband. Yet she was correct, morally true, and justified in her suspicions. It was Morteza's sinful behavior that wounded her, and it was his tapestry of lies that sent her into an emotional tail-spin, so that she doubted reality itself. Morteza's lies destroyed their marriage, not Mozhdeh's doubting. Doubt can move us to uncover sinfulness and lies, and we may well suffer on account of them, but doubt is necessary to reveal the truth, and the truth is essential.[36]

What we must not do is *remain* in doubt, because to remain in doubt is to remain in an unfinished work. Doubt is not a conclusion, doubt is a *process*. Agnosticism is lazy scholarship. One must examine the evidence and test the story tirelessly, until the final fact-filled step, or faith-filled leap, or flailing plunge can be accomplished.

In our next film, *The Song of Bernadette*, we will encounter an entire repertoire of doubters; even those who doubt the obvious, healing miracles at the grotto and the message of God's enduring love. If you think *The Song of Bernadette* is a story about faith, think again.

The Song of Bernadette[37]

Belief is not a very complicated notion. We make it complicated because we consider all the necessary steps that need to be taken before we can expel doubt and profess our belief. We want to nail our opinions to the wall and proclaim: "There, *that* is what I believe!" Knowledge requires a thorough examination, and while we may need to prove a theory or hypothesis by probing the material evidence, the very nature of belief is

36. We should recall that Willy Loman's lies were what severed his relationship with is son, Biff. The infidelity was terrible enough, but Biff doesn't call his father a cheat, he calls him a liar and a fake.

37. *Song of Bernadette*, directed by Henry King. Produced by William Perlberg, 1943. Not rated, suitable for all ages. Invite the kids!

such that it is *not* provable. If we require proofs then we are no longer talking about belief, we are talking about knowledge.

Belief is a judgment of the will; it is a decision made after we have worked through the processes of doubt and assented to the witnesses and authorities we trust. Belief says: "I choose to believe this," but it cannot prove its position, it can only trust its author, its witnesses, the lessons of its own reason, its own experiences, and its own perceptions.

One of the greatest Catholic films of all time is *The Song of Bernadette*. It is surely the first movie to come to mind when one thinks of classic Catholic cinema. Unfortunately, it tends to be passed over as overly sweet and childish; a story of adolescent girls and glowy visions accompanied by a soaring choir. I suppose this is true—it can be cheesy in places—but it really is a great film.

The Song of Bernadette was made in 1941 when the whole world was at war and when people were deeply traumatized by death and the disintegration of the social order. In times of great upheaval it is not surprising that people look for meaning and comfort and grace—a feminine grace, especially, I think—which they find in the beauty and simplicity of St. Bernadette and her encounter with the Mother of God at Lourdes.

Though we are inclined to think that *The Song of Bernadette* is a story about faith, it actually has a very different tale to tell. The faith of Bernadette Soubirous is simple and pure and rather matter-of-fact. She saw a beautiful lady at the town dump—a cesspool really—and the lady spoke to her and said some remarkable things, and the people were amazed. Bernadette's belief in what she saw and heard is unshakeable, she experienced a vision, but her faith in the things she experienced is really not the story.

The Song of Bernadette is a story about great doubt. Doubt is the force driving most of its other major characters. There is the doubt of Bernadette's parents at first, then the townsfolk, the priest, the mayor, the imperial prosecutor, the doctor, the chief of police, and even the nuns who teach at her school. In other words, *all of the vanguards of society* doubted Bernadette: her family, her friends, her community, her school, the church, the state, and the learned men of medicine, science, and the law. Every authority that the church teaches us to respect and regard doubted Bernadette's apparitions, and they doubted them profoundly. The movie wisely plays this up. These doubters discuss, debate, hypothesize, interrogate, challenge, confer, attack, and finally scatter in all directions, fragmented by this amazing event and Bernadette's simple assurance that it was true; she saw a beautiful lady in the grotto. That is why this is such a remarkable film, because it is an intelligent script with intelligent, modern characters, all contending with an event that *astounds* them to their core.

If you were an atheist, and you witnessed a miracle—a real miracle, not something that can be explained away—how would it change you? Would it make a believer out of you? When the twisted legs of a crippled child are straightened before your eyes, where will you be standing? Maybe you could profit by it, and so you will stand with the mayor, selling bottled water and attracting pilgrims to your impoverished little town. But what if, like the prosecutor, your pride got in the way? What if you thought you were better than the stupid peasants flocking to the miraculous pool and so, out of pride, you *chose* to succumb to cancer of the larynx rather than stoop to partake of the miraculous cure? Or what if you were like the old nun, eaten up with envy because you wanted—desperately needed—proof of God and God's assurance that your lifelong sacrifices were not in vain?

How do we respond when God makes himself known—through our Lady or through a simple peasant girl—and our own bungling egos get in the way? We poke at revelation like a scientist, interrogate it like a prosecutor, debate it like a clergyman, shame it like a nun, oppress it like a soldier, and jail it like a cop! These are the characters that people the story of *The Song of Bernadette*. It is their swan song, hardly hers. Bernadette's song does not go beyond her pure experience and her humble assertion: "I did see her." But in that proclamation we might hear the echo of a similar refrain: "My soul proclaims the greatness of the Lord; my spirit rejoices in God my savior."[38]

38. Luke 1:46.

6

Redemption

So faith, hope, love, remain, these three;
but the greatest of these is love.[1]

—ST. PAUL

The Theological Virtues

LET US REVISIT, FOR a moment, the cardinal virtues which we studied in our earlier chapters. We recall that these virtues can help us to avoid or resist the destructiveness of sin, and we gain these good habits through our own practiced efforts. This is why they are called *acquired* virtues. We build them up, through repetition and exercise, the way we might build up our muscles through a physical workout. We should remember, too, that these cardinal virtues cannot save us; they can only help us to be good so we might achieve happiness in this life. We use the power of our reasoning, for example, to discern what is true and decide how to act (prudence); we form right relationships in order to interact well with others (justice); we exercise courage so we might take necessary action, or acquire patience to endure hardships (fortitude); and we balance our passions and desires (temperance) for the sake of our own good, and that of the wider community.

1. 1 Cor 13:13.

The three theological virtues of faith, hope, and love, are very different in character from the cardinal virtues. St. Thomas extols these three,
promulgated by St. Paul, as the greatest of the virtues, but he is not simply
tagging three more good habits onto Plato's inadequate list. The theological virtues are not *acquired* good habits at all, they are *infused* and
uniquely interconnected with God's loving grace. The theological virtues
immerse us in the order of grace. And while they do work through us,
God is the exclusive *source* of these virtues. Just so, God is the sole *object*
(the destiny, the ultimate end) of these virtues as well.

We receive the theological virtues as gifts of grace. They are not
gained through our natural powers because our natural powers are incapable of knowing their object, their ultimate end, which is God. So we
must rely upon God to bestow these grace-filled virtues into our souls
(hence the infusion) and perfect our nature. They are poured into us as a
spiritual wealth, as living waters into sacred vessels, to make us holy and
lead us to salvation. Grace lifts up our limited nature and directs us to
unity with God. Grace takes our hand, if we allow it and are prepared for
it, to show us a different path. Grace heals us, strengthens us, enlightens
us, directs us, moves us, and calls us—without corrupting our free will—
always back to God. As we heard Reverend Toller tell Michael in *First
Reformed*: "Grace covers us all." In so doing, it not only helps us on our
spiritual journey, it *changes* who we are.

Redeemed by Christ in Faith

*Now faith is the substance of things hoped for,
the evidence of things not seen.*[2]

Faith, filled up with God's grace, believes those things true that God has
revealed as true. Faith cannot contradict the intellect, but neither is the
intellect capable of understanding everything that God knows.

Prudence is our natural guide in discerning the truth about worldly
things and in directing our actions according to that truth. Our integrity
is based on this honest desire to know, as we seek to anchor our lives
upon the rock of certainty. Yet the truth that we adopt relies heavily upon
our perceptions of reality and the power of our reasoning. And as we

2. Heb 11:1. (KJV)

know, our perceptions are often cloudy and the power of our reasoning is appallingly weak. "We see through a glass, darkly,"[3] St. Paul warns us before asserting, also, that "we walk by faith, not by sight."[4]

Faith, as a theological virtue, lifts up the limited way we know things and introduces us to those things hoped for in the yearning hollow of our hearts. Faith is not simply the natural act of believing that something is true, that is the work of prudence. Faith is directed towards the object of our deepest longing and our greatest concern.

In the natural order, we believe things are true because we experience them as true, or because others have told us they are true. We trust these witnesses based on their authority to proclaim true things. For example, I might believe that an airplane can be constructed and flown based upon a concept that is designed by some proper authority—say, an aeronautical engineer. I have every reason to trust in his authority; his credentials check out, his diagram makes sense, the building materials seem sound, and I have enough experience with aircraft to know that a structure built according to this design will fly. All of the principles check out. I might even stake my life on it. This is certitude.

But faith is not certitude. Faith takes us beyond our reasonable certainties. Faith is more than a belief in what witnesses or authorities tell us, and it is more than an intellectual assent. Faith dwells on ultimate things: with the meaning of our lives, the purpose of existence, and the destiny of our souls. Paul Tillich, the twentieth century Lutheran theologian, tells us that faith is concerned with the object of one's *ultimate concern*. In the same way, St. Thomas tells us that the object of faith is God. As a theological virtue intertwined with divine grace, both the object and the source of faith is God.

Faith, then, is a supernatural grace that perfects our reason, taking us beyond reason's limitations. It is seeded in the imagination, as we have the capacity to imagine what we do not know, where we long for faith's substance, faith's insights, and faith's assurance. We pray. We attend. We listen. This assurance can be as subtle as a whisper, or as jarring as a thunder clap. God speaks, and so Christ—the Word of God, the Incarnation, the Sacrament of God—enters creation to perfectly manifest God's reality to the world. Christ not only unfolds the pages of our sacred memory— what we might believe through the testimony of witnesses and authorities

3. 1 Cor 13:12. (KJV)

4. 2 Cor 5:7.

and prophets—Christ *is* the fulfillment of our ultimate concern. Christ manifests his two natures, the human and the divine, and images in his flesh our destiny to be joined to God forever. He is the revelation (what we believe in faith), the mystery (what we long for in hope), and the truth (who is Truth) that God is love; for "no one knows the Father except the Son and anyone to whom the Son wishes to reveal him."[5]

When faith is understood as a divine gift, it becomes a source of insight that turns us back to the Source of insight. In faith we discover the truth, not as some clouded perception of reality, but the Truth as a Person; Truth itself. It is Christ who speaks in me—the believer—from the witness of the gospels and by my own lived experience, but also through the intimate relationship I already share with him as a participant in his divine life. Christ is closer to me than I am to myself. This I believe in faith. This is my lived religion. This is my own being, living as a sacrament of God, where I am the visible sign but Christ in me is the greater reality.

If we can accept this on faith, then we might begin to recognize the spiritual treasure that God's good graces so eagerly pour forth.

I have been crucified with Christ; yet I live, no longer I, but Christ lives in me; insofar as I now live in the flesh, I live by faith in the Son of God who has loved me and given himself up for me.[6]

—*ST. PAUL*

Ordet[7]

It would seem impossible for a two hour movie to capture the sublime on screen; and not only capture it, but project it as transformational. Great artists have tried to do this in other mediums, and not without some epic successes (and heaven knows, mediocre artists have tried even harder). But few in cinema have managed to depict on film the depth of Christian faith and the power of God's presence in the world. Faith is too demanding, too radical, too contrary to the ordinary, indolent pattern of our lives.

5. Matt 11:27.

6. Gal 2:19–20.

7. *Ordet*, directed by Carl Theodor Dreyer. Produced by Carl Theodor Dreyer, 1955. (Danish) Not rated. Suitable for anyone old enough to read the subtitles.

But in our next film, *Ordet (The Word)*, we will connect with something that really is quite extraordinary, a matter of life or death, something utterly sublime and a true masterpiece.

Ordet is a deeply religious film that is particularly Protestant in its presentation and its theology. It is Protestant in some of the ways that Protestantism has fractured and failed the Christian church, but it is also Protestant in the ways that Protestantism has expressed the magnificence of Christian faith. These two extremes counter one another in the story, yet they are also artfully interwoven throughout, creating a dialectic of meaning, a harmony of voices, and a fullness of stereophonic depth.

Here, on the outskirts of a small Danish village in 1925, lives a comfortable family of well-off landowners. The Borgen farm is richly blessed, fertile, vast, but by no means opulent. It is, rather, a clean and tidy operation, bordered by the sea and steeped in the great faith tradition of its Lutheran forefathers.

Three grown brothers live at the farm under the paternal guidance of their widowed father, Morten Borgen.[8] Morten is a good and pious man, well on in years, and struggling with the weighty concerns of old age and a family that is drifting from its moorings. Because he has prayed and prayed for the healing of his son, Johannes—and to no avail—he has grown despondent in his faith. He admits that he is barely able to pray with conviction these days. Morten is of the Danish, mainline Lutheran sect known as *Grudtvigian,* which anchors its faith in Christ while enjoying a life filled with God's blessings. It is a practical faith and as earthy as the Borgen farm. If we pay close attention, we will hear the lowing of the cows, the song of the birds, and the whistling of the wind through the marsh reeds, all signs of a robust and fertile creation. Yet Morten is not a joyful man. He longs for the faith of his father—a minister of great renown whose portrait is neatly framed in the drawing room—and for the certainty of the old faith which his father once lived. Only Inger, his loving daughter-in-law, has the patience and kindness to temper his sorrowful moods.

Morten loves his three sons dearly, but they are grown and going their own ways. The old man fears that he is losing his grip on the ordered life

8. Like Dostoyevsky's *Brothers Karamazov*, each character can be viewed as a unique embodiment of a particular idea: great faith, great doubt, innocent goodness, noble wisdom, etc. But I would not wish to pursue this interpretation in these pages, as the power of the film might be lost by such a tangent. Though in itself it would make an intriguing study!

he cherishes. His eldest son, Mikkel, is married to Inger and they have two sweet little girls. Inger is expecting their third child which Morten hopes will be a grandson. As for Mikkel, he has rejected his father's religion for all of its rigidity and righteousness, and he no longer believes in God. When Inger comforts him, telling him that he has a good heart and that he will find God soon enough, he sighs in resignation. She asks him if he hasn't just a little faith in God, but he answers that he hasn't "even faith in faith." Only his complete devotion to his wife allows him any happiness in life.

The youngest son, Anders, has fallen in love with the tailor's daughter, Anne Petersen, a meek village girl whose father forbids her to associate with any of the Borgen landowners. Peter Petersen is of the Inner Mission sect, an austere, ascetic fragment of the Lutheran Danes.[9] Like the Manicheans, they hold that any joy in earthly things is an affront to the spiritual. The goods of this world must be rejected and replaced with the spiritual fruits of heaven. Petersen has formed a little home-church which welcomes just a handful of the purest town folk for meetings and prayer. Like Morten, the tailor is an unyielding master, the father of his own church and the minister of his own family. Rather than bend one fraction of an inch, these patriarchal icons only stiffen, then crack, and finally splinter into a thousand new fragments and churches; the logical end of which is an intractable congregation of one. It is ironic that the tailor, Peter, sits quietly by a lamp, stitching a seam of fabric together while he prays for unity in the divided church; especially when he brushes away young Anders, claiming that he is not a Christian and therefore not good enough to marry his daughter. It is also telling that the only natural things in his one-room life-denying world are small birds in cages.

Finally we have the middle son, Johannes. Old Morten had tremendous hope for Johannes. This son was so brilliant and devout that Morten was sure he would become a great prophet, one who would resurrect the faith of old. So he sent Johannes away to the university to study theology, but the young man returned to his home stricken with insanity. When the visiting minister asks after Johannes, wondering if it was a love affair that drove him to madness, Mikkel answers, "No, it was Søren Kierkegaard."[10] Johannes, in his madness, believes that he is Jesus Christ, but no one will

9. This somber Inner Mission offshoot of Lutheranism is the same Danish sect depicted in *Babette's Feast*.

10. It is an amusing line, but we should note that Kierkegaard's ideas do underpin the heart of this story; from his own admonishment of the Christian divisions he saw in his native Denmark, to his great theology on the quality of faith.

listen to him in his own house. As the story opens, we see him wandering in and out of the home and out beyond the sand dunes, proclaiming the words of Christ to the wind.

Johannes often preaches from the gospels, but he also pronounces his own astute observations to others when it is necessary. He sees death stalking the main room of the home, for instance, and he chides his family of believers for their lack of faith.

When Johannes meets the new parson for the first time, he speaks sorrowfully to this man of God—who is much more a man of the Enlightenment—as if he were speaking to the church herself.

At this first meeting, the minister is unaware of Johannes' malady, and so he greets him with a cheerful "Good day."

Johannes responds, "God be with you," and the minister is taken aback.

"I beg your pardon?"

"God be with you," he repeats, and the minister thanks him. "You don't know me," Johannes continues. "I am a bricklayer. I build houses but nobody will live in them. They like to build for themselves . . . even though they do not know how. Therefore, some of them inhabit half finished huts, others live in ruins, most of them wander about homeless . . . I am Jesus of Nazareth."

"Jesus. But how can you prove that?" the parson challenges him.

"Thou man of faith whose own self lacks faith! People believe in the dead Christ, but not in the living. They believe in my miracles from two thousand years ago, but they don't believe in me now."

"Miracles no longer happen."

"Thus speaks my church on earth, that church which has failed me, that has murdered me in my own name. Here I stand and again you cast me out. But woe unto you if you nail me to the cross again."

The minister watches the bizarre young man drift into another room, then mutters after him: "That is absolutely appalling."

Is it absolutely appalling? What an odd expression from this minister! How excellent and true are the words of mad Johannes! When the parson demands that Johannes "prove" that he is Jesus Christ, an astute audience might recollect Kierkegaard's own assertion: "You cannot prove God."

Though the men of Borgen Farm struggle with their doubts and loves and delusions, Inger gathers and consoles and holds the family together. She comforts old Morten in his despondency, speaks lovingly to her godless husband, Mikkel, and hopes to God in prayer for Johannes.

As for Anders, who is heartsick like a young Romeo pining over the daughter of his father's rival, Inger agrees to become his champion and plead his case to his father.

She does this by enticing old Morten with his favorite cakes, by filling his pipe with tobacco, and by serving up real coffee for him. Then she asks the old man to relent and give Anders his blessing to marry Anne Petersen, so Anders can find love in his life. But Morten refuses. The Petersens do not belong to his faith, and Anders is not strong enough to stand up for himself. Morten does not want to lose all of his sons. He says he cannot stand the look of "those funeral faces" among Peter Petersen's ascetic sect. No, he will not agree to it, and that is that. Inger then asks the old man if he has ever been in love. Morten, who seems incapable of looking anyone in the eye, curls his lips into a little smile while his staring eyes sparkle. "At least ten times," he almost grins. "That's just what I thought," she tells him, "That you have never *really* been in love." Morten walks away from her and explains, "Maren was a good wife to me, just the wife I needed," and "love comes with the years."

During this exchange, it is easy to see why the family all adore Inger, even in her mild, artful, and clever ways. While she and Morten dispute the merits of true love, Anders has already gone out to ask Petersen for Anne's hand, regardless of his obstinate father's approval. When Morten realizes that Inger's sweet cakes and soft words were only a diversion so Anders could go off on his own, he storms out of the house and then sulks at having been so lovingly duped. But Inger goes after him because he forgot his coat, and Morten cannot stay angry with her for long.

At the tailor's meager home Petersen informs Anders that his answer is "no" to the marriage. The timid boy asks why he is being rejected, is it because he is not good enough? "No, Anders, you are not good enough," Peter tells him, looping a thin thread through his hand-stitched seam. "You are not a Christian." Not a Christian?! How absurd is that? Anders says he is as much a Christian as Peter Petersen! But the tailor won't listen and ushers him to the door, offering his half-hearted regards to the Borgens.

Anders returns home in tears and with the news that Peter Petersen has rejected him. Now Morten is outraged; not for Anders' sake, mind you, but for the sake of his own family pride. How can that morose, destitute little tailor dare to claim that a Borgen is not good enough for his daughter? Riled up, Morten takes Anders back to town with him to confront Peter. The two are greeted politely, even warmly, but the facts remain, Anders is not of their faith. Petersen says he will not consent, but then he slyly adds "yet." Morten is hopeful. "Yet?" Then Peter moves in on him, seductively, and tries to lure Morten into joining his sect. "Come over to us," he pleads, knowing that Morten is unhappy and supposing that it is because he has lost God. But Morten is affronted by this seduction—perhaps because it strikes too close to the truth—and he ridicules Peter's dreary, miserable, lifeless, faith. "My faith is as warm as life, and your faith is as cold as death!" He calls for Anders and they prepare to leave.

The phone rings as they make for the door. It is Mikkel who tells Petersen that Inger is dangerously ill, and asks that his father please hurry home. The tailor is moved by this new crisis. How prophetic! Just as he was speaking of the dangers to Morten's soul, the Borgen farm is struck by calamity. "You sound as if you want Inger to die!" Morten gasps. Peter nods and suggests that it would be just the thing to bring the Borgens back to God. In a fury Morten grabs the tailor by both lapels and throttles him. Then he and Anders race their plow horse home.

Any hopes that Anders may have had for love are now dashed. His lost future, Mikkel's lost faith, Johannes' lost wits, and Morten's lost joy are all insignificant straw compared to the crisis that threatens Inger. It is Inger, loving Inger, who turns the story back around, because nothing would matter if she died. She is the one holding them all together and keeping them alive. Without Inger, they are nothing.

The doctor is already with his patient when Morten and Anders arrive home, and Mikkel is at her side, clasping her hand as she cries in agony. The night will be long, but Morten knows what he must do. He knows he must pray, though he can barely utter more than a submissive sigh, "Thy will be done," to the God he so adores.

We learn that the doctor must destroy the unborn child in order to save Inger's life. We are spared the graphic sight of it, but not the instruments, or the sounds, or the description of the baby "cut into four pieces" in the bottom of a pail. Is this a bloody image of the further fragmenting of Christ's body and his holy church? One wonders. The doctor then tells Mikkel that the crisis has passed.

Johannes enters the front room where his father sits with his head in his hands. "The Lord has come to take the child away, but you had the power to stop it if only you would believe."

"Go to bed, Johannes!" Morten pleads, because he cannot bear these prophecies of doom. When Johannes tells him that the man with the scythe has now come to fetch Inger, Morten trembles. "Keep quiet, man!"

"You still do not heed me."

"Johannes, no, this is madness and yet, what is madness and what is reason?"

"You are drawing nearer to God," the Kierkegaardian mystic answers. "It will only take one word . . . ."

But Morten's one word is "No! No! No! Go away!" And Johannes exits.

The doctor tells Morten that Inger is resting and that she will recover, and the old man is deeply relieved. Though he is grieved at the loss of the child—a boy, as Inger had promised him—he believes that God has answered his prayers.

The minister arrives at the home to inquire after Inger. Learning that she will recover, he and the doctor have a satisfying smoke and a cup of coffee together. The reverend thanks God for Inger's restored health, but the doctor decides to "tease" old Morten by asking him if he thinks it was a miracle of God or his own medical skills that saved the woman. It seems a very arrogant question to ask at a time like this, but the doctor is a modern agent of arrogance, much like the minister, so it is barely alarming. Old Morten, stalwart in his faith, professes that it was indeed a miracle of God. The modern men laugh in good fellowship and then leave together, while the exhausted old patriarch gets ready for bed.

Johannes re-enters the room and informs his father and Anders of a second death. Can they not see the man with the scythe and the hour glass? Did they not witness him leaving through the wall?

"Those are only the lights from the doctor's car," Morten tells him, and the deranged young man retreats again, dejected. To our shock, however, Inger *has* just died. Mikkel now leans into the doorway and tells them that Inger is dead. He felt her stiffen in his arms, then her lips turned blue and her eyes glassed over. They rush into her death room and stare in horror, then turn away in tears.

Little Maren, the oldest of Mikkel's daughters, has already asked Johannes to raise her mother if she should die, just as it happened in the Bible story. Johannes had to tell her that the others will not allow him to do it. But now Johannes enters the place where Inger lies cold and reaches out his hand to her. He speaks a few words, but he is then hurled backwards to the floor—shocked, as if by an electric charge—and he collapses dead away. His two brothers have to carry him out of the room. "Is . . . is he dead?" Morten is shaking with fear. Mikkel, straining under his brother's weight, mutters bitterly: "No, father. These are not the ones who die."

The radical, stunning, bizarre action of this sea-saw scene should stir the hearts of every Christian viewer. We know that these are modern times; and we know, secretly, that the doctor and the minister make perfectly good sense. Miracles don't happen anymore. We can understand Morten's compounded grief over Inger's death and the death of the child, and his impatience with Johannes' incessant, frightening prophecies. But most deeply, I think, we feel Mikkel's tremendous anguish and sorrow. How can he live another day when everything he has ever loved and worshiped is to be buried in the earth, "to rot, to rot, and rot?" These bloody and rotten and ghostly images are meant to upset us. Just as we saw in *House of Sand and Fog* with Esmail's death, Inger's death is so unexpected and so out of place that we are stunned by it. Were we not watching the other characters and presuming the story's conflicts were theirs to resolve? Conflicting faiths, forbidden loves, soothsaying madmen and all of those modern conceits; but no, the story is not theirs, it is Inger's. And her story is so quietly underplayed that we surely have missed it.

Now the large room is cleared away and Inger, clothed in white like a bride, lies in a white casket under the stilled clock and between two bright windows, shining like two angels on either side of her repose.

Johannes has awakened from his faint, but he has run away into the dunes again, and though the family and servants search everywhere for him, he cannot be found.

The funeral guests arrive and we can hear them singing a very bleak hymn about death: that while the young flowers bloom, the hail storm comes and knocks them all down; and while the little children play at dawn, by evening they are all cold and dead. A grim reminder of the hardship and swiftness of life and death in these times! The Borgen men remain stoic, though the heaviness of their grief bends them down to the earth in slow, stiff silence. They keep apart from the neighboring mourners.

Then Peter Petersen, his wife and their daughter, Anne, arrive. They come to pay their respects and, for Peter, to beg forgiveness of Morten. He regrets his angry words and apologizes for not turning the other cheek when Morten shook him. He is ready to make amends. Old Morten receives him politely, even warmly, and they exchange a necessary embrace. But Peter wants to make an announcement to all of them; and in a grand and generous gesture he offers the hand of his only daughter to Anders in marriage. The Borgen farm must not be left without a mother for their little girls. It is fitting and just and good. There is some hope for unity now. Pleased, Anders and Anne join hands and go into a far corner where they blend into the shadows.

Because of Peter's generous gesture, or perhaps on account of the love that Anders has now won, Mikkel bursts into tears, sobbing for Inger, his little sweetheart. He pleads that they not yet close the coffin lid.

Old Morten tries to comfort his son. "Her spirit is with God," he murmurs.

"But her body is here, and *I loved her body also!*" Mikkel weeps.

Our hearts must surely break for Mikkel at this most human moment. It is a telling moment, a critical moment, a moment that invites into it the very flesh of the Incarnation. "I loved her *body* also!"

Lightly, like a ghost who can pass through walls, Johannes appears and greets his father. His eyes are no longer fixed in a fanatical stare, and his voice is no longer strained and burnt. Something has happened to Johannes. Morten asks if he has regained his wits, and Johannes says yes, he has regained his wits. He looks on his father with love and then approaches the casket in the center of the room.

"Not one of you has had the idea of asking God to give Inger back to you again?" he chides them gently.

"Johannes, now you blaspheme God," old Morten cautions him.

"No, all of you blaspheme God with your lukewarm faith. Why is there not one among these believers who believes? Inger, you must rot because the times are rotten."

Then little Maren takes her uncle's hand and urges him to bring her mother back to life.

"The child . . . ." he murmurs, as if remembering something from a dream. "The greatest in the kingdom of heaven. Do you believe I can do it?"

"Yes, Uncle."

Johannes speaks clearly, gazing at Inger. "Jesus Christ, if it is possible, then give her leave to come back to life, give me the word that can make the dead come to life. Inger, in the name of Jesus Christ, I bid thee, arise!"

There is a long, significant, breathless wait. Then Inger's fingers, entwined in repose, loosen and fall away. Mikkel rushes over and her head tips toward him. Her weak arms reach out to him and he takes her up.

Morten and Peter grasp for one another. "It is the God of old, the God of Elijah, eternal and the same!"

As Inger and Mikkel entwine their arms, her first words to him are about their child, does he live? "Yes," Mikkel tells her. "He lives at home with God."

"With God?" she wonders at his new language of God.

"Yes, Inger, I have found your faith. Now life begins for us."

Inger then turns her face to him, her eyes streaked with tears, her mouth gnawing at his cheek in a very carnal and sensual kiss. It is meant to be carnal. She is meant to be enfleshed. The scene is meant to expose the Incarnation of Christ, who is divine but also human, and his bodily resurrection. This is Inger's triumph! Her sacramental moment.

The intrusion of grace that comes rushing in is a *force*, not a passive gift, but an absolute force that is thrust upon us, in our very flesh and in our very nature, because that nature is human and that nature is *Christ's*. Christ, who is the eternal infusion of life and grace and Life!

"Life, yes. Life."

"Yes."

"Life."

Our age is essentially one of understanding and reflection without passion. There is no more action or decision in our day than there is perilous delight in swimming in shallow water.[11]

—SØREN KIERKEGAARD

Søren Kierkegaard is best known for his theology of faith, one that requires a "leap" into the arms of God. This "leap of faith" is an expression that Kierkegaard himself never used, and yet he somehow became associated with its anti-intellectual religiosity. This *anti*-rational piety was actually quite contrary to his own beliefs. The claim that we must put reason aside and make a blind leap, trusting God without intellect and relying only upon correct doctrine to guide our ways, is an erroneous faith. It is not Kierkegaard's theology, his views are not so thinly stitched.

Kierkegaard's ideas were a reaction against the *over*-intellectualizing of Christianity by the theologians of medieval times, and by propaganda in his own "age of advertising." He claimed, rightly, that Christianity was more than "right thinking." The Christian mission is not expressed in proving God but in loving God. When the new minister challenges Johannes to "prove" that he is Jesus Christ, this challenge colors the minister as a man steeped in the language of modernity, yet thoroughly out of touch with the love of Christ.

The first and greatest commandment is to love God with all our heart, soul, mind, and strength. This is a love of our entire being, and

11. Kierkegaard, *The Present Age*, 33–36.

it is passionate. This pathos-filled love must not be a purely rational exercise—though reason is needed; nor should it be solely about accepting correct doctrines—though tradition and an historical memory are needed; and it certainly cannot be blind obedience to all the right rules—because conscience is essential. A conversion to Christ must be a conversion of our whole being: a complete spiritual, moral, corporal, *and* intellectual revolution that transforms our lives, because Jesus Christ is that radical. Christ's human life—his birth in a stable, his earthly ministry, his bloody death on the cross, and his physical resurrection—these are all bodily expressions of this passion-filled love.

What we see in *Ordet* is a wild swing from the life-weary pious (the Petersens) to the merely alive (the Borgens) to the corporeal life, death, and resurrection of Inger Borgen. Her life, like ours, is carnal and fully enfleshed; just as her death—in an agony that can be heard and closely felt, her baby cut to pieces—is carnal and fully enfleshed. Yet her bodily resurrection, which is after all what every Christian politely hopes for, must absolutely shock us with an insight that hurls us flailing back to God.

Redeemed by Christ in Hope

Those who abandon everything in order to seek God know well that He is the God of the poor . . . He is, above all, the God of those who can hope where there is no hope. The penitent thief who died with Christ was able to see God where the doctors of the law had just proved impossible Jesus's claim to divinity.[12]

—THOMAS MERTON

The Christian virtue of hope looks forward to our ultimate destiny. Hope is the second theological virtue which desires, above all, unity with God. There is no greater happiness than that union, yet we know by our own frailties and uncertainties and dejections that it is completely beyond our power to attain, and so we live in *longing* to be redeemed by Christ, and to be bought back from sin and alienation. We may crave riches, or power, or prestige—we may be captivated by those things that draw us away from God—but any fool knows that worldly goods will not bring lasting

12. Merton, *No Man is an Island*, 41.

joy. They rot and die as we will. Our true hope is in our one real happiness: unity with God. But because we are weak, and muddled, and struggling with faith, we may only reach for things we can see—those created pleasures that give us comfort. And while it is good to desire good things, they cannot fulfill our deepest longing, because they simply are not God.

Recall in *My Dinner with André,* that it was Wally who craved comfort and was content with mediocrity (a cold cup of coffee undefiled by a dead cockroach!) while it was André who longed for the sacramental and was ever restless. St. Augustine writes in his *Confessions:* "Because you have made us for yourself, our hearts are restless until they rest in you."[13] A restless heart is a good heart because it knows at the core of its being that it is not yet fulfilled. It hopes for the good, and then the Good.

That hope is the driving force in our next story and film, *Central Station.*

Central Station[14]

Central Station helps us to see how the prayers of the poor, who have only hope in hope, can work to rescue a despairing soul and an angry, lost, little boy.

Here we meet a retired school teacher, Dora, who supplements her meager pension by writing letters for illiterate people at the central train station in Rio de Janeiro. Her customers are an assorted mix of angry, frustrated, and broken people. We learn this from the letters they dictate. Dora may be educated, but she is no more impressive than her clients. She is bitter and selfish, an unattractive woman who never married. Though she charges her customers for postage, she only mails those letters that she deems worthy of the expense. The rest she either tears up or stuffs in her top drawer until she decides what to do about them; what her neighbor calls her *"purgatorio."*

On a routine day at the station, a woman and her nine year old son arrive at Dora's writing table. The mother had already dictated a scathing letter to the boy's father the day before, but now she has changed her mind and asks Dora to tear up that first note. She wants to have a new letter written and sent to the boy's absent dad. Our former school teacher

13. St. Augustine, *Confessions*, 21.

14. *Central Station,* directed by Walter Salles. Produced by Arthur Cohn, 1998. (Portuguese). Rated "R" for language, but it is very mild.

has little patience for the kid's unruly behavior and friction sparks quickly between them. But Dora writes the second letter for the woman, Aňa, who admits—woman to woman—that she secretly still loves the rascal. In her letter she asks if she might come to visit him, so the boy can finally meet his father. Dora is not impressed with the sentimental pining of the heart-sick Aňa, but she finishes the missive, is paid her fee, inserts a photo of the kid inside the folded pages, and adds it to her pile. Satisfied, the mother and her scowling child (who suspects the old lady is a cheat) leave the station.

Just as quickly, in the crowded city traffic, the boy's mother is struck and killed by a bus. The streets are so packed full of people that no one notices the orphaned boy. Officials will take care of the unfortunate woman and the people go on about their day. Dora pauses to gaze at the commotion in the street, learns of some traffic accident, and then packs up her letters and goes home.

For entertainment, she and her neighbor, Irene, giggle over the boastful stories they read in the day's letters. Dora reads Aňa's letter aloud, and is ready to tear it up as unworthy of the postage. Why unite a kind woman with some jerk who has abandoned her? He's obviously a drunkard who will only beat her and the kid. But Irene is touched, and she insists that Dora must send it off immediately so the family can be made whole again. Dora compromises and puts the woman's letter in her top drawer, her *purgatorio*, where it awaits some final judgment.

Meanwhile, the orphaned boy has nowhere to turn. His only connection in the city is the ugly, mean, old lady who has his absent father's letter, and on it his address. He stays and sleeps in the station until he can find her again. But when he does, she shoos him away, claiming to have already mailed the note. But this boy does not give up so easily. He doesn't know that his mother was killed in the accident. He presumes she will return for him once she recovers in the hospital. After days of waiting and harassing Dora for his father's letter, he finally learns that his mother will not return; that his mother is dead. Dora then offers to take the boy home with her, so he does not have to sleep in the train station and eat out of garbage cans. She does this, not out of generosity or pity, but because she has learned the boy is valuable to those who traffic in young children. So the orphan follows her home.

There he meets Dora's friend and neighbor, Irene. He introduces himself as Josué Fontenele de Paiva, and he takes to Irene because she is kind and pretty; and because Dora is neither. Then, while nosing about the apartment, Josué sees the drawer full of unsent letters, and recognizes his own photograph tucked in among the stash. It is true, she never mailed his mother's letter! Furious, he accuses Dora of lying to him. But she claims that she was just about to send it. He makes her "swear to promise" that she will never lie to him again, and she does, but it is a sworn promise she cannot keep.

The next morning she takes Josué across town and sells him to some shady characters for $2,000. Then she buys herself a new color TV and happily wheels it home. Dora never meant the boy any harm, nor did she imagine that he might be sold into the sex industry, or have his organs harvested by some medical black-market syndicate. She truly believes the story she was told, that he will be adopted by rich Americans, and that would be a far better fate for him than any government institution he might end up in in Brazil. When Irene learns what Dora has done she is horrified and she sounds the alarm, telling Dora that Josué is in great danger. Dora defends herself, claiming that the buyers were very good people. "There is a limit to everything, Dora," Irene chides her coldly.

The miserable, humid evening and her burning conscience keep Dora awake all night. Overcome with fear and remorse, she goes out first thing in the morning to retrieve the boy from the criminals' flat. Because she has already spent the money they paid her, she must steal Josué back from the furious villains. But she manages to trick them and then she and Josué escape in a taxi. But now what to do? Dora cannot go home, the mob will be looking for her there. So the two go to the bus station to embark on a thousand mile journey across Brazil to find the boy's father somewhere up north, "on another planet," "at the end of the world."

Hope is a constant virtue in our young hero, Josué. He has no doubt that they will find his father and that his father will love him. What he cannot tolerate, in his remarkable wisdom, is the bitter old woman who must accompany him. If he could travel alone he would, but he doesn't have the money and it's a long trip. He even asks Dora to give him the money so he can go on his own. Testing him, she hands him the bus ticket, and he boldly marches aboard. Thinking twice, she climbs onto the bus after him, flopping down in the seat beside him, but pulling the dividing armrest down so that their arms never touch! All she can think to do now is get this kid to his father somehow.

The bus trip reveals more of the hurt that has haunted Dora throughout her sad life. She buys a bottle of wine and drinks half of it, slurring her speech and telling the kid her story, all the while railing against the abuses of men. She calls one man on the bus a dirty name, giggles, and then complains to the boy about her own father who was a drunkard. He abandoned her mother, and her mother died shortly thereafter, "when I was your age," she says. Dora's life was not unlike Josué's life is now, only she clearly despises her old man. He was a train conductor, she tells Josué, but he got around pretty well on his own (meaning his infidelities). The boy listens, but he never follows her lead. He only speaks proudly of his own father, a man who abandoned him and his mother, a man he has never even met. Still, Josué boasts of his father's skills as a carpenter and he does not fail a fraction in his faith in him. (The father's name is Jesus, by the way, so you can guess where this might be going.)

When Dora finally passes out from the wine, Josué helps himself to the bottle and escapes to the back of the bus. There he entertains the passengers by drunkenly shouting out his paternal lineage to all of the weary, disgusted riders.

After this shameful event, Dora decides that she can go no further with the kid. She knows she is a bad influence on him, and so she tucks her remaining cash into the boy's backpack while he is sleeping, and instructs the bus driver to let the boy off at the right town. Then she leaves them at the next roadside stop and buys a ticket home to Rio.

While she waits, and after the north-bound bus has pulled away, she is horrified to see Josué sitting at a distant table by himself. What is worse, he has left his backpack on the bus along with all of her money! Now they are in a real crisis. Instead of being moved by the boy's desire to stay with her, she is furious that he has lost all of her cash. The bus to Rio has also just left, so there is nothing for them now but a wide, flat desert and a long, asphalt road. The ticket office gal isn't the least bit interested in their plight. They are both stuck and broke.

Everything Dora had hoped for, which was really very little, is now gone. If she hoped for a happy life, that ended a long time ago. If she wished only for a comfortable pension, a meager apartment, and a new color TV, those are lost, too. If she ever wanted to win Josué's affection, that chance has been blown to bits by her drunkenness and her impatient fury. The two linger in the café, hoping against hope, for some resolution.

Then a kindly truck driver shares his meal with the hungry pair, and offers them a lift in his truck. They eagerly climb aboard. Salvation at last! The driver is a Christian evangelist, devoted to Jesus, but something of a charlatan. He turns a blind eye when Dora and Josué both steal food from one of his clients; a store keeper he chummed up to as a great friend and fellow Christian. Still, they have to eat, and he giggles as he joins in the ill-gotten gains. For a while, anyway, times are good. When Josué says that he wants to be a truck driver when he grows up, Dora asks the driver to allow the boy to steer the big truck and blow the horn all along the highway. For a brief time, Dora experiences joy. They tell stories around a camp fire, and Dora speaks softly to the driver. They share a meal the next day, and then a beer, and then she takes his hands, her eyes shining for him; eyes that reveal all of the pain and lost trust and abandonment that she has known. Can this man maybe love her? Can he be her savior? Her father, her career, her friends, her retirement, her health, and this quarrelsome kid, have all failed her. So now, for the first time, Dora begins to reveal her vulnerability, and we do feel her pain! We didn't before, when she wore her mask of invincibility.

But hope in the things that the world has to offer is fleeting, and our hoped-for happy ending flees with it. True to form, the driver runs off—scared out of his wits—and he leaves Dora and Josué at some other roadside café, penniless and alone.

At least they are closer now to their destination, Bom Jesus do Norte. Dora pawns her wristwatch to purchase a ride from another truck driver who is transporting a band of dark skinned pilgrims to a holy celebration there. Crammed in on the flatbed with a dozen peasants, Josué accepts some beef jerky that a farmer shares, and he listens as the pilgrims sing holy hymns to the Virgin Mary of the Candlelight. He joins in the song, singing with them, because he knows the words that his mother had taught him. Josué is happy, without a care, knowing that he is going to his father.

When the two finally arrive at the house of Jesus de Paiva, the house that matches the address on the letter that Dora kept, they are stunned to learn that the family living there are no relation to Jesus. Jesus sold them this house long ago and then moved to "the new settlement," many miles further on, after winning a home there in some lottery. But Dora is also told, in a hushed whisper, that Jesus de Paiva lost everything he owned, including the new house, because of his drinking. Josué overhears this, and sullenly skulks away.

Now Dora is fading. Her heart is not strong and the stress is taking its toll. They trudge back to the pilgrimage site, to the shrine where night is falling and the crowds are swelling into a huge sea of human devotion. Dora has no love for this "godawful pilgrimage" and, panicking, she turns on the boy. "Hell, what did I ever do to God to deserve this?" she wails.

"You're a punishment! . . . Your parents should never have had you. Now it's me who has to put up with you. You're a curse, a curse!"

Josué bolts away from her and her wicked words and disappears into the crowd. Dora labors after him, calling his name and pushing through the throng of bodies and lit candles. Here are the prayerful, destitute pilgrims pleading to the Virgin Mary to hear their prayers, carrying torches and lighting firecrackers. Dora clamors into the shrine's vestibule where it is lighted wall-to-wall with waxy candles and dark icons. Even we can feel the sticky heat. Outside the pilgrims are shouting their prayers to God. What we hear: "I am praying with all my heart, with all my soul, Jesus!" "I am a Franciscan from the bottom of my heart, oh Jesus, bless my people!" "I suffer in my flesh, my bones, my blood; in my body, like our Lord, Jesus Christ." "Flood the darkness with light, Lord!" Dora staggers, perspiring, still calling for Josué. The icons blur and swim in the flames, Dora fights for air, the lights swirl, the chanting voices rise, a pinwheel explodes, and Dora collapses onto the concrete floor.

What the pinwheel reveals after its rockets die down is an icon of Our Lady of Perpetual Help; that is, the holy mother and child.

By morning the festivities are over. Dora is asleep in the dirt, her head resting on Josué's knee. He strokes her dark, stringy hair. Here is the holy icon juxtaposed, where the child consoles the wounded mother. The child is hopeful she will get better. He is hopeful she will love him. He is hopeful they will once again search for his father, Jesus. Now the story rolls over upon itself, and Dora opens her eyes. She awakens to the tender touch of this boy who has *not* abandoned her; this boy who is tougher than she could ever pretend to be; she awakens to an unknown grace and basks in its comfort.

At mid-morning the two drift through the abandoned fairgrounds that are strewn with confetti, the tattered remains of spent fireworks, and trash. There are still pilgrims wandering about, though the great devotion is over. The merchant booths are lively and active with fortune-tellers, icon sellers, and a man who will take your picture standing beside a cardboard cut-out of a saint. Then Josué gets an idea. He tells Dora to set up a table beside the photographer and starts hawking like a professional barker: "Letters! Send a letter home! A message to a saint! Only one buck!" Dora is flabbergasted at his brazen salesmanship, but she is also very impressed. The people wander over, then they get in line, and Dora starts writing.

Now we can hear the very heart—the very sanctified heart—of these poor people, the poorest of the poor. These are not the same missives we heard at the beginning of the film, those dictated by the illiterate citizens of Rio. No, there is no boasting or cursing or cheating demands made here. These letters are composed by the meek pilgrims who, owning absolutely nothing, speak only of gratitude. They do not ask the saint for a color TV, what good would it do them? Instead they send their letters as prayers of thanksgiving: "Thank you, Jesus, for answering my prayers, my husband has stopped drinking." "I am now the happiest man in the world!" "I walked all the way here . . . ." "I am fulfilling a vow . . . ." And the sweet farmer who removes his hat to dictate his prayer: "Thank you baby Jesus, for bringing us rain this year. I came to Bom Jesus to set off ten colored rockets in your honor."

"Hoopla!" Dora responds, scribbling.

With Dora's letters and Josué's enterprise, they take in a fistful of cash. They are rich! Now, with money to spare, they have their own pictures taken with the saint—two in fact, one for each of them—and then Josué buys Dora a blue dress as a gift. They stay at a hotel overnight, in a real bed, and in the morning they get ready to board the bus that will take them to the new settlement. But first Dora walks over to the post office to mail all of the letters. No more lies, no more thieving, no more *purgatorio*. Even if the letters are addressed to a saint in heaven, Dora will buy the proper postage and send them off.

When the two arrive at the new settlement, "the end of the world" as the ticket agent describes it, they discover that the father has indeed moved on. Now Josué's hopes fade, as the two stand among the rows of block houses wondering what to do. Dora has exhausted every possibility to help Josué, there is really nothing left for them but to start over. She elbows him playfully and asks if he would like to come live with her. She tells him that she would like it if he did. "I really would." Slowly he nods and agrees and they shake hands on it. This would be a nice ending, but it isn't quite.

Word has made its way around the projects that a woman and child are looking for Jesus de Paiva. A young man who has been working on a roof approaches them and introduces himself as Isáias, the son of Jesus. Josué shrinks behind Dora, suspicious of this older half-brother. But Isáias invites the two home where they meet Moisés, the other brother, at a house they have claimed as squatters. Moisés is a carpenter, like his father, and he shows Josué how to use the lathe, carving out a toy top for him.

The older boys then tell Dora that their father was a drinker and that he went off somewhere and has never returned. Isáias asks Dora if she might read a letter that their father had sent to Aňa, which made its slow way to them; a letter that they are both unable to read. Dora takes the envelope and reads the note aloud. In it we learn that their father, Jesus, was all the while looking for Aňa in Rio. He wrote to her, but his letters got lost or delayed in the mail. He asks her to wait for him in the new house, as he will be returning there soon.

How ironic that his letters got delayed in the mail! You can see it on Dora's face. Are they sitting in her top drawer, perhaps? Whether this tragedy was or was not the direct consequence of Dora's *purgatorio*, we do not know, but it doesn't really matter. Her disdain for the illiterate poor— those people who trusted her and paid her out of their meager funds—is a tremendous sin against them, and it has borne out its consequences. Her fun little letter-game took vicious advantage of the destitute, and—as we have seen in so many other films—these mean little sins often lead to catastrophe. Dora does share some responsibility for this broken family. This is subtly revealed in her expression now, and when she places the two lost envelopes together at last, beneath a portrait of Jesus and Aňa.

If we would be Christ to one another, then Christ can bring us together in love. But so long as we will not, Christ cannot. This is Dora's lesson in hope. What Josué longed for in steadfast faith he may soon win with his father's return. What Dora longs for, however, is only now taking shape.

In the morning, while the boys sleep, Dora sneaks away from the house to catch the first bus out of town. She knows that this is where Josué belongs, that his brothers are good and their father loving. She will return to Bom Jesus, and start her life over again from there. We can only trust that she will be set aright.

Josué, who really does love her, is shown running after her bus as it departs but he cannot keep up, and Dora does not see him. Calmly, she takes out her pen and paper and starts to write to him:

Josué,

I haven't sent a letter to anyone for a while, but I am sending you this one now. You were right. Your father will come back, and he surely is all you say he is. I remember riding with my father in his train. I was just a little girl, but he let me blow the whistle the whole time. When you're driving down the road in your big truck, remember that I was the first person to have you put your hand on the wheel.

It will be better for you to stay with your brothers. You deserve much more than I can give you. If you miss me one day, look at the picture we took together. I'm telling you this because you, too, may forget me.

I long for my father. I long for everything.

—Dora

Prayer is the desire for God . . . brought about by grace.[15]
—*ST. JOHN CHRYSOSTOM*

Central Station is clearly a film about hope. But if we think it is about Josué's strong hope that he will find his father, then we have been successfully distracted from the truer theme. As in *The Song of Bernadette,* the character who is steeped in virtue (be it faith or hope or love) is not the true subject of the story. These characters are fine on their own, they don't need a story to challenge them or grace to change them. It is the doubters who besiege Bernadette with their crippled, miserable doubt who need the redemptive act that good stories must rely on. They have the conflict to resolve. Theirs is the transformational tale. In the same way, the driving force in *Central Station* is not Josué's search for his father so much as it is Dora's hope for meaning in her life. It is her bitter, self-reliant *despair* that has been crushing her spirit to the point of death. Only when she has reached this threshold of despair is she able to hear the powerful prayers of the poor all around her and accept the outpouring of God's grace. Only now, through the healing virtue of hope, does she recognize the power of the child who never leaves her. These are the lights that ignite her transformation, like ten colored rockets for the baby Jesus, bursting into flame and launching her into the realm of a very tender redemption.

"Hoopla!"

The Lord is close to the brokenhearted
and saves those whose spirit is crushed.[16]

---

15. Chrysostom, *Homilies,* #6.

16. Ps 34:19.

Redeemed by Christ in Love

Love never fails.[17]

—ST. PAUL

We are redeemed by Christ in faith, hope, and love. In *Ordet*, we witnessed the astounding act of resurrection, wholly and bodily, through the faith of a little child and her fanatical uncle. In *Central Station*, we discovered the healing power of hope that is intrinsically tied to our yearning for God. Yet, of the theological virtues, love is the greatest of the three. In its ordinary way, love is also the central theme of most dramas. But in this context we are talking about divine love, *agape*,[18] the love of God, the love by God, and the Love that *is* God.

Agape is self-giving, and *agape* is the pinnacle of the Christian story of redemption. It cannot be divorced from the greatest commandment, which is to love God and love one another, and it cannot be taken down from the cross.

To my mind, this Christian, self-giving love is best expressed through three essential qualities: the heroic (the messianic rescue), the sacrificial (the price one pays), and the redemptive (the reparation and reunification of the beloved). Each one of these qualities is expressed in the life, death, and resurrection of Jesus; and each one is bound uniquely to the cross. The cross is heroic, it is the summation of every practiced virtue; it is sacrificial, as it gives every earthly value away; and it is redemptive, because it buys back from destruction—at a great price—those it will save. The cross is also poorly understood. We recall what St. Paul tells us: "the message of the cross is foolishness to those who are perishing, but to us who are being saved it is the power of God."[19]

On the theme of Christian love, let us now explore each of these three qualities individually, and through three illustrative films. As we endeavor to recognize what Christian love is, we might first consider what it most assuredly is not.

17. 1 Cor 13:8.

18. *Agape* is the Greek word for *caritas*, which is the Latin word we translate into *charity*. This is why the greatest virtue is often called charity.

19. 1 Cor 1:18.

The Heroic

Shane [20]

Shane is a thoroughly American film by every definition. It is a story about goodness and those values our culture most esteems: rugged individualism, family cohesion, and the struggle of good, working people against the fierce and the powerful. Set before a stunning—absolutely stunning—backdrop of the Rocky Mountains, *Shane* tells the story of a simple family who have settled a homestead in Wyoming cattle country. They farm a modest piece of ground, but their homes and crops stand in the way of the greedy cattlemen who want to dominate the wide range with their grazing herds. Though the story is unique in its historical setting, it is universal in its theme and mythic scope. What do good people want but to work and love and raise their families in peace? And yet it is the greed and sinfulness of others that interfere with their humble aims.

What is needed—as Jesus' own followers would insist—is a Messiah to rescue them from their oppressors. They need a hero, a prince, or a Superman, to fight their battles for them, because they cannot do it on their own. Like the men of the Phoenix, they try individually, and they fail, and they die. Then in rides Shane, the good, the noble, and the very able hero. He is adored by children, admired by women, respected by men, and despised by the greedy evildoers.

My point is not to stress that *Shane* is a cliché (although it is), my point is to show that *Shane* is universal; it is a man-made myth told a million times in a million different languages by as many different cultures. Shane is the virtuous hero. He has achieved excellence. He is the white-hatted good guy who is the champion of the downtrodden. Review the seven saving virtues and you might see how Shane embodies every single one of them, right down to that handshake with Miriam!

The homesteading farmer, Joe Starrett, is a decent man, hard-working, gentle, yet admittedly a little slow. Miriam, his good wife, is a loving spouse and a sweet mother to their son, Joey. But as a woman she is weak, and she is depicted in her feminine weakness. Secretly, she longs for Shane (which we might balk at, but it is there). Joey is a typical farm

---

20. *Shane*, directed by George Stevens. Produced by George Stevens, Paramount Pictures, 1953. Not rated. Suitable for all ages, with the usual violence of fist fights and gun slayings found in most Westerns of that era.

boy and the story is told through his innocent eyes so that we might see this well-worn fable afresh.

As for the homesteaders, they are so befuddled by the cattlemen's threats to their families and farms that they cannot form any kind of unity in response to their oppression. Every one of these many characters needs Shane. He must deliver them from their enemies. He is the only one good and able enough to do it. And if he has to die for them then, by gum, let him die for them! It has always been so. Prometheus stole fire from the gods and gave it to human kind, and he was eternally punished for it (bound to a rock to have his liver eaten out each day by an eagle sent from Zeus). Superman spun the world around backwards in order to reverse time and save humanity, even at great personal risk. Jesus died on the cross as the hoped-for Messiah of an oppressed Israel. And Shane shoots up a barroom full of bad guys to save the farmers' farms. No movie tells this simple story as beautifully as *Shane*. We crave its telling, again and again. "Come back, Shane!" "We love you, Shane!" "Father needs you! And Mother wants you, I know she does." "*Shane!!* Come back!"

Shane is uniquely American because the film promotes the values of our boot-strap lifting individualism, that frontier spirit, and the goodness of community—as well as its ineptness. It celebrates the child's faith in his upright hero and, let's face it, it celebrates the power of the gunman and his gun.

Yes, Shane is heroic. He risks his life to save the families. He forces his way into the place of the father, to fight the father's fight and to save him from certain death. Shane does this because he loves the child and his mother and the goodness of their humble lives. His truly is a sacrificial love; indeed, he may even die from his wounds, we just don't know. And Shane's sacrifice produces a good outcome: the homesteaders are liberated from their oppressors, the land is free to settle according to distributive justice, and the better people prosper.[21] Yet, while Shane is certainly a hero who makes an heroic sacrifice, this really is *not* Christian valor. He might be a very useful champion of courage, a crusader for a just cause, but he is a killer, too, and we should not forget that.

---

21. Of course you wouldn't want to look too deeply at the history of this American settlement, or you might see beneath the surface to where tens of thousands of murdered souls lie buried. That is the problem with delving too deeply into fables, they tend to float, not on purity, but on blood.

Shane is a folk hero, and that is fine, but we must not reduce the role of Christ to the status of a folk hero, one who saves our sorry selves from bad men and then rides off into the sunset. Jesus *failed* as a folk hero. Jesus failed as the champion of Israel on Israel's messianic terms. Jesus did not destroy the Roman oppressors as the Zealots had hoped. Instead, he forgave them. Jesus told his followers to love their enemies, and then he was crucified by those same foes, goaded on by the people he had come first to save. Jesus was, on the level of pure fable, an heroic letdown.

Our cultural virtues and values must sometimes be cut and turned like plowed earth before a single seed can be planted, and I mean to do this with *Shane.*

As Christians, we should not place our hope on the shoulders of great men, lest they shoot up a barroom to rescue us and call it justice. That kind of justice will destroy the world. Nor should we presume that our great saints will save us, while we hide behind locked doors and let them take up the labor of discipleship. *We* are all called to that work! Those homesteaders, with enough courage and a little compromise and with faith in one another, might well have corralled the cattle barons. This is what Joe Starrett encouraged them to do. Some chose to take on their oppressors alone, and we saw the result of their bravado with the death of the impetuous "Stonewall." If they had only listened to Joe, however, and persisted as a community against injustice—in *solidarity* with one another—they might well have succeeded in securing the land for their farms and families. Instead, they hid themselves or ran or relied upon the sacrifice of a Promethean hero, where gunplay and death soon followed.

This is not what Christ calls us to do. We are told to put our swords away. We are asked to take up our cross and stagger under the weight of God's unnerving plan. That is Christian heroics. Because without the cross and its demands, love is dead. Reverend Toller knew this, remember, in *First Reformed;* that is why he lashed out at his feminine admirer who only wanted to soothe him: "You are a stumbling block to me!" he shouted. Toller had a cross to bear, and he chose to carry it. This is just why Jesus rebuked Peter, saying: "Get behind me, Satan! You are a stumbling block to me, for you are not setting your mind on the things of God, but on the things of men."[22]

The lesson of *Shane* is just that. It is a fable of men, not God.

22. Matt 16:23. (WEB)

The Sacrificial

Shane knew that he might win in a gun battle against Wilson, the strongman who was hired by the cattle barons to intimidate the farmers. Shane was once a renowned gunslinger himself, and an excellent one. He also knew that he was riding into an ambush, but he accepted the danger for the sake of justice, and because of the love he felt for Joey's family. Like Tom Joad, Shane craved decency, and he fought for a noble cause. And while his sacrifice was heroic, it is not the heroic work of a Christian disciple. It is just decent in the usual and common ways of the world, but it falls short of Christian love, which does not go looking for a fight.

Still, every nation and tribe throughout history has had to rely upon its warriors to make a similar sacrifice. And we can understand why young people might heed their country's call and go off to war. There may be a hundred just causes and a hundred good reasons to join in war's grueling adventures. But I have to wonder, what would make a young man sacrifice his life in war when every worthy reason for it is removed? What drives him to go "over the top" when his sure death cannot be justified by any loyalty, or honor, or mission, or consequence, or hope for success?

Taking our queue from Juror #8 and his rational method of elimination in *Twelve Angry Men,* let us question every single motive for self-sacrifice that drives the heart of our next hero, Archy Hamilton, because only then will the truth drop like ripened fruit into our waiting hands.

Gallipoli [23]

Gallipoli tells the story of a young man living a cowboy life on his parents' ranch in Western Australia. Archy Hamilton is passionate about running and, encouraged by an adventurous uncle, he trains to compete in the local track races. His dream is to become the fastest sprinter in the country. At a nearby meet, Archy wins the sprinting competition and then answers the clarion call of the recruiters who have sponsored the event. They are looking for healthy young men to enlist and fight in Britain's war against Germany. Archy is eager to join up but, being underage, he is refused by the recruiting officer.

The next morning, Archy meets a suave but penniless competitor, Frank Dunne, who partakes in Archy's unfinished breakfast. The two hit

23. *Gallipoli,* directed by Peter Weir. Produced by Patricia Lovell and Robert Stigwood, 1981. Rated "PG" for mild war violence, but nothing very graphic.

it off and together they pal around the outback as they head for Perth, where Archy is sure he will be accepted into the Light Horse regiment. Frank has zero interest in joining the military. His Irish ancestry sparks little fervor for fighting on behalf of England, or in a war (WWI) that has no apparent purpose. He laughs at Archy's earnest patriotism that can't even explain his country's mission. Still, out of affection for his young pal and utter boredom at home, he reconsiders and decides to join the Light Horse along with Archy. However, while Archy proves himself to be an excellent horseman and is accepted into the regiment, Frank is a city kid who has never even saddled a horse. His comical trial on horseback sends him packing off to the infantry.

Most of the movie centers on the friendship of these two young men, and then the friendship Dunne forms with three other mates who march and carouse and practice the art of war in Egypt, where they are temporarily stationed. When Archy meets up with Frank again, during their war games in the Egyptian dunes, he is ecstatic and he requests a transfer to the infantry from the Light Horse so they can serve together.

Soon they are moved by ship to the Dardanelles and Gallipoli, a narrow channel that links the Black Sea to the Mediterranean. It is a strategic passageway and it is heavily guarded by enemy Turks. Because both of our heroes are sprinters, Archy and Frank are assigned the duty of messengers, running orders from headquarters to the dug-in trenches of an impossible cliff-side front. The Turks, entrenched above them with machine guns, can easily mow down anything that rises above the lower horizon. It is a total lockdown, but when the orders are given to attack, wave after wave of young ANZAC[24] soldiers leave their trenches and are butchered not five feet from the sandbags.

The question that must be asked here is "why?" The movie makes it perfectly clear that there are no real, actual, current, or imagined objectives. The mission is impossible. A man cannot climb a sandy cliff into the face of machine gun fire and survive. The casualties are enormous. And when the communication lines are broken, even the orders are conflicting and suspect. This battle—or for that matter the entire war—has no clear purpose. The British troops, who were presumably being protected by the ANZACs (who were used as a diversionary force) have already safely landed and are "sipping tea on the beach" of their objective. To attack now, to climb out of an entrenched sand pit and stagger up a vertical

24. Australian New Zealand Army Corps.

cliff against machine gun fire, is utterly pointless; and its pointlessness is thoroughly made. These soldiers know that there is no reason to leave their trenches and die. They know there is no advantage, no mission, and no possibility for success, yet the order is "go" and they go. Heroically, even the sergeant goes over the top, reckoning that "I can't ask my men to do what I won't do myself."

Death comes to each one of us. The readiness is all. It is a lesson we hear in *Hamlet*, and echoed again in *Never Let Me Go*, where the useful purpose of the clones' deaths is at least a reason for their sacrifice. In *Gallipoli*, even the utility of the soldiers' death is removed from the equation. There is no reason for them to die. So why do they go?

These actions must give us pause and force us to question the intentions of the human heart. What would you do? When all true meaning has been stripped from a command that orders you to die, would you still obey it? Why? What is the point? You are not fighting for your country, your country is a world away. It is not for a greater good because there is no greater good even imagined by this war. It is not for the mission of your platoon because that mission has already been accomplished. The order to go is clearly the result of broken communications between the soldiers at the front and the commanders at the rear. The soldiers who are prepared to die know this absolutely, and still they stumble to their deaths at the sound of the whistle. Not even the fastest runner can save them.

The only answer I can give to this question has already been revealed in every scene of this film. The soldiers went to their deaths out of love. Not out of a sense of duty or obedience or honor or apple pie. They went because the mate next to them was going, and because the mates in front of them had already gone, and out of love for their buddies they died. That is it. We are able to die out of love for one another, out of self-giving friendship, out of *caritas, agape*. This self-sacrificing love has no reasons. It is a human quality and a human triumph that transcends any rational purpose, because its source is grace and its destiny is God, is Love. Though it may take the absurdity of an absurd war to strip away all of the confusing motives that might otherwise justify that sacrifice, in the end we know that it is love that drove the soldiers to their deaths, and that it is *only* the love that triumphs.

The Redemptive

The necessity of redemption is a theme found in most religious faiths. It is common because guilt is common; and guilt is common because sin is universal. If there was no sin, even original sin, there would be no need for redemption. The mistake we often make, universally, is to point out and try to fix other people's sins. The true spiritual voyager reflects and seeks out redemption for his or her own failings.

Most of us are familiar with Christian redemption—though traditions do differ on the role Christ plays as Redeemer and regarding our own responsibilities as disciples—but I suspect few grasp the significance that other faiths place on the necessary act of redemption. It seems a little peculiar. When a faithful Muslim tells a lost young man that "there is a way to be good again," what are Christians to think? What is that foreign, non-Christian way to justification?

The Kite Runner [25]

Sin, penance, and redemption are the themes that carry *The Kite Runner* from Islam in Afghanistan to great acclaim in the Christian West. First a novel and then a motion picture, *The Kite Runner* tackles the theme of reparation after the great sin of betrayal.

It is the story of two boyhood friends of different life stations, living in Kabul, Afghanistan, in the 1970s. Amir is the son of a secular, wealthy businessman, a widower, living in good times before the Soviet invasion. Hassan is the son of their house servant, Farid. Hassan and Farid are Hazaras, an ethnic people considered racially inferior by the Afghanis.

The two boys are close in age and very close as friends, almost brothers, but it is not an equal friendship. Hassan adores Amir. He waits on him, tags after him, praises the stories Amir writes, and chases down his kites. Hassan also seems to possess uncanny insight, a mystical way of knowing that he has formed through prayer and true piety.

Amir loves being adored by Hassan, but Amir is a weak boy. He is shy, suspicious, fearful, and unable to stand up to the bullies who mock his friendship with that dirty little Hazara boy. Amir's father is disappointed in his bookish son. He admires Hassan, the servant boy, who is bold as well as humble, and he criticizes Amir's weakness. "A boy who

25. *The Kite Runner*, directed by Marc Forster. A Participant Productions Production, 2007. (Dari). Rated "PG 13" though there is a child-rape scene that is disturbing.

won't stand up for himself becomes a man who won't stand up for anything," he tells his best friend, Rahim. Amir overhears his father berate
him and is ashamed. It is Rahim who goes to comfort him and assure him
of his father's love.

Longing for his father's approval, Amir enters a kite battling contest
and wins against all the boys of his neighborhood. Hassan, who is Amir's
partner and strategist, rejoices with his young hero over the victory. The
crowd lifts Amir on to their shoulders and Amir's father cheers him from
his balcony. Hassan then offers to chase down the fluttering, conquered
kite as a trophy for his beloved pal. "For you, a thousand times over!" he
cries out to Amir, loping after the prize through the narrow alleyways.

Hassan does retrieve the kite, but he is quickly confronted by three
older boys, bullies who demand that he turn the kite over to them. But
Hassan will not give up Amir's trophy, so they beat him, and then their
leader assaults the boy in a brutal rape. Amir arrives in time to witness
the atrocity, but he is frozen in fear and then flees.

Life changes now. Neither boy speaks of the assault. The winning
kite is framed with great honor by his father, but it only reminds Amir
of his cowardice. He can no longer bear Hassan's affection. His very existence seems to fill Amir with shame. In an attempt to rid himself of his
guilt Amir decides to rid himself of Hassan. He does so by hiding his own
birthday gift, an expensive wristwatch, under Hassan's pillow and then
falsely accusing Hassan of the theft. Amir's father forgives Hassan, but the
servant boy and his humble father are so stunned by the false accusation
that they leave the household in tears.

Then the Soviets invade.

We fast-forward a dozen years. Amir and his father have fled Afghanistan and are living now in California. Amir has become a successful
writer, but he has not forgotten Hassan who must have endured tremendous suffering in their war-torn home. Hassan, the sacrificial goat to
Amir's treason. Hassan, the good servant, the defending friend, the pious
mystic, the slaughtered lamb. What has become of him in that devastated
country? While Amir can have his future and his safety bought for him
by a clever and wealthy father with the right bloodlines, Hassan has no
choice but to endure tragedy.

Amir's father works two jobs to put Amir through college, he min-
gles with the Afghani community in the Bay Area, and he finds Amir a
good wife to marry. But his joy does not last long, and he is stricken with
an illness—perhaps cancer—and dies.

After his death, Amir receives a phone call from Rahim Khan, his father's closest friend who is living in exile now in Pakistan. "Amir," he tells him, "come home. There is a way to be good again." Indeed? What is that way? It isn't revenge, because Amir is already a miserable man who loathes himself for his cowardice and his jealousy and his betrayal. He has spent ten years avenging himself on himself. He can't go back to Afghanistan, the Taliban would kill him. What can he possibly do to atone for his sins against Hassan? But the elder friend tells him to come and see him in Pakistan, because he is not well.

For the first time in his life Amir takes a risk. After his father's death, and with the loving support of his wife, he has learned something essential about the demands of love. Rahim is dying. Rahim always stood up for him. He will go.

So Amir travels to Pakistan to visit his dying friend. There he learns the wild and wonderful and terrible truth that Hassan was also his father's son; his own half-brother. His father had relations with his serving maid after his wife's death, and Hassan was their beloved offspring. Hassan later married and had a son, Sohrab, but Hassan and his wife were both murdered by the Taliban, and the boy is now in an orphanage somewhere near Kabul. Will Amir endanger his life to save the boy? Is that what it will take "to be good again?" Die for the other? Die out of obedience to this greatest love?

With the help of a driver arranged by Rahim, Amir ventures into Afghanistan. There he sees the destruction of his country, brought on by war with the Russians and the rise of the Taliban. Everything is in ruins. Armed, bearded thugs patrol the streets. The trees have all been cut down for firewood, and the women drift behind their escorts like shadows swathed in sheets. The half-time show at a soccer match is the stoning spectacle of a woman and man who were caught in an adulterous affair. It is absolutely appalling.

Amir learns of an orphanage where Sohrab may be living, and so he visits there. The man who cares for the children admits that he sells the children to the Taliban from time to time, to get enough money to feed the rest of the orphans. What else can he do? Amir's nephew, he is ashamed to say, has been sold into prostitution to the Taliban leaders.

Now, like Orpheus in Hades, or Doggie as Bodhisattva, Amir must descend into the depths of hell to rescue Sohrab. Hell, in this setting, is a Taliban camp. Its leader is the same bully who antagonized Amir when they were young, and who sodomized Hassan. This leader recognizes

Amir at once and, knowing that Amir is a coward, he begins to beat him unmercifully, claiming that it is the price he must pay for the boy. But Sohrab, like his father, is bold and skilled with a sling shot. He shoots his enemy in the face, taking out his eye, and giving him time to lead a bloodied and broken Amir out of the fortress and into their waiting car. They return to America together.

Sohrab is thoroughly traumatized by his ordeal, but Amir and his wife provide a tender and loving home for him in California. And though the boy does not warm to his new home quickly, we are given great hope for him in the final scene of the film.

It is a sunny day in the park, east of San Francisco Bay. Seeing kites aloft over the green waters, Amir buys a colorful kite from a vendor and eagerly goads a reluctant Sohrab into joining the fun. The boy shakes his head, not knowing what to do, so Amir pulls the kite aloft on his own and into the brisk winds. He hands the spool of string to Sohrab, and they are quickly challenged by another kiter who wants a dog-fight. Amir is ecstatic. He tells Sohrab about Hassan, the boy's wise father, and how he guided Amir to victory with his excellent battle strategies. The two kites swirl over the bay until the string of the enemy flyer is cut, and the dislodged victim flutters away.

Amir, as giddy as a child, cheers their victory. But Sohrab is bewildered, dazed, unsure of all the excitement, still holding loosely the spool of string.

"Do you want me to run that kite down for you?" Amir asks him breathlessly. The boy nods. Then Amir races off, joyfully loping over the hills to retrieve their prize, crying out: "For you, a thousand times over!"

This is redemption.

When we consider the three previous films individually, we can see how they illustrate three great qualities of human love: what is heroic (*Shane*), what is sacrificial (*Gallipoli*), and what is redemptive (*The Kite Runner*). Love has many more qualities, of course, and some of the other films we have studied here have given us a number of differing portraits; from the childlike, to the romantic, to the long-suffering and the reverential. Yet these three traits—the heroic, the sacrificial, and the redemptive—best express Christian love, I think, because Christ is all of these things, and perfectly so. There is something of the divine in these qualities, as Christ is divine; and there is something very human about them too, just as Christ is human. This is why, when we watch a non-Christian film that captures a significant truth about human love, it will not only move us, it will grip and rattle us with its power. The quality of human love, uplifted by grace and directed toward God, always shines through the darkness, even remotely, even on the silver screen.

The Absolute

Love—or *agape*, or *caritas*, or self-giving charity—is the greatest of the greatest virtues. We have just reflected upon three films that depict the extent and the limits of the human heart, as our heroes struggle to express the heroic, the sacrificial, and the redemptive qualities of love. This love, as a theological virtue, takes us beyond our own capacities. The *source* of this charity, remember, is God; and the *object* of this charity, remember, is God. And because God is love, love—as the greatest virtue of the greatest virtues—is an absolute good.

Our task as Christian disciples is to point to Christ, to imitate Christ, and to be Christ to the world. Through the course of this book, we have reviewed a number of great films that can help to form us in the ways of Christian discipleship. We have learned to discard our false self and embrace the true; we have rejected sin and exercised the virtues; we have prepared ourselves for the action of grace in our lives, learning that we receive this grace through the sacraments of the church as well as in our everyday encounters in the world; we have seen how our heroes struggle against their fallen natures and still allow themselves to be lifted up by grace, tested by suffering, thwarted by evil, and troubled by doubt; yet always and constantly redeemed by the actions and virtues of Christ.

My hope is that these films have helped guide us on our pilgrim's progress to Christian discipleship; and that our reflections on their themes might better prepare us to grasp who we are, what makes us strong, what lifts us up, what throws us down, and what speaks to us of an unimaginable destiny of love.

Jesus gave us two great commandments, to love God and to love our neighbor. Loving God, the absolute good, is an irrefutably good action. But to love our neighbor as we love ourselves? How does that manifest the virtue of love when the object of that love is the absolute goodness of God? This is not some secondary tenet, an afterthought that Jesus tagged on to his first most laudable command. Our Lord tells us that the second commandment is *like* the first, equal in importance, and just as essential. St. John makes it clear: "For whoever does not love his brother whom he has seen, cannot love God whom he has not seen."[26]

Now we must consider the double-nature of love's great commandment and find one last film that is worthy, in its depth and scope, to take on the magnitude of Christian love. It really does seem necessary to cap our study with one wholly epic, powerful, and stunning work of cinema in order to bring so many of our sacred themes to light. Fortunately, and by the grace of God, we have that *magnum opus* in *Schindler's List*.

Schindler's List[27]

"The list is an absolute good."

—ITZHAK STERN

What is an absolute good? God is an absolute good, surely, but can a list of people's *names* be absolutely good? The people themselves might be moderately good, but hardly *absolute*. The whole idea seems preposterous. We are not absolute people, we are particular people, each with an individual identity, a personal name, and a unique destiny.

Yet Thomas Merton tells us that there is, at the center of our being "a point of nothingness which is untouched by sin and by illusion, a point of pure truth, a point or spark which belongs entirely to God . . . This little point of nothingness and of absolute poverty is the pure glory of God in us."[28] If the first of the greatest commandments is to love God, and if the second is *like it*, to love our neighbor, then the object of those two loves must converge. And they do converge, like a sacrament, because we are particular in the outward sign of our lived lives, yet absolute in our deepest reality.

26. 1 John 4:20.

27. *Schindler's List*, directed by Steven Spielberg. A Steven Spielberg / Amblin Entertainment production, 1993. Rated "R" for violence, adult themes, and some sexual situations.

28. Merton, *Conjectures of a Guilty Bystander*, 146.

Oskar Schindler was a Nazi and a financial opportunist. He was too clever to be taken in by the racist ideologies of the Nazi party, and he held no suffocating loyalties; not to his country, his wife, his church, or his God. He was just a low-level entrepreneur, shrewd in his business dealings and willing to cooperate with an evil regime that helped him advance his bottom line. He had little regard for the law, civil or moral, especially when it interfered with his finances. Most of his previous schemes had failed him, but then he discovered the one crucial factor that had been missing from all of his earlier ventures, the greatest money-making business of them all, "war."

With masterful charm, Schindler ingratiates himself into the powerful Nazi elite. He spends exorbitant sums buying them gifts, celebrating their successes, having his picture taken with the high brass to barter influence with the wartime industrialists, and making a name for himself among these newest war lords.

After the Germans invade Poland, Schindler sets himself up as an enamel-works manufacturer in Krakow, making cookware for the German army. There he can hire three hundred Jewish laborers at slave wages (which is nothing) and go into production. He doesn't have the money to fund his factory and he doesn't want to do the work—that is for his Jewish staff to tend to—what Schindler does well is the marketing, the "presentation" as he calls it. And he makes a lot of money.

Oskar Schindler is married, but he is habitually unfaithful. He is Catholic, but he uses the darkened church interior only for his networking; as a hideout for secret, black-market dealings, and never for prayer. He is a patriot, but he doesn't risk his life soldiering in battle. Instead, he pins his patriotism onto his lapel—a Nazi swastika in gold—and contracts with the Nazi military for his industrial goods. They provide the perfect structure for his enterprise because armies always need cookware and because the Nazi's control the purse strings. As an amoral profiteer, he gleefully thrives in the lawless landscape of war, greed, and desperation.

What would it possibly take to shock such a man back to justice and the moral law? If his faith, his family, and his human decency can't turn him, what on earth will?

This is the central question of the film. It is also the theme posed for us in *My Dinner with André*. Wally, you may recall, in his dinner conversation with André, asks what it would take to awaken a bored and sleeping audience. André says he once proposed using a real, severed human head from the city morgue to pass through the audience during a production of Euripides' play, *The Bacchae*. He wanted the audience to experience the bloody events in the play as *real*. When the protagonist, Pentheus, is decapitated and torn to shreds by the women of Thebes—including his own mother—the audience ought to experience this horror as a genuine atrocity. André claims that only the theatre can rouse a catatonic populace, because modern humanity has fallen asleep to real reality. He hoped that the grotesque, severed head would get that point across.

Schindler's List does something quite like André's shocking proposal.

With painful and often graphic imagery, the film takes its audience through the experiences and the suffering of the Jewish Poles as they are first barricaded into ghettos, then corralled into concentration camps, then driven into death camps, and finally forced into the gas chambers. But it also leads us on a very human tour as well; one where the Jewish faces become known to us, and where their Jewish names are repeatedly named. We are meant to know these very real survivors of the Nazi genocide. Consider how often the use of lists is depicted in the film—by the Germans and by the Jews—and how often the Jewish names are read aloud. These names will be remembered; we are not meant to forget them.

For now, however, Oskar Schindler is only motivated by the free labor that his Polish Jews provide. Still, he does resent the interference of the occupying government when it tries to deport his laborers, or when a Nazi soldier playfully shoots and kills one of his workers—a one-armed old man—deeming him "twice as useless" to their war effort. Affronted by this vile action, Schindler lodges a formal complaint to the Nazi authorities, claiming that the old man was one of his skilled press operators, an "essential worker." But that sporting murder also upsets Schindler at a level we did not expect to find in him. It wounds him at the very heart of his humanity. It offends his latent sense of justice, and it cuts to the center core of his truer self.

Then there is another scene that we must not overlook. This is one of the few colorized moments in an otherwise black and white tour of horror; one that depicts the confused trauma of a lost little girl. The child wears a red coat. Though the color is muted, it does stand out. It is significant. The scene depicts the Nazis cleansing the ghetto of its occupants, and slaughtering with machine guns every Jewish family living there. The little girl, dazed, is looking around for an escape. Schindler watches her plight from the vantage of a high hill, looking down with alarm as the liquidation takes place. He follows the little girl's red coat as if he were seeing color for the very first time, while she wanders through the massacre. Schindler sees this appalling reality with newly shocked eyes. He is being awakened, not only to the general evil all around him, which he knew, but to the unique and *particular good* of that single, significant child, which he did not know. It is as if he were seeing the truth of war for the first time and in all of its horror. War is not some convenient and lucrative vehicle for his marketing portfolio, it is very real and very evil. The severed head has been tossed.

In a later scene, when the dead bodies from the ghetto are being exhumed, unearthed, and transported—only to be burned in the pyre of holocaust—Schindler spies a fragment of red cloth protruding from behind a stack of grey corpses. This dreadful image finally turns him completely. It is meant to. It is meant to turn us, too. It is so intentionally placed—that coat is the only colored thing in the film besides the candles that are lit in prayer—that we simply must regard it as absolutely essential to the story. Why that one little girl? Who is she? Does it even matter who she is? She is not a character we recognize from any other scene in the story. We have never seen her before. If she is a symbol, what does she stand for? If she is a representative, for whom? What is the consequence of her wandering, her suffering, her death, and her unearthing into the light of day? Why is she depicted in color, like the candles of the Shabbat? What grace hath wrought!

Oskar Schindler is changed by it. Though he maintains the persona of an efficient Nazi businessman, even to his closest Jewish staff, Schindler turns and devotes his war effort to rescuing every single worker in his factory from death. He flatters Göth, the German commandant who oversees the work camp, bribing him with payoffs as he begins to purchase back his workers, one by one. He will transport them all to Czechoslovakia and to a new munitions factory that he is establishing in his home town. Because they have been bought and paid for, he has Göth's assurance that the Nazis will not arrest them or interfere with his plans. His effort is costing him a fortune.

Schindler's Jewish accountant, Itzhak Stern (the brains behind Schindler's success) composes a list of the workers, typing in their names, one by one. The names are spoken, repeated, and visibly displayed by the tapping typewriter. With every pay-off another life is saved, until at last there are eleven hundred of them. These purchased people are known, comically to the Germans, as Schindler's Jews *(Schindlerjuden),* and the Nazis snicker at Oskar's extravagance. Oskar laughs, too. And though Göth suspects that Schindler is engaged in some illicit enterprise, he is willing to go along with it because he is making a lot of money himself. The Nazis suspect that Schindler is up to no good, but no one suspects that he is up to redemption.

Oskar Schindler spends every last dime he ever made in his industries to purchase back his workers from the death camps. In Czechoslovakia he sabotages his own munitions factory, telling Stern that he does not want a single artillery shell to fire. To complete his moral turn around, Oskar tells his wife—in church, no less—that no doorman will ever mistake her for his mistress again.

When the war is ended the Nazis flee their occupied lands, and Schindler and his wife must flee along with them. As they prepare their escape, Oskar laments that he did not manage to save more people. He confesses that he could have done more. Dressed in prison rags as camouflage, he grieves for that one last life he might have rescued if only he had sold his car, or hocked his gold Nazi pin. Itzhak Stern, our quieter hero, assures him that he did "so much." Eleven hundred people have their lives because of him, and so will their descendents. Then Stern presents Schindler with a gold ring on behalf of all the workers—gold that was melted down from the gold teeth offered by the *Schindlerjuden*—with this inscription from the Talmud: "Whoever saves one life saves the world entire."

What Schindler has done, risking his life to save his Jewish workers, has saved the world, entirely. This is the culmination of our own formative theme as Christian disciples: to *be* Christ to the world. Christ died for the redemption of humanity, a buy-back from death and non-being and decay. Oskar Schindler, though an opportunist and a rogue, had enough of the spark of God in him to be transformed by grace. Grace changes who he is. The great virtue of love has thoroughly turned him from a nameless war-monger into a legend for the age. Like the Roman centurion who only recognized the Son of God after he had been crucified in front of his own eyes, Schindler, as a witness to the holocaust and to the deepest real reality before his shocked eyes, can make the same audacious claim: here is Christ crucified, surely the Son of God.

Love demanded it, grace exposed it to his eyes, and he acted.

What love demands are eyes opened to see clearly the reality before us. What is real can seem overwhelming when it is presented in its entirety, as a generality, or as a utility. But the utility is nothing. The generality is nothing. The presentation is nothing. Only the truly real, those *particular* people who have faces and names (their outward sign) listed in the book of life, only their truth as the image of God (the underlying grace) is absolutely good; because we have been claimed by Christ, the Sacrament of God; because God is Love and Life and Truth, so that all who live—*in their particularity*—are holy, transparent, and lit-through with the Divine.

How magnificent, really, that a cinematic work of art can bring the absolute good into such a Light.

We are living in a world that is absolutely transparent, and God is shining through it all the time. This is not just a fable or a nice story, it is true. And this is something we are not able to see. But if we abandon ourselves to Him and forget ourselves we see it sometimes and we see it maybe frequently: that God manifests Himself everywhere, in everything—in people and in things and in nature and in events and so forth. So that it becomes very obvious that He is everywhere, He is in everything, and we cannot be without Him. You cannot be without God. It's impossible, it's just simply impossible.[29]

—*THOMAS MERTON*

29. Merton, *Essential Writings*, 67.

Discussion Questions

THE FOLLOWING REVIEW QUESTIONS are provided for your use with family and friends, in the classroom, on social media, or to promote discussion at a literary or movie club setting.

1. *My Dinner with André*

What is Wally's overriding concern in joining André for dinner?

What would he prefer to be doing?

Is Wally suffering for his art? How is that expressed? Or is Deby, perhaps, suffering for his art? What do you think?

Why is André so cheerful when he and Wally first meet, yet he says he feels terrible? Is this a ruse? Is he putting on an act?

What triggers Wally's first moment of self-reflection? How does he respond?

If André had never suggested that the theatre, Wally's beloved occupation, was failing the people, would Wally have ever cared about André's plight?

When André suggests that comfort is dangerous, how does Wally react? Has it become personal now?

What does André suggest his production team do to wake up his audience?

When does Wally experience this awakening? Or does he?

How does Wally's taxi-ride home show that Wally has changed in the way he perceives the world?

What role does "wonder" play in our religious perspective? Why do we lose that sense of wonder as we age? Can we regain it? How? Will we? How might that regained perspective be a dangerous undertaking?

2. *Death of a Salesman*

What are Willy Loman's values? List them. Cross off any that do not apply to you.

Does he ever achieve even one of these goods?

Who does Willy admire most?

How did his brother, Ben, achieve his riches? How is that significant?

What is Linda Loman's truth? How does she speak it?

What does Linda value most? What becomes of her most cherished values? Why?

What is Biff's truth?

Will Biff's self-knowledge ever make a change in him? How?

What does Biff value most?

What about Happy? Will Happy ever ponder any of these themes?

What does Happy continually promise his parents? Do you believe him? Is he happy?

What is happiness according to the standards of each character? List them.

Biff is a good man who is able to see his own failings, as well as his father's. Yet Willy is a weak man, who can accuse Biff of hateful spite and then praise him for his magnificence, all in the same breath. How does this dramatic, chaotic, duality express our human condition?

3. *All About Eve*

What does Margo Channing think of herself?

What does Margo fear most?

How does Eve ingratiate herself to Margo?

Why won't Margo listen to her friends?

Why does she doubt her fiancé?

Why does Margo berate her friendships?

How does Addison DeWitt ingratiate himself to Eve?

Does Margo's greatest fear come true?

What does that truth do to her, or for her?

What will become of Eve?

4. *The King of Masks*

How does Wang regard family and social traditions? How does this help/hinder him in his life?

What does justice mean? What is it?

How might the theme of *masks* interact with the identity of each character? How do the characters regard themselves?

Why do you think an effeminate opera singer, a man playing the operatic roles of women, accentuates the theme of masks and identity?

Why aren't little girls valued or wanted in this poverty-stricken culture?

Besides gender, what other masks are perpetuated by social norms? Are they good or are they corrupting? How would you determine their goodness or their tendency to corrupt?

How does Doggie save Wang from his imprisonment? What motivated her to attempt this dangerous stunt?

What Buddhist religious theme does her daring action imitate? What Christian theme?

5. *Anastasia*

What emotions or values or principles are driving Anna to go along with the fraudulent scheme, pretending to be Anastasia? Is she moral in this regard?

Why are the Russian exiles eager to have Anna crowned Grand Duchess Anastasia?

Why does General Bounine lose interest in the project and in the money he might receive? If it is because he loves Anna, then why not marry her and join the royal family as her royal consort, which would provide a great station in life and much wealth? Why does the couple flee?

If you only had this film to go on, would you believe that Anna was, indeed, Anastasia?

Why does the dowager empress dismiss the revelers at the end of the film, suggesting that Anna was actually a fraud?

6. *My Life as a Dog*

Why does Ingemar see his life "as a dog?" What happens to the dogs in his life and in his reflections? Does he fear the same thing will happen to him?

How does Ingemar deal with the great turmoil and grief in his life? Can you give examples from scenes in the film?

Why does Ingemar seem to fit comfortably in the odd little factory town? How many oddities can you find in the townsfolk? What are Ingemar's own oddities?

What events throw Ingemar into great anguish at the end of the film. What fear must he finally face?

Is he unwanted? Will he be abandoned, left to die, or be destroyed?

How does he come to realize that he is loved and cared for? What does the uncle do? His friends? The townsfolk?

How does love and nurturing guide a young person on the path to their true self? Why might this be so?

What is the "true self?"

7. *The Burmese Harp*

If you had to choose—as this Japanese platoon must choose—would you prefer to surrender and live, using your life to rebuild the country you love? Or would you presume that surrender dishonors the dead, and continue fighting to the death, as befits a noble calling?

What turns Mizushima from a dutiful soldier, following orders and volunteering to undertake a dangerous mission, to a pacifist monk who is horrified by war?

If Mizushima wants to go home, as he claims, how is it that his true self will not allow him to do what he wants most?

How has his true self been revealed to him? Is it by reason? Logic? Emotion? Or something else?

What is grace, and how/why is it given?

Does Mizushima have a special calling or vocation?

8. *House of Sand and Fog*

Each of the four main characters in this film are flawed in some tragic way. Identify the vices that afflict them, using a scene from the film to support your view.

How are the main characters victims of the sins of others, as well as perpetrators? Can you identify the sins that occurred before the events in the movie, that may have inflicted damage on these characters?

How is Esmail different from the four adult characters?

What does Esmail do to counteract the flaws he sees in his father? His mother? In Lester and Kathy?

How do the sins of the four main characters impact others? Are they able to see the consequences of their actions on the innocent people around them?

Why do things continue to get worse, not better, for everyone involved, directly or indirectly?

Are the consequences of sin a punishment by God? Why or why not?

Were the wrong choices made freely by the main characters? Could they have made a better choice? Explain.

Were there better options available to them? Identify the scenes where these better opportunities were presented but not taken.

How is the issue of freedom entangled with the workings of sin?

The imagery of birds is used throughout this film, in different scenes and under different circumstances. Are these depictions allegorical? If so, what do you think the bird images are attempting to show?

9. *Flight of the Phoenix*

What justification can you find for the survival of some of the unsavory characters?

If the good survive and the sinful die off, then why is the good doctor killed, and why does Sergeant Watson survive?

Captain Towns is proud and wrathful; but Dorfmann is also proud. What makes Dorfmann a more successful agent in their escape, compared to Towns?

How does Dorfmann justify drinking more than his share of the rationed water? Do you agree with his justification? How is it similar to Colonel Behrani's logic regarding Kathy Nicolo's irresponsibility and the county's incompetence?

Why is cooperation stronger than individual virtue?

Define solidarity as per church teaching.

Is a strong, good person more likely to lift up the weak; or is the weak, flawed person more likely to pull down the strong? How is this dilemma presented in the film? Can you identify those scenes that depict the weaker man shouldering more of the work; and the stronger man weakening and tearing down the work? Is this a valuable paradox, or is it just our experience in an absurd world?

10. *Captains Courageous*

How many vices can you attribute to young Harvey Cheyne? Describe the scene that depicts each.

What virtues does Harvey learn and put into practice? Describe each scene that portrays this learning.

Who are Harvey's instructors in the virtues? Manuel, surely, but can you identify any others? What do they teach?

How does the cohesion of the virtues work in Captains Courageous?

Compare the cooperative work of this crew with the castaways in *Flight of the Phoenix*. How do they differ? How are they the same?

Besides the circumstances, how is Manuel's death similar to Esmail's death? How is it dissimilar? What does Manuel's death achieve that Esmail's death does not? Why do you think that is?

Does nature or human failure factor into the death of Manuel? If both, what is nature's role in human suffering? What is the role of human failure?

Identify the Christian message in this film. How are the Christian virtues different or more developed than the pagan virtues?

Is Manuel a Christ figure? Explain.

Describe Harvey's new course and the changes his character has undergone. How will these changes impact his future life?

11. *Twelve Angry Men*

What reason does Juror #8 give for his first "not guilty" vote?

Are the other jurors attentive to their duty? Give examples of inattention.

Why didn't the defense lawyer examine the prosecutor's witnesses the way Juror #8 does?

What is justice? What does it mean to give to each his due? What is his or her due?

How does the virtue of prudence direct our due process or judicial system?

How does the re-enactment of the murder scene fill out or enflesh the testimony of the witnesses?

How does this enfleshed rendering expose the errors of those testimonies? Why might that be important?

12. '12'

What are the classic images of grace found in this film?

How does the Mother of God figure into the story? Who might have been the human agent of grace in the life of Juror #1? Why is that important?

Is the bird an angel, or the Holy Spirit, or an image of freedom, or just an annoying pest? Why does it defecate on the cabby's forehead?

What was the cabby doing when he was struck with the bird droppings? Why might that be important?

Is it pity, or is it justice, or is it mercy that is most prevalent in this story? Can you distinguish these concepts, one from the other?

What sets mercy apart from justice?

Why is the scene of the war zone repeated so often; what is its Christian message? Why the human arm? Is it just to repel us, or awaken us, like André's use of the severed head? Or is there an underlying Christian theme? What is sacred in Christian theology?

13. *A Man for All Seasons*

What is conscience? Why does the church put such great emphasis on conscience?

How does prudence guide the judgment of conscience?

How does prudence direct the moral judgments of Sir Thomas More?

What action does he take to preserve his integrity, his safety, and the safety of his family?

How does conscience uphold the rule of law in a just society?

Is the monarchal rule of King Henry VIII just?

How does individual conscience lay the foundation for democracy?

When Sir Thomas says the devil will turn once the laws are all made flat, what does he mean?

William Roper states that he is willing to destroy the law to get at the devil. Lester is also willing to corrupt the law in *House of Sand and Fog*. How is this attitude problematic? Where does it lead? Where did it take Lester?

14. *Roma*

How is Cleo depicted?

How do all of the other characters differ from Cleo?

If Cleo is an image of grace, how does that grace manifest itself?

How is it thrashed and betrayed in the story?

How is that grace salvific?

How does this feminine quality of grace imitate the redemptive action of Christ?

Can a land, or a culture, or a person be a bearer of grace?

What is grace? How is it made real?

15. *First Reformed*

Why was Michael unable to accept Toller's paradox of hope and despair?

Is Toller able to accept his own paradox?

Why does Toller react so strongly against the loving advances of the music director?

Why does Toller take on Michael's crusade to save the earth?

Compare Reverend Toller's failing health to the polluted earth. How are they similar? How are they different?

How does Mary intrude into Toller's life?

Is grace intrusive? Is it passive, active, direct, demurring, a whisper, or a shout? (Or all of the above?)

Is the leadership of the Abundant Life mega-church corrupt? Is this church mildly or seriously askew? Is it conducting business as usual and doing what it takes to survive, or is it gainfully cooperating with evil?

Does the venial sin of mundane inattentiveness seem more dangerous than blatant corruption? Why or why not?

How are we, ourselves, similar in the affairs of our own lives?

Why did Jesus say that you cannot serve God and money? Why are they incompatible?

What is our response to grace?

Has grace been offered to you in your life? Did you recognize it? Did it change you?

How are the sacraments fountains of grace?

16. *Ocean Heaven*

Why does the father want to kill his son? Does he believe in an afterlife?

How does Dafu express his feelings?

What is Dafu's relationship with the sea creatures?

What attracts him to the clown girl?

What associations can you make between the images that make up Dafu's world, and the feelings he has that he cannot express? Can you list them?

Does Dafu grieve for his dead mother? How is that shown?

Does he later grieve for his dead father?

Why does he go to the flower at the graveside?

Does the sea turtle represent eternal life?

What are the graces of baptism?

What are the gifts of the Holy Spirit?

How have they been active in your life?

17. *The Mission, Part I*

What is the point of penance?

What restitution does Rodrigo need to pay back? What does he need to restore?

Why did he choose to climb the waterfall with his weaponry in tow?

Whose forgiveness is he seeking?

Who imposed the penance?

Why does the one priest cut the rope and let Rodrigo's burden go? Why does Rodrigo retrieve it?

Do the indigenous people forgive Rodrigo? Why do you think so (or not)?

Does God forgive him? Why do you think so (or not)?

Does he forgive himself? Why do you think so (or not)?

How is the institutional church portrayed in this film?

How is the church as the People of God portrayed in this film?

How is the church as the Mystical Body of Christ portrayed in this film?

How do these qualities of the church differ? How are they alike?

Which characters embody each aspect of the church?

Are the missionaries saving the people? Are they contributing to their demise?

Is it a sin to enslave people?

17. *The Mission, Part II*

What is the role of the priest? How is that role portrayed in this film?

How is the sacramental action of Christ kept alive in this world?

How is Fr. Gabriel different from the other priests? When they defend the people with weapons, and he stays to die with the people, does this make him a coward?

What is the focus of Fr. Gabriel's procession? What does he carry aloft? Why is that so significant?

How does Fr. Gabriel's death, depicted through the eyes of Rodrigo, change Rodrigo, even in the few seconds he has left before he dies? Why do you think this is?

Does Rodrigo's last sigh reveal the condition of his soul?

18. *Babette's Feast*

The Incarnation sanctifies the human person, as Christ is both divine and human. Two natures, one person, in the unity of the Holy Trinity. How does *Babette's Feast* approach this mystery?

How does the French Catholic Babette regard the ascetic piety of these Lutheran elders?

Why do they regard good food, drink, sexual attraction, and pleasure in marriage as impediments to heaven?

How does Babette adapt to their austere spirituality?

Why does Babette spend her entire winnings on a feast for the sisters and their friends?

How is this feast akin to the Eucharistic meal?

Do the good, material things of the earth detract us from our right worship of God?

19. *Driving Miss Daisy*

Why is Hoke so patient with Miss Daisy? Is it just to get along and keep his job, or has he been taught that virtue?

What in Hoke's life has taught him the virtues of patience, humility, kindness, and fortitude?

Can suffering teach us good habits?

What are Miss Daisy's saving qualities?

Why does she get along with Idella, but not Hoke? She says that she and Idella "know how to stay out of each other's way." Isn't this a kind of segregation right inside her own home? Is it holy? Can it be? Do they ever form a friendship?

Hoke cannot stay out of Miss Daisy's way, his job requires him to carry her to her appointments. How does Miss Daisy eventually respond to Hoke's intrusion in her life? How does she grow?

What opens her eyes to racism? When does it get personal?

If Miss Daisy grows, how does Hoke grow? Does he need to? Or does he only need to endure?

Christ told us to serve one another. What problems can arise from this teaching when the serving people are also the oppressed, either because of race, age, gender, or class?

Hoke and Miss Daisy form a final Eucharistic friendship that is holy. One serves the other, with a shared will and a shared purpose. Do you have these kinds of friendship in your life?

20. *Becket*

What are the gifts of the Holy Spirit? These are given at baptism, and confirmation completes our baptism. How is this evident in the life of Thomas Becket, and in how he changes throughout the film?

Identify scenes that show Thomas questioning his destiny and purpose.

Is it grace that leads him, unwillingly, into the priesthood?

Even if it is a political stunt, how is God working within the context of his missteps and mistakes?

How does grace work within that context?

King Henry II expects loyalty, but at the price of truth and at the expense of the honor of God. Who wins?

How does this story foreshadow *A Man for All Seasons*? What are the similarities? The differences?

What prepares Archbishop Becket for martyrdom?

Is King Henry's penance real? Is it believable? Or is it just another political stunt?

Will King Henry change?

21. *Ryan's Daughter*

What is the purpose of marriage?

How does marriage imitate Christ's love for his church? How does it imitate God's covenant with Israel?

What is a sacrament of vocation?

Besides matrimony, what is the other sacrament of vocation?

How are they alike? How are they different?

Why did Tom Ryan betray his own people? What was the price of that betrayal?

Why does Rosy betray her marriage vows? What is the price of that betrayal?

Why do the villagers betray this couple? What vices and sins are at work in their lives?

How are these sins perpetuated by their living conditions? What perpetuates that disorder?

How is Charles an inattentive accomplice in Rosy's unfaithful behavior?

What is the role of Fr. Hugh in this drama?

Do his actions in running guns to the Irish rebels betray his priestly character? How are his actions different from the Jesuits' actions in *The Mission,* who defended the mission people with weaponry?

Do you think Rosy and Charles will stay together?

What gives you that hope (or doubt)?

22. *Shadowlands*

Does Dillard's paradoxical quote: "if you want to live, you have to die," remind you of Reverend Toller's paradox, that we live our lives between hope and despair?

Is suffering evil?

Why do we suffer at all? How does Lewis answer this monumental question?

Do you accept his (Joy's) answer, that it is just the way things are, that it is "the deal?"

Is this akin to accepting that suffering is a mystery we can't understand? Is it a satisfying answer?

Is Douglas lost? Why does Lewis allow Douglas to reject prayer and faith?

What does Lewis say about prayer?

How is prayer regarded, practiced, taught, and emphasized in this film?

Should we pray for *grace*? Should we pray for *healing*? Should we pray for a *miracle*?

How is the sacrament of the anointing of the sick a prayer for all of these things?

23. *Departures*

How is Daigo crippled in his ability to live his life?

Would you agree that the loss of his mother and the abandonment by his father have hindered Daigo's ability to take a risk, act with courage, live his life with fervor and meaning?

How does Mika enable his weaknesses?

How does his boss redirect him? What images are used to show this?

How does the virtue of reverence change Daigo?

How does the mastery of his art change him?

Is his job a true calling? A vocation? How can we know?

Does Daigo's last act of reverence for his father give us a sign that he has matured into a loving and forgiving son?

How is his art an honoring of death and a celebration of life?

Do you expect that he will now find the courage to live life without fear?

24. *Force Majeure*

Who would you save, really? Have you ever been in a similar situation? How did you react?

The courage to risk one's life to save another is a practiced virtue. What other virtues might be needed to overcome our tendency to preserve our own life first?

How does Tomas' confession change the other characters? Or does it?

Who among the six main characters is most admirable? Why?

When the family is separated on the ski slopes, who brings them back into cohesion? What might that mean, overall?

Is Mats as noble as he thinks he is? How does he change, or does he? What makes you think so?

Is Ebba always on the side of truth and righteousness? Why or why not?

When does she stumble?

Does Ebba ever realize that she might be wrong?

How is the splintering of this family depicted in their trek down the mountain? How are the family members positioned? What does their silence suggest?

25. *The Grapes of Wrath*

Can a society sin?

When does fear become a sin?

Why are the well-off so afraid of the migrants? What do they fear most? Is their fear justified?

Which characters are most attractive and admirable? Which are the least attractive?

What events or manners or words mark Casey as a Christ figure?

How is Ma Joad portrayed that might suggest her rock-solid role as the church?

How does Tom learn; is it by example, by preaching, by experience? All three? Give instances from the film that show Tom's maturation.

Who are Tom's teachers?

What avenue of hope is offered to these pilgrims? How is it depicted?

How is the Transcendentalist tradition exemplified in this film? How does it differ from Catholicism?

The novel ends on a very dark note, the movie on a high note. Why do you think that is?

26. *Jean de Florette*

Is Jean de Florette a skeptic or a believer?

What role does nature seem to play in this film?

Is nature completely indifferent to our struggles? How is Jean's concept of God portrayed?

Jean is a good man, but he suffers greatly and loses everything. What is the point of such a story?

Would this film be able to stand alone, without its sequel (Manon des Sources) to bring it full circle?

Are men like César and Ugolin believable in their cunning callousness?

Is Jean more believable in his goodness?

When your prayers are not answered, or when the answer is "no," does it jar your own faith?

Are prayers magical? What happens when the magic ends?

Jean does not pray for the grace to endure his trials, he prays for rain. When the rains don't come his frustrations overwhelm him. His faith abandons him. His actions grow desperate. And his desperation kills him. What does this say about the way we believe and pray and function in the world?

27. *Manon des Sources*

Is Ugolin a sympathetic character? Do you ever feel sorry for him?

What about César? When César says that "there is no such thing as fate!" what do you think he means?

How many instances of fated circumstances can you find in this film, or in *Jean de Florette*?

What is set above fate? What moved Manon to unblock the region's water supply?

What turns Manon's conscience to do this good act? Is it prudence? Is it mercy? Is it love?

How does conscience and human will override the happenstance of fate?

How is the church depicted in this film? Why? Is it because the church is foolish, or because the characters have such a low regard for the church? Or is it because superstition is an affront to true faith? What do you think?

When César is confronted with the truth, do the fates that he derided finally win their vengeance? Is that the point?

What about César's turn to confession and penance, is it real? Is it believable?

Is it possible that he finds salvation? Why do you think so? Or why not?

28. *Europa '51*

What marks saintly people as peculiar? As crazy? Can you name a few saints who were thought to be out of their minds?

How far can sanctity take us from our comfortable couches, our comfortable roles?

Would André Gregory approve of Irene's ministrations?

How does suffering trigger Irene's call to serve the poor?

How does Irene cross the lines of respectable behavior into a radical lifestyle?

How is sanctity radical?

Is the call to holiness a turn so sharp that we can properly call it radical?

How might we distinguish between the bizarre, crazy actions of a fanatic and the bizarre crazy actions of, say, a St. Francis or St. Thérèse?

Who proclaims the saints? Why does the church delegate or allow that proclamation to the laity?

29. *The Usual Suspects*

Is Keyser Söze real? Or is he a spook story? A figure meant to distract the investigators?

Have you ever experienced the devil as a personal presence? Do you believe the devil exists?

Do you believe in Jesus? Was Jesus being metaphorical when he spoke of Satan as real?

Was Keaton believable as Keyser? Did you believe that angle?

How many twists and turns can you count in this film?

Did any of Verbal's cohorts, besides Keaton, actually exist in reality? How do you know?

How is Keyser Söze different from the depiction of Satan in other demonically-themed films (such as *The Exorcist*)? Which is more frightening?

What does violence and cruelty reveal about the devil?

Why does violence against the human body—in shootings, threats, tortures, etc.—blaspheme Christ?

How is the sanctity of human life denigrated by violence of this kind?

Does evil in itself exit?

How does evil manifest itself in our lived experience? Where is it coming from?

What qualities or gifts are necessary to our human nature, yet still allow evil to enter the world?

30. *Fargo*

Is evil caused by human pathology, supernatural spirits, or the natural tendency toward decay?

St. Thomas says that evil is a void where the good ought to be; a kind of non-being. Does this seem plausible? How can we speak of non-being as existing? If we cannot, what is evil?

What seems to be missing in the criminal characters in *Fargo*? What is the good that ought to be there?

Who is most culpable for the evil done in this film? Is it the psychopath, the greedy idiot, the dishonest car salesman, or the oppressive father-in-law? Who freely chooses to do evil?

Why does Jerry Lundegaard contract to have his wife kidnapped? What does he really fear most?

How does Mike Yanagita trigger a revelation in Margie? What is it?

How is innocence depicted in this film? Does it have a holy quality, or does it just seem childish?

How does a place like Minnesota convey a sense of innocence?

31. *Au Revoir les Enfants*

Why does the civil law stray from God's law?

When a civil or social law is unjust, should it be followed? What does St. Augustine say regarding unjust laws? What should we do?

Why does Joseph trade with the school boys and the black market?

Why do the boys harass Joseph?

If they had been kind to him, would he have turned on them?

Why are the French boys so unruly? How might this give them an advantage in the resistance against the Nazi occupation? How is it a disadvantage?

Why does Père Jean single out Julien to befriend Jean Bonnet?

How is their adversarial friendship tested?

Why don't the French citizens, the clergy, and the students, respect Nazi law?

Is the Nazi law moral? Should it be opposed? What should the good people do?

32. *Never Let Me Go*

"The end justifies the means." How does this film challenge this moral precept?

What is utilitarianism?

Why might the church refute society's reliance on this ideology?

Can you give some examples of socially acceptable solutions to problems like disease, war, and personal morality from a utilitarian perspective?

Upon what does the church base her social morality?

The doctrine that we are made in the image of God and that Christ has sanctified humanity by the action of the Incarnation are the basis for our human dignity. From this basis we assert our human dignity, from which arise our human rights and liberty. How might this perspective address the moral conundrum found in *Never Let Me Go*?

Can an atheistic perspective assent to human dignity and human rights? When humanity is the highest good, would it not also follow that human dignity should be paramount?

Should human beings be used as commodities? What about as labor, when paid a meager wage? What about slavery? What about prostitution? Should an individual be allowed to sell his own kidney? How might these uses of our personal freedom conflict with social morality?

Why do the clones go so meekly to their deaths?

Are they human beings with immortal souls? Can their capacity to love, or their ability to express themselves through art, prove that they have souls? Why would art prove such a thing?

Does a fetus have human rights? Does a vegetative, comatose individual? A frozen embryo? With conjoined twins, when one twin's brain is deteriorating, who should be saved?

33. *Fireworks Wednesday*

Which of the warring spouses seems most believable at the beginning of the film?

Does the husband, Morteza, ever gain your sympathies? When and why?

Does Rouhi seem to be meddling in dangerous territory? Do you ever fear for her safety?

When do your suspicions turn to the beautician? Do you believe her? Why?

When Morteza strikes his wife in the street, how do your sympathies shift?

Does Rouhi seem to be following some process of doubt, the way Juror #8 does in *Twelve Angry Men*, for example? Is she rational, prudent, wise, cunning, or is she too easily swayed by the changing circumstances? Why is that important?

When circumstances change it is natural for our judgments to change as well. Is this wisdom? What quality or characteristic or virtue directs the will when there is chaos all about?

Do you have hope that this marriage will be saved? Why or why not?

34. *Song of Bernadette*

Compare this film to Europe `51. How do they touch on the similar themes of sanctity and sanity?

Who is the first person (or people) to believe in Bernadette? Why?

Who are the many who do not believe her story?

Why does the priest even doubt her?

Are the religious sisters correct to doubt and exercise caution?

Why do some believe for the sake of their own gain? Who are they? Are they worse than those who doubt because they cannot assent to such a miracle?

Why won't the imperial prosecutor submit his cancer to the miraculous waters?

What is the message of Lourdes?

Does this film capture the sanctity of St. Bernadette? How does it do this?

Is belief the same thing as faith? How might they differ?

35. *Ordet*

What causes Mikkel to lose his faith? What makes Inger so steadfast in hers?

What causes Johannes to lose his wits? Is it only Kierkegaard, or something more?

What causes Anders so much turmoil? Does he care about the differences in the two families' faith traditions?

Why has Morton lost his joy? Why can't he pray?

Is Peter Petersen correct when he senses that Morton has lost God?

What happens to the church when it will not tolerate questioning or new ideas?

How large is Peter's congregation?

How is the faith of Johannes a testament to the great emphasis on faith that is found in the Protestant traditions?

How are the doctor and the reverend alike?

Do you believe in miracles?

How is this ultimately Inger's story?

Why is "life" repeated so often in the last scene?

What is the quality of faith as a virtue?

36. *Central Station*

What is the tone and the content of the letters dictated at the Rio train station?

How do the letters differ from the ones dictated by the poor pilgrims in Bom Jesus do Norte?

What might this difference mean?

How does Josué change, if at all, over the course of the journey?

Why does he admire Irene, preferring her over Dora? Is he being fair?

What meaning can you draw from the way Josué proclaims his many names and patrimony?

How does Dora change over the course of the journey?

What is Dora's most painful life experience? How does that impact her entire life?

Why does the truck driver abandon her?

What event or experience in her travels impacts Dora the most? How does it change her for the good?

Why did Josué's father leave his family on so many occasions? Is he working, drinking, searching for Aña? What gives you hope that he will return?

What gives you hope that Dora will find salvation?

When she writes to Josué, saying: "I long for my father. I long for everything," how is her father and "everything" interconnected? Does this echo St. Augustine's restless heart? Explain.

What is the quality of hope as a virtue?

37. *Shane*

Is Shane a Christ figure or a messiah figure? What is the difference?

Is Shane willing to die for the homesteaders?

Why didn't he let Joe fight his own battles?

What about the townsfolk, are they noble characters? Why or why not?

What virtues do they seem to lack?

The families are good people, but is their goodness enough? Who or what do they need?

Compare Shane to Jim Casey in *The Grapes of Wrath*. How are they similar in their roles? How different? How is Tom Joad like or unlike Shane?

Why should we not look to the hero to save us?

If the townsfolk had found common ground and purpose, could they have won out over the cattlemen? What would it take?

Contrast the difference between democracy and authoritarian monarchy. Now contrast the difference between the rule of law and despotic rule. How is the conflict of the townsfolk against the cattlemen similar to these ideological differences? What would St. Thomas More do? What would Jesus do?

Shane lived by the gun and will likely die by the gun. What lesson is learned here?

How is this film quintessentially American in its mythic imagery and lore?

38. *Gallipoli*

Why was World War I fought? What was its objective?

What was the objective of the British military at Gallipoli?

When did the British obtain their objective?

What did the British think of the Aussie soldiers? How were the Australian troops used?

Why was Archy eager to join the war effort in Europe? What were his motives?

Did Archy's uncle's stories instill in him a sense of adventure?

Why did Frank join up? What were his motives?

How is love expressed by these men?

List as many expressions of friendship and love as you can from the scenes in this film.

Why did the soldiers go over the top to certain death when all of the usual motives were stripped away?

Was it still their duty to go? Why?

Do you agree it was out of love?

Does this make their deaths any less tragic?

Is sacrificial love, with no good outcome, still holy and good?

39. *The Kite Runner*

Why does Amir believe his father does not love him?

How does his father show his disdain for Amir's gentle character? Does he ever reject him, or is that only Amir's impression?

Why is Amir so afraid of the bullies and unable to fight them? Why is Hassan unafraid?

What words of comfort does Rahim (his father's best friend) give to Amir? Do they help?

Why does Amir like to write stories? Who loves these stories the most? Why can't Hassan read?

Why does Amir enter the kite fighting contest?

How does the brutal rape of Hassan destroy the friendship between the two boys?

Why does Amir turn on Hassan?

Are Amir and his father devout Muslims? How does his father express his disdain for Amir's fundamental Islamic teachers?

Is Amir's father brave? How is his bravery portrayed? What impact does his father's example of courage have on Amir? Does he learn from his example? From his death?

Why does the grown Amir return to the Middle East?

What inspires his new found courage?

Why is there a theme of redemption in a film about Islamic morality?

Is there an action of grace in this film? What is it?

Could this have been a Christian story? How might it have been differently portrayed?

When do we see Amir at prayer? How is this similar to Behrani's desperate prayer?

What does the word "Islam" mean?

40. *Schindler's List*

Give five attributes that illustrate Oskar Schindler's vices. How are his vices overcome?

Can you find five corresponding virtues?

When does grace enter into Schindler's life? How is it depicted?

Who is the brains and strength behind Schindler's enterprise?

How does war augment his successes?

How do the victims of that same war achieve success for him?

How often are names and lists referenced in this film? Why are names so important? Is it just a form of remembrance?

What is it that is holy about a person's name?

Who is the girl in the red coat? Does she have a name? Why not?

Why are the Shabbat candles in color? What is the interconnection of the two colorized images?

How is God shining throughout this film?

What kind of terror rose in your heart when the Nazi shrieked with joy and horror, as he trampled on the mass of dead corpses? What kind of diabolical paradox is that?

Why is the particularity of human life sanctified?

How does God manifest his love in the world?

Is it possible that a human portrait is also a *spiritual* painting? Explain, using themes from *Schindler's List* and the sacramental theology that you have learned.

Bibliography

New American Bible. Iowa Falls, Iowa: World Bible, 1987.

Catechism of the Catholic Church. New York: Image; Doubleday, 1995.

Augustine, Saint. *Confessions.* Middlesex: Penguin, 1961.

Benedict XVI, Pope Emeritus. "In Truth, Peace." Presented on the 39th World Day of Peace, Rome: 2006. http://www.vatican.va/content/benedict-xvi/en/messages/peace/documents/hf_ben-xvi_mes_20051213_xxxix-world-day-peace.html.

Chrysostom, St. John., *On Wealth and Poverty.* New York: St. Vladimir's Seminary Press, 1984.

———. "Prayer is the Light of the Soul." Rome: Pontifical University of Saint Thomas Aquinas.

———. *Sentences.* Independently published, 2019.

Clark, Mary T., ed. *An Aquinas Reader, Selections from the Writings of Thomas Aquinas.* New York: Image; Doubleday, 1972.

Dillard, Annie. *Pilgrim at Tinker Creek.* New York: Harper and Row, 1974.

Flannery, Austin, OP., ed. *Vatican Council II: The Conciliar and Post Conciliar Documents.* Indiana: Liturgical Press, 1975.

Gustafson, Hans. "Collapsing the Sacred and the Profane: Pan-Sacramental & Panentheistic Possibilities in Aquinas and Their Implications for Spirituality." *The Heythrop Journal,* HeyJ (2011) 1–14. DOI: *10.1111/j.1468–2265.2011.00684.x.*

Hamilton, Edith and Huntington Cairns, eds. "The Republic." In *The Collected Dialogues of Plato.* New Jersey: Princeton University Press, 1961.

Hopkins, Gerard Manley. *Poems of Gerard Manley Hopkins.* Edited by Robert Bridges. London: Humphrey Milford, XCVIII.

Kierkegaard, Søren. "Two Ages: A Literary Review." In *The Present Age and the Difference Between a Genius and an Apostle.* Trans. Alexander Dru. New York: Harper Torchbooks, 1940.

Mattison, William C. *Introducing Moral Theology: True Happiness and the Virtues.* Grand Rapids: Brazos, 2008.

McElroy, Robert W. *The Search for an American Public Theology.* New Jersey: Paulist Press, 1989.

Merton, Thomas. *Conjectures of a Guilty Bystander.* New York: Doubleday, 1966.

———. *Essential Writings,* selected and edited by Christine M. Bochen. Matrix: Modern Spiritual Masters Series. New York: Orbis, 2000.

———. "Hagia Sophia." In *Emblems of a Season of Fury.* New York: New Directions, 1961.

———. *The Inner Experience*. San Francisco: Harper, 2004.

———. *New Seeds of Contemplation*. New York: New Directions, 1961.

———. *No Man is an Island*. New York: Dell, 1955.

———. *The Sign of Jonas*. New York: Harcourt, Brace, 1956.

———. *A Thomas Merton Reader*, edited by Thomas P. McDonnell. New York: Image, Doubleday, 1974.

O'Connor, Flannery. *Mystery and Manners, Occasional Prose, selected and edited by Sally and Robert Fitzgerald*. New York: Farrar, Straus and Giroux, 1957.

Pegis, Anton C., ed. *The Basic Writings of St. Thomas Aquinas*. New York: Random House, 1945.

Pieper, Joseph. *The Four Cardinal Virtues*. Indiana: University of Notre Dame, 1966.

Ratzinger, Joseph Cardinal (Pope Emeritus Benedict XVI). "Conscience and Truth." Presented at the 10th Workshop for Bishops. Dallas: 1991. http://www.yumpu.com/en/document/read/42290046/joseph-ratzinger-conscience-and-truth-communio-37–2010.

Film Bibliography

Aldrich, Robert, director. *Flight of the Phoenix*. An Associates and Aldrich Production, 1965.

Attenborough, Richard, director. *Shadowlands*. Produced by Richard Attenborough, 1993.

Axer, Gabriel, director. *Babette's Feast*. A Nordisk Film Production, 1987.

Beresford, Bruce, director. *Driving Miss Daisy*. A Zanuck Company Production, 1989.

Berri, Claude, director. *Jean de Florette*. A Pierre Grunstein, Alain Poiré Production, 1986.

Berri, Claude, director. *Manon des Sources*. A Pierre Grunstein, Alain Poiré Production, 1986.

Coen, Joel and Ethan, directors. *Fargo*. A PolyGram Filmed Entertainment Production, 1996.

Cuarón, Alfonso, director. *Roma*. Produced by Alfonso Cuarón, Gabriela Rodriguez, and Nicolás Celis; Netflix, 2018.

Dreyer, Carl Theodor, director. *Ordet*. Produced by Carl Theodor Dreyer, 1955.

Farhadi, Asghar, director. *Fireworks Wednesday*. Produced by Jamal Saadatian, 2006.

Fleming, Victor, director. *Captains Courageous*. A Metro-Goldwyn-Mayer Production, 1937.

Ford, John, director. *The Grapes of Wrath*. A Darryl F. Zamuck Production, 1940.

Forster, Marc, director. *The Kite Runner*. A Participant Productions Production, 2007.

Glenville, Peter, director. 1964. *Becket*. A Hal Wallis Production, 1964.

Hallström, Lasse, director. *My Life as a Dog*. A Waldemar Bergendahl Production, 1985.

Ichikawa, Kon, director. *The Burmese Harp*. Produced by Masayuki Takagi, Nikkatsu Corporation, 1956.

Joffé, Roland, director. *The Mission*. A Goldcrest Films Production, 1986.

King, Henry, director. *Song of Bernadette*. Produced by William Perlberg, 1943.

Lean, David, director. *Ryan's Daughter*. A Faraway Production, 1970.

Litvak, Anatole, director. *Anastasia*. A 20th Century Fox Production, 1956.

Lumet, Sidney, director. *Twelve Angry Men*. An Orion-Nova Production, 1957.

Malle, Louis, director. *Au Revoir Les Enfants*. A Louis Malle Production, 1987.

Malle, Louis, director. *My Dinner With André*. A George W. George Production, 1981.

Mankiewicz, Joseph, director. *All About Eve*. A Daryl Zanuck Production, 1950.

Mikhalkov, Nikita, director. '*12*'. Three T Productions, 2007.

Östlund, Ruben, director. *Force Majeure*. A Beofilm Production, 2014.

Perelman, Vadim, director. *House of Sand and Fog*. Bisgrove Entertainment, Cobalt Media Group Production, 2003.

Romanek, Mark, director. *Never Let Me Go*. A DNA Films Production.

Rossellini, Roberto, director. *Europe '51*. A Roberto Rossellini Production.

Salles, Walter, director. *Central Station*. Produced by Arthur Cohn, 1998.

Schlondorff, Volker, director. *Death of a Salesman*. H. M. Television Company. A Roxbury and Punch Production of Arthur Miller's play (an adaptation), 1985.

Schrader, Paul, director. *First Reformed*. A Killer Films Production, 2017.

Singer, Bryan, director. *The Usual Suspects*. A Bad Hat Harry Production, 1995.

Spielberg, Steven, director. *Schindler's List*. A Steven Spielberg / Amblin Entertainment Production, 1993.

Stevens, George, director. *Shane*. Produced by George Stevens, Paramount Pictures, 1953.

Takita, Yōjirō, director. *Departures*. A Tokyo Broadcasting System Production, 2008.

Tianming, Wu, director. *The King of Masks*. Samuel Goldwyn Film, a Shaw Brothers (H. K.) Production, 1996.

Weir, Peter, director. *Gallipoli*. Produced by Patricia Lovell and Robert Stigwood, 1981.

Xue, Xiao Lu, director. *Ocean Heaven*. A William Kong Production, 2010.

Zinnermann, Fred, director. *A Man for All Seasons*. A Fred Zinnermann Production, 1966.

Printed in the USA
CPSIA information can be obtained
at www.ICGtesting.com
LVHW011344250124
769841LV00033B/26

STARGAZING
2007

MONTH-BY-MONTH GUIDE TO THE NORTHERN NIGHT SKY

HEATHER COUPER & NIGEL HENBEST

HEATHER COUPER and NIGEL HENBEST are inter-nationally recognized writers and broadcasters on astronomy, space and science. They have written more than 30 books and over 1000 articles and are the founders of an independent TV production company, specializing in factual and scientific programming.

Heather is a past President of both the British Astronomical Association and the Society for Popular Astronomy. She is a Fellow of the Royal Astronomical Society, a Fellow of the Institute of Physics and a Millennium Commissioner. Nigel has been Astronomy Consultant to New Scientist magazine, Editor of the Journal of the British Astronomical Association, and Media Consultant to the Royal Greenwich Observatory.

ACKNOWLEDGEMENTS

All star maps by Wil Tirion/Philip's, with extra annotation by Philip's.
Artworks © Philip's.
All photographs from Galaxy.
8 Michael Stecker
12 Dave Tyler
17 Paul Andrews
20, 32, 40, 44, 52 Robin Scagell
24, 48 Nick King
28 David Cortner
37 Michael Maunder

Published in Great Britain in 2006
by Philip's, a division of Octopus Publishing Group Ltd,
2–4 Heron Quays, London E14 4JP

Text: Heather Couper & Nigel Henbest (pp. 6–53)
Robin Scagell (pp. 61–64)
Philip's (pp. 1–5, 54–60)

ISBN-13 978-0-540-08941-3
ISBN-10 0-540-08941-9

Printed in China

Details of other Philip's titles and services can be found on our website at: **www.philips-maps.co.uk**

Title page: Whirlpool Galaxy M51 (Nick King/Galaxy)

CONTENTS

The sight of diamond-bright stars sparkling against a sky of black velvet is one of life's most glorious experiences. No wonder stargazing is so popular. Learning your way around the night sky requires nothing more than patience, a reasonably clear sky and the 12 star charts included in this book.

Stargazing 2007 is a guide to the sky for every month of the year. Complete beginners will find it an essential night-time companion, while seasoned amateur astronomers will find the updates invaluable.

THE MONTHLY CHARTS

Each pair of monthly charts shows the views of the heavens looking north and south. They're useable throughout most of Europe – between 40 and 60 degrees north. Only the brightest stars are shown (otherwise we would have had to put 3000 stars on each chart, instead of about 200). This means that we plot stars down to 3rd magnitude, with a few 4th-magnitude stars to complete distinctive patterns. We also show the ecliptic, which is the apparent path of the Sun in the sky.

USING THE STAR CHARTS

To use the charts, begin by locating the north pole star – Polaris – by using the stars of the Plough (see March). When you are looking at Polaris you are facing north, with west on your left and east on your right. (West and east are reversed on star charts because they show the view looking up into the sky instead of down towards the ground.) The left-hand chart then shows the view you have to the north. Most of the stars you see will be circumpolar, which means that they're visible all year. The other stars rise in the east and set in the west.

Now turn and face the opposite direction, south. This is the view that changes most during the course of the year. Leo, with its prominent 'Sickle' formation, is high in the spring skies. Summer is dominated by the bright trio of Vega, Deneb and Altair. Autumn's familiar marker is the Square of Pegasus, while the winter sky is ruled over by the stars of Orion.

The charts show the sky as it appears in the late evening for each month; the exact times are noted in the caption with the chart. If you are observing in the early morning you will find that the view is different. As a rule of thumb, if you are observing two hours later than the time suggested in the caption, then the following month's map will more accurately represent the stars on view. So, if you wish to observe at midnight in the middle of February, two hours later than the time suggested in the caption, then the stars will appear as they are on March's chart. When using a chart for the 'wrong' month, however, bear in mind that the planets and Moon will not be shown in their correct positions.

THE MOON, PLANETS AND SPECIAL EVENTS

In addition to the stars visible each month, the charts show the positions of any planets on view in the late evening. Other planets may also be visible that month, but they won't be on the chart if they have already set, or if they do not rise until early morning. Their positions are described in the text, so that you can find them if you are observing at other times.

We've also plotted the path of the Moon. Its position is marked at three-day intervals. The dates when it reaches First Quarter, Full Moon, Last Quarter and New Moon are given in the text. If there is a meteor shower in the month we mark the position from which the meteors appear to emanate – the *radiant*. More information on observing the planets and other Solar System objects is given on pages 54–57.

Once you have identified the constellations and found the planets, you'll want to know more about what's on view. Each month, we explain one object, such as a particularly interesting star or galaxy, in detail. We have also chosen a spectacular image for each month and described how it was captured. All these pictures were taken by amateur astronomers. We list details and dates of special events, such as meteor showers or eclipses, and give observing tips. Finally, each month we pick a topic related to what's on view, ranging from lunar eclipses to light pollution and space missions, and discuss it in more detail. Where possible, all relevant objects are highlighted on the maps.

FURTHER INFORMATION

The year's star charts form the heart of the book, providing material for many enjoyable observing sessions. For background information turn to pages 54–57, where diagrams help to explain, among other things, the movement of the planets and why we see eclipses.

Although there's plenty to see with the naked eye, many observers use binoculars or telescopes, and some choose to record their observations using cameras, CCDs or webcams. For a round-up of what's new in observing technology, go to pages 61–64, where equipment expert Robin Scagell shares his knowledge.

If you have already invested in binoculars or a telescope then you can explore the deep sky – nebulae (starbirth sites), star clusters and galaxies. On pages 58–60 we list recommended deep sky objects, constellation by constellation. Use the appropriate month's maps to see which constellations are on view, and then choose your targets. The table of 'limiting magnitude' (page 58) will help you to decide if a particular object is visible with your equipment.

Happy stargazing!

The start of the New Year is the most exciting time for appreciating the magnificence of the starry sky. Darkness falls early, and the nights are often frosty and very clear. Centrestage of the heavens is the glorious constellation of **Orion**, fighting his adversary, **Taurus** the Bull – accompanied by his trusty hounds, **Canis Major** and **Canis Minor**.

These constellations include many of the brightest stars in the sky – including the most brilliant of all, **Sirius**, which lies down towards the south in Canis Major. Sirius forms one end of a great arc of stars lying to the left of Orion, which stretches from **Procyon** (in Canis Minor) through **Pollux** and **Castor** (in **Gemini**) to **Capella** (in **Auriga**), which soars almost overhead this month.

▼ The sky at 10 pm in mid-January, with Moon positions at three-day intervals either side of Full Moon. The star positions are also correct for 11 pm at the

JANUARY'S CONSTELLATION

This month it has to be **Orion** – the most recognizable constellation in the sky. And it's one of the rare star-groupings that really looks like its namesake – a giant of a man with a sword below his belt, wielding a club above his head. Orion is fabled in mythology as the ultimate hunter. The constellation is dominated by two brilliant stars: blood-red **Betelgeuse** at top left (known to generations of sci-fi fans as 'Beetlejuice') and the even more brilliant blue-white **Rigel** at bottom right.

The two stars could hardly be more different. Betelgeuse is a cool, bloated, dying star – known as a red giant – over 300 times the size of the Sun. But Rigel is a vigorous young star more than twice as hot as our Sun (its surface temperature is around 12,000°C), and over 50,000 times as bright. The famous 'belt of Orion' is made up of the stars **Alnitak** (left), **Alnilam** and **Mintaka** (right) – below which hangs Orion's sword, the lair of the great **Orion Nebula** (see January's Picture).

WEST

PISCES

TRIANGULUM

Square of Pegasus

PEGASUS

ANDROMEDA

Algol

Epsilon

Deneb

CEPHEUS

THE MILKY WAY

CASSIOPEIA

PERSEUS

Capella

Zenith

CYGNUS

Polaris

NORTH

HERCULES

DRACO

URSA MINOR

URSA MAJOR

Radiant of Quadrantids

The Plough

CANES VENATICI

The Sickle

BOÖTES

LEO

NE

VIRGO

EAST

beginning of January, and 9 pm at the end of the month. The planets move slightly relative to the stars during the month.

PLANETS ON VIEW

Just after sunset, look to the southwest to spot the brilliant planet **Venus**, shining at magnitude -3.9. The 'Evening Star' appears higher in the sky as the month progresses.

As Venus sets, **Saturn** is rising in the east, and is visible all night long. It lies close to the bright star Regulus, which marks the heart of Leo (the lion). Saturn is noticeably the brighter of the two, at magnitude +0.1. And because it's a planet it shines with a steady light, while Regulus twinkles like all the stars.

If you're an early bird, look out for the giant planet Jupiter rising at around 5 am in the southeast. It shines at magnitude -1.8, in the constellation Ophiuchus (the serpent-bearer), near to the more familiar star-pattern of Scorpius (the scorpion).

The dim planet **Uranus** (magnitude +5.9) lies low in the west after sunset, setting at around 8.30 pm in the constellation Aquarius. Keen observers can spot it mid-month lying just to the left of the naked-eye star lambda Aquarii.

Mercury, **Mars** and **Neptune** all lie too close to the Sun to be seen this month.

MOON

On 6 January the waning Moon lies near to Saturn (a few hours before moonrise in Europe, people in eastern Asia will see the Moon pass right in front of Saturn, when both are below the horizon as seen from the UK). The following night it skims past Regulus. On the morning of 15 January the thin

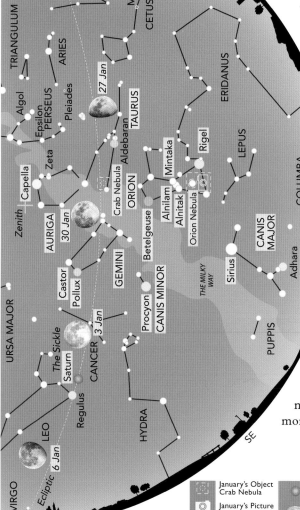

	MOON		
Date	**Time**	**Phase**	
3	1.57 pm	Full Moon	
11	12.44 pm	Last Quarter	
19	4.01 am	New Moon	
25	11.01 pm	First Quarter	

January's Object
Crab Nebula

January's Picture

Radiant of
Quadrantids

Saturn

Moon

EAST

crescent Moon rises near Antares, with brilliant Jupiter farther over to the left. On the evening of 20 January a very narrow crescent forms a striking pair with Venus. As the sky gets dark on 27 January the Moon is right in front of the Pleiades (Seven Sisters) star cluster.

SPECIAL EVENTS

3 January: Earth is at perihelion, its closest point to the Sun.

3 January: It's the maximum of the **Quadrantid** meteor shower. These shooting stars are tiny particles of dust shed by a now burnt-out comet called 2003 EH1. The solid grains burn up as they enter the Earth's atmosphere. Perspective makes them appear to emanate from one spot in the sky, the *radiant* (marked on the star chart). This is a poor year for observing the Quadrantids because bright moonlight will drown out the fainter meteors.

JANUARY'S OBJECT

This month, we home in on Taurus the Bull – particularly the small region above his 'lower horn'. At this spot, in 1054, Chinese astronomers witnessed the appearance of a 'new star', which outshone all the other stars in the sky. Visible in daylight for 23 days, it remained in the night sky for nearly two years. But this was no new star: it was a supernova, that is, an old star on the way out – which exploded because it was overweight.

Today we see the remnants of the star as the **Crab Nebula**, so named by the nineteenth-century Irish astronomer Lord Rosse because it resembled a crab's pincers. The debris is still expanding from the wreckage, and now measures 15 light years across.

At the centre of the Crab Nebula is the core of the dead star, which has collapsed to become a pulsar. This tiny but super-dense object (only the size of a city, but with the mass of the Sun) is spinning around furiously 30 times a second and emitting beams of radiation like a lighthouse. You can just make out the Crab Nebula through a small telescope, but it is small and faint.

> **◉ Viewing tip**
> It may sound obvious, but if you want to stargaze at this most glorious time of year, dress up warmly! Lots of layers are better than a heavy coat (for they trap air next to your skin), heavy-soled boots stop the frost creeping up your legs, and a woolly hat really will stop one-third of your body heat escaping through the top of your head. And – alas – no hipflask of whisky: alcohol constricts the veins, making you feel even colder.

◄ *The Orion Nebula, captured in California by Michael Stecker through a Takahashi 200 mm f/4 reflector on Fujicolor HG400 film. Two separate 45-minute exposures were combined in photo processing software.*

JANUARY'S PICTURE

1600 light years away, the **Orion Nebula** is part of the nearest region of massive star formation to our planet. Easily visible to the unaided eye, the nebula is 30 light years across, and is illuminated by the searing radiation from a clutch of young stars. The Orion star-region has the capacity to create half a million baby suns.

JANUARY'S TOPIC
The Zodiac

This year, giant planet Jupiter lumbers around in the constellation of Ophiuchus. But don't planets usually sit around in well-known signs of the Zodiac, like Leo, Gemini or Taurus? Not entirely true. When our familiar constellation patterns were drawn up in Mesopotamia and Greece over 2000 years ago, astronomers noticed that the Sun, Moon and planets kept to a distinct band in the sky. They divided this special band into the constellations of the Zodiac, and assigned one star-pattern for each month of the year, in order to locate these important moving objects. Today we know that this celestial highway is a result of our Solar System being largely flat, and so everything orbits in the same plane. Misguided astrologers have taken this up, interpreting the positions of the planets and the Sun as omens for humankind – in particular, where the Sun is placed against the stars during your birth-month. But you think you're a Gemini? You're likely to be a Taurus. The reason for this is that everything has slipped back since the time of the Greeks. Due to the Moon's gravity, the Earth's axis wobbles – a phenomenon called *precession*. This means that the positions of the Sun and planets, relative to the background stars, shift over a period of 26,000 years. In addition, when you look in detail, you find that this celestial highway crosses a thirteenth constellation – Ophiuchus. So if you believe that you're a Sagittarian, you're probably an Ophiuchan.

'Star' of the month is ringworld **Saturn**, at its closest to the Earth this year – and shining more brightly than anything in the late evening sky except **Sirius**, the most brilliant star of all. And when Saturn is exactly opposite the Sun on 10 February, watch out for a brief surge in the planet's brightness (see February's Picture).

Compare Saturn with Sirius, and you'll notice an easy way to tell the difference between a planet and a star – even without a telescope! Saturn shines with a steady light (like all the planets), while Sirius twinkles constantly. This has nothing to do with Sirius itself, but a lot to do with Earth's atmosphere. Looking at the stars through the atmosphere is like looking at your surroundings from the bottom of a swimming pool. As the water shifts and ripples, you get a distorted view. Earth's atmosphere is similarly always on the move, making all the stars appear to twinkle. A planet, however, appears larger in our skies, and so its light is less distorted.

FEBRUARY'S CONSTELLATION

Crowned by glorious **Sirius**, **Canis Major** is the larger of **Orion's** two hunting dogs. He is represented as chasing **Lepus**, the Hare (a very faint constellation below Orion), but his main target is Orion's chief quarry, **Taurus** the Bull (take a line from Sirius through Orion's belt, and you'll spot Taurus on the other side). From the UK, the Greater Dog is too low in the sky to be a brilliant sight. But Arabian astronomers, at lower latitudes, accorded great importance to Canis Major. Without fail, they saw the constellation as a dog. **Canis Minor** lies to Orion's left, and the Indians regarded both cosmic dogs as being 'watchdogs of the Milky Way' (the galaxy runs between the two constellations). To Sirius' right is the star **Mirzam**, whose Arabic name means 'The Announcer'; the presence of Mirzam heralded the appearance

▼ The sky at 10 pm in mid-February, with Moon positions at three-day intervals either side of Full Moon. The star positions are also correct for 11 pm at the

WEST
CETUS
PISCES
19 Feb
Ecliptic
ANDROMEDA
TRIANGULUM
ARIES
Pleiades
PEGASUS
Algol
PERSEUS
Capella
CASSIOPEIA
AURIGA
THE MILKY WAY
Zenith
Deneb
CEPHEUS
Polaris
URSA MAJOR
URSA MINOR
CYGNUS
NORTH
DRACO
The Plough
CANES VENATICI
LYRA
Vega
HERCULES
BOÖTES
VIRGO
CORONA BOREALIS
Arcturus

EAST

beginning of February, and 9 pm at the end of the month. The planets move slightly relative to the stars during the month.

of Sirius, one of the most venerated stars in the sky. Just below Sirius is a beautiful star cluster, **M41**. This loose agglomeration of over a hundred young stars – 2500 light years away – is easily visible through binoculars, and even to the unaided eye. It's rumoured that the Greek philosopher Aristotle, in 325 BC, called it 'a cloudy spot' – the earliest description of a deep sky object.

PLANETS ON VIEW

The first half of February is the best period this year to see elusive **Mercury** in the evening sky: it's at its greatest apparent distance from the Sun on 7 February. Venus advantageously acts as a guide: after sunset, look to the west to spot Venus as the brilliant Evening Star. As the sky darkens, scan the sky to the lower right of Venus (binoculars will help) to find a 'star' that's around one-twentieth of Venus' brightness. This is Mercury, shining at magnitude -0.5.

Venus (magnitude -3.9) is gradually approaching the Earth. It's setting at around 7 pm at the beginning of February, and well after 8 pm by the end of the month.

The ringed planet **Saturn** is now up all night long, shining at magnitude 0.0 in Leo (the lion), near to the constellation's brightest star, Regulus. It's directly opposite the Sun in the sky on 10 February (see February's Topic).

Jupiter (magnitude -2.0) is rising in the southeast at around 3.30 am, in the constellation Ophiuchus.

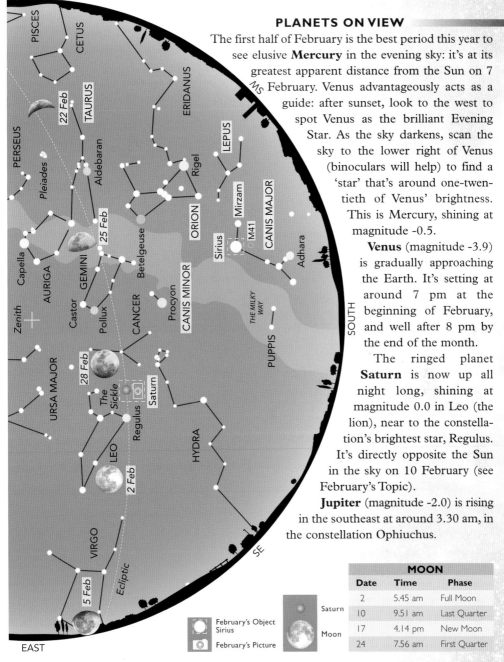

February's Object
Sirius

February's Picture

Saturn

Moon

MOON		
Date	Time	Phase
2	5.45 am	Full Moon
10	9.51 am	Last Quarter
17	4.14 pm	New Moon
24	7.56 am	First Quarter

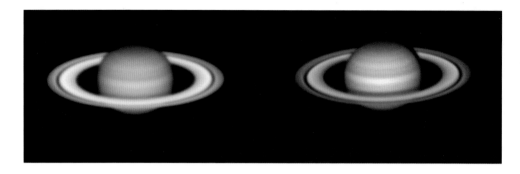

Distant **Uranus** is too low in the evening sky for easy viewing, but there's a good opportunity to spot it with binoculars or a small telescope on the evening of 7 February, when it lies immediately to the right of Venus. The two planets provide a striking contrast, with the Evening Star shining 8000 times brighter than the +5.9-magnitude Uranus.

Mars and **Neptune** are both hidden in the Sun's glare in February.

MOON

On 2 February, the Full Moon just grazes past Saturn. The night of 7/8 February sees the Moon pass Spica, the brightest star in Virgo (the virgin). The crescent Moon lies to the lower right of Jupiter on the morning of 12 February; and near to Venus on the evening of 19 February. On the night of 23/24 February (between about 10 pm and 1 am) the Moon passes in front of the Pleiades star cluster, hiding three of the Seven Sisters.

SPECIAL EVENTS

On **28 February** NASA's New Horizons spacecraft, heading for Pluto, swings by the giant planet Jupiter.

FEBRUARY'S OBJECT

This is the month of the brightest star in the sky – **Sirius**. It isn't a particularly luminous star: it just happens to lie nearby, at a distance of 8.6 light years. The 'Dog Star' is accompanied by a little companion, affectionately called 'The Pup'. This tiny star was discovered in 1862 by Alvan Clark when he was testing a telescope, but it had been predicted by Friedrich Bessel nearly twenty years earlier, when he'd observed that something was 'tugging' on Sirius. The Pup is a white dwarf: the dying nuclear reactor of an ancient star which has puffed off its atmosphere. White dwarfs are the size of a planet but have the mass of a star: because they're so collapsed, they have considerable gravitational powers – hence Sirius' wobble. The Pup is visible through medium-powered telescopes.

⊙ **Viewing tip**

When you first go out to observe, you may be disappointed at how few stars you can see in the sky. But wait for around twenty minutes, and you'll be amazed at how your night vision improves. The pupil of your eye is getting larger to make the best of the darkness. Observers call this 'dark adaptation', and it also involves the increased production in the retina of a chemical called rhodopsin, which dramatically increases the eye's sensitivity.

◀ Saturn at opposition (left), and two weeks later (right). Dave Tyler from Flackwell Heath, Buckinghamshire, UK, took these images with a Celestron 355 mm Schmidt Cassegrain with a Barlow lens to make it f/37, using a Lumenera 075 black-and-white CCD camera and RGB filters. These pictures were taken on 27 January and 10 February 2006 respectively.

FEBRUARY'S PICTURE

When Saturn lies opposite the Sun in the sky – as seen from the Earth – it can suddenly appear surprisingly bright, even to the unaided eye. This surge at the time of opposition occurs because the ice particles making up the rings reflect sunlight brilliantly – rather like car headlights illuminating a road sign head-on. While the rings brighten, Saturn's gassy globe appears little different. A few days later, when Saturn and the Sun are out of alignment, the planet's overall brightness returns to normal. This year, 'opposition' takes place on 10 February.

FEBRUARY'S TOPIC
Saturn

On 10 Feburary ringworld Saturn is at opposition – opposite the Sun in the sky, which means that it's at its closest distance to Earth (admittedly, 1227 million kilometres away!). But it will shine brightly in the sky in the constellation of Leo at a magnitude of 0.0. Seen through a small telescope, Saturn looks like a model: a suspended puppet of a world, surrounded by its famous rings – resembling a graphic from a movie. But it's real, and the planet's rings (made of billions of chunks of ice) would stretch nearly all the way from Earth to the Moon.

NASA's Cassini spacecraft is currently in orbit about Saturn, homing in on its mighty family of moons. So far, 47 have been discovered. Cassini, with its European lander-probe Huygens, has laid bare some of the secrets of Saturn's biggest moon Titan, revealing that it has a dense atmosphere and vestiges of oceans of liquid methane. Astronomers had suspected this all along – but the real eye-opener has been another moon, Enceladus. 500 km across, it is the most reflective object in the Solar System. Its surface appears to have been recoated by recent explosions from ice-volcanoes, which provide a source of warmth for this tiny world. Astronomers are beginning to speculate that there might be primitive life on its surface.

It's a busy month for the **Moon**! It takes part in two eclipses (one of them a spectacular total eclipse of the Moon that will be visible from the UK), and takes the chance to obscure the bright star **Regulus** and the planet **Saturn**.

Also this month, the nights become shorter than the days as we head into Spring. The official start of the new season is 21 March – the Vernal (Spring) Equinox. At this time the Sun moves over the equator on its way from the southern hemisphere of the sky to the northern hemisphere.

▼ The sky at 10 pm in mid-March, with Moon positions at three-day intervals either side of Full Moon. The star positions are also correct for 11 pm at the

MARCH'S CONSTELLATION

Ursa Major (the Great Bear) – whose brightest stars are usually called the Plough – is jointly with **Orion** the most famous constellation. Orion's fame is clear to see: its stars are brilliant, and make up a very powerful image of a giant dominating the sky. In contrast, those of the Plough are fainter, and most people today have probably never seen a horse-drawn plough, from which the constellation takes its name. In fact, some children call it 'the saucepan', while in America it's known as the Big Dipper.

But the Plough is the first constellation that many get to know. There are two reasons for this. First, the two end stars of the 'bowl' of the Plough point directly towards the Pole Star: also known as **Polaris**, it's the star that lies directly above the Earth's North Pole. As the Earth spins on its axis, the stars rise and set, while the Pole Star stays still – because we are actually rotating *under* Polaris. Locating the Pole Star is a sure way to find the direction of north. And because the Plough is so close to Polaris, it never sets, as seen from northern latitudes – and this is why it is such a familiar sight.

The seven stars of the Plough are quite a rarity: unlike in most constellations, several of the stars lie at the same distance *beginning of March, and 10 pm at the end of the month (after BST begins). The planets move slightly relative to the stars during the month.*

and were born together. The middle five stars are all moving in the same direction (along with brilliant **Sirius**, which is a member of the group). Over thousands of years, the shape of the Plough will gradually change, as the two 'end' stars go off on their own paths.

PLANETS ON VIEW

Venus is a striking sight in the evening sky, shining at magnitude -4.0 and setting about three hours after the Sun. The Evening Star is gradually approaching the Earth, though it's still comparatively small even seen through a telescope.

High in the south you'll find **Saturn**, between the constellations Leo (the lion) to its left and Cancer (the crab) to its right. At magnitude +0.1, the ring-world dominates the late evening sky.

Jupiter rises at around 2 am, in the constellation Ophiuchus (the serpent-bearer). As the Earth approaches Jupiter, this giant of the Solar System brightens in March from magnitude -2.0 to -2.3.

Mercury is at greatest western elongation on 22 March, but is lost in the twilight as seen from the UK. **Mars**, **Uranus** and **Neptune** are too close to the Sun to be visible this month.

MOON

The morning of 2 March sees the Moon partially occulting (hiding) Saturn (see Special Events), and in the evening the Moon passes near to Regulus. On 3 March

WEST

EAST

MOON		
Date	Time	Phase
3	11.17 pm	Full Moon
12	3.54 am	Last Quarter
19	2.42 am	New Moon
25	7.16 pm	First Quarter

Saturn

Moon

March's Object
Polaris

there's a total eclipse of the Moon. On the morning of 12 March the Last Quarter Moon stands directly below Jupiter. The Moon lies near Venus on 21 March, and is back near Saturn on 28 March. Finally, the Moon occults Regulus in the early morning of 30 March (3.30–4.20 am).

SPECIAL EVENTS

On **2 March**, between 2.40 and 2.57 am, Saturn is hidden behind the Moon as seen from some parts of the UK. These times apply in London, where Saturn is partially occulted: the amount of obscuration and times will vary according to your location.

The evening of **3 March** sees a total lunar eclipse visible from the UK (see March's Topic) – the only total eclipse of the year.

19 March, from 0.38 to 4.25 am, sees a partial eclipse of the Sun – visible from eastern Asia, but not from the UK.

The Vernal Equinox, on **21 March** at 0.07 am, marks the beginning of Spring, as the Sun moves up to shine over the northern hemisphere.

25 March, 1.00 am: British Summer Time starts – don't forget to put your clocks forward (the mnemonic is 'Spring forward, Fall back').

MARCH'S OBJECT

The Pole Star – **Polaris** – is a surprisingly shy animal, coming in at the modest magnitude of +2.1. Polaris lies at the end of the tail of the Lesser Bear (Ursa Minor), and it pulsates in size, making its brightness vary slightly over a period of four days. But its importance throughout recent history centres on the fact that Earth's north pole points to Polaris, so we spin 'underneath' it. It remains stationary in the sky, and acts as a fixed point for both astronomy and navigation. But over a 26,000-year period, the Earth's axis swings around like an old-fashioned spinning top (the phenomenon of precession), so our 'pole stars' change with time. Polaris will be nearest to the 'above pole' position in 2100, before the Earth wobbles off. Famous pole stars of the past include **Kochab** in Ursa Minor, which presided over the skies during the Trojan Wars of 1184 BC. In 14,000 years time, brilliant **Vega**, in Lyra, will be our pole star.

MARCH'S PICTURE

This month's total lunar eclipse takes place on the evening of 3 March. The Moon disappears into the Earth's shadow for about an hour, but may not become completely invisible. If our planet's atmosphere is clear, sunlight is bent around to fall on the lunar surface, causing a reddish glow, as our image shows.

◉ *Viewing tip*

This is the time of year to tie down your compass points – the directions of north, south, east and west – as seen from your observing site. North is easy: just latch onto Polaris, the Pole Star. But the useful extra in March is the Spring Equinox, when the Sun hovers over the equator. This means that it rises due east, and sets due west. And at noon, the Sun is always due south. So remember those positions relative to a tree or house around your horizon.

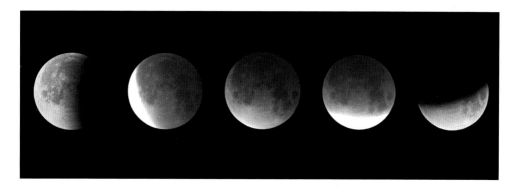

▲ Composite of the stages of the total lunar eclipse seen on 9 November 2003. Paul Andrew used a 200 mm Schmidt-Cassegrain and Canon 10D digital camera to capture this image from near Dover, Kent, UK. The composite was made using photo processing.

MARCH'S TOPIC
Total Eclipse of the Moon

On 3 March the Full Moon will disappear. But don't worry – wait an hour and our familiar satellite will once again become resident in our skies. The occasion is a total eclipse of the Moon, which takes place when our companion, which reflects light from the Sun, moves into the Earth's shadow. When the Moon is Full – opposite the Sun, and behind the Earth – the slight inclination of its orbit to ours (about five degrees) means that it normally avoids being plunged into darkness. But not on 3 March. Between 10.43 pm and 11.58 pm, the whole of Europe and Africa will witness the spectacle of the Moon skulking in the shadows.

Our satellite may not totally disappear from view. If the Earth's atmosphere is clear, enough sunlight can be refracted around its edge to cast an eerie red glow on the eclipsed Moon. A cloudy Earth means that the Moon completely vanishes. It's fascinating to observe the behaviour of animals when this happens. On one occasion – in Colombia – we were amused to hear a bullfrog, waxing loud with his mating call, being stunned into silence for sixty minutes! You'll see the Earth's shadow start to eat into the Moon at 9.30 pm, and the party will be over at 1.12 am on 4 March.

Glorious **Venus** is turning all heads as she blazes in the evening sky, far brighter than any star. And the Evening Star forms a picturesque grouping with the Seven Sisters – the **Pleiades** – in the second week of April.

Two ferocious beasts ride high in April's sky: **Ursa Major** (the Great Bear) almost overhead, with Leo (the lion) below. Between **Leo** and the southern horizon sprawls **Hydra**, the water snake, which straggles over 100 degrees – getting on for one-third of the way round the entire sky. A distinctive quadrilateral of stars marks out **Corvus** – a crow perched on the snake's back.

To the east (left) of Leo lies the ancient constellation of **Virgo**, represented as a Y-shape of stars extending from 1st-magnitude **Spica**, meaning 'ear of corn'. Above blue-white Spica lies the orange giant star **Arcturus** – a glorious contrast in colours when viewed through binoculars.

APRIL'S CONSTELLATION

Like Orion, **Leo** is one of the rare constellations that looks like its namesake – in this case, an enormous crouching lion. Leo is one of the oldest constellations, and commemorates the giant Nemean lion that Hercules slaughtered as the first of his labours. According to legend, the lion's flesh couldn't be pierced by iron, stone or bronze – so Hercules wrestled with the lion and choked it to death.

Leo is dominated by his head – the familiar '**sickle**', which looks like a back-to-front question mark. At the base of the sickle is the bright blue-white star **Regulus** (see April's Object). Leo's end is marked by **Denebola**, which in Arabic means 'the lion's tail'. Just underneath the main 'body' of Leo are several spiral galaxies: nearby cities of stars like our own Milky Way. They can't be seen unaided, but a sweep along the lion's tummy with a small telescope will reveal them.

▼ The sky at 11 pm in mid-April, with Moon positions at three-day intervals either side of Full Moon. The star positions are also correct for midnight at the beginning of

WEST

ORION
Betelgeuse
NNW
Venus
TAURUS
Pleiades
Venus
19 Apr
Ecliptic
Algol
AURIGA
GEMINI
22 Apr
PERSEUS
Capella
Castor
Pollux
ANDROMEDA
CASSIOPEIA
URSA MAJOR
NORTH
Polaris
URSA MINOR
The Plough
Zenith
CEPHEUS
Kochab
BOÖTES
THE MILKY WAY
Deneb
DRACO
CORONA BOREALIS
CYGNUS
Vega
Radiant of Lyrids
HERCULES
LYRA
OPHIUCHUS
NE

EAST

April, and 10 pm at the end of the month. The planets move slightly relative to the stars during the month.

PLANETS ON VIEW

The evening skies are dominated by glorious **Venus**, shining at magnitude -4.1 and setting almost four hours after the Sun: Venus is up so late that – unusually – it appears on our star charts. Through a small telescope you can see the Evening Star as a small globe, three-quarters lit by sunlight. On 10–12 April you'll find Venus near the Pleiades (Seven Sisters) star cluster.

Saturn still lies on the borders of Leo (the lion) and Cancer (the crab). At magnitude +0.3, it's fading now that the faster-moving Earth is drawing away.

On the other hand, **Jupiter** is brightening as the Earth approaches. It's currently at magnitude -2.4, in the obscure constellation Ophiuchus (the serpent-bearer). Jupiter rises at about 2 am at the start of April, and at 11.30 by the end of the month.

The planets **Mercury**, **Mars**, **Uranus** and **Neptune** are lost in the Sun's glare in April.

MOON

On 3 April the Moon lies near Spica, the brightest star of Virgo (the virgin). On the morning of 7 April it's close to Antares, in Scorpius (the scorpion), and the following morning passes below Jupiter. The crescent Moon lies to the right of Venus on 19 April. On 24 and 25 April the Moon is near Saturn. And on 30 April the Moon passes Spica once more.

SPECIAL EVENTS

22 April: It is the maximum of the **Lyrid** meteor shower, which – by per-

WEST

THE MILKY WAY

GEMINI · Procyon · CANIS MINOR · Castor · Pollux · CANCER · URSA MAJOR · The Sickle · 25 Apr · Saturn · Regulus · LEO · Denebola · HYDRA · Zenith · CANES VENATICI · Virgo Cluster · M87 · 28 Apr · Porrima · CORVUS · The Plough · Arcturus · Spica · SOUTH · BOÖTES · VIRGO · Ecliptic · CORONA BOREALIS · SERPENS · 2 Apr · LIBRA · HERCULES · OPHIUCHUS · SE · EAST

April's Object — Virgo Cluster
April's Picture
Radiant of Lyrids

Venus
Saturn
Moon

MOON		
Date	Time	Phase
2	6.15 pm	Full Moon
10	7.04 pm	Last Quarter
17	12.36 pm	New Moon
24	7.35 am	First Quarter

spective – appear to emanate from the constellation of Lyra. The shower, consisting of particles from a comet called Thatcher, is active between 19 and 25 April. Usually it generates a desultory ten shooting stars per hour, but occasionally we have seen it being a little more generous. This should be a good year for observing the Lyrids, as moonlight will not interfere.

APRIL'S OBJECTS

It is 'objects' this month – and big ones, too. If you have a small telescope, sweep the 'bowl' formed by Virgo's 'Y' shape, and you'll detect dozens of fuzzy blobs. These are just a handful of the thousands of galaxies making up the **Virgo Cluster**: our closest giant cluster of galaxies, lying at a distance of 55 million light years.

Galaxies are gregarious. Thanks to gravity, they like living in groups. Our Milky Way, and the neighbouring giant spiral the Andromeda Galaxy, live in a small cluster of about 30 smallish galaxies called the Local Group.

But the Virgo Cluster is in a different league; it's like a vast galactic swarm of bees. What's more, the cluster's enormous gravity holds sway over the smaller groups around, including our Local Group – thus making a cluster of clusters of galaxies: the Virgo Supercluster.

The galaxies in the Virgo Cluster are also mega. Many of them are spirals like our Milky Way – including the famous

⊙ **Viewing tip**
The Sun is a fascinating astronomical object, especially when its surface is marked by dark sunspots – but be careful. Never use a telescope or binoculars to look at the Sun directly: it could blind you permanently. Fogged film is no safer, because it allows the Sun's infrared (heat) rays to get through. The best way to observe the Sun is to project its image through binoculars or a telescope onto a white piece of card

'Sombrero Hat', which looks just like its namesake – but some are even more spectacular. The heavyweight galaxy of the cluster is **M87**, a giant elliptical galaxy emitting a jet of gas over 4000 light years long and travelling at one-tenth the speed of light.

APRIL'S PICTURE

On 10–12 April you'll find brilliant Venus close to the tiny Pleiades star cluster. The 500 stars of the Pleiades lie nearly 400 light years away; in contrast, Venus is our closest celestial neighbour. It appears so brilliant because its dense sulphuric acid clouds reflect sunlight so efficiently.

APRIL'S TOPIC
The Date of Easter

Christmas comes but once a year, and always on 25 December. The celebration is almost certainly a christianized version of an age-old pagan festival, which marked the occasion of the Winter Solstice – when the days were at their shortest, but starting to become longer again. But why is there no fixed date for Easter, which traditionally commemorates the crucifixion and resurrection of Christ? This year, Easter Sunday falls on 8 April – but it can take place as late as 25 April, or as early as 22 March.

The date of Easter is set by the events described in the New Testament. Easter Day was the Sunday when Jesus was observed to rise from the dead. It followed the Last Supper, which was a Passover meal. And the date of Passover is the first Full Moon after the Spring Equinox. So the date of Easter can be summed up as 'the first Sunday after the first Full Moon after the Spring Equinox'. The Spring Equinox this year falls on 21 March, the first Full Moon afterwards is on 2 April – and the following Sunday is 8 April. The last time it fell on the earliest possible date was back in 1818; and we won't see an Easter as late as 25 April until the year 2038.

The two most brilliant planets sit astride the evening skies: Venus in the northwest after sunset, with Jupiter rising over in the southeast. The summer constellations are starting to put in an appearance, and we always get excited when we see **Arcturus**, the brightest star of **Boötes** – it means that long torrid days are on the way.

▼ The sky at 11 pm in mid-May, with Moon positions at three-day intervals either side of Full Moon. The star positions are also correct for midnight at the beginning of

MAY'S CONSTELLATION

Up in the northern sky hangs a star-pattern making the unmistakable shape of a capital 'W'. To ancients, this constellation represented Queen **Cassiopeia** of Ethiopia, who ruled with her husband King **Cepheus**.

Cassiopeia misguidedly boasted that her daughter **Andromeda** was more beautiful than the sea nymphs. The sea god, Poseidon, was so incensed that he sent a ravaging monster (Cetus). It could only be appeased by the sacrifice of Andromeda – but she was rescued by the hero **Perseus**. Cepheus, Andromeda and Perseus are also immortalized by constellations lying near to Cassiopeia.

The Chinese saw Cassiopeia as three star groups, which included a chariot and a mountain path. Unusually, the central star in Cassiopeia is known today by its Chinese name – Tsih (the whip). This star is unstable in brightness. Some 70,000 times brighter than the Sun, it spins around at breakneck pace flinging out streams of gas.

Cassiopeia has seen two more extreme variable stars – supernovae, where an entire star has blown apart. One was seen by Danish astronomer Tycho Brahe in 1572. The other exploded in around 1660 as a surprisingly dim supernova, but its expanding gases form the most prominent radio source in the sky, Cassiopeia A.

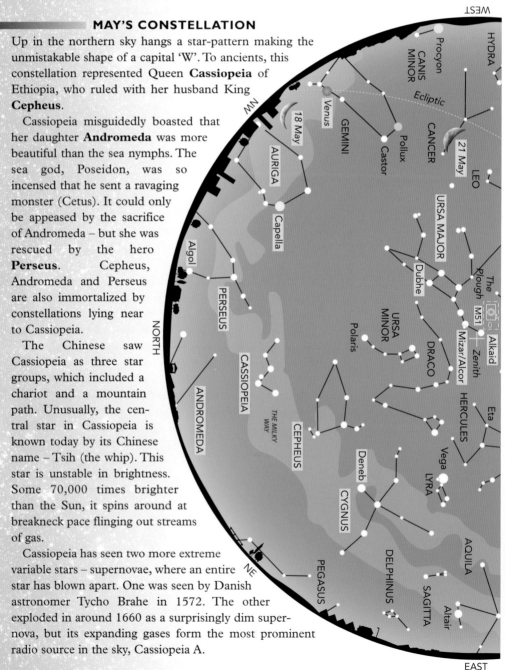

May, and 10 pm at the end of the month. The planets move slightly relative to the stars during the month.

PLANETS ON VIEW

Venus is absolutely stunning this month. It's not yet at its brightest, nor at its greatest angular distance from the Sun, but it sets so late (well after midnight) that the brilliant jewel of the Evening Star is set against the black velvet of completely dark night skies. During May Venus increases in brightness from magnitude -4.1 to -4.3, and moves from Taurus (the bull) into Gemini (the twins). On 8–10 May it lies near the lovely star cluster M35. At the very end of the month Venus is line with the twin stars Castor and Pollux.

During the second half of May you may glimpse **Mercury** (around magnitude 0), very low down in the southwest after sunset.

The ringed planet **Saturn** is well placed for viewing during the late evening. At magnitude +0.5, it lies between Leo (the lion) and Cancer (the crab) and sets at around 2.30 am.

You'll find giant **Jupiter** rising at around 10.30 pm in the southeast, in the constellation Ophiuchus (the serpent-bearer). At magnitude -2.5, it's brighter than anything else in the night sky bar the Moon and Venus.

Mars, **Uranus** and **Neptune** are all lost in the bright morning twilight.

MOON

On the nights of 5/6 and 6/7 May the Moon lies below Jupiter. The crescent Moon makes a lovely close pairing with Venus on 19 May; the following night it's near the celestial twins Castor and Pollux. And on 21 May the Moon just skims the Praesepe

	MOON	
Date	**Time**	**Phase**
2	11.09 am	Full Moon
10	5.27 am	Last Quarter
16	8.27 pm	New Moon
23	10.02 pm	First Quarter

Venus
Jupiter
Saturn
Moon

May's Picture

WEST

CANCER
Saturn
Regulus
HYDRA
The Sickle
24 May
LEO
URSA MAJOR
CORVUS
The Plough
CANES VENATICI
27 May
VIRGO
Spica
Ecliptic
HYDRA
CENTAURUS
SOUTH
Mizar/Alcor
Zenith
M51
Alkaid
BOÖTES
Arcturus
SERPENS
LIBRA
Eta
CORONA BOREALIS
Rasalgethi
2 May
HERCULES
OPHIUCHUS
SCORPIUS
Antares
Jupiter
AQUILA
THE MILKY WAY
SE
SERPENS
Altair

EAST

◄ *Whirlpool Galaxy M51. This beautiful photograph was taken by Nick King, using a Vixen 200 mm f/6.4 reflector with a Canon 300D digital camera modified for astronomical work. Astonishingly, it was captured in light-polluted Harrow, Middlesex, UK – but Nick used an Astronomik CLS light-pollution filter to cut through the glow. He took eleven ten-minute exposures at ISO 800.*

(Beehive) star cluster in Cancer (the crab). The following evening the Moon occults Saturn (see Special Events). The Moon is near the bright star Spica on 27 May, and Antares on 31 May.

SPECIAL EVENTS

5 May: It is the maximum of the Eta Aquarid meteor shower, tiny pieces of debris shed by Halley's Comet burning up in Earth's atmosphere. Bright moonlight will interfere with seeing the shooting stars this year.

On **22 May** the crescent Moon moves in front of (occults) Saturn. The occultation occurs before the sky is dark, so you'll need a telescope to monitor events. As seen from London, the occultation lasts from 8.08 to 9.16 pm – and times will vary slightly according to your location.

MAY'S OBJECT

Home in on the 'kink' in the tail of **Ursa Major** (the Great Bear), and you'll spot the most famous pair of stars in the sky – **Mizar** (magnitude +2.4) and **Alcor** (magnitude +4.0). Generations of astronomers have referred to them as 'the horse and rider', and students have long been taught that the pair are a classic double-star system, orbiting in each other's embrace. But *are* Mizar and Alcor an item? It seems not. Although they both lie about 80 light years away, they are separated by three light years – nearly the distance from the Sun to our closest star, Proxima Centauri. Undoubtedly, Mizar is a complex star system, having a companion visible through a telescope which is itself double (four stars involved in total). But Alcor appears to be an innocent bystander. Although it shares its path through

◉ *Viewing tip*

Venus is dazzling this
month – so dazzling, in
fact, that it's difficult to
view. If you have a small
telescope, don't wait until
the sky gets totally dark:
Venus will appear so bright
that it'll be hard to make
out any of the very subtle
markings in its clouds. Best
to wait until just after the
Sun has set (not before, or
you risk catching the Sun
in your field of view) – and
you'll see a much fainter
crescent Venus against a
pale blue sky.

space with Mizar, the two are just members, along with many
others, of the 'stellar association' of Ursa Major. Unlike most
constellations, the stars of the Great Bear are genuinely linked
by birth (apart from **Dubhe** and **Alkaid**, at opposite ends of
the central 'Plough'). So let's hear 'independence for Alcor'!

MAY'S PICTURE

Lying just below the stars of the Plough, the Whirlpool Galaxy
(M51) is a survivor of a cosmic traffic accident. The tiny companion galaxy above M51 struck its bigger neighbour hundreds
of millions of years ago. It now lies far in the background – but
the collision's legacy is clear to see. It led to a burst of star formation in the Whirlpool, resulting in the glorious spiral arms we
see today.

MAY'S TOPIC
Star Names

Why do the brightest stars have such strange names? It's
because they date from antiquity, and have been passed
down through the generations ever since. The original
Western star names – like the original constellations – were
probably Babylonian or Chaldean, but few of these survive.
The Greeks then took up the baton, the name of the star
Antares being a direct result. It means 'rival of Ares' because
its red colour rivals that of the planet Mars ('Ares' in Greek).

The Romans were not particularly interested in astronomy, but nevertheless left their mark on the sky. **Capella**, the
brightest star of **Auriga**, has Roman roots: the name is a
diminutive of *capra* (goat), and means 'the little she-goat' (a
slight understatement for a star over 100 times brighter than
the Sun).

The Arabs were largely responsible for the star names we
have inherited today. Working in the so-called 'Dark Ages'
between the sixth and tenth centuries AD, they took over the
naming of the sky; this explains the number of stars beginning with 'al' (Arabic for 'the'). **Algol**, in the constellation
Perseus, means 'the demon' – possibly because the Arabs
noticed that its brightness seemed to 'wink' every few days.
Deneb, in **Cygnus**, also has Arabic roots; it means the tail
(of the flying bird).

But the most remembered star name in the sky is Orion's
Betelgeuse (visible in the winter months). For some time it
was gloriously interpreted as 'the armpit of the sacred one'.
But the 'B' in Betelgeuse turned out to be a mistranslitera-
tion – and so we're none the wiser as to how our distant
ancestors really identified with this fiery red star.

Venus and Jupiter are slugging it out for attention this month. **Jupiter** should have the limelight, because the giant planet is at its closest point to the Earth this year: but it's low down in the sky, on the borders of **Ophiuchus** and **Scorpius**. **Venus** is riding high – and brilliantly – in the northwest after sunset.

It's just as well that both these planets are bright, because June nights in the UK hardly get properly dark. The hours of darkness depend critically on your latitude. If you are north of the Arctic Circle (66.5° north latitude), the Sun doesn't set at all. It just dips down towards the northern horizon, then moves up in the sky again, producing the phenomenon of the Midnight Sun.

At more temperate latitudes, the Sun is now setting at its most northerly point along the horizon. This unique time of year was certainly picked out by our distant ancestors, who built great monuments such as Stonehenge.

JUNE'S CONSTELLATION

A tiny celestial gem, **Corona Borealis** (the northern crown) rides high in the skies of early summer. In legend, it was the crown given as a wedding present from Bacchus to Ariadne. It really looks like a miniature tiara in the heavens, studded at its heart with an ultimate jewel – the blue-white star **Gemma** (magnitude +2.2). Gemma is a member of the Ursa Major association of stars (as is Sirius), and all move together in the same direction through space. Within the arc of the crown resides a remarkable variable star, **R Corona Borealis**. It normally hovers around the limits of naked-eye visibility – 6th magnitude – but, unpredictably, it can drop to magnitude +14. That's because sooty clouds accumulate above the star's surface and obscure its light. The tiny crown also possesses another bizarre variable star, **T Corona Borealis**, which behaves in the opposite way to its celestial

▼ The sky at 11 pm in mid-June, with Moon positions at three-day intervals either side of Full Moon. The star positions are also correct for midnight at the beginning of

June, and 10 pm at the end of the month. The planets move slightly relative to the stars during the month.

compatriot. It usually skulks around at magnitude +11 (out of the range of binoculars), but then suddenly flares to magnitude +2. This 'Blaze Star' last erupted in 1946. It's what astronomers call a 'recurrent nova' – a white dwarf star undergoing outbursts after dragging material off its companion.

PLANETS ON VIEW

Venus is a brilliant Evening Star all month, brightening from magnitude -4.3 to -4.4. But the bright summer nights are catching up with the planet, which starts to descend into the twilight after its greatest angular separation from the Sun on 9 June. On 13 June Venus passes just above the Praesepe (Beehive) star cluster in Cancer (the crab), and on 30 June it approaches Saturn.

To the left of Venus you'll find the fainter planet **Saturn**, currently shining at magnitude +0.5. The planets converge throughout the month, reaching closest approach between 30 June and 1 July. After 10.30 pm Venus and Saturn are joined by the second brightest planet, **Jupiter** (magnitude -2.6), rising in the southeast in the constellation Ophiuchus (the serpent-bearer). Jupiter is opposite to the Sun in the sky – and at its nearest and brightest – on 6 June (see June's Topic).

Neptune is visible low in the southeast before dawn in Capricornus (the sea-goat), but you will need a telescope to see this faint world (magnitude +7.9).

WEST

EAST

SOUTH

SE

Venus

Jupiter

Saturn

June's Object M13

June's Picture

Moon

MOON		
Date	Time	Phase
1	2.04 am	Full Moon
8	12.43 pm	Last Quarter
15	4.13 am	New Moon
22	2.15 pm	First Quarter
30	2.49 pm	Full Moon

Mercury is at greatest eastern elongation on 2 June, but is hidden in the twilight glow as seen from the UK. **Mars** and **Uranus** are also lost in the Sun's glare in June.

MOON

In the early morning of 1 June the Full Moon lies immediately below giant planet Jupiter. The crescent Moon appears close to Venus on 18 June (it actually occults the planet that afternoon, between 3.01 and 4.20 pm, but you'll need a telescope to observe this). It lies near Regulus the following night. On 27 June the Moon passes below Antares, with Jupiter above both.

SPECIAL EVENTS

6 June: NASA's Messenger's spacecraft flies past Venus on its way to Mercury.

21 June, 7.06 pm: It is the Summer Solstice. The Sun reaches its most northerly point in the sky, so 21 June is Midsummer's Day, with the longest period of daylight. Correspondingly, we have the shortest nights.

JUNE'S OBJECT

At the darkest part of a June night, you may spot a faint fuzzy patch way up high in the south. Through binoculars it appears as a gently glowing ball of light. With a telescope you can glimpse its true nature: a cluster of almost a million stars, swarming together in space.

This wonderful object is known as **M13**, because it was the thirteenth entry in the catalogue of fuzzy objects recorded by the eighteenth-century French astronomer Charles Messier. We now classify M13 as a 'globular cluster'. These great round balls of stars are among the oldest objects in our Milky Way Galaxy, dating back to its birth some 13 billion years ago.

In 1974 radio astronomers sent a message towards M13, hoping to inform the inhabitants of any planet there of our existence. There's only one problem: M13 lies so far away that we won't be receiving a reply until AD 52,200!

> ⊚ *Viewing tip*
> A medium-sized pair of binoculars can reveal Jupiter's four largest moons, but you have to use them carefully. Balance your elbows on a fence or a table to minimize wobble – the magnification of the binoculars magnifies the wobble as well! You should see the moons strung out in a line either side of Jupiter's equator.

JUNE'S PICTURE

Observers sometimes report sudden outbursts in the sky that last for only seconds. These are caused by the solar panels from the Iridium communications satellites catching the Sun – making a flash brighter than the most brilliant stars. Even in the light nights of June, Iridium flares are easily visible.

JUNE'S TOPIC
Jupiter

Jupiter is particularly bright this month. On 6 June it's at 'opposition' – meaning that it's opposite the Sun in the sky, and at its closest to the Earth. 'Close' is a relative term, however – the planet is still over 640 million kilometres away. But Jupiter is vast (at 143,000 km in diameter, it could contain 1300 Earths), and as it's made almost entirely of gas, it's very efficient at reflecting sunlight.

Although Jupiter is so huge, it spins faster than any other planet in the Solar System. It rotates every 9 hours 55 minutes, and as a result its equator bulges outwards; through a small telescope it looks a bit like a tangerine crossed with an old-fashioned humbug. The humbug stripes are cloud belts of ammonia and methane stretched out by the planet's dizzy spin.

Space missions to Jupiter have revealed how active the planet is. It has a fearsome magnetic field that no astronaut would survive, with huge eruptions of lightning, and it radiates more energy than it receives from the Sun. The core is so squashed by the planet's mighty bulk that it simmers at a temperature of 20,000°C. In fact, had the planet been 50 times heavier, the core would have been capable of sustaining nuclear reactions, and Jupiter would have become a star.

In some ways, Jupiter has a lot in common with a star. It commands its own 'mini-solar system' – a family of over 60 moons. The four biggest are visible in good binoculars, and even to the unaided eye (if you are really sharp-sighted). We remember a 78-year-old lady at an evening class asking, 'What are those little dots either side of Jupiter?'

These four are worlds in their own right – Ganymede is even bigger than the planet Mercury. But two vie for 'star' status. The surface of Io is erupting – incredible geysers erupt plumes of sulphur dioxide 300 km into space. Brilliant white Europa probably contains oceans of liquid water beneath a solid ice coating, where alien fish may swim …

◄ *Flare from an Iridium communications satellite, seen in a twilight sky. David Cortner, in North Carolina, USA, took several separate brief exposures on a Canon 20D, and combined them in photo processing software.*

It's all change in the planetary arena. After six months in the footlights, Venus and Saturn now leave the evening stage. In their place comes **Jupiter**, with Mars hoving into view as it heads towards a starring role near the end of 2007.

It's not so easy to navigate the stars at night, as the bright summer skies collude with a period of year marked by big sprawling faint constellations that are studded with only a few brilliant jewels of 1st-magnitude stars.

The easiest way to find your way around is to use the brightest stars as signposts. Over in the west is the great Summer Triangle, its corners marked by **Vega**, **Deneb** and **Altair**. Well to the right of Vega is the slightly brighter **Arcturus**, in kite-shaped **Boötes**. Between these two 1st-magnitude stars lie the hourglass-shaped constellation of **Hercules** and the distinctive circlet of stars making up **Corona Borealis** (the northern crown).

JULY'S CONSTELLATIONS

Visually not the most thrilling area of the sky (we'll admit), but **Ophiuchus** and **Serpens** are two of the most ancient constellations in the heavens. Their mythology is fascinating. In legend, Ophiuchus was the son of Apollo, named Aesculapius. He became a fabled surgeon, serving on the voyage of the *Argo*, and even restoring dead people back to life. Eventually, his fame reached King Minos of Crete, whose son had died of a wasting disease. Minos pleaded with Aesculapius to revive him. Aesculapius refused, explaining that the prince would only revert to his former condition if resuscitated. The king flung him into a dungeon, where serpents writhed over his body. The surgeon was so desperate that he killed one of the serpents – but then another arrived, with a herb in its mouth, which it then applied to its companion's body. The dead serpent immediately sprung into

▼ The sky at 11 pm in mid-July, with Moon positions at three-day intervals either side of Full Moon. The star positions are also correct for midnight at the beginning of

WEST

VIRGO
LEO
The Sickle
CANES VENATICI
The Plough
BOÖTES
URSA MAJOR
HERCULES
DRACO
URSA MINOR
Polaris
Zenith
AURIGA
NORTH
Capella
CASSIOPEIA
CEPHEUS
THE MILKY WAY
Deneb
CYGNUS
PEGASUS
PERSEUS
Algol
TRIANGULUM
ANDROMEDA
Square of Pegasus
NE
PISCES

EAST

July, and 10 pm at the end of the month. The planets move slightly relative to the stars during the month.

life – and both serpents wriggled off, leaving a supply of the healing herbs. Aesculapius applied the magic balm to the dead prince; lo and behold, he was restored to life in perfect condition! For their labours to humankind, the gods placed Aesculapius and his trusty serpent in the sky.

The name of the brightest star in the constellation of Ophiuchus, **Rasalhague** (magnitude +2.1), means 'head of the serpent charmer'. And Serpens – representing the snake twisted around Aesculapius – is the only constellation that is split into two separate parts.

PLANETS ON VIEW

Venus reaches its maximum brightness on 14 July (magnitude -4.5), but it's losing the magnificence of earlier in the year as it drops down into the twilight: by the end of the month you'll be hard pushed to see it at all. On 12 July Venus passes Regulus, the brightest star in Leo. Through a telescope you'll see its shape change from half-lit to a crescent.

We're losing sight of **Saturn**, too. In the first week of July you can still make out the ringed planet (+0.6 magnitude) as the 'star' to the right of brilliant Venus, before it sinks into the evening twilight.

Giant **Jupiter** (magnitude -2.5) is now dominating the evening skies – even though it lies low in the south in the constellation Ophiuchus, just above the more familiar Scorpius with its red giant star Antares. In July's last few days Jupiter seems to have five bright moons instead

WEST

21 July
VIRGO
Spica
MS
24 July
LIBRA
LIBRA
Arcturus
BOÖTES
CORONA BOREALIS
SERPENS
SCORPIUS
Antares
27 July
SOUTH
Jupiter
OPHIUCHUS
DRACO
Zenith
Vega
LYRA
LYRA
Epsilon
HERCULES
Rasalhague
SERPENS
SAGITTA
Deneb
CYGNUS
AQUILA
THE MILKY WAY
SAGITTARIUS
Altair
DELPHINUS
PEGASUS
CAPRICORNUS
30 July
Neptune
Ecliptic
SE
PISCES
5 July
Uranus
AQUARIUS
Antares

EAST

		MOON	
	Date	**Time**	**Phase**
Jupiter	7	5.53 pm	Last Quarter
Uranus	14	1.04 pm	New Moon
Neptune	22	7.29 am	First Quarter
Moon	30	1.48 am	Full Moon

July's Object Antares

July's Picture

of four: the interloper is the star omega Ophiuchi.

After skulking in the morning twilight all year, **Mars** now appears in the night sky. Shining at magnitude +0.6, in the constellation Aries, the Red Planet rises at 1.30 am at the beginning of July and at 0.20 am by the end of the month.

Uranus (magnitude +5.8) and **Neptune** (magnitude +7.8) rise at around 11 pm – in Aquarius and Capricornus respectively – though you'll need optical aid to see these distant worlds.

Mercury reaches greatest western elongation on 20 July, but is lost in the twilight as seen from the UK.

▲ The planet Jupiter in the constellation of Scorpius. Robin Scagell, in St Lawrence Bay, Essex, UK, photographed this region of the sky with a 20-second exposure on Kodak Ektachrome 1600 film, using a 24 mm lens on a Canon A1 camera.

MOON

On the night of 8/9 July the Moon passes to the upper right of Mars. The thin crescent Moon lies just below Saturn on 16 July, with brilliant Venus to the left. On 21 July the Moon is near Spica, the brightest star in Virgo. Jupiter lies to the upper right of the Moon on 25 July, with Antares directly to the Moon's right.

SPECIAL EVENTS

7 July: Earth is at aphelion, its furthest point from the Sun. That's a cool 152 million km (94.5 million miles).

JULY'S OBJECT

Look low in the south this month for a baleful red star that marks the heart of the constellation of **Scorpius**. 600 light years away, **Antares** is a bloated red giant star near the end of its life. Its name means 'the rival of Mars' – and you can see why. Running out of its central supplies of nuclear fuel, its core has shrunk and heated up, causing its outer layers to billow out and cool. Now Antares is over 500 times bigger than our Sun, 10,000 times more luminous, and at least 15 times heavier. Placed at the centre of our Solar System, it would engulf all the planets out to Mars. And its size isn't constant. Antares' gravity hasn't got to grips with its extended girth, making the star swell and shrink – changing in brightness as it does so. The giant star has a small blue companion (magnitude +5), which is hard to see against Antares' glare. Just visible in a small telescope, the star circles the red giant every 878 years. Eventually, Antares's core will collapse completely, and it will explode as a brilliant supernova.

JULY'S PICTURE

Spotting low-down Scorpius – dominated by red giant star Antares – is a sure sign that summer has come. At this time of the year, Earth looks out towards the constellations of Scorpius and Sagittarius: the star-packed regions that mark the centre of our Galaxy. The planet Jupiter (at opposition in June) joins the stars of the celestial beast in this image.

JULY'S TOPIC
DAWN to the asteroids

This may seem like déjà vu: yes, we did feature the DAWN mission to the asteroids in *Stargazing 2006*. But the mission was postponed, cancelled, and then reinstated. So we hope this month really does see this daring NASA mission blasting off on its way to the asteroid belt. Its twin targets are Ceres (the biggest at 930 km across) and Vesta (the brightest). It will orbit both asteroids for a year or more, to check them out at close quarters. The mission's aim is to investigate the formation and evolution of our Solar System. Asteroids and comets are the building-blocks of planets, and give us clues to our origins – perhaps even the origin of life itself.

The two asteroids couldn't be more different, which is why NASA has chosen them as targets. Ceres evolved with water present, and there may even be frost or water vapour on its surface today. Vesta, on the other hand, originated in hot and violent circumstances. By studying the two asteroids, DAWN will be looking back to the earliest days of our Solar System.

'The sky is so amazing in the south of France: you get to see so many shooting stars,' friends have often said to us. 'Mid-August must be the time you regularly take your summer holidays' is our reply – and we are invariably right!

It doesn't take a Sherlock Holmes to make this deduction. The dark skies of southern France do help in seeing what's going on in the sky. But there's only one time of year – outside deep winter – when the sky is full of shooting stars. August is the meteor-month.

If you are in southern latitudes on holiday, the other stunning sky-sight of August is the softly glowing Milky Way – looking like luminous clouds – down on the southern horizon. Here we are looking towards the centre of the Galaxy that we inhabit.

AUGUST'S CONSTELLATION

Low down in the south there's a constellation shaped rather like a teapot. The handle lies to the left; and the spout to the right!

To the ancient Greeks, the star-pattern of **Sagittarius** represented an archer, with the torso of a man and the body of a horse. The 'handle' of the teapot is his upper body, the curve of three stars to the right his bent bow, while the end of the spout is the point of the arrow, aimed at Scorpius, the fearsome celestial scorpion.

Sagittarius is rich with nebulae and star clusters. On a clear night (preferably from a southern latitude), sweep Sagittarius with binoculars for some fantastic sights. Above the spout lies the wonderful **Lagoon Nebula** – visible to the naked eye on a very dark night. This is a region where stars are being born. Between the Teapot and the neighbouring constellation Aquila, you'll find a bright patch of stars in the Milky Way (catalogued as **M24**). Raise your binoculars higher to spot another star-forming region, the **Omega Nebula**.

▼ The sky at 11 pm in mid-August, with Moon positions at three-day intervals either side of Full Moon. The star positions are also correct for midnight at the

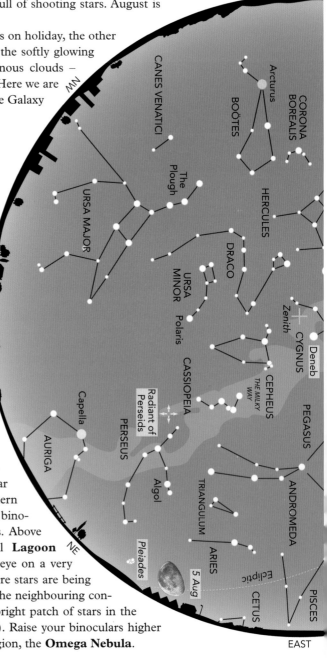

beginning of August, and 10 pm at the end of the month. The planets move slightly relative to the stars during the month.

With very clear skies you might spot a fuzzy patch, above and to the left of the Teapot's lid. This is the globular cluster **M22**, a swarm of almost a million stars that lies 10,000 light years away.

PLANETS ON VIEW

The night belongs to **Jupiter**, now that Venus has shifted off the scene. At magnitude -2.3, the giant planet dominates the sky from its low perch in Ophiuchus. Jupiter starts the month near the star omega Ophiuchi, which (through binoculars) looks like a fifth bright moon for the planet.

As Jupiter sets – around midnight – **Mars** is rising in the northeast, in Taurus. The faster-moving Earth is catching up with the Red Planet so it brightens during the month, from magnitude +0.5 to +0.3. In the second week of August Mars passes below the Pleiades (Seven Sisters) star cluster. Around 22 August Mars lies near the red giant star Aldebaran in Taurus – compare its colour with the Red Planet.

Between Jupiter and Mars lie two faint outer planets. **Uranus**, at magnitude +5.7, is in Aquarius; on 28 August it passes very close to the star that marks a sharp bend in the constellation's outline, phi Aquarii (magnitude +4.2). **Neptune** (magnitude +7.8) is inhabiting Capricornus and comes to opposition on 13 August.

Mercury and **Saturn** are hidden

WEST

EAST

CORONA BOREALIS — SERPENS — LIBRA — 22 Aug — SCORPIUS — Jupiter

DRACO — Vega — LYRA — HERCULES — OPHIUCHUS — SAGITTA — Altair — AQUILA — THE MILKY WAY — SERPENS — Omega Nebula — M24 — M22 — Lagoon Nebula — 25 Aug — SAGITTARIUS

Zenith — Deneb — CYGNUS — SUMMER TRIANGLE — DELPHINUS — Neptune — CAPRICORNUS — SOUTH

ANDROMEDA — Square of Pegasus — PEGASUS — 28 Aug — PISCIS AUSTRINUS

Uranus — AQUARIUS — Ecliptic — SE

PISCES — 31 Aug — CETUS

| | August's Object | Summer Triangle |
| | Radiant of Perseids |

	Jupiter
	Uranus
	Neptune
	Moon

MOON		
Date	Time	Phase
5	10.19 pm	Last Quarter
13	0.02 am	New Moon
21	00.54 am	First Quarter
28	11.35 am	Full Moon

in the Sun's glare. **Venus** is also drowned out by the Sun's light for most of August, but reappears as the Morning Star at the end of the month.

MOON

On 2 August the Moon passes close to Uranus, and it occults the Pleiades on 6/7 August (see Special Events for details of both). On 21 August the First Quarter Moon lies directly under Jupiter, with Antares in between.

SPECIAL EVENTS

On the morning of **2 August**, at around 1.30, the Moon is one moon-width above Uranus – giving you a great chance to spot this elusive planet (with good binoculars or a small telescope).

There's a striking sight on the night of **6/7 August**, when the Moon occults several members of the **Pleiades** (Seven Sisters) star cluster, with Red Planet Mars just below.

12/13 August: This is the maximum of the **Perseid** meteor shower. You'll see Perseid meteors for several nights around the time of maximum. We should be in for an excellent show this year, as moonlight won't interfere.

On **28 August** there's a total eclipse of the Moon, visible from all around the Pacific Rim – but not from the UK.

AUGUST'S OBJECT

The **Summer Triangle** is very much part of this season's skies (and it hangs around for most of the autumn, too). It's made up of Vega, Deneb and Altair – the brightest stars in the constellations of Lyra, Cygnus and Aquila respectively. The trio of stars makes a striking pattern almost overhead on August evenings.

The stars may seem to be almost the same brightness, but they're very different beasts. **Altair** – its name means 'flying eagle' – is one of the Sun's nearest neighbours, at a distance of nearly 17 light years. It's about ten times brighter than the Sun and spins at a breakneck rate of once every 6.5 hours – as compared to around once every 30 days for our local star.

Vega, just over 25 light years away, is a brilliant white star nearly twice as hot as the Sun. In 1850 it was the first star to be photographed. Today's more sensitive instruments have revealed that Vega is surrounded by a dusty disc, which may be a planetary system in the process of formation.

While **Deneb** – meaning 'tail' (of the swan) – may appear to be the faintest of the trio, the reality is different. It lies a staggering 3200 light years away (a newly measured distance from the Hipparcos satellite). To appear so bright in our skies, it must be truly luminous. We now know that Deneb is over 200,000 times brighter than our Sun – one of the most brilliant stars known.

> ◉ **Viewing tip**
>
> Have a Perseids party! You don't need any optical equipment – in fact, telescopes and binoculars will restrict your view of the meteor shower. The ideal viewing equipment is your unaided eye, plus a sleeping bag and a lounger on the lawn. If you want to make measurements, a stopwatch and clock are good for timings, while a piece of string will help to measure the length of the meteor trail.

► *A Perseid meteor. Michael Maunder captured this chance appearance of the shooting star streaking across the heavens during a three-minute exposure of the sky using ISO 400 film.*

AUGUST'S PICTURE

Early August is a brilliant time to see shooting stars. The Perseids – debris from Comet Swift-Tuttle – stream into the atmosphere and burn up at the rate of roughly one per minute. Without moonlight interfering, 2007 is an excellent year to witness this cosmic fireworks display.

AUGUST'S TOPIC
A Phoenix Arises from the Ashes

The crash of NASA's Mars Polar Lander in 1999 caused huge disappointment. But this month a new space-probe will be launched towards the same destination: Mars' north pole. Phoenix will land in late May 2008, after a ten-month journey. Unlike the recent Martian probes, which have had their descents cushioned by airbags, no one is taking any chances with this mission. Phoenix will have a proper, controlled system of thrusters to guide it down safely. Its mission is to look for water and ice at the pole cap.

'We know there's plenty of water frozen into Mars at high latitudes,' observes mission leader Peter Smith, from the University of Arizona. 'And we've designed Phoenix to tell us more about this region as a possible habitat for life.' Phoenix has a prehensile robotic arm two metres long, which will be able to take soil samples at a depth of 50 centimetres. While the highly successful rovers Spirit and Opportunity roamed the dry, desert regions of Mars, the new probe will encounter a totally different environment. 'We're going down and dirty on the surface of Mars,' comments Smith. 'We're going to get muddy, while the rovers got dusty.'

This month we may still be treated to the warm sunny days of an Indian summer, but to astronomers winter begins on 23 September. On the Autumn Equinox, the Sun crosses the equator and moves down to the southern hemisphere of the sky.

In the night sky, the Summer Triangle – **Deneb**, **Vega** and **Altair** – is shifting over to the west. Rising in the east are the autumn star-patterns, commencing with the distinct Square of **Pegasus** (the flying horse), followed by the princess **Andromeda** and her mother **Cassiopeia** and her suitor **Perseus**.

SEPTEMBER'S CONSTELLATION

With a pedigree stretching back to antiquity (although it's hardly one of the most spectacular constellations), **Aquarius** is part of a group of 'watery' star-patterns which includes **Cetus**, **Capricornus** and **Pisces**. There's speculation that the ancient Babylonians associated this region with water because the Sun passed through this zone of the heavens during the rainy season, from February to March. They saw the faint central four stars of Aquarius as a water jug, being poured by a man.

In long-exposure images Aquarius boasts one of the most glorious sights in the sky, and it's visible as a faint celestial ghost in binoculars or through a small telescope. The **Helix Nebula**, half the diameter of the Full Moon in the sky, is a star in its death throes. The Helix is a planetary nebula, and, at 450 light years away, it's one of the nearest known. (The term 'planetary nebula' comes from eighteenth-century amateur astronomer William Herschel, after its resemblance to a planet when viewed in a telescope.) Once a red giant star, the Helix is the result of the aged star puffing off its unstable, distended atmosphere into space – forming a beautiful spiral shroud around its collapsed core. This central core is a white

▼ The sky at 11 pm in mid-September, with Moon positions at three-day intervals either side of Full Moon. The star positions are also correct for midnight at *the beginning of September, and 10 pm at the end of the month. The planets move slightly relative to the stars during the month.*

dwarf star: bereft of nuclear power at the end of its life, it will gradually ebb away to become a cold black cinder.

PLANETS ON VIEW

The giant planet **Jupiter** is brilliant in the southwest after sunset, at magnitude -2.1. It lies in the constellation Ophiuchus, above better-known Scorpius, and sets at around 10 pm.

Mars is rising in the northeast at about 10.30 pm, in Taurus. It's at magnitude +0.1 and brightening as Earth speeds towards the Red Planet. On the night of 16 September Mars lies near the Crab Nebula, an exploding cloud of gas from a supernova.

Distant **Uranus**, in Aquarius, is at opposition this month (see Special Events). **Neptune**, in Capricornus, shines at magnitude +7.8.

Look out for Venus and Saturn resuming their frolics in the morning sky. **Venus** appears first, as the brilliant Morning Star. At the start of September, Venus rises at 4.45 am at magnitude -4.3, appearing as a distinct crescent shape when viewed through a telescope. But it quickly pulls away from the Sun, to end the month rising at 3.10 am, having brightened to -4.5 and filling to a 'half-moon' shape.

Saturn (magnitude +0.7) follows behind Venus, lying to its lower left near Regulus, the brightest star of Leo.

Mercury reaches its greatest eastern elongation from the Sun on 29 September, but it's too low in the twilight to be easily seen from the UK.

WEST

SERPENS
OPHIUCHUS
HERCULES
SERPENS
SAGITTARIUS
THE MILKY WAY
20 Sept
Vega
LYRA
Albireo
AQUILA
Altair
SAGITTA
DELPHINUS
CAPRICORNUS
Deneb
CYGNUS
Enif
Neptune
23 Sept
Zenith
PEGASUS
PISCIS AUSTRINUS
GRUS
SOUTH
CEPHEUS
Scheat
Square of Pegasus
Uranus
Helix Nebula
Fomalhaut
ANDROMEDA
AQUARIUS
Ecliptic
TRIANGULUM
PISCES
26 Sept
ARIES
Harvest Moon
CETUS
TAURUS
ERIDANUS
Mira
SE

EAST

		MOON	
	Date	**Time**	**Phase**
Mars	4	3.32 am	Last Quarter
Uranus	11	1.44 pm	New Moon
Neptune	19	5.48 pm	First Quarter
Moon	26	8.45 pm	Full Moon

September's Object Uranus
September's Picture

MOON

On 3 and 4 September the Moon lies near Mars. The morning of 9 September sees the thin crescent Moon forming a lovely pair with brilliant Venus, low in the east. On 18 September the Moon lies to the lower left of giant planet Jupiter, with Antares to the right.

SPECIAL EVENTS

On **10 September** Uranus is at opposition, meaning that it's opposite the Sun in the sky and at its closest point this year. Shining at magnitude +5.7, it is just visible to the naked eye – and you can certainly pick it out with binoculars. There's an extra signpost during the first half of September: Uranus lies right next to the slightly brighter star phi Aquarii (magnitude +4.2), which forms the left-hand extremity of the constellation.

On **11 September** there's a partial eclipse of the Sun, visible from southern regions of South America and Antarctica, but not from the UK.

23 September, 10.51 am: Autumn Equinox. The Sun is over the equator as it heads southwards in the sky, and day and night are equal.

SEPTEMBER'S OBJECT

If you're very sharp-sighted and have extremely dark skies, you stand a chance of spotting **Uranus** – the most distant planet visible to the unaided eye. It's at magnitude +5.7 in Aquarius (our constellation of the month). Discovered in 1781 by William Herschel, Uranus was the first planet to be found since antiquity. Then, it doubled the size of our Solar System. Uranus is a gas giant like Jupiter, Saturn and Neptune. Four times the

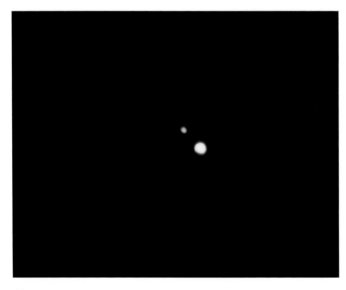

◀ Double star Albireo in Cygnus. Robin Scagell took this five-second exposure on ISO 400 film through a 220 mm f/8 reflecting telescope from Ickenham, Middlesex, UK.

◉ Viewing tip
Try to observe your
favourite objects when
they're well clear of the
horizon. When you look
low down, you are seeing
through a large thickness
of the atmosphere – which
is always shifting and
turbulent. This turbulence
makes the stars appear to
twinkle. Low-down planets
also twinkle, but because
they subtend tiny discs the
effect is less marked.

diameter of the Earth, it has an odd claim to fame: it orbits the Sun on its side (probably as a result of a collision in its infancy, which knocked it off its perch). As with the other gas giants, it has an encircling system of rings. But these are nothing like the spectacular edifices that girdle Saturn: the eleven rings are thin and faint. It also has a large family of moons: 21 named ones and six unnamed ones. Many of us were disappointed when the Voyager probe flew past Uranus in 1986 to reveal a bland, featureless world. But things are hotting up as the planet's seasons change. Streaks and clouds are appearing in its atmosphere. And in 2007 the Sun will be directly over the equator of Uranus. So expect surprises!

SEPTEMBER'S PICTURE

Albireo – the star that marks the 'head' of Cygnus the Swan – is actually two stars in orbit around each other. Seen through a small telescope, the duo forms the most beautiful double star in the sky. The brighter star is yellow; its companion is blue. The Victorian astronomer Agnes Clerke described the components as 'golden and azure'.

SEPTEMBER'S TOPIC
The Harvest Moon

It's the time of year when farmers work late into the night, bringing home their ripe crops before Autumn sets in. And traditionally they are aided by the light of the 'Harvest Moon' – a huge glowing Full Moon that seems to hang constant in the evening sky, rising at the same time night after night. At first sight, that doesn't seem possible. After all, the Moon is moving around the Earth, once in just under a month, so it ought to rise roughly one hour later every night. But things in the sky are hardly ever that simple...

The Moon follows a tilted path around the sky (close to the line of the ecliptic, which is marked on the chart). And this path changes its angle with the horizon at different times of year. On September evenings, the Moon's path runs roughly parallel to the horizon, so night after night the Moon moves to the left in the sky, but it hardly moves downwards. The consequence is that the Moon rises at around the same time for several consecutive nights. This year, Full Moon on 26 September rises at 6.33 pm (ideal for harvesting); it rises just 13 minutes earlier the evening before, and 12 minutes later the night after.

The evenings are now drawing in, providing splendid views of the night sky at relatively social hours – especially at the end of the month, when the clocks go back and we lose the summer's extra hour of evening light.

On display is the great Square of **Pegasus**, high in the south. Below the celestial flying horse we find some constellations of a distinctly aqueous nature, including **Aquarius** (the water-carrier) and that strange creature **Capricornus**, which is depicted in old star charts as half-goat and half-fish. Way down to the south is **Piscis Austrinus** (the southern fish), with one of our favourite stars – 1st-magnitude **Fomalhaut**, barely peeking above the horizon as seen from the UK.

OCTOBER'S CONSTELLATION

It has to be said that **Pegasus** is one of the least interesting constellations in the sky. How did our ancestors manage to see the shape of an upside-down winged horse in what is no more than a large, barren square of four medium-bright stars?

In legend, Pegasus sprang from the blood of Medusa the Gorgon when **Perseus** (nearby in the sky) severed her head. In fact, all pre-classical civilizations have their fabled winged horse, and we see them depicted on Etruscan and Euphratean vases.

The star at the top right of the square – **Scheat** – is a red giant more than 100 times wider than the Sun. Close to the end of its life, it pulsates irregularly, changing in brightness by about one magnitude. **Enif** (the nose) – outside the square to the lower right – is a yellow supergiant. A small telescope, or even good binoculars, will reveal a faint blue companion star.

Just next to Enif – and Pegasus' best-kept secret – is the beautiful globular cluster **M15**. You'll need a telescope for this one. M15 is around 50,000 light years away, and contains

▼ *The sky at 11 pm in mid-October, with Moon-positions at three-day intervals either side of Full Moon. The star positions are also correct for midnight at the*

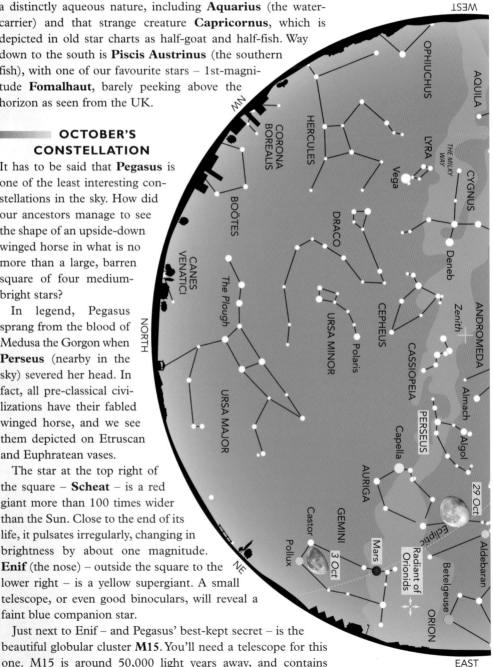

beginning of October, and 9 pm at the end of the month (after the end of BST). The planets move slightly relative to the stars during the month.

about 200,000 stars.

PLANETS ON VIEW

In the early evening, look out for brilliant **Jupiter** (magnitude -1.9) in the southwest. Lying in the constellation Ophiuchus, the giant planet sets at around 8.30 pm.

After Jupiter has set, **Mars** rises at around 9.30 pm in the northeast, in Gemini. As the Earth moves ever closer, the Red Planet steadily brightens, from magnitude 0.0 at the start of October to -0.6 by the end of the month – making it brighter than any of the stars visible in the evening sky.

The faint planet **Neptune** (magnitude +7.9) lies in Capricornus, and sets at about 1.30 am. You'll need a telescope to see it.

Its sister planet, **Uranus**, is just visible to the naked eye – but binoculars will be a big help. It's in Aquarius, shining at magnitude +5.8, and is up all night.

Venus is a brilliant Morning Star, shining at magnitude -4.4 and rising at around 3 am (it's at its greatest elongation from the Sun on 28 October). This month we see Venus in totally dark skies, so it's a good time to check out the theory that it's bright enough to cast shadows.

Saturn (magnitude +0.8) lies nearby, in the constellation Leo. During October these two planets, and Leo's brightest star Regulus, perform a celestial dance. The month starts with Venus to the upper right, Regulus in the

WEST

SERPENS
THE MILKY WAY
AQUILA
20 Oct
CYGNUS
SAGITTA
Altair
DELPHINUS
M15
Enif
AQUARIUS
Neptune
CAPRICORNUS
PISCIS AUSTRINUS
Deneb
Andromeda Galaxy
ANDROMEDA
PEGASUS
Scheat
Square of Pegasus
Uranus
23 Oct
Fomalhaut
CASSIOPEIA
Zenith
Ecliptic
SOUTH
PERSEUS
Almach
M33
26 Oct
PISCES
CETUS
Algol
TRIANGULUM
ARIES
Mira
Pleiades
TAURUS
ERIDANUS
Aldebaran
Betelgeuse
ORION
Rigel

EAST

SE

●	Mars
○	Uranus
○	Neptune
●	Moon

October's Object
Andromeda Galaxy

October's Picture

Radiant of Orionids

MOON		
Date	Time	Phase
3	11.06 am	Last Quarter
11	6.01 am	New Moon
19	9.33 am	First Quarter
26	5.51 am	Full Moon

middle and Saturn to the lower left. As the days pass, Venus swings downwards and to the left. There's a spectacular grouping with the Moon on 7 October (see Special Events). Venus passes Regulus on the morning of 9 October, and Saturn on 15 October.

Mercury is too close to the Sun to be seen this month.

MOON

On 2 October the Moon lies near Mars. The morning of 7 October sees the Moon near Venus, Saturn and Regulus (see Special Events). On 15 October the crescent Moon lies beneath Jupiter. The Moon comes very close to Uranus on the night of 22/23 October: at around 2 am, use binoculars or a small telescope to view the Moon and you'll see Uranus as the 'star' horizontally to its left. On 27 October, the Moon occults the Pleiades (see Special Events). Mars is near the Moon again on 30 October.

SPECIAL EVENTS

The early morning of **7 October** (at around 5 am) sees a spectacular grouping of the crescent Moon with brilliant Venus, along with Leo's brightest star Regulus (right next to the Moon) and Saturn to the lower left. Between 6.15 and 6.55 am the Moon moves in front of Regulus, but you'll need a telescope to see this in the brightening dawn sky.

21 October: This is the maximum of the **Orionid** meteor shower. These meteors are debris from Halley's Comet, burning up in Earth's atmosphere and appearing to spray out from the constellation Orion.

On the night of **27/28 October**, the Moon moves in front of some of the stars of the **Pleiades** (Seven Sisters) cluster. The occultations begin at 11.33 pm and finish at around 1.20 am (for London; times will differ slightly in other locations).

28 October, 2 am: End of British Summer Time. Clocks go backwards by an hour.

OCTOBER'S OBJECT

This month's object just has to be the **Andromeda Galaxy**, M31 – for most of us, the most distant object visible to the unaided eye. (The Triangulum Galaxy, **M33**, is fractionally fur-

◄ Oxfordshire, UK was the
location where Robin Scagell
photographed the constellation
Delphinus. He used a 135 mm
lens on ISO 200 film for the
three-minute exposure.

ther away, but is only tentatively visible from dark desert locations.) Andromeda, as seen from the UK, looks like a fuzzy dinner plate on its side in the sky – and it extends to four times the
diameter of the Full Moon. Thanks to data from the Hipparcos
satellite, it turns out to be even more remote than we original-
ly thought – at 2.9 million light years away.

When observing this amazing object through binoculars or a
small telescope, you have to pinch yourself to remember that
you're looking at 400,000 million stars (Andromeda is one of
the biggest spiral galaxies known). It's a great shame that it is
presented at such a steep angle to us that we can't see more of
its amazing spiral structure.

OCTOBER'S PICTURE

Traditionally regarded as a summer constellation, the delightful star-pattern of Delphinus – the Dolphin – is still high in the
skies of October. This small-but-perfectly-formed group of
stars looks like the beautiful maritime mammal that the ancient
Greeks associated with saving sailors plunged into the high
seas.

OCTOBER'S TOPIC
Jodrell Bank

Fifty years ago this month a new British institution hit the
world between the eyes. On 4 October 1957 the Leviathan
of Cheshire – Jodrell Bank's brand-new radio telescope –
swung into action for the first time. The huge dish, 76
metres (250 feet) across, tracked the carrier rocket that loft-
ed Russia's Sputnik I into space. It was a spectacular
achievement, and proved that if Russia could launch rockets
like this they could also send ICBMs across our planet. A
decisive moment in our world's history, it made Jodrell Bank
an international icon.

Since then, the mightily-engineered telescope has seen
calmer waters, exploring the far wider universe. The massive
Mark I dish (an astronomical equivalent of the Forth
Bridge) was at the forefront of the new discipline of radio
astronomy: looking at the universe through radio waves,
instead of light. In particular, it has conducted in-depth
research into pulsars – rotating neutron stars. These are the
corpses of giant suns that have exploded, leaving spinning
remnants behind them. And at the other end of the spec-
trum, the Lovell Telescope (recently renamed after its
founder, Sir Bernard Lovell) has been used to search for life
– as part of a worldwide project to track down radio waves
emanating from other living beings in the universe.

◉ **Viewing tip**
At a distance of 2.9 million
light years, the Andromeda
Galaxy is the furthest
object easily visible to the
unaided eye. But it's large
and extended, and a little
difficult to spot. The trick is
to memorize the star
patterns in Andromeda
and look slightly to the
side of where you expect
the galaxy to be. This
technique – called 'averted
vision' – causes the image
to fall on a part of the
retina that is more light-
sensitive than the central
part, which is designed to
see fine detail.

It's truly autumn now, and that's reinforced by what we see in the sky above us. The faint, sprawling constellations of **Pegasus**, **Andromeda**, **Pisces** and **Cetus** make the heavens look lacklustre – a reflection of the autumnal landscape here on Earth.

As the evening progresses, though, we'll start to see brighter stars and constellations rise in the sky. Leading the way is **Taurus** (the bull) with the lovely little star cluster of the **Pleiades** (the Seven Sisters). Accompanying the bull is the charioteer – the constellation **Auriga** with its bright leading star **Capella**.

Following on are **Orion** and **Gemini**. They are traditionally the constellations of winter, and a reminder that the hardest season is still to come – but they are also the promise of more wonderful skysights.

NOVEMBER'S CONSTELLATION

Another faint, wet constellation! **Cetus**, in legend, is the sea monster that was about to devour the princess **Andromeda** before the hero **Perseus** rescued her (the story also involves Cetus being turned to stone by the head of a gorgon). Cetus, like neighbouring Aquarius, is a constellation of unspectacular stars – except for one. **Mira** (meaning 'The Wonderful') was discovered in 1596 by David Fabricius, a disciple of the fabled astronomer Tycho Brahe. He noticed that over an eleven-month period it changed in brightness massively. Normally it varies between 3rd and 10th magnitude, but William Herschel in 1779 saw it as looking almost as bright as Aldebaran (magnitude +0.85). Mira is the prototype pulsating red giant – a star so distended that it can't control its atmosphere. At its minimum luminosity Mira is only about as bright as our Sun, but it can swell to become 1500 times brighter. This star out of

▼ The sky at 10 pm in mid-November, with Moon positions at three-day intervals either side of Full Moon. The star positions are also correct for 11 pm at the *beginning of November, and 9 pm at the end of the month. The planets move slightly relative to the stars during the month.*

hell is estimated to be 700 times the diameter of our Sun, and has a white dwarf in orbit around it which exchanges matter with its red giant companion. Eventually Mira will puff off its unstable atmosphere, to become a planetary nebula like the Helix (see September). This year Mira reaches maximum brightness in March, and fades from sight in September.

PLANETS ON VIEW

Jupiter's brief dominance of the evening sky is now over. The planet (magnitude -1.8) sets in the southwest at around 6 pm at the beginning of November, and it soon disappears into the twilight glow.

The night sky is now the domain of **Mars**. As the Earth approaches Mars, the Red Planet doubles in brightness this month from magnitude -0.6 to -1.3. Lying in Gemini, Mars rises at around 7 pm and is visible all night long.

Neptune (magnitude +7.9) still skulks in Capricornus, setting at around 10 pm. It's followed by **Uranus**, in Aquarius, which shines at magnitude +5.8 and sets at 1 am.

Just after midnight, **Saturn** rises in the east. It glows at magnitude +0.8 under the belly of Leo (the lion).

Venus is brilliant in the dark skies before dawn, rising at around 3 am. As fast-moving Earth pulls away from the Morning Star, Venus' magnitude drops from -4.4 to -4.2 – still far brighter than anything else apart from the Moon. During the month, Venus moves from Leo to Virgo, passing the latter's

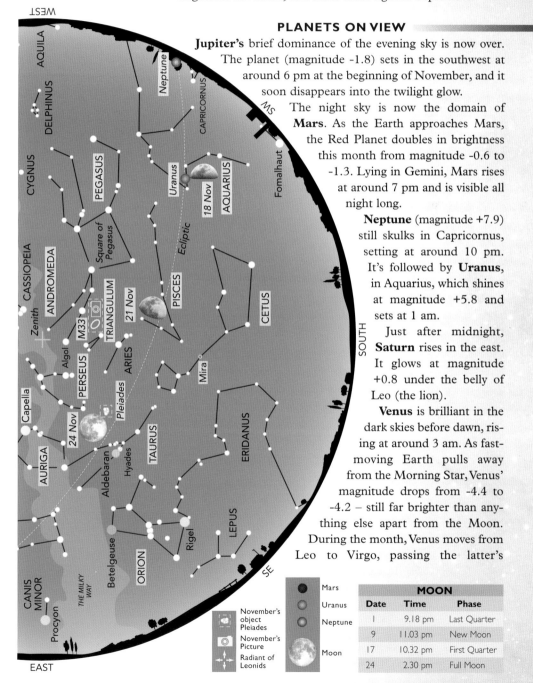

		MOON	
	Date	**Time**	**Phase**
	1	9.18 pm	Last Quarter
	9	11.03 pm	New Moon
	17	10.32 pm	First Quarter
	24	2.30 pm	Full Moon

- Mars
- Uranus
- Neptune
- November's object Pleiades
- November's Picture
- Radiant of Leonids
- Moon

brightest star Spica on the mornings of 29 and 30 November.

Between 7 and 17 November you may just catch **Mercury** very low down in the east in the morning twilight (at around 5.30 am). Mercury (magnitude -0.5) is at its greatest elongation from the Sun on 8 November, and you'll see Spica (magnitude +1.0) lying just to its right.

MOON

The waning crescent Moon lies near to Saturn on the night of 3/4 November, near to Venus on the mornings of 5 and 6 November, and to the upper right of the Mercury-Spica pair on the morning of 7 November. On the night of 26/27 November the gibbous Moon passes close by Mars. 28 November sees the Moon move right in front of the Praesepe (Beehive) star cluster. And on the last night of the month it approaches Saturn again.

SPECIAL EVENTS

17 November: It is the maximum of the **Leonid** meteor shower. A few years ago this annual shower yielded literally storms of shooting stars (many thousands an hour), but the rate has gone down as the parent comet Tempel-Tuttle, which sheds its dust to produce the meteors, has moved away from the vicinity of Earth.

NOVEMBER'S OBJECT

'A swarm of fireflies tangled in a silver braid' – this evocative description of the lovely **Pleiades** (or Seven Sisters) star cluster was coined by Alfred, Lord Tennyson, in his 1842 poem 'Locksley Hall', and how accurate it is. Very keen-sighted observers can pick out up to eleven stars, but most mere mortals have to content themselves with six or seven. These are just the most luminous in a group of 500 stars, lying about 400 light years away (although there's an ongoing debate about the precise distance). The brightest stars in the Pleiades are hot and blue, and all of the stars are young – less than 80 million years old. They were born together, and have yet to go their separate ways. The fledgling stars have blundered into a cloud of gas in space, which looks like gossamer on webcam images. But they're still a beautiful sight to the unaided eye or through binoculars.

NOVEMBER'S PICTURE

M33 *may* be the faintest and most distant object visible to the unaided eye. Observers in desert locations claim to have seen this sprawled-out galaxy – which is over three million light years away – without optical aid. The Triangulum Galaxy lies close to the Andromeda Galaxy in our autumn skies.

NOVEMBER'S TOPIC
Light Pollution

We once received a letter from a lady in Kent, saying, 'Before the War, we could see so many stars. But they're not there any more. Have they faded?' No – light pollution is the culprit. Our skies are crammed with particles of dust, coming from sources like car exhausts and factory emissions. Couple this with badly-designed streetlighting – and, hey presto, the stars disappear. It's not just an aesthetic issue. It's calculated that each year the UK throws away £52 million and two power-stations worth of energy in badly-designed lighting. It is robbing us of our vision of the skies – and contributing to global warming. It isn't even making our lives any safer from crime, for research shows that more crimes are committed in well-lit areas.

What's to be done? The Clean Neighbourhoods Act – which addresses, among other nuisances, noise and light pollution – should make a difference. And lighting engineers are actively working on new designs for streetlights that point the light down, not up. We hope that this will bring us our vision of the dark night sky again. Otherwise, the only recourse will be to sit under the artificial skies of a planetarium.

◀ *Spiral galaxy M33, captured by Nick King from Harrow, Middlesex, UK. Nick's equipment was a Starlight Xpress SXV-H9 CCD camera and an 80 mm Megrez refractor. The total exposure time was 2 hours 25 minutes.*

The year closes with the Red Planet dominating the sky – with a rare brush past the Moon early on Christmas Eve, when **Mars** lies in line with the Moon, Earth and Sun.

To compete with Mars, the sky is putting on its annual display of luminous stars. The great hunter **Orion** alone contains 10% of the brightest 70 stars in the sky. He's accompanied by the most brilliant star of all, **Sirius** – the Dog Star in the constellation of **Canis Major** (the Great Dog).

DECEMBER'S CONSTELLATION

Taurus is very much a second cousin to brilliant **Orion**, but a fascinating constellation nonetheless. It's dominated by **Aldebaran**, the baleful blood-red eye of the celestial bull. Around 68 light years away, and shining with a magnitude of +0.85, Aldebaran is a red giant star, but not one as extreme as neighbouring **Betelgeuse**. It is around three times heavier than the Sun. The 'head' of the bull is formed by the **Hyades** star cluster. The other famous star cluster in **Taurus** is the far more glamorous **Pleiades**, whose stars – although further away than the Hyades – are younger and brighter.

Taurus has two 'horns' – the star **El Nath** (Arabic for 'the butting one') to the north, and **Zeta** (which has an unpronounceable Babylonian name meaning 'star in the bull towards the south'). Above this star is a stellar wreck – literally. In 1054 Chinese astronomers witnessed a brilliant 'new star' appear in this spot, and it was visible in daytime for weeks. What the Chinese actually saw was an exploding star – a supernova – in its death throes. And today, we see its still-expanding remains as the **Crab Nebula**. It's visible through a medium-sized telescope.

▼ The sky at 10 pm in mid-December, with Moon positions at three-day intervals either side of Full Moon. The star positions are also correct for 11 pm at the

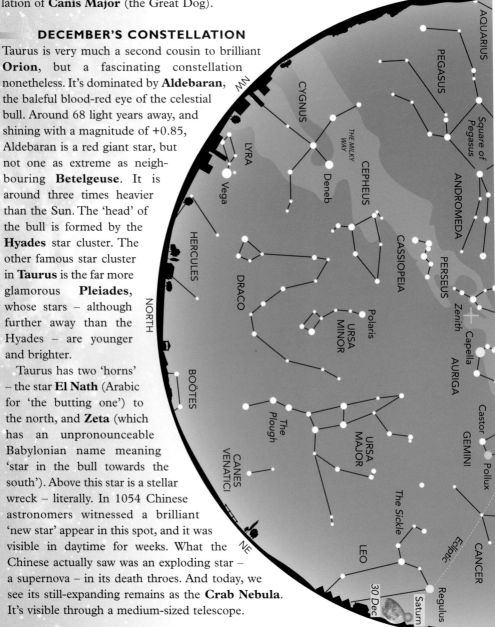

beginning of December, and 9 pm at the end of the month. The planets move slightly relative to the stars during the month.

PLANETS ON VIEW

Mars is 'star' of the month, reaching its closest point to Earth on 17 December – a 'mere' 88 million km away – and opposition (in line with the Sun and the Earth) on 24 December. It shines in the constellation Gemini all night long, its magnitude reaching a maximum of -1.6, more brilliant than any of the stars.

At around 10 pm **Saturn** is rising in the east. The ringed world lies under the constellation Leo and shines with a magnitude of +0.7.

In the constellation Capricornus is the dim planet **Neptune** (magnitude +7.9), setting at about 8.30 pm. It's followed by +5.9-magnitude **Uranus**, in Aquarius, which sinks below the horizon at 11 pm.

Brilliant Morning Star **Venus** is shining at magnitude -4.1. It rises at 3.30 am at the start of December, but as late as 5 am at the month's end. At the start of the month Venus lies near to Spica, the brightest star in Virgo. It moves down into Libra, to end the year on the borders with Scorpius. **Mercury** and **Jupiter** are hidden in the Sun's glare this month.

MOON

The Moon is in the vicinity of Saturn on 1 December. On the mornings of 5 and 6 December the crescent Moon lies near brilliant Venus. The Moon passes Neptune on 14 December (see Special Events). It occults members of the Pleiades (Seven Sisters) on 21 December, between 9.20 and 11.15 pm. On 24

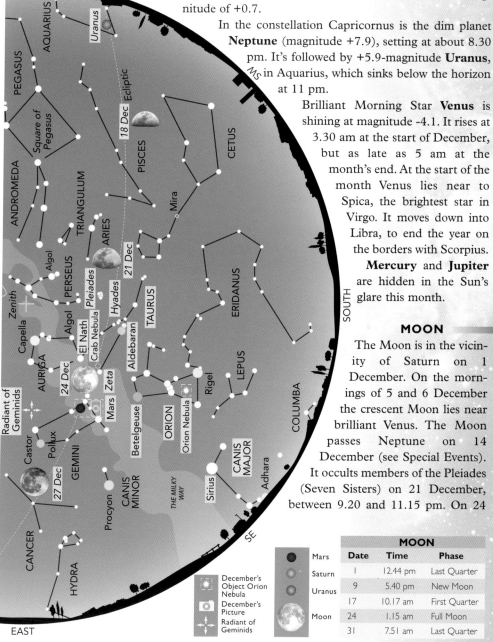

	MOON		
Mars	**Date**	**Time**	**Phase**
Saturn	1	12.44 pm	Last Quarter
	9	5.40 pm	New Moon
Uranus	17	10.17 am	First Quarter
Moon	24	1.15 am	Full Moon
	31	7.51 am	Last Quarter

December's Object Orion Nebula
December's Picture
Radiant of Geminids

December the Moon is very near Mars (see Special Events), and on 28 December it's back in the region of Saturn.

SPECIAL EVENTS

13 December: This is the maximum of the **Geminid** meteor shower, which lasts from 7 to 16 December. The meteors, being debris shed from an asteroid called Phaethon, are quite substantial – and hence bright. This is a good year for observing them, as moonlight won't interfere.

The evening of **14 December** sees the Moon very near Neptune, providing a rare opportunity to identify this dim world. At around 6.30 pm focus a small telescope on the Moon. Follow a line connecting the 'horns' of the Moon upwards, by one-and-a-half moon-diameters. Here you'll find three faint stars in a row: Neptune is the 'star' in the middle.

22 December, 6.08 am: Winter Solstice. As a result of the tilt of Earth's axis, the Sun reaches its lowest point in the heavens as seen from the northern hemisphere: we get the shortest days, and the longest nights.

Early on **24 December** the Full Moon skims past Mars: the two are just a hair's breadth apart at 3.45 am. As seen from eastern Europe, the Moon will occult the Red Planet.

DECEMBER'S OBJECT

Looking at Orion's Belt on a clear night, you'll detect a fuzzy patch below the line of stars. Through binoculars, or a small telescope, the patch looks like a tiny cloud in space. It is a cloud, but at 30 light years across, it's hardly small. Only the distance of the **Orion Nebula** – 1600 light years – diminishes it. Yet it

◉ **Viewing tip**

It's time for thinking about Christmas presents – but be cautious if you've your eye on a telescope for your loved one. Unscrupulous mail-order catalogues, selling 'gadgets', often advertise small telescopes that boast huge magnifications. Beware! This is known as 'empty magnification' – blowing up an image that the lens or mirror simply doesn't have the light-grasp to get to grips with. A rule of thumb is to use a maximum magnification no greater than twice the diameter of your lens or mirror in millimetres. So if you have a 100-mm reflecting telescope, go no higher than 200X.

◄ *Robin Scagell prepared this composite image of the planet Mars and the Moon when the Red Planet was close to opposition in 2005. The Moon image was captured with an exposure of 1/125 second on ISO 64 film with a 220 mm f/8 reflector. Mars was imaged with by a 203 mm Schmidt-Cassegrain telescope at f/40 on Toucam 740 webcam, and the composite consists of approximately 1000 frames.*

is the nearest region of massive star formation to Earth, containing at least 150 fledgling stars (protostars), which have condensed out of the gas.

This 'star factory' is lit by fierce radiation from a small cluster of newly born stars called 'the Trapezium', which are beautiful to look at through a small telescope. The Orion Nebula is just part of a huge gas complex in the Orion region which may have enough material to make 500,000 stars in the future.

DECEMBER'S PICTURE

On Christmas Eve, Mars will be at its closest to Earth for two years, and it will form a stunning tableau with the Moon in our skies. Both worlds are not only beautiful celestial sights, but they are also destinations which humankind might visit within our lifetimes.

DECEMBER'S TOPIC
The Christmas Star

Brilliant Mars, high in the sky this festive month, will focus attention as to the nature of the Christmas Star. What was the object that drew the Magi towards Bethlehem?

Any answers to this are rooted in the mists of antiquity and hearsay. But first of all, we need to establish the date of Christ's birth. It was certainly not AD 1, but a date somewhat before that (a cleric in the sixth century AD trying to establish the dates of important events made a counting error).

So what might have been in the sky to lure the Magi from the East? In 5 BC Chinese astronomers reported a comet in the sky. Or it might have been a nova. But King Herod said that at the time of Christ's birth he was not aware of any celestial portent, so this fifth-century BC comet can't be the 'Christmas Star'.

The key fact is that the Magi were astrologers. And in 7 BC they worked out that the planets Jupiter and Saturn would draw together on three occasions to create a rare 'triple conjunction'. To astrologers, Jupiter was the king of the planets and Saturn the planet of the Jews. The message was clear: the King of the Jews was about to come into the world.

So there was no brilliant star. But taking together all the astronomical evidence, David Hughes – an expert on the Christmas Star – reckons that the best-guess date for Christ's birth is 15 September 7 BC. An early excuse for a Christmas celebration!

There's always something to see in our Solar System, from planets to meteors or the Moon. These objects are very close to us – in astronomical terms – so their positions, shapes and sizes appear to change constantly. It is important to know when, where and how to look if you are to enjoy exploring Earth's neighbourhood. Here we give the best dates in 2007 for observing the planets and meteors (weather permitting!), and explain some of the concepts that will help you to get the most out of your observing.

THE INFERIOR PLANETS

A planet with an orbit that lies closer to the Sun than the orbit of Earth is known as *inferior*. Mercury and Venus are the inferior planets. They show a full range of phases (like the Moon) from the thinnest crescents to full, depending on their position in relation to the Earth and the Sun. The diagram shows the various positions of the inferior planets. They are invisible at *conjunction* and best viewed at their eastern or western *elongations*.

Magnitudes
Astronomers measure the brightness of stars, planets and other celestial objects using a scale of *magnitudes*. Somewhat confusingly, fainter objects have higher magnitudes, while brighter objects have lower magnitudes; the most brilliant stars have negative magnitudes! Naked-eye stars range from magnitude −1.5 for the brightest star, Sirius, to +6.5 for the faintest stars you can see on a really dark night. As a guide, here are the magnitudes of selected objects:

Sun	−26.7
Full Moon	−12.5
Venus (at its brightest)	−4.6
Sirius	−1.5
Betelgeuse	+0.4
Polaris (Pole Star)	+2.0
Faintest star visible to the naked eye	+6.5
Pluto	+14
Faintest star visible to the Hubble Space Telescope	+31

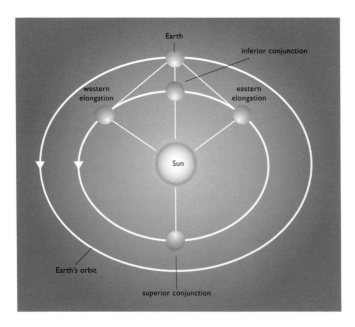

◄ At eastern or western elongation, an inferior planet is at its maximum angular distance from the Sun. Conjunction occurs at two stages in the planet's orbit. Under certain circumstances an inferior planet can transit across the Sun's disc at inferior conjunction.

Mercury

In early February 2007 Mercury is at its greatest elongation (east) of the Sun and is visible during dusk after sunset. It may just be visible low in the southwest again in late May. In early November, it is at its greatest elongation (west) and is visible in the dawn before sunrise.

⬤ Maximum elongations of Mercury in 2007		
Date	Time (UT)	Separation
7 Feb	17:39	18° 13' 55" east
22 Mar	01:47	27° 44' 26" west
2 Jun	09:56	23° 21' 57" east
20 Jul	14:59	20° 19' 28" west
29 Sep	16:08	25° 58' 58" east
8 Nov	20:31	18° 58' 34" west

Maximum elongation of Venus in 2007		
Date	Time (UT)	Separation
9 Jun	02:44	45° 23' 27" east
28 Oct	15:05	46° 27' 59" west

Venus

From the beginning of 2007 until its peak in June and early July, Venus is an increasingly prominent evening object. From mid-August it is an early morning object, reaching its greatest elongation (west) on 28 October.

THE SUPERIOR PLANETS

The superior planets are those with orbits that lie beyond that of the Earth. They are Mars, Jupiter, Saturn, Uranus, Neptune and Pluto. The best time to observe a superior planet is when the Earth lies between it and the Sun. At this point in the planet's orbit, it is said to be at *opposition*.

▶ *Superior planets are invisible at conjunction. At quadrature the planet is at right angles to the Sun as viewed from Earth. Opposition is the best time to observe a superior planet.*

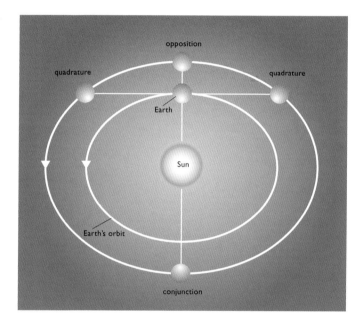

Progress of Mars through the constellations	
Early Jan	Ophiuchus
Mid Jan–late Feb	Sagittarius
Late Feb–early Apr	Capricornus
Early Apr–early May	Aquarius
Mid May–late June	Pisces
Late June–late July	Aries
Late July–late Sep	Taurus
Late Sep–late Dec	Gemini

Mars

Mars is best placed for viewing late in the year. Its closest approach to the Earth is on 17 December and it is at opposition on 24 December. Its progress through the constellations is shown in the table at left.

Jupiter

Jupiter lies in the constellation of Ophiuchus for most of 2007, until it moves into Sagittarius in December. It is best placed for observing during summer and early autumn, after it reaches opposition on 6 June.

Saturn

Saturn is in Leo for the whole of 2007. It is at opposition on 10

February and is at its best for observing from January to June and again from November onwards.

Uranus

Throughout 2007 Uranus lies in the constellation of Aquarius, so for much of the early part of the year it is drowned out by the glare from the Sun. Visibility improves during the summer and it reaches opposition on 10 September.

Neptune

Neptune spends 2007 in the constellation of Capricornus. It is not visible in the early part of the year, and is best viewed in the summer. By July it is above the horizon all night, and it reaches opposition on 13 August.

Pluto

Pluto is very faint, magnitude 14, and difficult to locate even in the largest amateur instruments. Some astronomers do not even regard it as a planet.

SOLAR AND LUNAR ECLIPSES

Solar eclipses

There are two partial solar eclipses in 2007, on 19 March and 11 September. The former will be seen from south and south-east Asia and western Alaska, while the latter is visible only from southern South America and part of Antarctica.

Lunar Eclipses

There are two total lunar eclipses in 2007. The first is on 3 March: the whole eclipse is visible from Europe, Africa and the Middle East, while in Asia and Australasia it will be partly visible before moonset and in the Americas partly visible after moonrise. The second is on 28 August: the whole eclipse can be

Astronomical distances

For objects in the Solar System, like the planets, we can give their distances from the Earth in kilometres. But the distances are just too huge once we reach out to the stars. Even the nearest star (Proxima Centauri) lies 25 million million km away. So astronomers use a larger unit, the *light year*. This is the distance that light travels in one year, and it equals 9.46 million million km.

Here are the distances to some familiar astronomical objects, in light years:

Proxima Centauri	4.2
Betelgeuse	427
Centre of the Milky Way	24,000
Andromeda Galaxy	2.9 million
Most distant galaxies seen by the Hubble Space Telescope	13 billion

◄ Where the dark central part (the umbra) of the Moon's shadow reaches the Earth, a total eclipse is seen. People located within the penumbra see a partial eclipse. If the umbral shadow does not reach Earth, an annular eclipse is seen. This type of eclipse occurs when the Moon is at a distant point in its orbit and is not quite large enough to cover the whole of the Sun's disc.

Dates of maximum for selected meteor showers	
Meteor shower	date of maximum
Meteor shower	date of maximum
Quadrantids	3/4 January
Lyrids	21/22 April
Eta Aquarids	5/6 May
Perseids	12/13 August
Orionids	21/22 October
Leonids	17/18 November
Geminids	13/14 December

seen from the Pacific Ocean, while in the Americas it is visible before moonset and in south and southeast Asia and Australasia it can be seen after moonrise. It is not visible from Europe or Africa.

METEOR SHOWERS

Shooting stars – or *meteors* – are tiny particles of interplanetary dust, known as *meteoroids*, burning up in the Earth's atmosphere. At certain times of year, the Earth passes through a stream of these meteoroids (usually debris left behind by a comet) and a *meteor shower* is seen. The point in the sky from which the meteors appear to emanate is known as the *radiant*. Most showers are known by the constellation in which the radiant is situated.

When watching meteors for a coordinated meteor programme, observers generally note the time, seeing conditions, cloud cover, their own location, the time and brightness of each meteor and whether it was from the main meteor stream or not. It's also worth noting any details of persistent afterglows (trains) and fireballs, and making counts of how many meteors appear in a given period.

▶ *Meteors from a common source, occurring during a shower, enter the atmosphere along parallel trajectories. As a result of perspective, however, they appear to diverge from a single point in the sky.*

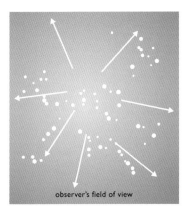

observer's field of view

Angular separations

Astronomers measure the distance between objects, as we see them in the sky, by the angle between the objects, in degrees (symbol °). From the horizon to the point above your head is 90 degrees. All around the horizon is 360 degrees.

You can use your hand, held at arm's length, as a rough guide to angular distances, as follows:

Width of index finger 1°
Width of clenched hand 10°
Thumb to little finger on outspread hand 20°

For smaller distances, astronomers divide the degree into 60 arcminutes (symbol ′), and the arcminute into 60 arcseconds (symbol ″).

COMETS

Comets are small bodies in orbit about the Sun. Consisting of frozen gases and dust, they are often known as 'dirty snowballs'. When their orbits bring them close to the Sun the ices evaporate and dramatic tails of gas and dust can sometimes be seen.

A number of comets move round the Sun in fairly small, elliptical orbits in periods of a few years; others have much longer periods. Most really brilliant comets have orbital periods of several thousands or even millions of years. The exception is Comet Halley, a bright comet with a period of about 76 years. It was last seen in 1986.

Binoculars and wide-field telescopes provide the best views of comet tails. Larger telescopes with a high magnification are necessary to observe fine detail in the gaseous head (coma). Most comets are discovered with professional instruments, but a few are still found by experienced amateur astronomers.

Deep sky objects are 'fuzzy patches' that lie outside the Solar System. They include star clusters, nebulae and galaxies. To observe the majority of deep sky objects you will need binoculars or a telescope, but there are also some beautiful naked eye objects, notably the Pleiades and the Orion Nebula.

The faintest object that an instrument can see is its *limiting magnitude*. The table gives a rough guide, for good seeing conditions, for a variety of small- to medium-sized telescopes.

We have provided a selection of recommended deep sky targets, together with their magnitudes. Some are described in more detail in our 'Object of the month' features. Look on the appropriate month's map to find which constellations are on view, and then choose your objects using the list below. We have provided celestial coordinates, for readers with detailed star maps. The suggested times of year for viewing are when the constellation is highest in the sky in the late evening.

Limiting magnitude for small to medium telescopes	
aperture (mm)	limiting magnitude
50	+11.2
60	+11.6
70	+11.9
80	+12.2
100	+12.7
125	+13.2
150	+13.6

RECOMMENDED DEEP SKY OBJECTS

Andromeda – autumn and early winter

M31 (NGC 224) Andromeda Galaxy	3rd magnitude spiral galaxy, RA 00h 42.7m Dec +41° 16'
M32 (NGC 221)	8th magnitude elliptical galaxy, a companion to M31. RA 00h 42.7m Dec +40° 52'
M110 (NGC 205)	8th magnitude elliptical galaxy RA 00h 40.4m Dec +41° 41'
NGC 7662 Blue Snowball	8th magnitude planetary nebula RA 23h 25.9m Dec +42° 33'

Aquarius – late autumn and early winter

M2 (NGC 7089)	6th magnitude globular cluster RA 21h 33.5m Dec –00° 49'
M72 (NGC 6981)	9th magnitude globular cluster RA 20h 53.5m Dec –12° 32'
NGC 7293 Helix Nebula	7th magnitude planetary nebula RA 22h 29.6m Dec –20° 48'
NGC 7009 Saturn Nebula	8th magnitude planetary nebula; RA 21h 04.2m Dec –11° 22'

Aries – early winter

NGC 772	10th magnitude spiral galaxy RA 01h 59.3m Dec +19° 01'

Auriga – winter

M36 (NGC 1960)	6th magnitude open cluster RA 05h 36.1m Dec +34° 08'
M37 (NGC 2099)	6th magnitude open cluster RA 05h 52.4m Dec +32° 33'
M38 (NGC 1912)	6th magnitude open cluster RA 05h 28.7m Dec +35° 50'

Cancer – late winter to early spring

M44 (NGC 2632) Praesepe or Beehive	3rd magnitude open cluster RA 08h 40.1m Dec +19° 59'
M67 (NGC 2682)	7th magnitude open cluster RA 08h 50.4m Dec +11° 49'

Canes Venatici – visible all year

M3 (NGC 5272)	6th magnitude globular cluster RA 13h 42.2m Dec +28° 23'

M51 (NGC 5194/5) Whirlpool Galaxy	8th magnitude spiral galaxy RA 13h 29.9m Dec +47° 12'
M63 (NGC 5055)	9th magnitude spiral galaxy RA 13h 15.8m Dec +42° 02'
M94 (NGC 4736)	8th magnitude spiral galaxy RA 12h 50.9m Dec +41° 07'
M106 (NGC4258)	8th magnitude spiral galaxy RA 12h 19.0m Dec +47° 18'

Canis Major – late winter

M41 (NGC 2287)	4th magnitude open cluster RA 06h 47.0m Dec –20° 44'

Capricornus – late summer and early autumn

M30 (NGC 7099)	7th magnitude globular cluster RA 21h 40.4m Dec –23° 11'

Cassiopeia – visible all year

M52 (NGC 7654)	6th magnitude open cluster RA 23h 24.2m Dec +61° 35'
M103 (NGC 581)	7th magnitude open cluster RA 01h 33.2m Dec +60° 42'
NGC 225	7th magnitude open cluster RA 00h 43.4m Dec +61 47'
NGC 457	6th magnitude open cluster RA 01h 19.1m Dec +58° 20'
NGC 663	Good binocular open cluster RA 01h 46.0m Dec +61° 15'

Cepheus – visible all year

Delta Cephei	Variable star, varying between 3.5 and 4.4 with a period of 5.37 days. It has a magnitude 6.3 companion and they make an attractive pair for small telescopes or binoculars.

Cetus – late autumn

Mira (omicron Ceti)	Irregular variable star with a period of roughly 330 days and a range between 2.0 and 10.1.
M77 (NGC 1068)	9th magnitude spiral galaxy RA 02h 42.7m Dec –00° 01'

Coma Berenices – spring

M53 (NGC 5024)	8th magnitude globular cluster RA 13h 12.9m Dec +18° 10'
M64 (NGC 4286) Black Eye Galaxy	8th magnitude spiral galaxy with a prominent dust lane that is visible in larger telescopes. RA 12h 56.7m Dec +21° 41'
M85 (NGC 4382)	9th magnitude elliptical galaxy RA 12h 25.4m Dec +18° 11'
M88 (NGC 4501)	10th magnitude spiral galaxy RA 12h 32.0m Dec.+14° 25'
M91 (NGC 4548)	10th magnitude spiral galaxy RA 12h 35.4m Dec +14° 30'
M98 (NGC 4192)	10th magnitude spiral galaxy RA 12h 13.8m Dec +14° 54'
M99 (NGC 4254)	10th magnitude spiral galaxy RA 12h 18.8m Dec +14° 25'
M100 (NGC 4321)	9th magnitude spiral galaxy RA 12h 22.9m Dec +15° 49'
NGC 4565	10th magnitude spiral galaxy RA 12h 36.3m Dec +25° 59'

Cygnus – late summer and autumn

Cygnus Rift	Dark cloud just south of Deneb that appears to split the Milky Way in two.
NGC 7000 North America Nebula	A bright nebula against the back- ground of the Milky Way, visible with binoculars under dark skies. RA 20h 58.8m Dec +44° 20'
NGC 6992 Veil Nebula (part)	Supernova remnant, visible with binoculars under dark skies. RA 20h 56.8m Dec +31 28'
M29 (NGC 6913)	7th magnitude open cluster RA 20h 23.9m Dec +36° 32'
M39 (NGC 7092)	Large 5th magnitude open cluster RA 21h 32.2m Dec +48° 26'
NGC 6826 Blinking Planetary	9th magnitude planetary nebula RA 19 44.8m Dec +50° 31'

Delphinus – late summer

NGC 6934	9th magnitude globular cluster RA 20h 34.2m Dec +07° 24'

Draco – midsummer

NGC 6543	9th magnitude planetary nebula RA 17h 58.6m Dec +66° 38'

Gemini – winter

M35 (NGC 2168)	5th magnitude open cluster RA 06h 08.9m Dec +24° 20'
NGC 2392 Eskimo Nebula	8–10th magnitude planetary nebula RA 07h 29.2m Dec +20° 55'

Hercules – early summer

M13 (NGC 6205)	6th magnitude globular cluster RA 16h 41.7m Dec +36° 28'
M92 (NGC 6341)	6th magnitude globular cluster RA 17h 17.1m Dec +43° 08'
NGC 6210	9th magnitude planetary nebula RA 16h 44.5m Dec +23 49'

Hydra – early spring

M48 (NGC 2548)	6th magnitude open cluster RA 08h 13.8m Dec −05° 48'
M68 (NGC 4590)	8th magnitude globular cluster RA 12h 39.5m Dec −26° 45'

M83 (NGC 5236)	8th magnitude spiral galaxy RA 13h 37.0m Dec −29° 52'
NGC 3242 Ghost of Jupiter	9th magnitude planetary nebula RA 10h 24.8m Dec −18°38'

Leo – spring

M65 (NGC 3623)	9th magnitude spiral galaxy RA 11h 18.9m Dec +13° 05'
M66 (NGC 3627)	9th magnitude spiral galaxy RA 11h 20.2m Dec +12° 59'
M95 (NGC 3351)	10th magnitude spiral galaxy RA 10h 44.0m Dec +11° 42'
M96 (NGC 3368)	9th magnitude spiral galaxy RA 10h 46.8m Dec +11° 49'
M105 (NGC 3379)	9th magnitude elliptical galaxy RA 10h 47.8m Dec +12° 35'

Lepus – winter

M79 (NGC 1904)	8th magnitude globular cluster RA 05h 24.5m Dec −24° 33'

Lyra – spring

M56 (NGC 6779)	8th magnitude globular cluster RA 19h 16.6m Dec +30° 11'
M57 (NGC 6720) Ring Nebula	9th magnitude planetary nebula RA 18h 53.6m Dec +33° 02'

Monoceros – winter

M50 (NGC 2323)	6th magnitude open cluster RA 07h 03.2m Dec −08° 20'
NGC 2244	Open cluster surrounded by the faint Rosette Nebula, NGC 2237. Visible in binoculars. RA 06h 32.4m Dec +04° 52'

Ophiuchus – summer

M9 (NGC 6333)	8th magnitude globular cluster RA 17h 19.2m Dec −18° 31'
M10 (NGC 6254)	7th magnitude globular cluster RA 16h 57.1m Dec −04° 06'
M12 (NCG 6218)	7th magnitude globular cluster RA 16h 47.2m Dec −01° 57'
M14 (NGC 6402)	8th magnitude globular cluster RA 17h 37.6m Dec −03° 15'
M19 (NGC 6273)	7th magnitude globular cluster RA 17h 02.6m Dec −26° 16'
M62 (NGC 6266)	7th magnitude globular cluster RA 17h 01.2m Dec −30° 07'
M107 (NGC 6171)	8th magnitude globular cluster RA 16h 32.5m Dec −13° 03'

Orion – winter

M42 (NGC 1976) Orion Nebula	4th magnitude nebula RA 05h 35.4m Dec −05° 27'
M43 (NGC 1982)	5th magnitude nebula RA 05h 35.6m Dec −05° 16'
M78 (NGC 2068)	8th magnitude nebula RA 05h 46.7m Dec +00° 03'

Pegasus – autumn

M15 (NGC 7078)	6th magnitude globular cluster RA 21h 30.0m Dec +12° 10'

Perseus – autumn to winter

M34 (NGC 1039)	5th magnitude open cluster RA 02h 42.0m Dec +42° 47'
M76 (NGC 650/1) Little Dumbbell	11th magnitude planetary nebula RA 01h 42.4m Dec +51° 34'

NGC 869/884	Pair of open star clusters
Double Cluster	RA 02h 19.0m Dec +57° 09'
	RA 02h 22.4m Dec +57° 07'

Pisces – autumn

| M74 (NGC 628) | 9th magnitude spiral galaxy |
| | RA 01h 36.7m Dec +15° 47' |

Puppis – late winter

M46 (NGC 2437)	6th magnitude open cluster
	RA 07h 41.8m Dec −14° 49'
M47 (NGC 2422)	4th magnitude open cluster
	RA 07h 36.6m Dec −14° 30'
M93 (NGC 2447)	6th magnitude open cluster
	RA 07h 44.6m Dec −23° 52'

Sagitta – late summer

| M71 (NGC 6838) | 8th magnitude globular cluster |
| | RA 19h 53.8m Dec +18° 47' |

Sagittarius – summer

M8 (NGC 6523)	6th magnitude nebula
Lagoon Nebula	RA 18h 03.8m Dec −24° 23'
M17 (NGC 6618)	6th magnitude nebula
Omega Nebula	RA 18h 20.8m Dec −16° 11'
M18 (NGC 6613)	7th magnitude open cluster
	RA 18h 19.9m Dec −17 08'
M20 (NGC 6514)	9th magnitude nebula
Trifid Nebula	RA 18h 02.3m Dec −23° 02'
M21 (NGC 6531)	6th magnitude open cluster
	RA 18h 04.6m Dec −22° 30'
M22 (NGC 6656)	5th magnitude globular cluster
	RA 18h 36.4m Dec −23° 54'
M23 (NGC 6494)	5th magnitude open cluster
	RA 17h 56.8m Dec −19° 01'
M24 (NGC 6603)	5th magnitude open cluster
	RA 18h 16.9m Dec −18° 29'
M25 (IC 4725)	5th magnitude open cluster
	RA 18h 31.6m Dec −19° 15'
M28 (NGC 6626)	7th magnitude globular cluster
	RA 18h 24.5m Dec −24° 52'
M54 (NGC 6715)	8th magnitude globular cluster
	RA 18h 55.1m Dec −30° 29'
M55 (NGC 6809)	7th magnitude globular cluster
	RA 19h 40.0m Dec −30° 58'
M69 (NGC 6637)	8th magnitude globular cluster
	RA 18h 31.4m Dec −32° 21'
M70 (NGC 6681)	8th magnitude globular cluster
	RA 18h 43.2m Dec −32° 18'
M75 (NGC 6864)	9th magnitude globular cluster
	RA 20h 06.1m Dec −21° 55'

Scorpius (northern part) – midsummer

M4 (NGC 6121)	6th magnitude globular cluster
	RA 16h 23.6m Dec −26° 32'
M7 (NGC 6475)	3rd magnitude open cluster
	RA 17h 53.9m Dec −34° 49'
M80 (NGC 6093)	7th magnitude globular cluster
	RA 16h 17.0m Dec −22° 59'

Scutum – mid- to late summer

| M11 (NGC 6705) | 6th magnitude open cluster |
| Wild Duck Cluster | RA 18h 51.1m Dec −06° 16' |

| M26 (NGC 6694) | 8th magnitude open cluster |
| | RA 18h 45.2m Dec −09° 24' |

Serpens – summer

M5 (NGC 5904)	6th magnitude globular cluster
	RA 15h 18.6m Dec +02° 05'
M16 (NGC 6611)	6th magnitude open cluster,
	surrounded by the Eagle Nebula.
	RA 18h 18.8m Dec −13° 47'

Taurus – winter

M1 (NGC 1952)	8th magnitude supernova remnant
Crab Nebula	RA 05h 34.5m Dec +22° 00'
M45	1st magnitude open cluster, an
Pleiades	excellent binocular object.
	RA 03h 47.0m Dec +24° 07'

Triangulum – autumn

| M33 (NGC 598) | 6th magnitude spiral galaxy |
| | RA 01h 33.9m Dec +30° 39' |

Ursa Major – all year

M81 (NGC 3031)	7th magnitude spiral galaxy
	RA 09h 55.6m Dec +69° 04'
M82 (NGC 3034)	8th magnitude starburst galaxy
	RA 09h 55.8m Dec +69° 41'
M97 (NGC 3587)	12th magnitude planetary nebula
Owl Nebula	RA 11h 14.8m Dec +55° 01'
M101 (NGC 5457)	8th magnitude spiral galaxy
	RA 14h 03.2m Dec +54° 21'
M108 (NGC 3556)	10th magnitude spiral galaxy
	RA 11h 11.5m Dec +55° 40'
M109 (NGC 3992)	10th magnitude spiral galaxy
	RA 11h 57.6m Dec +53° 23'

Virgo – spring

M49 (NGC 4472)	8th magnitude elliptical galaxy
	RA 12h 29.8m Dec +08° 00'
M58 (NGC 4579)	10th magnitude spiral galaxy
	RA 12h 37.7m Dec +11° 49'
M59 (NGC 4621)	10th magnitude elliptical galaxy
	RA 12h 42.0m Dec +11° 39'
M60 (NGC 4649)	9th magnitude elliptical galaxy
	RA 12h 43.7m Dec +11° 33'
M61 (NGC 4303)	10 magnitude spiral galaxy
	RA 12h 21.9m Dec +04° 28'
M84 (NGC 4374)	9th magnitude elliptical galaxy
	RA 12h 25.1m Dec +12° 53'
M86 (NGC 4406)	9th magnitude elliptical galaxy
	RA 12h 26.2m Dec +12° 57'
M87 (NGC 4486)	9th magnitude elliptical galaxy
	RA 12h 30.8m Dec +12° 24'
M89 (NGC 4552)	10th magnitude elliptical galaxy
	RA 12h 35.7m Dec +12° 33'
M90 (NGC 4569)	9th magnitude spiral galaxy
	RA 12h 36.8m Dec +13° 10'
M104 (NGC 4594)	Almost edge on 8th magnitude
Sombrero Galaxy	spiral galaxy.
	RA 12h 40.0m Dec −11° 37'

Vulpecula – late summer and autumn

| M27 (NGC 6853) | 8th magnitude planetary nebula |
| Dumbbell Nebula | RA 19h 59.6m Dec +22° 43' |

EQUIPMENT REVIEW

' I 've always wanted a telescope.' Many people have said that, but were never able to realize their dream. At one time, telescopes were expensive and hard to find in the marketplace, but these days they are more affordable and user-friendly than ever before, and are widely available from specialist suppliers or from reputable Internet sources.

But this availability has brought its own problems, because there are now so many different products available. The good news is that without spending a fortune you can buy a perfectly serviceable telescope which will give you years of good observing. Once out of the very cheapest end of the market there are many buys worth having, though some traps exist for the unwary. The old maxim 'If it seems too good to be true, it probably is' still applies!

So how should you narrow down your choice? Broadly speaking there are three optical designs and two mounting options, though not every permutation of these is available. The optical systems are the refractor, the reflector and the catadioptric, while the mountings are the altazimuth and the equatorial, both of which can be computer-controlled.

▼ A GO TO instrument with an aperture of 130 mm, the Celestron 130 SLT will locate a wide range of objects having first been directed to any three bright stars or planets in the sky. Cost, about £300.

Types of telescope

Refractors have enjoyed a resurgence of interest in recent years. These are the classic telescopes, with a lens at the top of the tube to collect the light and an eyepiece to magnify the image at the bottom. They are straightforward to use and to maintain, and can give superb images, but at the cheaper end of the market they suffer from false colour – for example, objects can appear surrounded by blue fringes. But good modern instruments tend to be better designed than formerly, and in the more expensive instruments – usually described as APO or ED – false colour has been almost completely eliminated. These are equally suitable for visual or photographic use, and they give a comparatively wide and sharp field of view.

A reflecting telescope uses a mirror rather than a lens to collect the light. The eyepiece is usually at the top of the tube, viewing at right angles to the main tube. The images are free from false colour and the telescopes are cheaper, size-for-size, than refractors, particularly in the larger instruments. But they require more maintenance and care than refractors.

Catadioptric telescopes combine the two systems to produce compact instruments that are capable of high performance, at least in theory. They are invariably more expensive than similar-sized basic refractors or reflectors, but some of the most popular telescopes are of this design. There are three main designs: the Maksutov, popular in smaller instruments; the Schmidt-Cassegrain for medium-sized instruments; and the Ritchey-Chretien, which is being introduced at the high quality end of the market.

The telescope's mount is just as important as the optics. Altazimuth mounts allow simple up-and-down and side-to-side movements, and in their basic form are fine for quick viewing, particularly at low magnifications, but are impractical for most imaging purposes (that is, taking photos or digital images). However, with the addition of computer control and motors, many of their drawbacks are eliminated. Equatorial mounts have one axis inclined at an angle to the horizon in order to facilitate the tracking of objects as they move through the sky – this is invaluable for long-exposure photography.

GO TO mounts can be of either type, but the essential difference is that sensors on the axes tell a built-in computer where they are pointing, once they have been aligned on the sky. All types of mounts can be motorized, making it much easier and smoother to track an object as it moves across the heavens. Until you have viewed an astronomical object at even a moderate magnification of, say, 100 times, you don't appreciate the speed of the movement caused by the Earth's daily rotation, and how important it is to be able to track objects smoothly.

In practical terms, whatever the type of telescope, there is another feature affecting your choice: the focal ratio of the telescope. The telescope's aperture (the size of the main mirror or lens) affects the brightness of the images in general, but the focal ratio affects the magnifications that the telescope will give, and the sort of objects you can observe. A telescope with a short focal ratio (say, f/4 or f/5) has a short and stubby tube, and is ideal for comparatively low-magnification wide-field observing such as deep-sky observing of nebulae,

▲ *Jupiter, as photographed through the Celestron 130SLT using a Philips ToUcam webcam and a Celestron Barlow lens (not supplied with the telescope).*

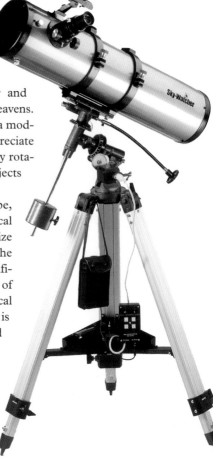

▶ *One of the most popular instruments available is the Sky-Watcher Explorer130M, a 130 mm reflecting telescope. This has now been upgraded to the Explorer 130PM, with an improved parabolic mirror, at the same price of about £200.*

WEBSITES

Celestron are imported by David Hinds Ltd of Tring – www.dhinds.co.uk

They are available through several outlets.

Vixen are imported by Orion Optics of Crewe – www.orionoptics.co.uk

The Pop-up Observatory website is www.popoutside.com

Meade telescopes are available from several outlets, including www.telescopehouse.co.uk

Sky-Watcher telescopes are imported by Optical Vision – www.opticalvision.co.uk; and are available through several outlets.

clusters and galaxies. At the other end of the scale, a telescope with a long focal ratio – f/12, for example – will normally have a long tube and will be more suited to high-magnification observing of planets where wide field is not an issue. That said, catadioptric telescopes are designed to squeeze a long focal length into a short tube, and are widely used for deep-sky observing, so there are no hard and fast rules. In general, however, short focal length telescopes are better suited to dark-sky use, while in the suburbs where light pollution is an issue, it is better to have a longer focal ratio.

This year's innovations

Celestron have recently introduced some interesting additions to the range available. The astronomical community is buzzing with interest about the SkyScout, which is a hand-held device that will identify any of 6000 objects in the sky visible to the naked eye. It combines a GPS unit, identifying your precise location, with gravitational and magnetic sensors that measure direction and tilt, and also a database of the sky. In practice you simply turn it on and point it at an object in the sky, and it will give you details of that object either on a scrolling display or in audio form through an earpiece. It will also direct you to any object in its database.

At the time of writing working models of the SkyScout were not available, so its accuracy remains to be tested. But people are speculating that if it works as advertised, it could turn any telescope into a GO TO telescope – or more accurately a 'push-to' telescope. Mounted on a simple telescope, for example, it should be able to lead you to locate any object in its database. However, at £349 it could easily cost more than the telescope itself!

▼ The Celestron SkyScout, which will tell you the name of any naked-eye object in the sky that you can centre through its non-magnifying optical system.

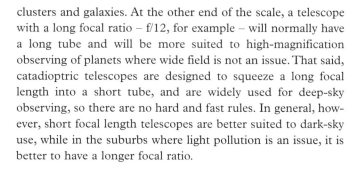

Celestron now also have a useful new GO TO system, known as SLT, on their beginners telescopes. Their arch-rivals Meade have patented the 'level and north' system for providing the initial orientation of GO TO telescopes. Rather than pay a royalty to Meade to use this system, Celestron have developed the SLT telescopes which require that you enter just your time, date and location, and that you roughly level the mount. Then you point the telescope at any three bright objects in the sky. You don't need to know which objects they are – even the Moon and planets will do.

The system appears to work well, and beginners may find it easier to use than the Meade ETX approach. The SLT telescopes are available in four models, with 80 and 102 mm refractors and 114 and 130 mm reflectors.

Another new GO TO instrument is the Vixen Skypod 110.

This is an integrated 110 mm reflecting telescope on a sturdy GO TO tabletop mount which has the same Star Book system as their larger Sphinx mount. This shows you a sky map which you can use to select the object you wish to observe. The telescope can be replaced by a larger instrument if required, and mounted on a tripod. At £699 for the tabletop model it is more expensive than the equivalent ETX, but its stylish design and handy controls make it an interesting alternative.

Pop outside

The British weather is the main enemy of the observer, and on many nights the clouds roll over as soon as you set up your telescope. Advanced amateurs have their own observatories, allowing them to observe within minutes of the skies clearing and also providing shelter from the wind. But a new design of portable observatory will make life easier for those with neither the space nor the budget for a permanent building.

The Pop-up Observatory is a novel design of tent based around two metal hoops. It folds up to a circular package less than a metre across, yet can be erected or dismantled within three or four minutes, though windy conditions are a problem as with any tent. There is generous space inside for a telescope and observer, though it is better suited to a telescope with a short tube mounted well off the ground. The view of the sky is somewhat restricted by the material surrounding the structural hoops, but the tent can be unpegged and turned fairly easily. At £250 it is cheaper than a solid building, yet still allows you to keep your telescope outside for a period of time without having to dismantle it after every session.

▲ Vixen's Skypod 110 telescope on GO TO mount, in basic tabletop mode. A field tripod is available for an extra £100 allowing the mount to take a large instrument on a standard dovetail fitting.

▶ The Pop-Up Observatory, shown housing a Meade LX90 200mm Schmidt-Cassegrain telescope. All four upper segments of the observatory can be opened, and a rain cover is included to keep the interior dry. It folds into a carrying bag with a diameter of less than 80 cm and a weight of 9 kg. Assembled it is 2 m high and 2 m across the base.